KEMP

THE HISTORICAL SERIES OF THE REFORMED CHURCH IN AMERICA
NO. 86

KEMP

The Story of John R. and Mabel Kempers,
Founders of the Reformed Church in America
Mission in Chiapas, Mexico

Pablo A. Deiros

WILLIAM B. EERDMANS PUBLISHING COMPANY
Grand Rapids, Michigan / Cambridge, UK

Wm. B. Eerdmans Publishing Co.
2140 Oak Industrial Drive SE, Grand Rapids, Michigan 49503
PO Box 163, Cambridge CB3 9PU UK
www.eerdmans.com

Printed in the United States of America

All photos courtesy of the Joint Archives of Holland, unless otherwise noted.

Library of Congress Cataloging-in-Publication Data

Names: Deiros, Pablo Alberto, 1945- author.
Title: Kemp : the story of John R. and Mabel Kempers, founders of the
   Reformed Church in America mission in Chiapas, Mexico / Pablo A. Deiros.
Description: Grand Rapids, Michigan : Eerdmans Publishing Company,
2016. |
   Series: The historical series of the Reformed Church in America ; 86 |
   Includes bibliographical references and index.
Identifiers: LCCN 2015047545 | ISBN 9780802873545 (pbk. : alk. paper)
Subjects: LCSH: Kempers, John R., 1900-1995. | Kempers, Mabel, 1902-2003.
|
   Missionaries--United States--Biography. | Missionaries--Mexico--Biography.
   | Reformed Church in America--Clergy--Biography. | Reformed Church in
   America--Missions--Mexico--Chiapas--History. | Chiapas (Mexico)--Church
   history--20th century.
Classification: LCC BV2832.2.K43 D45 2016 | DDC 285.7092/2--dc23 LC
record available at http://lccn.loc.gov/2015047545

To Dr. Charles Van Engen and his wife Juanita (Jean Taylor)

For their efforts and commitment to the cause of Christ
and for their recognition of John and Mabel Kempers,
whom they deeply loved, this book is dedicated.

The Historical Series of the Reformed Church in America

The series was inaugurated in 1968 by the General Synod of the Reformed Church in America acting through the Commission on History to communicate the church's heritage and collective memory and to reflect on our identity and mission, encouraging historical scholarship which informs both church and academy.

www.rca.org/series

General Editor
    Rev. Donald J. Bruggink, PhD, DD
    Western Theological Seminary
    Van Raalte Institute, Hope College

Associate Editor
    George Brown Jr., PhD
    Western Theological Seminary

Editorial Associate
    JoHannah Smith

Production Editor
    Russell L. Gasero

Commission on History
    James Hart Brumm, MDiv, Blooming Grove, New York
    David M. Tripold, PhD, Monmouth University
    Douglas Van Aartsen, MDiv, Ireton, IA
    Matthew Van Maastricht, MDiv, Milwaukee, Wisconsin
    Linda Walvoord, PhD, University of Cincinnati

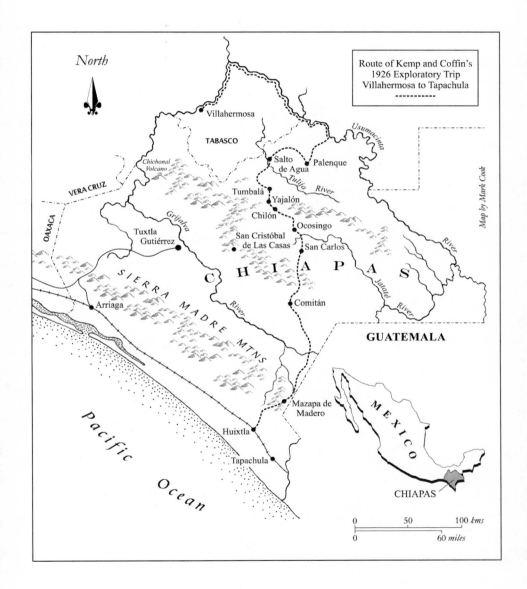

North

Route of Kemp and Coffin's
1926 Exploratory Trip
Villahermosa to Tapachula
- - - - - - - - - - -

Map by Mark Cook

Villahermosa

TABASCO

*Chichonal
Volcano*

VERA CRUZ

OAXACA

Grijalva

Tuxtla
Gutiérrez

Usumacinta

Salto
de Agua   Palenque

Tulijá   River

Tumbalá
Yajalón
Chilón
Ocosingo

San Cristóbal
de Las Casas   San Carlos

River

C H I A P A S

River

Jataté   River

Arriaga

Comitán

GUATEMALA

S I E R R A   M A D R E   M T N S

M E X I C O

Mazapa de
Madero

Huixtla

Tapachula

P a c i f i c

O c e a n

CHIAPAS

| 0 | 50 | 100 *kms* |

| 0 | | 60 *miles* |

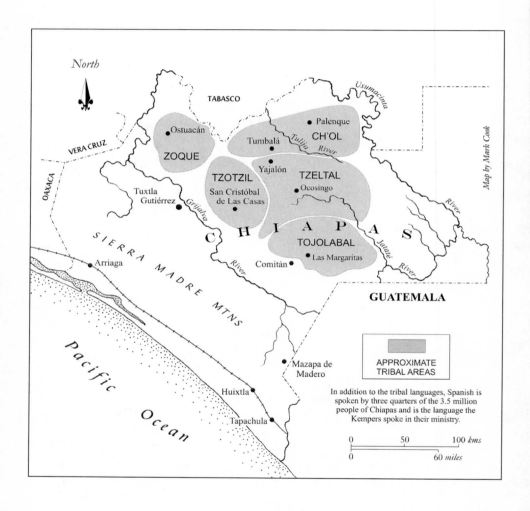

North

TABASCO

VERA CRUZ

OAXACA

Ostuacán

ZOQUE

Tuxtla
Gutiérrez

SIERRA MADRE MTNS

Arriaga

Pacific Ocean

Usumacinta

Palenque

Tumbalá   CH'OL

Yajalón

TZOTZIL   TZELTAL
San Cristóbal   Ocosingo
de Las Casas

C H I A P A S

River   TOJOLABAL

Comitán   Las Margaritas

Tulijá River

Grijalva

River

Jataté River

River

GUATEMALA

Mazapa de
Madero

Huixtla

Tapachula

Map by Mark Cook

APPROXIMATE
TRIBAL AREAS

In addition to the tribal languages, Spanish is
spoken by three quarters of the 3.5 million
people of Chiapas and is the language the
Kempers spoke in their ministry.

| 0 | 50 | 100 *kms* |
| 0 | | 60 *miles* |

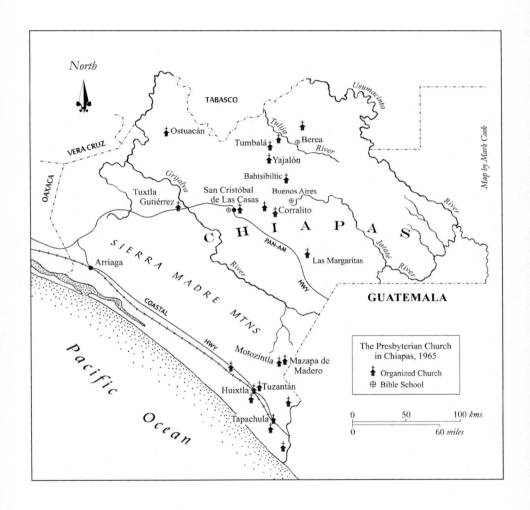

North

TABASCO

Ostuacán

VERA CRUZ

OAXACA

Tumbalá

Tulijá

Berea

River

Yajalón

Bahtsibiltic

Grijalva

Tuxtla
Gutiérrez

San Cristóbal
de Las Casas

Buenos Aires

Corralito

Usumacinta

C H I A P A S

River

PAN-AM

Las Margaritas

Jataté

River

SIERRA

Arriaga

River

HWY

MADRE

MTNS

GUATEMALA

COASTAL

HWY

Motozintla

Mazapa de
Madero

The Presbyterian Church
in Chiapas, 1965

✝ Organized Church
⊕ Bible School

Pacific

Huixtla

Tuzantán

Tapachula

Ocean

0   50   100 *kms*

0   60 *miles*

Map by Mark Cook

Contents

List of Illustrations

Foreword

Samuel Zwemer in the Middle East, Ida Scudder in India, Harvey and Lavina Hoekstra in Ethiopia, and Arlene Schuiteman in Africa are examples of pioneer Reformed Church in America (RCA) missionaries who founded, guided, and propelled important and globally recognized missions movements in their parts of the world. In the history of missions, John R. and Mabel Kempers are of the same caliber and importance in terms of their missionary life and work in Chiapas, Mexico. What the Kempers began in 1925 eventually grew into hundreds of large, vibrant churches speaking Spanish and five Mayan languages and organized in sixteen presbyteries with over three hundred thousand believers in 2015. The Presbyterian Church in Chiapas, fruit of the ministry of the Kempers, is now larger than the total membership of the RCA. It is important that we tell the story of the Kempers to show the fruit of the missionary vision of RCA churches and church members, to tell the story of the Holy Spirit's work in missions, to learn the basic principles of doing missions anywhere in the world, and to motivate young and old alike to participate in Christ's mission locally and globally.

Several of us have dreamed, thought, and prayed about this book for more than thirty years. We envisioned this to be a missionary biography that would tell the story "like it was," of how John and Mabel Kempers—as individuals and in their actions—went about doing missions in Chiapas, Mexico. This would not be a book of family memoirs; it would be a book from which many others involved in missions could learn much. We wanted this missionary biography to be suitable and interesting reading for church study groups as well as for college or seminary courses in missions. We wanted this book to be fascinating and inspiring reading for members of the church. And we hoped it would also contribute to the literature of the history of missions, particularly that which took place in Latin America.

For many years, we searched and prayed for just the right person to write this biography. In 2010 I was in Sioux Center, Iowa, speaking at First Reformed Church, the home church where John Kempers grew up. Several descendants of the Kempers extended family attend First Reformed, and many others live in that area. After the morning worship, I was invited to the home of Roger Kempers, grandnephew of John R., to meet with around fifteen members of the Kempers family. I shared with them our dream of telling the story of John and Mabel. They were enthusiastic about the project and offered valuable advice and helpful ideas. They pointed out that many of today's young adults are very interested in the stories of people who have made a difference, who have made important contributions in their field. Young adults today are more interested in the stories of missionaries' lives and actions than in the theoretical concepts of Christian missions work; these concepts are taught through the stories of those who have gone before.

The ninetieth anniversary of the arrival of John and Mabel Kempers in Chiapas would come in 2015. The story needed to be told—to the glory of God!—but still, we had neither the funding nor the right person to write the book. In the fall of 2013, however, the right person finally emerged: Dr. Pablo Deiros, premier historian of the church and missions in Latin America. Pablo is fully bilingual in Spanish and English. He is the author of over forty books, several on missions history. Some years ago, Pablo and his wife, Norma, were in Chiapas to teach a course on the history of the Latin American church and its mission. At that time, they became familiar with the work of the RCA in Chiapas. Former pastor of the Central Baptist Church in Buenos Aires, Argentina, Pablo was my colleague for many years on the faculty of Fuller Theological Seminary. He then became president of the large Baptist International Seminary in Buenos Aires, and in 2013, he was about to retire. I presented the idea of this project to Pablo and was so pleased that he was willing to join this project, to gather the data, do the research, and write the book. The time to publish this story had come.

My next step was to contact Dr. Roger Kempers, eldest son of John and Mabel, to ask for approval and advice. I asked Roger to talk with his siblings, Joy Fuder, David Kempers, and Margery Wiegerink to find out if they would also approve the project. Roger provided us with a biography of his own, in which he describes what it was like to grow up in Chiapas. All four Kempers children endorsed the project and have been very encouraging and helpful. In April of 2014, Pablo had the opportunity to personally interview each of them. He told me it was a moving and inspirational experience to talk with them.

During the fall of 2013, I contacted all retired RCA missionaries who had served in Chiapas. They were excited to hear that, after so many years of hoping and dreaming, the biography of the Kempers was going forward. At that point, I was ready to compose a formal proposal for the project, including the estimated cost. I sent the proposal to the First Reformed Church in Sioux Center, Iowa, as well as to the extended Kempers family, the retired RCA Chiapas missionaries, and other friends and family. First Reformed Church designated its Thanksgiving offering that fall for this project and offered to set up and administrate a related fund. Many who were contacted sent donations, and almost overnight, we had the funding for this endeavor! What a blessing!

In April 2014, Pablo and I traveled to Holland, Michigan, where we discovered that there was a treasure trove of original documents at the Joint Archives of Holland. The extensive collection of documents that Rev. Sam Hofman and Dr. Roger Kempers had gathered and donated to the Joint Archives, along with my own collection of files that John Kempers had left me years ago, provided an invaluable amount of information. Pablo was amazed at the extensive documentation available for his research. He discovered that John Kempers (known affectionately as "Kemp") had made extensive comments, notations, and explanations in the margins of many original documents, essentially directing any future researcher along a pathway of information. Working through these documents, Pablo kept exclaiming, "Kemp keeps telling me where to find things and how to understand them!" Pablo remarked that he felt as if Kemp himself were dictating the book.

Such extensive documentation and Kemp's own organization, notations, and explanations motivated Pablo to write this book in the first person, present tense, a more contemporary way to write history.

Pablo wrote the story as if he were the protagonist, recalling events as they unfolded. Early in the writing process, Pablo began calling this an "imaginative autobiography." By "imaginative" Dr. Deiros did not imply that the story was not true or that it was something merely created in someone's imagination. No. All the facts, background explanations, stories, and descriptions come right out of the documents originally written by Kemp himself. By "imaginative" Pablo means that he, the writer of the book, placed himself in the scenes and stories that Kemp described and wrote about them as if Kemp himself were writing about them. The book provides a deep, broad, and thorough understanding of the political, economic, religious, and social issues transpiring in Mexico and Chiapas during the missionary period of John and Mabel Kempers. Pablo expanded and explained Kemp's own short, pithy observations written in the margins of the original documents.

This project was truly a group endeavor. Sam and Helen Hofman, lifelong RCA missionaries in Chiapas from 1958 to 2000, provided invaluable and untiring help. They drew from their extensive knowledge of Chiapas, the RCA mission there, and the church in Chiapas to help with many editorial details. They also selected the photos and wrote the captions. The assistance of Anita (Van Engen) and John Bateman was a God send. They helped Pablo and me set up the computer, scanner, Cloud account, and many other digital details that were essential for this success of this project.

Donald J. Bruggink, general editor of the RCA Historical Series, has provided remarkable assistance, wise counsel, enthusiastic support, and close collaboration which have been invaluable in the shaping of this book, and the RCA Historical Commission has graciously accepted the book for publication in the RCA Historical Series.

Geoffrey Reynolds and Lori Trethewey of the Joint Archives of Holland provided access to the documents, the scanning of documents, and very attentive personal support. Jacob E. Nyenhuis and his colleagues at the Van Raalte Institute (VRI) received us with open arms and were immensely helpful and supportive throughout the entire project. Nella Kennedy of the VRI helped us translate back into English a detailed travelogue that Kemp wrote in 1925 and 1926, when he and Mabel were on their way to Mexico for the first time. Kemp had sent it to Sioux Center, where it was translated into Dutch for publication in the local newspaper. JoHannah Smith of the VRI also helped us so much with her thorough and careful copy editing, providing a smooth-flowing narrative.

When the biblical writer Luke wrote his two-volume work called Luke-Acts, he did not finish his work. The book of Acts has no ending. It simply stops with Paul under house arrest in Rome. I believe Luke did that intentionally, because he knew that the Holy Spirit would continue to work and mobilize the church in missions. Following Luke's perspective, I believe the Holy Spirit was continuing the book of Acts through the lives of John and Mabel Kempers. It is my prayer that this story may inspire and challenge many to commit themselves even now to participate in Jesus' mission locally and globally. To God be the glory.

Dr. Charles Van Engen
Fuller Theological Seminary
Founding President and CEO
Latin American Christian Ministries

January 2016

Preface

This book is not a biography, much less, the presentation of missionary heroes to stir the Christian vocation to apostolic achievements in distant lands. My main objective was to write a literary creation, in spite of my many limitations to do that in a language other than my mother tongue. This book is not an anthology, even though it is based on solid documentation in both primary and secondary sources. In the writing and organization of this book, I worked freely, moving along the lines of the inspiration provoked by the information collected. I find it in fact rather difficult to determine to what literary genre this book belongs: biography, narrative history, essay, epic poem, chronicle, testimony, or inspirational prose. Perhaps it belongs to all or to none. Technically speaking, however, it looks like narrative history.

Narrative history is the practice of writing history in a story-based form. In this case, I have tried to produce a modern narrative. The traditional way of writing narrative history is to focus on chronological order, creating an event-driven story, centered around individuals, actions, and intentions. Conversely, modern narrative typically focuses on structures and general trends. A modern narrative will break from rigid chronology when the historian believes it will explain the concept better. Also, this type of historic craft might use different sociological, political, economic, and religious factors to show how common human beings are protagonists of significant events.

In a nutshell, all that I want to do in this book is to tell a story, the story of two very special people: John ("Kemp") and Mabel Kempers. In attempting this, I will try to respond to the when, where, and (hopefully) *why of* their lives, which have caused thousands of people in Chiapas, Mexico, and various other parts of the world to praise God for their contribution to the progress of his Kingdom. In this sense, this narrative will seek to identify certain events that occurred during their extended period of service as missionaries, the larger significance or context of these events, and who the important participants were.

My goal in this work is to relate what has happened in the dimensions of time and space around the lives and ministries of John R. Kempers and his wife Mabel Van Dyke. They themselves, however, are not the center or core of this narrative history; they are the *reason* to tell a story that transcends them. This book is the recollection of God's divine redemptive action in an unknown part of Mexico called Chiapas. I have sought to write this in such a way that the reader will feel that what has happened in the course of time and in a particular corner of the world can happen again and again when the story of faith is told.

The way I have decided to organize the materials is chronological, but the events are not subject to chronology. They move in the arena of time without too much respect for the past, present, or future. The indication, however, of a given year and place for each episode helps one to better understand the historical context of these events. In some cases, the narrative cannot be situated in any particular moment or place, simply because I do not know the when and where of the episodes. In other cases, it is so because they do not belong to time and space, but to eternity.

Pablo A. Deiros

Acknowledgments

The ninetieth anniversary (2015) of the arrival of John and Mabel Kempers in Mexico as the first missionaries of the Reformed Church in America offered an opportunity to write a narrative history of their ministry in that remote land. The idea and initiative of the Reverend Dr. Charles Van Engen to honor these outstanding servants of the Lord ended up with my assuming the enormous responsibility of telling this captivating story. Dr. Van Engen and his wife Juanita (Jean Taylor) were 100 percent involved in promoting and managing this project right from the beginning. They searched for the author, gathered the necessary funds, and made all the required contacts for this book to be published with excellence and efficiency.

As the author of this work, I am greatly indebted to First Reformed Church in Sioux Center, Iowa, for their generosity in providing most of the funds, collecting a special offering to that effect. To this offering was added the significant contribution of the entire balance of the Kempers Scholarship Fund administered by the family and the church. Several other people also granted contributions.

John and Mabel's children are also worthy of my deep gratitude. The four of them—Dr. Roger Dyke Kempers, Dr. David Warren Kempers, Mrs. Kathleen Joy Kempers Fuder, and Mrs. Margery Ann Kempers Wiegerink—graciously assisted me by granting interviews which added valuable information to amplify the story. Former Reformed Church missionaries in Chiapas were also of great assistance as I had the opportunity to converse with most of them in person: J. Samuel and Helen Hofman, Henry (Hank) and Charmaine Stegenga, Jim and Sharon Heneveld, Vern and Carla Sterk, Charles and Jean Van Engen, and Alan and Sue Schreuder. I am also indebted to the published materials of Dorothy Dickens Meyerink and Rev. Hugo Esponda Cigarroa.

A special mention and recognition should be given to Geoffrey D. Reynolds, director of the Joint Archives of Holland, Michigan, and Lori Trethewey, office manager and able assistant. They were more than kind and generous with me in the rather short time that I spent in Holland, working with the well-organized files of the Kempers. I am also indebted to all the members of the Commission on History who, under the chairmanship of the Reverend Dr. Donald J. Bruggink, trusted me and made the decision to include this book in the Historical Series of the Reformed Church in America. Each member gave me particular encouragement as regards this project and professional assistance in gathering materials, offering positive criticism, and reading the manuscript. In a special way, I am indebted to the patience and longanimity of JoHannah Smith, who carefully copy edited my manuscript and gave me most helpful advice for its improvement.

The historical research for this book was made possible with the priceless assistance of Dr. Charles Van Engen and the Reverend J. Samuel Hofman. Both of them served as Reformed Church missionaries to Chiapas. Van Engen kept with him an important collection of documents (letters, articles, brochures, etc.) entrusted to him by Dr. John R. Kempers. He made significant suggestions to improve this work and contributed relevant historical data. Hofman assisted me as my right hand man with the heuristic research in the Joint Archives files and also shared with me the correspondence that Kemp and Mabel maintained with him and his wife Helen throughout the years. I am also deeply indebted to Sam and Helen Hofman for their thoughtful reading of this manuscript with helpful revisions and for sifting through thousands of photographs to choose those and write captions for those that best tell our story. I do not have words to express my gratitude to these outstanding scholars and partners in this project.

Special words of love and gratitude to my wife Norma, who had to live with the insufferable process of my research and writing of this book; through several months of intensive work, she willingly cooperated in this venture. Her reading and correction of my limited English enhanced the quality of its redaction.

My last but not least expression of gratitude goes to the Lord. The Word says that we should give honor to those who deserve honor, and be grateful. The Lord is the only one who deserves all the glory and acknowledgment in the making of this book, since he alone played the central role in the story that follows.

Soli Deo Gloria!

Chronology

1900: John R. Kempers (JRK) was born to John Kempers and Annie Rozeboom on February 19 in Sioux Center, Iowa.

1901: Leonard S. Ingram visited Tuxtla Gutiérrez, capital of Chiapas, and did personal evangelism. Abraham Quilos and Tranquilino Castillo, colporteurs, arrived in Mazapa de Madero. City president Pablo de la Cruz and secretary Felipe López of Mazapa received Bibles. Organization of the General Synod of the National Presbyterian Church in Northern Mexico.

1902: Edwin McDonald visited Tuxtla Gutiérrez and tried cottage meetings.

Mabel Van Dyke (MVD) was born to William E. Van Dyke and Christina Leusenkamp in Holland, Michigan.

1903: The Mission Board of the General Synod of Mexico sent Francisco Rodriguez y Rodriguez to minister in Tuxtla and Ocozocoutla.

1904: José Coffin graduated from the Presbyterian Seminary in Mexico City. Francisco Rodríguez y Rodríguez initiated the Christian Endeavor Society in Tuxtla Gutiérrez.

1905: José Coffin and his wife returned to Tabasco to begin ministry.

1908: The railroad connecting Arriaga and Tapachula along the Pacific Coast was completed.

1909: Church services were discontinued in Tuxtla Gutiérrez and Ocozocoautla until 1919.

1910: The Mexican Revolution began.

1912: The General Synod of the National Presbyterian Church in Mexico could not have meetings for five years until 1917 because of the Revolution.

1913: First converts began the church in Tapachula.

JRK began high school in Sioux Center and later transferred to the Northwestern Academy in Orange City.

1914: The Cincinnati Plan was created by six denominations with missionaries in Mexico.

1915: JRK heard Mrs. Walter C. Roe preach at First Reformed Church in Orange City, Iowa.

1916: Representatives of American denominations with mission endeavors in Latin America met in Panama for the Panama Congress on Christian Work in Latin America.

1917: JRK graduated from Northwestern Classical Academy on June 18.

1917-20: Venustiano Carranza served as president of Mexico. The Mexican Constitution of 1917 greatly restricted religious activities.

1918: The church group in Tapachula rented a property which became the location of the Presbyterian church Jesus Christ the Savior.

1920: Presbyterian ministers Eligio Granados and José Coffin from Tabasco baptized a large group of converts in Tumbalá, Chiapas.

1920-24: Alvaro Obregon was president of Mexico.

1922: The Tapachula congregation was organized as a church.

JRK began studying at Princeton Theological Seminary.

1924-28: Plutarco Calles served as president of Mexico.

1925: Four representatives of the Boards of Domestic Missions visited the Coffins in Tapachula.

John and Mabel Kempers were married; later in the year, they arrived in Orizaba in the state of Veracruz, Mexico.

1926: The Kempers arrived in Tapachula, Chiapas. José Coffin and JRK took almost three months to cross the state of Chiapas.

1926-29: The Cristeros along with Catholic militants waged war against the Mexican government.

1927: Church properties were expropriated by the Mexican government. The church building in Mazapa was completed.

1928: Alvaro Obregon was reelected president of Mexico and then assassinated.

1929: Bert and Harriet Heneveld Kempers arrived in Tapachula.

1930: JRK and his brother Bert made an extensive three-week trip through central Chiapas. JRK left Chiapas to assist the Presbyterian mission (Central Presbyterian Church) in Guatemala City for eight months.

1931: Julián de la Cruz, Epigmenio Jacob Trigueros, Enrique Hernández, Israel Jacob, and Heriberto López de la Cruz came from Mazapa to study with JRK. The National Presbyterian Church of Mexico established its own seminary in Coyoacán, Mexico City.

Dr. Gustavus A. Watermulder of the Board of Domestic Missions visited the Kempers in Tapachula and encouraged their move to Tuxtla Gutiérrez. In April they moved from Guatemala City to Tuxtla Gutiérrez and opened a program to train national pastors. JRK promoted the construction of a church in Tuxtla Gutiérrez.

1932: Margarito Hernández López studied for nine months with John Kempers. New arrivals from Mazapa for the Bible Institute were Natalio Bravo, Juan López, and Margarito Bravo. The government of Chiapas, following the federal government, limited the number of clergy to one for every sixty thousand inhabitants and closed every church in the state on May 31.

1933: Margarito Hernández López studied only four months in the home of John and Mabel Kempers.

1934: Lazaro Cárdenas was elected president of Mexico.

1936: Margarito Hernández López finished his studies in the home of the Kempers.

1937: Rev. Ezequiel Lango from Mexico City began his ministry in Tuxtla Gutiérrez.

1938: Wycliffe Bible Translators arrived in Chiapas.

The Kempers returned to Tuxtla Gutiérrez for two years.

1939: The first church building was constructed in San Cristóbal de Las Casas. The geographical division of Chiapas occurred for the pastoral care of Rev. Coffin and Rev. Lango.

1940: Genaro de la Rosa was ordained in May to become pastor of the Tapachula Church.

John and Mabel Kempers moved to San Cristóbal de Las Casas for six months and back to Tuxtla Gutiérrez in June.

1941: Construction began on a church building in Tumbalá in Ch'ol territory. It was completed in 1943.

1943: The first Convention of the Union of Christian Endeavor Societies was held in Tuxtla Gutiérrez. Rev. Isidro Estrella began his ministry in Yajalón. Garold and Ruth Van Engen arrived in Chiapas to work with the Ch'ol churches in Yajalón and Tumbalá.

1944: Rev. Ezequiel Lango left Chiapas and returned to Mexico City.

1946: The first Missionary Aviation Fellowship (MAF) airplane arrived in Chiapas.

1947: The Chiapas Union of Women's Societies was organized. The confrontation between Rev. Isidro Estrella and JRK occurred at the Presbytery meeting in Comalcalco, Tabasco. Rev. José Coffin was elected the first moderator of the General Assembly of the National Presbyterian Church of Mexico at its organizational meeting in Mexico City.

1948: Daniel Aguilar Ochoa was ordained to pastor the church in San Cristóbal de Las Casas. Garold and Ruth Van Engen settled permanently in San Cristóbal de Las Casas where Garold began a printing and publishing ministry. Retirement took them to Orange City, Iowa, in 1978.

1949: Margarito Hernández López, Bartolomé Solórzano, and Nehemías García López were ordained as pastors. The Chiapas Presbytery was organized. José Coffin left Chiapas and returned to Tabasco.

1950: JRK was awarded an honorary doctorate in divinity from Hope College in June.

1952: Albert and Nita De Voogd began ministry among the Ch'ol people. After ten years, they returned to Michigan in 1963.

1956: Paul and Dorothy Meyerink arrived at Corralito to work among the Tzeltal people. After five years, they moved to Buenos Aires Ranch to establish the Tzeltal Bible School. They retired in 1993.

1958: Two Tzeltal ministerial candidates, Francisco Gomez and Manuel López, began their theological studies in the home of the Kempers and continued later in the Instituto Bíblico de Chiapas (Chiapas Bible Institute).

1959: Sam and Helen Hofman arrived at Corralito to work with the Tzeltals and later moved to Buenos Aires Ranch to teach in the Bible school. They retired in 2000. Henry and Charmaine Stegenga began to work with the Ch'ols in Berea. They returned to the United States in 1978 due to Henry's illness.

1961: Juan Trujillo Velasco was ordained as the first Ch'ol minister.

1963: Francisco Gomez Sanchez was ordained as the first Tzeltal minister.

1965: Kemp and Mabel retired from the Chiapas Mission at age sixty-five and moved to Mexico City to be on the faculty of the Presbyterian Theological Seminary for the next four years.

1969: Kemp and Mabel retired in Seal Beach, California, and became active members and teachers in Lake Hills Community Church in Laguna Hills, California.

1972: The National Presbyterian Church of Mexico celebrated its centennial and declared a moratorium on receiving funds and personnel from outside Mexico.

1975: The Kempers were invited guests at the General Assembly meeting of the National Presbyterian Church of Mexico to celebrate the fiftieth anniversary of their arrival in Mexico.

Kemp and Mabel celebrated their fiftieth wedding anniversary with their family in Holland, Michigan.

1988: The Synod of Chiapas was organized, comprised of three presbyteries.

1995: Kemp and Mabel moved to Holland, Michigan. JRK died on November 27.

2003: MVD died on December 13.

CHAPTER 1

New Century, New Life

In his good time and with his infinite wisdom, God works his perfect plan throughout history and in the lives of his people. On the nineteenth of February in the year 1900, God brought into this world a tiny servant, one whom he would train and equip, along with his future wife, to serve the people of Chiapas, Mexico, for forty-five years.

That tiny servant was I, born to Annie Rozeboom (1872-1946) and John Kempers (1877-1953), who owned a farm some 4.7 miles north of Sioux Center, Iowa.[1] I was given the name John Rozeboom. I came to appreciate "John" because of its biblical implications and the good character of the apostle who first enjoyed it, but "Rozeboom" I did not like. Perhaps this is the reason why, throughout my life, I have always signed my name "John R. Kempers." And not one of the many officials who wrote and checked my identification documents ever knew that I had another name. For those, however, who were of

---

[1]   For the general background of Dutch immigrants to Iowa see, Johan Stellingwerff, ed., *Iowa Letters: Dutch Immigrants on the American Frontier*, Robert P. Swierenga, ed.; Walter Lagerwey, trans. (Grand Rapids: Eerdmans, 2004).

I grew up on this prosperous farm in northwest Iowa (*courtesy Roger Kempers*)

a closer acquaintance, I was simply "Kemp." I was baptized in First Reformed Church in Sioux Center, Iowa, the church where I retained my membership for many years.[2]

My family was numerous. I had ten siblings: Gerrit J., Bert, Bernard, Marion, Minnie, Dena, Hermina, Johanna, and Betty. There was also another boy who passed away when he was a little baby. I was number three in that Iowa farm family. We grew up in a rural setting, where I learned from my early days to be industrious, innovative, hard-working, and dependable. These traits would serve me well in my missionary career. But the most important aspect of my Dutch heritage was an unshakable faith in God and his providence and a belief that, with the Lord's help, I could do the work he set before me.[3]

My personal documents certified what I saw in the mirror: at five feet eleven inches tall, I had a medium complexion with blue eyes and brown hair. My military discharge from the army said that I had never fired a weapon, had no (mounted) horsemanship, had not participated in any battle, and was of good physical condition.[4] In other words, by the time I had reached my eighteenth birthday, I was a good-looking, thin, and physically strong young man. I have always been very fond of sports, particularly tennis, which I would eventually play from time to time on the mission field in Chiapas. Tennis was the only recreation I enjoyed in addition to my many travels around the state of Mexico to share the gospel and my involvement in a significant amount of construction. Tennis was also my only opportunity to be in contact with wealthy people and with those who had influence in the higher social spheres of the very aristocratic dominant elites in Chiapas.

[2]   Charles Van Engen (CVE), "John Kempers: A Modern Day Apostle," sermon delivered at the funeral service of John R. Kempers (JRK), Dec. 7, 1995, First Reformed Church, Sioux Center, Iowa, in Joint Archives of Holland, Michigan (hereafter JAH).

[3]   Dorothy Dickens Meyerink (DDM), "Seventy Years of Missionary Service: John and Mabel Kempers—Pioneers of the Faith, Part 1," *Missionary Monthly* (August-September 1995): 11.

[4]   According to the Honorable Discharge from the US Army, Dec. 15, 1918, in JAH.

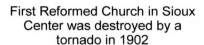
First Reformed Church in Sioux
Center was destroyed by a
tornado in 1902

The year of my birth also ushered in a new century. But sadly, when midnight came on the last day of the passing century, many people around the world thought that hope for humanity had been lost. The nineteenth century was so full of sin that many had come to the conclusion that God's wrath had overflowed, and his judgment was now at hand. But the new century was born; the twentieth century was on its way, and it forged ahead as if nothing had happened. The inhabitants of Chiapas continued in the same houses, living and surviving among the same mountains and valleys of southern Mexico— to the disenchantment of the devout, who were probably expecting paradise, and to the relief of sinners, who found that this isolated region of the world was not so bad after all, if one makes comparisons.

For the country of Mexico as well, the year 1900 was a year of new beginnings. The consolidation of the central powers in Mexico during the Porfiriato (General Porfirio Díaz's long dictatorial rule, 1876-1911) had repercussions on the deeper integration process of Chiapas to the economic life of the country and the strengthening of the state government during the last years of the nineteenth century and the first years of the twentieth. The state political evolution, however, remained quite at the margins of the national conflicts during this period. By then, the wealthier elites of ranchers, cattle raisers, and businessmen of Tabasco, and increasingly those of Oaxaca, had an influence on the balance of power in Chiapas. At the turn of the century, the economy in the region was stagnant. Business continued to be conducted in the

The Sioux Center church gave us strong support
throughout our ministry

same way that had existed in the state when it was incorporated to the
Mexican Republic (September 1824). The means of transportation were
oxcarts or canoes and, more extensively, native porters. The regions
were not connected among themselves. In most cases, it was easier to
communicate with Guatemala or the neighboring states of Oaxaca,
Tabasco, and Veracruz. In general, the state of Chiapas was somehow
without communication, and a good number of its communities were
essentially isolated. Various efforts to develop the necessary and more
modern infrastructure were not successful. National and international
investments were absent.

With the turn of the century, however, all of this changed. In
Chiapas, the change of the century brought important novelties,
namely economic investments. But the revitalization, however,
was not balanced. Some regions such as the Soconusco (the Pacific
coastal area), Palenque, Pichucalco, Comitán, and the valleys in the
department of Tuxtla benefited more than others. As a result of this
process, the traditional conflict for political supremacy between the
highlands of Chiapas and the central valley was resolved in 1892 with
the establishment of the town of Tuxtla Gutiérrez as the capital city of
the state. Everyday politics, however, continued to be dominated by the
power of the various regional *caudillos* (leaders), never to be questioned
by the claims of the natives. Additionally, in 1892, an agreement was

signed with Guatemala regarding the border between the two countries which assured the sovereignty of the state of Chiapas.

The most significant event in the first few years of the new century was the construction of the Pan-American Railroad. Increased economic activity in Chiapas was the catalyst for this initiative. This railroad extended for about 250 miles, connecting Arriaga and Tapachula. By 1908 the rail was finished with the addition of the tracks joining Tapachula with Tehuantepec. Later in our missionary work, this rail was for us very much like the Roman roads for the apostle Paul on his missionary travels. For many years, those steamy and puffing machines were our only transportation both inside and outside of the state. Some roads were added or improved with the new century. One of them connected Arriaga (where the railway station of the Pan-American Railroad was) with Tuxtla Gutiérrez, the town of Chiapa (renamed in 1881 Chiapa de Corzo), San Cristóbal de Las Casas, and Comitán. The railroad, however, could not be constructed toward the inland regions because of the difficult terrain and the lack of resources.[5]

During the first ten years of the century, Chiapas received some telephone and telegraph lines that connected the principal cities of the state and the rest of Mexico through Simojovel and Tabasco. When Mabel and I arrived in Chiapas in 1926, we had the great blessing of enjoying this connectivity and communication with the principal towns in the region, the country, and our motherland. We could never have enough words of gratitude to God for Thomas Alva Edison and his inventions which brought light and music to the new century. We did not take for granted the contributions of Alexander Graham Bell and his talking apparatus, improved with Edison's addition of the microphone. Maybe in Iowa or Michigan these devices were too common to be appreciated. But for us in Chiapas, they were a gift from God that came with the new century. We came to appreciate the importance of communication in missions work in a foreign land. Means of travel and lines of communication have been vital throughout the history of missions.

---

[5] Emilio Zebadúa, *Breve historia de Chiapas* (Mexico: El Colegio de México and Fondo de Cultura Económica, 2003), 114-16.

CHAPTER 2

The Bible Came First

In the work of the Kingdom, consistent teaching of the Word of God right at the beginning of the Christian testimony of the gospel assures a solid foundation in the faith. The "pure, spiritual milk"[1] of the Word of God was already nourishing the lives of the few new Chiapaneco believers when I was still an infant. And like that young church grew strong on the Word of God, my mother provided me with all the necessary nutrients that helped me grow into a healthy and strong person. I would not have survived the stress and physically demanding conditions of our lives and ministries in Chiapas, if not for the healthful nourishment and environment of my childhood.

As is the case with most countries in Latin America, so also in Mexico it was the introduction of the Bible that opened the way to Protestant missionaries. The Bible, placed in the hands of men and women who were willing to read it and receive its message, played a major role in the planting of evangelical churches in this country. For centuries, the Bible had been almost unknown in Mexico. Its

---

[1]   I Peter 2:2 (NIV).

distribution had been forbidden in New Spain (Mexico) by decree of the Pope and the king. The Roman Catholic Church intended to keep the colony free of the "poison" of the Reformation, and the Inquisition backed up that intent. But after independence from Spain, and in spite of many difficulties, Bible colportage work flourished. Many stories are told of churches and congregations established solely by the testimony of a Bible reader who had shared with others the reality of his or her discovery.

John A. Mackay, who served for a number of years as a Presbyterian missionary to Peru and later as president of Princeton Theological Seminary, wrote in a book I read with great interest that to the British and Foreign Bible Society belonged the honor of having introduced Latin America to the perennial source of Christian thought and experience. According to Mackay, the new Christians showed up not with a sword but with a Bible. The fact is that between 1804 and 1807, the society published twenty thousand copies of the New Testament in Portuguese. These books were distributed mostly in towns located along the coast of Brazil, through traders and sailors interested in the diffusion of the scriptures. Mackay stated that the distribution of the Bible started in this way, which according to the best opinion in Latin America, has satisfied the greatest need of the spiritual life of the continent.[2] It seems to me then, that the first planned efforts to propagate the gospel in Latin America were done with the presentation and distribution of the Bible.[3] No doubt, the Holy Spirit worked in a remarkable manner through the scriptures to reveal to many people the living Christ. Evangelical churches sprang up in unusual and unexpected places. Many said that the pattern was clear: first the Bible, then a convert, then a church.[4]

In Mexico, after its independence from Spain in 1821 and in spite of the growing predominance of liberal and mostly anticlerical regimes, the circulation of the scriptures was hindered by political and military instability and by the resistance of the Roman Catholic Church. Yet, John C. Brigham, then a missionary of the American Board of Commissioners and soon to join the American Bible Society staff, wrote in 1823 that in the cities of Spanish America "the Scriptures sold rapidly for a time and then the demand entirely ceased." Years later,

[2]   Juan A. Mackay, *El otro Cristo español: un estudio de la historia espiritual de España e Hispanoamérica* (Mexico: Casa Unida de Publicaciones, 1952), 231.
[3]   Sante Uberto Barbieri, *El país de Eldorado* (Buenos Aires: La Aurora, 1962), 38.
[4]   William R. Read, Victor M. Monterroso, and Harmon A. Johnson, *Latin American Church Growth* (Grand Rapids: Eerdmans, 1969), 38-39.

despite the fact that the Mexican Constitution of 1867 prohibited—rather ambiguously—the burning of Bibles or even their banning by hostile priests and local officials, colporteurs were harassed by hired or incited *bandidos*. Mexicans who accepted the "Protestant" scriptures were often excommunicated. Poverty, illiteracy, and civil war left a country desolate and in which peddling books was difficult.[5]

Nevertheless, the work of Bible distribution in Mexico was notable by the end of the nineteenth century and the beginning of the twentieth. Hiram P. Hamilton had served for twenty-six years as the American Bible Society agent in Mexico when he died in 1905. His work was continued by his wife Frances Snow Hamilton, who proved to be as courageous and determined as she was efficient. Years later, Hazael T. Marroquin was not only the first Mexican agent appointed by the society but also the first "national" agent installed anywhere.[6] In spite of this auspicious progress in the distribution of the scriptures throughout the country, Chiapas remained outside the reach of the major Bible societies.

The first missionaries to come to Chiapas were simple laypeople who brought the Bible with them as colporteurs. Colporteurs are those who sell or give away small portions of scripture or gospel tracts. The idea (and word) comes from France, where *col* (neck) and *porter* (to carry) were combined to refer to peddlers who carried on their backs boxes of their wares for sale around the countryside. Colporteurs were employed by missionary agencies (especially Bible societies) and traveled mostly across rural areas selling or trading their products. Colporteurs were used widely in Latin America, and in many regions, they were the first to share the good news of the gospel. All of them were hard working and devout individuals, willing to walk seemingly endless miles and face severe persecution in the hope of bringing printed scriptures to people who otherwise would never have access to them.[7] Some of them were martyred, and their shed blood became the seed of the Kingdom in many places.

The distribution of the Bible, regardless of the resistance by both government and clergy, became a growing and constant phenomenon throughout the nineteenth century and especially at the beginning of the twentieth century, even in isolated places like Chiapas. Because

---

5   Creighton Lacy, *The Word Carrying Giant: The Growth of the American Bible Society* (Pasadena, CA: William Carey Library, 1977), 75, 116.
6   Ibid., 178-79.
7   *Evangelical Dictionary of World Missions*, A. Scott Moreau, ed. (Grand Rapids: Baker Books, 2000), 210.

of this, colporteurs were able to produce the largest results with the smallest expenditure of means. That was the case with the arrival of two colporteurs (Abraham Quilos and Tranquilino Castillo) in Mazapa de Madero, Chiapas, coming from San Marcos, Guatemala. They brought with them the Bible and the gospel to southern Chiapas. They had been converted through Presbyterian missionary work in Guatemala. They placed Bibles in the hands of town officials in the village of Mazapa. The president and secretary were converted, and this humble highland village became a beacon of light for that area. Guatemalan coffee pickers (*tapiscadores*) also brought the gospel to coffee ranches near the town of Tapachula, and a congregation was formed in this commercial center, located by then at the end of the railroad traversing the Soconusco.

Someone once remarked that colporteurs were "the first to give out the blessed Word of God in the state of Chiapas without any other objective than to obey the mandate of 'Go and preach.'"[8] A pioneer of the Presbyterian work in Mexico, Rev. Edwin McDonald, reported in 1904, "Everywhere in the state, we find the good results of the work of the colporteurs of the American Bible Society. Many people have kept their books and have read them in spite of the prohibition of the priests and the threat of excommunication for all who dare to read them."[9] One of the major difficulties in Chiapas was the lack of versions of the Bible in the major languages of the state, other than Spanish. In Chiapas there were six principal indigenous languages, plus several dialects for each one. At the end of the nineteenth century, Mexico had at least fifty-three indigenous languages with no written alphabet. In the southern state of Chiapas, the situation was even more complicated. The difficult travel conditions were one thing, but mainly the hostile—often violent—reaction to the sale of the Bible (the Roman Catholic Church outlawed the reading of the Bible by any person other than clergy) made evangelizing difficult. In Mexico religious intolerance had been taught by the Roman Catholic hierarchy for centuries.

Protestant missionaries in Mexico quickly realized that the oral approach to evangelization was more appropriate, since no one could object to the presentation of the gospel in that format. Furthermore, the majority of the Chiapanecan population neither understood Spanish, the official language, nor wrote their indigenous languages. Another possible interpretation is that the monopolistic nature of the Roman Catholic hierarchy did not want the indigenous populations to

---

[8]   Comisión de Historia, *Bodas de Oro: 1902-1952* (Tuxtla Gutiérrez, Chiapas: Iglesia Evangélica Presbiteriana Nacional "Getsemaní," 1952), 2.

[9]   Ibid.

learn Spanish because, if they did, they would potentially be exposed to Protestantism. Nor did the Roman Catholic hierarchy want the indigenous populations to have access to the gospel in their native tongue, lest they become independent of the clergy.

Interestingly enough, the first attempts of an evangelical testimony in Chiapas had a lot to do with the introduction of the Bible to the Spanish-speaking population.

CHAPTER 3

Mabel Van Dyke

In his infinite wisdom and grace, God brought into this world on February 7, 1902, my future wife and life partner to the mission field of Chiapas, Mexico. On this day, my dear Mabel was born. She brought even more beauty and sweetness to the home of Christina Leusenkamp and William E. Van Dyke, in Holland, Michigan. She was the crowning jewel in the precious crown of the Van Dykes, together with their four other children: Edward, Lillian, Milton, and Russell. Lillian did not marry, but was a highly intelligent and outstanding high school teacher and will most probably outlive us all.[1]

Third Reformed Church in Holland, Michigan, has always been Mabel's home church. This was the church of her great-grandparents, who were charter members, and of her grandparents and parents. Her father served as an elder. Here she received baptism, confessed publicly her faith in the Lord, and expressed her intent to follow him. Here she was nurtured and trained for missionary life and service for Jesus Christ. A pastor of this congregation, Rev. James M. Martin, officiated at our marriage and asked for God's blessing upon us. This church helped

---

[1]   Lillian Van Dyke (1897-2002) passed away at 105 years of age in Holland, Michigan.

us during our Mexico career and retained Mabel's name on its list of members until recent years when we joined Lake Hills Community Church in Laguna Hills, California. It was in Third Reformed Church too that our children Roger and Joy made confession of faith and were members for a time, and all four of our children received baptism here as well.[2]

Mabel received her elementary education in Holland and was awarded her eighth grade diploma in Ottawa County on June 3, 1916. Her high school education was also completed in Holland, where she graduated and received her diploma on June 17, 1920.[3] Later, on July 14, 1924, she graduated *cum laude* from Hope College and received the gold medal awarded in those days to the girl judged to be the most distinguished of the class. Regretfully, the gold medal was stolen by a customs agent when we first entered Mexico through the port of Veracruz in 1925. For a year she taught English and French in Big Rapids High School, Michigan. Her work was interrupted when she married me on August 13, 1925.

Before she married me, Mabel Van Dyke had a crucial decision to make, which would impact the rest of her life. I was in my final year of study at Princeton Theological Seminary and had thoughts of becoming a missionary to Mexico. I was wondering if my bride-to-be was serious about following me. But shortly after I announced my desire to go to Mexico, she made her approval clear, writing on January 30, 1925:

> My Very Own Boy,
>
> Don't be wondering any more about what I will answer you—or whether or not I still am ready to go anywhere with you. Dear, I have been thinking, thinking—and I want to do that— just that with you. You wanted me to have to struggle with all the opposition to my decision. You wanted me to see all the darkness and privation it involves. And, Kemp, I have. Hard it was, even though I knew all along that I wanted that if you did. But, honey, I am ready. But it wasn't as you thought it would be: first the brightness and enthusiasm. No, that came after all the other. First, it was all a horrible blur, sort of stunning me. But a whole day and a night of thinking and praying has ended in the brightness I see now.

---

[2]   Mabel Van Dyke (MVD), "Thoughts on Our Golden Wedding Anniversary," p. 2, in JAH.

[3]   These diplomas are in JAH.

Dear, I wish one thing, though. Won't you write to Mom and Dad and tell them, ask them? It does concern them much, and I do want to consider them. I am old enough to know what I want, and they, of course, will never refuse to let us do what we wish, you and I. But, Kemp, dear, they are my parents, my own Mother and Father, who have given me life and who love me, and I am theirs, though I am yours. I will write them too, honey, but I think you should too, and it would please them so much! I know, Kemp, it won't be easy; instead it will be hard, hard for you. But I know it is right. Mother, as you say, wants us or hoped we might stay here, and she seems to have the idea from something you said, that we will be. This plan will mean her letting me go sooner than she has hoped for. I will write them about it, not till I hear from you once more. Please, honey?

As for our year of becoming accustomed to each other, dearest, this will be just as well, even better. Don't you think? I do! We will be so much more dependent upon each other, and we will mean all happiness and comfort to each other there. And honey, we will be happy in our work. It will be work of course, and we will become weary, I know. But with each other—and for our Christ—we will make it fun too! I know we will. We won't let ourselves be unhappy! And this I am sure of too. No matter what our home will be made of, the house, I mean. Love will always be there, always. Kemp, we will make it dear, with a few things that we may have, our own things, yours and mine, and it will be colorful and restful for us.

It isn't much they allow us to live on. But, well, maybe so, we won't want or need rather so much there. Kemp, it doesn't look hopeless and darkness to me. I can see lonesomeness for things we have now, and things we have loved together here among our own people. But, dear, I can see happiness in service, in working together for the God that has been so good to us. And always I can see us—husband and wife, and boy and girl—loving each other, and showing our love with tenderness and care for each other. This will mean an earlier wedding, won't it? We had wanted it later. But, well, we have each other enough to marry right now.

Kemp Dearest, your letter, I will always keep it. I love it! I love you! You are a dear boy to your girl, and you are a dear, dear husband to your wife. I am not afraid to go anywhere with you— my man! Write me soon, honey! I must wait so long to know what you are thinking of me and my thoughts and my decision. Kemp, I am your wife—for always and forever.

Your very own. Mabel.[4]

This was a remarkably mature letter for a twenty-two-year-old woman, born and raised in Holland, Michigan. It was realistic. She knew that living in remote southern Mexico would be tough. She knew that we would be leaving behind much that we had cherished and that there would be plenty of sacrifices ahead. But her dedication and courage welled up within her, as did her love for me. On January 31, 1925, she wrote:

> Dearest One,
>
> Just a note this must be, Kemp, to tell you how much I do love you—and always will. And I want to tell you once again, dear, how certain I am that I want to go with you to Mexico. You don't doubt do you, the certainty my letter told you of? . . . Honey, I have decided that if, after we had this chance to take a real place in Christ's work, I had refused to accept that place, I would have regretted it all my life.[5]

My answer was not delayed, and I wrote back immediately, on February 2:

> Your answer was read with moist eyes—of course it thrilled me and made me thank our God for you. Honey, I have been all wrong. I vaguely had a fear lest perhaps you simply might consent to go because I am your man and then I thought that perhaps after the novelty and romance of it was gone, you would not be happy and that it then might be doubly hard for both of us. But when I read your special last night, I knew and I now know that it won't be that I will be cheering you, but you will be the sweet young woman, my wife, with your devotion for the work and for me who will be doing that for me constantly.
>
> I am glad you thought it through seriously and that you were alone to think. You say you are ready, and I know you are, and we will do our best so that neither of us need ever be sorry for being ready now. . . . There will be times before and even after going, when we will wonder whether we really are doing the right thing and whether it isn't perhaps our love for adventure that is

4   MVD to JRK, Jan. 30, 1925, in JAH.
5   MVD to JRK, Jan. 31, 1925, in JAH.

carrying us on. But we are decided now, and we haven't decided recklessly. So now if anything prevents our going, it will have to be something other than our wills.

Honey, we looked at the dark side but there is a bright side, too. . . . I didn't go to bed for a long time and then when I did, I put your letter under my pillow. . . .the most significant letter that has ever passed between us, and the most dear, too![6]

This was my Mabe, the very special woman that God had given me as a partner for life and ministry. We spent forty-five years ministering together to the people of Chiapas, Mexico, often traversing Mexico's southernmost state on mule or horse as the first Reformed Church in America missionaries to live in Chiapas, working with missionaries and pastors from the National Presbyterian Church in Mexico. In this way, and in human terms, we helped to give birth to the church in Chiapas. It was not an easy task. We had to learn the language, share our faith, and start churches, sometimes under arduous conditions. The task was often hard and occasionally looked impossible. But Mabel kept her word and was by my side totally committed in love to her Lord and to me.

She was a heroine to me right from the early days of our missionary service in Chiapas. Fulfilling our ministry duties was grueling, especially in facing the risks of traveling through the mountainous, undeveloped areas near the Guatemalan border. Several months after arriving in Chiapas in May 1926, I traveled with a Presbyterian missionary across the rugged terrain to meet those to whom we would be ministering. Mabel stayed in a rented house in Tapachula, since the trip was expected to take only two weeks. But it took almost two months!

One night in Ocosingo, I became violently ill with vomiting and diarrhea. By midnight I was too weak to get out of my hammock. During that night, Mabe, far off in Tapachula, heard me calling her. She got out of bed and hurried to the door, thinking that I was home at last. She opened the door, but no one was there. She closed the door and did the one positive thing she could still do for me: she prayed. I survived that night and the next day with the help of an American doctor who just happened to be staying nearby. After one day of recovery, I was back in the saddle again—half alive—and on the long, weary trail toward Tapachula. On arriving there two weeks later, I wrote, "If it takes two months to cross the state, how shall we ever cover it?"

---

[6]   JRK to MVD, Feb. 2, 1925, in JAH.

For Mabel it must have been a traumatic beginning, living in the very humble two-room house in dusty, hot Tapachula, struggling to learn Spanish in an unfriendly world, left alone for nearly two months, and almost becoming a widow before we could even celebrate our first wedding anniversary. Most couples at that point would have sent a telegram to New York asking for money for a return trip to the United States. But Mabel agreed that our motto would be "Chiapas para Cristo" (Chiapas for Christ). And together we started to work toward that goal. The isolation, the rugged travel conditions, and the serious health hazards never frightened her. Nor did they deter her decision to stay by me in the work of the Kingdom, despite the fact that Chiapas was in political chaos, struggling through the last violent years of the Mexican Revolution.[7]

---

[7]   J. Samuel Hofman (JSH), "Mabel Kempers's Eulogy," presented at the memorial service for Mabel (Van Dyke) Kempers at Third Reformed Church, Holland, Michigan, January 4, 2004, in JAH.

CHAPTER 4

Early Beginnings

There is no more blessed experience than to grow up in a Christian home. My parents were not extraordinary people whose names are engraved in marble as outstanding citizens. But both of them were good parents, who were faithful to communicate to their children the love of God and the fundamental truths of the gospel. At a very early age, I learned to love Jesus and was taught Bible verses and simple Christian songs. My long life as a servant of the Lord did not begin when we went to Chiapas as missionaries. It began when I was a little child in a farmhouse filled with the Spirit of God and nurtured by the love of my parents. I have often thought that working in the Lord's vineyard is exactly the same. As the parable of the mustard seed illustrates, small beginnings result in great things. Faith planted early in the soul of a child will endure forever and bring amazing fruit.

The state of Chiapas is about half the size of my native Iowa. It is a remote and neglected green jewel snuggled up against Guatemala. Geographically and culturally, it should have been a part of Guatemala. But in 1824, following the Mexican War of Independence, when both

The spectacular Maya ruins of Palenque reveal a very advanced
ancient culture (*courtesy J. Samuel and Helen Hofman*)

Mexico and Guatemala broke free from Spain, Chiapas chose to become
part of Mexico.[1]

Scattered over the surface of Chiapas are archeological sites
where scientists try to read the history of past ages. One of the most
remarkable sites is Palenque, part of the Ancient Maya Empire, which
is perhaps as old as Christianity. The Bonampak ruins were discovered
in the eastern part of the state and have caused a sensation. There may
even be other ruins buried in the jungles, awaiting discovery by modern
man. The ruins in Chiapas and in all of Mexico are of temples or
buildings connected with religious rites. This seems to indicate either
the importance of religion in the lives of these people groups or the
power of the priests over the inhabitants.

In the eastern jungles lived the Lacandones, descendants of the
Old Maya people who spoke the Maya tongue more purely than any
of the other tribes. These natives had never accepted Roman Catholic
influence nor government control. In homespun cotton clothes, they
tilled patches of land in the jungle and painstakingly practiced their
complicated ancient religious rites.

The upbringing of most Chiapanecos was totally different from
my upbringing in a Dutch Reformed environment. All of the indigenous
habitants in Chiapas were bound by the fetters of witchcraft and fear of

[1]   JSH, "The History of the Chiapas Mission," *Reformed Review* 58, no. 1 (Autumn
2004): 1.

the medicine man, who controlled the conduct of the tribe, threatening anyone who deviated from tribal custom. Along with witchcraft, there was the prevalent belief in the Nagual—the belief that people were teamed with animals into which the spirits of the persons were believed to pass at night to roam the countryside. A native would not kill a jaguar, because in so doing, he might be killing the person of the Nagual. So firm was this belief that the Chiapanecos would recount many cases where a prowling animal was shot at night, and a corresponding hole appeared in the body of a human being. Adopting the outward forms of civilization is easier than forgetting ancient superstitions.

Colonial Roman Catholicism was able to erect enormous church buildings in heavily populated indigenous sections. Tecpatán, Sabanilla, and Tumbalá had tremendous ancient structures which had crumbled to ruins. Indigenous beliefs lived on, and pagan rites were incorporated into Roman Catholic worship. The occasional conscientious priest who attempted to institute reforms met unyielding resistance. The Tojolabal natives continued to worship upright stones in caves, kissing them, and burning incense before them. That, to them, was worshiping the "soul of the corn," and thus they hoped to ensure supernatural blessings on their corn crop. The sun was the object of worship of many Aborigines. Four of the five monolingual tribes were of Maya descent, and all used a form of the word *Tat* (our father) to address the sun. Strangely enough, some Catholic priests encouraged them in this belief.[2] It is not that easy to get rid of beliefs and practices that you have learned since your childhood. The only power that can change a pagan heart and let the seed of the gospel be planted is the power of the Holy Spirit. This power was made manifest from the very beginning of the evangelical testimony in Chiapas.

The gospel was introduced to Chiapas from three directions: Mexico City, Guatemala, and Tabasco, the state to the north of Chiapas. Chiapas was a spiritually parched land, and no one person or group can be credited with having introduced the gospel to this region. The Catholic Church had a spiritual monopoly, dating back to the Spanish Conquest in the 1520s. The Catholicism that arrived was medieval Catholicism, unchallenged and unrefined by the Reformation and the Renaissance. In the centuries that followed, the remote and rugged terrain, the scarcity of priests, and the illiteracy of the people produced

---

[2] JRK, "How the Gospel Came to Chiapas," n.d. brochure, pp. 14-16, in JAH. See also, JRK, "How the Gospel Came to Chiapas," *The Church Herald* (November 5, 1954), 4-5, 20-21.

a Catholicism that was more animistic than Christian. The good soil of Chiapas desperately needed the good seed of the gospel.[3]

The first of these three introductions of the gospel was the testimony coming from the capital city of the country. From 1901 to 1904, English and American missionaries from Mexico City visited Chiapas. In 1901 Mr. and Mrs. Leonard S. Ingram and their daughter (an English family) arrived in Tuxtla Gutiérrez, and after six months of personal evangelism in the marketplace, the quarters, and from house to house, they moved on to San Cristóbal de Las Casas, withdrawing soon thereafter and returning to Mexico City. Mr. Ingram was a layperson related to the Plymouth Brethren, who worked independently, without any support from a missionary board or society.

In February 1902, Mr. and Mrs. Edwin McDonald arrived in Tuxtla and tried cottage meetings. In spite of the fears of the few local believers, they were soon able to have regular public services.[4] The McDonalds were well received by the Tuxtlecos, but as soon as the Roman Catholic bishop began his work of opposition and persecution against them, as well as against the first believers, popular discontent was expressed. In the face of these circumstances, believers were encouraged by the powerful testimony of their pastor. The house they used for worship was closed, but six other homes were opened weekly to study the Word of God. Before the McDonalds' retirement to Mexico City in 1904, elders were ordained in Tuxtla and in Ocozocoautla, a nearby town. They organized the first consistory of the church, the Sunday school, and the evangelization work with Simón García and Adelaido Petriz as leaders, and they baptized the first believers. This is how they succeeded in planting the seeds of Presbyterianism in Tuxtla Gutiérrez, the capital city in central Chiapas. Later in 1905 and 1906, Rev. McDonald returned to this city on evangelistic tours; the first was nineteen days, and the second was seven. The incipient congregation was also encouraged by letters from Dr. Arcadio Morales, who was very interested in the work in Chiapas.[5]

In 1903 the Missions Board of the General Synod of Mexico agreed to send to the church in Tuxtla a preacher named Francisco Rodríguez y Rodríguez, who accompanied the work done by Rev. McDonald. He served in Tuxtla and Ocozocoautla, and by November 1903, he was totally in charge of the church. He was the one who interested

3   JSH, "The History of the Chiapas Mission," 1-2.
4   Hugo Esponda, *El presbiterianismo en Chiapas: orígenes y desarrollo* (Mexico: Publicaciones El Faro, 1986): 197-200.
5   Comisión de Historia, *Bodas de Oro*, 2-3.

the congregation in youth work. One of the fruits of his efforts was the organization of the Sociedad de Esfuerzo Cristiano (Christian Endeavor Society) on October 14, 1904. Its twenty members chose the name Por Cristo y por su iglesia (For Christ and his church) for the society. From 1905 to 1908, Rodríguez continued to fulfill his ministry. After 1909 there was no more news about this leader. The chaos of the Mexican Revolution that erupted in 1910 and continued through the following years made further visits and contacts impossible. Services were discontinued in both places (Tuxtla and Ocozocoautla) for many years (1909-19). The group in Tuxtla reorganized later as a Christian Endeavor Society. It was this nucleus with whom Mabel and I began our work in 1930 and which was developed into a large church with its outlying congregations.[6]

The second introduction of the gospel into Chiapas came from Tabasco. In 1908 a valiant Mr. Sutherland crossed from that state into the northern side of Chiapas reaching Yajalón (*yash' lum*, green land), where he interested young Gonzalo Astudillo, and Chilón, where he recruited Gerónimo Arévalo. Many years later, Rev. Eligio M. Granados from Tabasco came and was able to hold services both in Yajalón and in Chilón with the help of these two believers. In Chilón shooting broke up the meeting, but people were converted and began to do personal evangelism. These people were later found by José Coffin and me on our exploratory trek in 1926.[7]

The third introduction of the gospel in Chiapas occurred when missionaries from Guatemala crossed the border and visited the Mam-Quiché indigenous town named Mazapa de Madero around 1902. Pablo de la Cruz, the town president, accepted the gospel, and because of his influence, the good news spread rapidly. These natives became a missionary people, doing personal work in their native tongue in all the neighboring mountain villages and holding their services in the Spanish language. Because of diminishing rainfall, some of the Mazapa people were forced to migrate, thus forming two new congregations, thereby reducing the size of the mother church. One of the chapels of the Consistory of Mazapa was at an altitude of ten thousand feet. The pastor of the church and of the congregations in the entire area was a native Mazapa aboriginal, capable of using three languages.

Meanwhile, down in the southwestern tip of Chiapas, Guatemalans coming to pick coffee on the plantations of the region

---

[6] JRK, "How the Gospel Came to Chiapas," 2.
[7] Ibid.

introduced the gospel. The resulting group of believers requested a leader from Mexico City. It was this petition that brought Rev. José Coffin to Chiapas in 1920, where he remained until 1949. There were a good number of new believers that ended up serving as leaders in the newborn churches. Manuel Molina was one of them. Considered the black sheep in his home in San Cristóbal de Las Casas, he drifted from place to place until he found the gospel in Tabasco. His experience sent him home, where he fought fanaticism in that hyper-clerical center and started a group which became the Las Casas church, whose pastor was also a native of that city.

In the years that Coffin was in Chiapas under the Northern Presbyterian Mission (before the Reformed Church adopted the work), in spite of difficulties of travel due to sporadic revolutionary fire, he was able to visit several of these groups. Four consistories were organized, and chaplains selected from the groups were appointed to take charge of the congregations.[8] One of the singular ways of Coffin to provide leadership to the newly organized congregations was to appoint *capellanes* as soon as possible. This method was effective in helping the small groups have their own native leadership, but it proved to be very risky in placing at the head of congregations some people who were neophytes and who were superficially trained for the ministry.

When Mabel and I arrived in Chiapas, we found this picture of the work. At the beginning, I tried my best to adjust myself to Coffin's ways. But shortly thereafter, I realized the weak points of his strategy. Most of all, I perceived that the work as a whole in the state of Chiapas was too much centered on one person: José Coffin. Churches and leaders were a reflection of his personality and methods. There were many positive aspects of his ministry, but I could also see dangerous features that could have serious consequences in the future of the work.

---

[8]   Ibid., 3, 4.

CHAPTER 5

Mazapa de Madero

If ever there was an isolated place in Chiapas, it was Mazapa de Madero, where it was impossible to move in a straight line for one hundred yards. In visiting the small town of Mazapa de Madero, I realized how difficult it is to move on a rugged terrain interrupted by creeks and trenches and plagued with steep ups and downs. But I saw again how God in his sovereignty gave me as a young child a large farmhouse full of siblings and the great outdoors to learn to walk and run and climb. I became strong and agile; I learned to move quickly and carefully, and God prepared me physically for the ministry ahead.

The town of Mazapa de Madero is located in the high region of Chiapas, southeast of the capital city. It is in the Sierra Madre mountains and close to the border with Guatemala, at an altitude of 3,300 feet above sea level. The Sierra Madre del Sur range cuts through Chiapas, raising magnificent but formidable mountains, leaving little level land and only a narrow strip of coast to the south. Mazapa is a small border town at the foot of the Tacanah volcano. Here is the source of the branches of the Mezcalapa and Grijalva rivers that cross Chiapas and Tabasco and pour out their waters into the Gulf of Mexico. This town is all that is left of the ancient empire of the Ketchekels in Mexican territory.

Scattered about and separated by these great barriers, there were believers. A Protestant group might be a single family living at a high altitude, a few families of peons on a coffee plantation in the lower highlands, or a sizeable congregation like the indigenous church of Mazapa de Madero. Their geographical isolation, as well as the diversity of sources from which they had received the gospel, made them individualistic and independent.[1]

The converted natives of Mazapa were profoundly religious, moral, and humble. They also had a missionary spirit. They carried forward their missionary work in spite of the wars. Twice they had to enlarge their primitive chapel while the revolution of Carranza was in full swing, during which they suffered in person and property. During the second revolution by the Cooperatives, they built the parsonage. By 1927 they had finished putting up the walls of a new chapel, since the congregation had grown so much that the former was no longer adequate. Coffin had laid the cornerstone, and on that occasion, he also received five new members into the church on confession of faith, married five couples, and baptized twenty-three children.[2]

The name Mazapa means "deer river," and the town is part of a region known as Mariscal. Throughout the centuries, the local inhabitants had been involved in agriculture, cultivating corn, beans, sugar cane, and other vegetables for domestic consumption, particularly potatoes in the higher elevations. By the beginning of the twentieth century, most of the natives were Maya and speaking the Mam language. Religion always played a significant role in this community, and despite the influence of the Roman Catholic Church, the population kept many of its traditional beliefs and practices.

Syncretism, as the fusion of two or more distinct systems of belief and practice, had always been characteristic of indigenous popular religiosity. The imposition by force of Roman Catholicism did not put an end to the old religious traditions. This bellicose evangelization resulted only in many native parishioners practicing their own ritualistic behavior outside the confines of the institutional church. Folk Catholicism, the use of some elements of the Catholic faith in

---

[1]   Mabel Van Dyke Kempers, *Chiapas for Christ: Chiapas para Cristo* (New York: Board of Domestic Missions, Reformed Church in America, 1958), 7.

[2]   José Coffin, "Mazapa, Chiapas, Mexico," *The Christian Intelligencer* (November 16, 1927), 729.

The Holy Spirit Presbyterian Church in Mazapa is the mother church of southern Chiapas (*courtesy J. Samuel and Helen Hofman*)

a noninstitutional setting, is a clear example of this phenomenon, particularly in remote and isolated places like Mazapa.

The evangelical testimony was not immune to this syncretistic process. Although evangelical Protestants have always represented a direct challenge to the Roman Catholic Church in issues of doctrine and as the closest religious alternative to Catholicism, we too have struggled to keep biblical faith unpolluted by the traditional native religions. We have always tried to be a very close substitute for folk or popular Catholicism, but we have to admit that, in places like the Mariscal, we have known some failures.

In the Mariscal region, the beginnings of the Presbyterian testimony are linked to the work of lay missionaries and leaders. In 1901, just a few months before the eruption of the Santa María volcano in neighboring Guatemala in 1902, two of these lay witnesses arrived in Mazapa, coming from San Marcos, Guatemala. Abraham Quilos and Tranquilino Castillo came as Spanish-speaking colporteurs, with the mission of selling and distributing Bibles and Bible portions. In those years, the local population was shrouded in ignorance and superstition, manipulated by shamans and fear. Alcoholism prevailed and all sorts of social problems with it. The only two people in the town who were able to read and write were the municipal president and his secretary. The first was Pablo de la Cruz, and the second was Francisco López. Since they were the only possible customers for the two colporteurs in this small town, the colporteurs visited them and presented their product. Both were interested, and each bought a Bible.

This contact was very significant because it represented the first step in the introduction of the gospel in Mazapa, which later became the cradle of the Presbyterian work in the Mariscal area. De la Cruz and López began to read the Bible together with their families, trying to understand it the best they could. In 1902, a few months after the visit of the colporteurs, the Santa María volcano erupted in Guatemala not far from Mazapa. The whole region remained in darkness for several days due to the falling ashes, which had serious consequences for the crops. De la Cruz and López tried to bring comfort and strength to the population, telling them that the disaster they were suffering was the consequence of the fulfillment of prophecies recorded in the Bible. The message had a positive effect, and in the midst of these dramatic circumstances, the people came to know the Word of God.

Ten years after the arrival of the two colporteurs, two Christian women also came from Guatemala. A woman, forty-eight years of age, Antonia Marroquín, accompanied by her twenty-five-year-old daughter, Hercilia Marroquín, were escaping from the abuses of a Guatemalan army general who was obsessed with the younger lady. They left Guatemala City and went to San Marcos, but this man followed them there, forcing them to continue to Huehuetenango and then to Cuilco. Finally, they were compelled to move across the border to Mazapa de Madero, after staying for a while in Bacantón de Altamirano, where Hercilia was appointed as teacher of the local school. Not being able to obtain enough food for two, they continued to Mazapa. In arriving at this town, they went to see the local authorities to explain their situation and needs. De la Cruz and López were surprised when, after expressing their needs, the women showed them a Bible, wrapped in a shawl, and shared with them their faith in Jesus Christ. De la Cruz invited them to come to his house, where later they explained the gospel again, and the head of the house and his wife, Anastasia Gutiérrez, confessed Jesus Christ as Savior. Regretfully, López never wanted to accept the message of salvation, in spite of his initial interest.

From this starting point, the work in Mazapa continued to develop. By the end of 1910, there was already a group of sixteen confessing believers. This group invited people from the congregation in San Marcos, Guatemala, to come and help them. Among those who came were Flaviano Hernández and Eduviges Laparra, who stayed for about two months with the small group, teaching them the Bible and some hymns and Christian songs.

Their Christian testimony did not go forth without opposition. The gospel was rejected as a new religion, particularly by some Roman Catholics. The conclaves of believers were dispersed by stones that rained over them and curses that assaulted them. Pedro de la Cruz and Felipe Jacob, the leaders of the congregation, had the enormous responsibility of speaking for the group. With perjury, the opponents managed to send to jail a number of believers, accusing them of minor misdemeanors. The time these believers spent in prison was a blessing, because it became an extraordinary opportunity to share the good news with other inmates.

Very early, the group in Mazapa related to the congregation in Tapachula, which was more mature in doctrine and better connected with the Presbyterian Church. It was not unusual for the men from Mazapa to go down to Tapachula (*tierra caliente*, hot land) to work for four or five months each year on the coffee plantations. In 1918, however, two brothers from Tapachula, José León Coronado and Jesús Martínez, visited the Mazapa congregation, which met on Saturday evenings due to certain Adventist influences. On June 6, 1920, the Presbyterian Church in Mazapa was organized and given the name of Espíritu Santo (Holy Spirit), being among the first churches in the state of Chiapas. They also dedicated their first church building, constructed on a site donated by Pablo de la Cruz. The first national pastor in Mazapa was Margarito Hernández López who was born in Finca Argovia (Tapachula) in 1904. He received his initial bible training in 1934 in our house in Tuxtla Gutiérrez, where he spent nine months. The following year, he could attend only four months, because Mabel and I went to the United States on furlough. Finally, he finished his studies in 1936 and was ordained in 1949.[3]

---

[3]   Esponda, *El presbiterianismo en Chiapas*, 24-39.

CHAPTER 6

Presbyterian Missions in Mexico

During my secondary studies at Northwestern Academy in Orange City, Iowa, I had the opportunity not only to study the Latin language but also to be introduced to the best of Latin literature. Among the various works that I had the pleasure to read was Plutarch's *Parallel Lives*, a series of compared biographies of great Greek and Latin men. During my childhood, I experienced something like "parallel lives." As I was growing up, gaining knowledge, and learning so many skills and abilities that would later be crucial to my ministry in Chiapas, many events occurred that set the stage on which Mabel and I would carry out our mission. I have always believed that these parallel experiences did not happen by chance, but on purpose, according to God's eternal purpose in Jesus Christ.

Mabel and I have been considered the "pioneers" of the Reformed Church in America missionary work in Chiapas. But we were not the first missionaries to bring a Reformed testimony to this Mexican state. Rev. José Coffin, a Presbyterian leader from Tabasco, came to Chiapas five years before we arrived. The Presbyterian testimony arrived in Mexico quite early during the nineteenth century. In fact, Presbyterians were the first to initiate Protestant work in this country. The first missionaries to come, however, were able to build upon the foundations that had been laid by faithful individuals like G. Mallet Prevost, Melinda Rankin, and various others. Four Presbyterian missionary boards have done valuable work in the country—the Northern Presbyterians, the Southern Presbyterians, the Associate Reformed, and the Cumberland Presbyterians. The majority of the work was done by the Presbyterian Board of the North. The Southern Presbyterians were working in the states of Tamaulipas and Nuevo León, with girls boarding schools in Brownsville and Linares. The Associate Reformed Board was in three states: Veracruz, Tamaulipas, and San Luis Potosí. The Cumberland Presbyterians were in Aguas Calientes and Guanajuato, each of which had a girls boarding school.

The Presbyterian Board of the North began its work in 1872 when four missionaries with their wives went to Mexico City. They found that there were already a number of independent Protestant congregations, many of whom soon joined the different mission boards. One of these early workers, Rev. Arcadio Morales, noted for his eloquence and his evangelistic zeal, was a leading preacher of this mission. The work was organized at first as two separate missions in northern and southern Mexico. It was then divided into three presbyteries, and in 1901, the Synod of Mexico was formed, uniting all the work of the Northern and Southern Presbyterian Boards. This synod was not under the control of any ecclesiastical body in the United States. The American missionaries and the native Mexican pastors were on equal footing as members of the synod, with the one aim of raising up a self-supporting and self-extending Presbyterian Church in Mexico. They had their own home mission board.

By 1905 this board had a large and prosperous mission in Mexico City, including three congregations, five preaching halls, six day schools, a Girls Normal and Boarding School, fourteen Christian Endeavor Societies, and twelve Sunday schools. This was only a sample of the work being done in other missionary stations. Not only was a large evangelistic and educational work being done but also much literary work was undertaken.[1]

There is something interesting to note that had a significant influence on our missionary strategy when we began our work in

---

[1]   Francis E. Clark and Harriet A. Clark, *The Gospel in Latin Lands: Outline Studies of Protestant Work in the Latin Countries of Europe and America* (New York: Macmillan, 1909), 199-201.

Chiapas. Unlike the missions in Asia and Africa, but like those elsewhere in Latin America, the Mexico Mission of the Northern Presbyterians had not concentrated its members in strong central stations but had distributed them in smaller groups. For administrative purposes, the mission was organized into only two stations. What was known as the Central Station, founded in 1872 in Mexico City, included Veracruz from 1897 and Oaxaca from 1919. The other station known as the Peninsula and constituted in 1915, included the three states of Yucatán, Campeche, and Tabasco and the territory of Quintana Roo, with resident missionaries at Merida and Tabasco. It was precisely in Tabasco that Coffin learned this strategy from the missionaries and later taught it to us.

The same can be said of the key role that the printed page played in our mission in Chiapas. The printed page had been used extensively by the first Presbyterian missionaries. Early in the history of the mission, Rev. Henry C. Thomson started the first Protestant paper in Mexico, *Antorcha Evangélica* (Evangelical torch).[2] In 1885 another paper called *El Faro* (The lighthouse) was issued, and many religious tracts and illustrated Sunday school cards and lesson helps were published by Mission Press. A hymnbook was also published, which proved to be very helpful in the work. In 1883 Rev. Joseph M. Greene raised money for Mission Press which, in 1919, merged with the Methodist Press in Mexico City. At the same time, the Presbyterian and Methodist papers merged into a new paper under the name *El Mundo Cristiano* (The Christian world). This was later discontinued as a union paper, and the mission had an excellent Presbyterian journal of its own, *El Heraldo Evangélico* (The evangelical herald).

The Northern Presbyterian Mission had not undertaken medical work beyond aiding one or two clinics staffed by Mexican physicians and nurses, but it had given high priority to its educational work. It had a large number of small day schools, a preparatory school for boys at Coyoacán, large normal schools for girls at Saltillo and San Ángel (a suburb of Mexico City), the Turner-Hodge School both for boys and girls at Mérida, Yucatán, and three Bible schools for training lay workers. Theological education was begun in two schools at Tlalpán and Monterrey, which were merged in 1885 but closed in 1894. In 1897 a seminary was opened in Coyoacán. This later merged with Union Theological Seminary in Mexico City. But in January 1931, the

---

[2]   Unpublished English translations of foreign titles are capitalized sentence style per *Chicago Manual of Style*, 16th ed. (Chicago: University of Chicago Press, 2010), 533.

National Synod established its own seminary in Coyoacán, where most of the Mexican Presbyterian leaders had been trained. Most of these institutions were doing fine work and prospering, until they were forced to close due to government regulations.[3]

These imposed limitations ended up to be a blessing for the work, because the National Church was earnestly grappling with the increased responsibilities imposed upon it by the restrictions which the government had placed upon foreign missionaries. In this way, the national work could be developed with the removal of a great hindrance in the proclamation of the gospel in Latin America, namely, its apparently foreign character, its foreign sources of support, and the control of the evangelical enterprise by foreigners. The churches in Mexico were obliged by these religious laws to take on a thoroughgoing nationalization, which was most beneficial for their spiritual life.

In short, the more important, substantial, and fruitful missionary work in Mexico was carried out by devout Presbyterian missionaries. Their hearty fellowship with those of other denominations was a major factor in the unity and spirit of brotherhood, which characterized our own participation later as missionaries sent by the Reformed Church to Chiapas. We adapted to their ways, at least at the beginning of our work, and we learned important missiological lessons from their experience. When we arrived on our own mission field in Chiapas, two parallel lives came together, our rather short preparation and the well-trained experience of the Presbyterian missionaries and national workers who had preceded us.

[3]   Arthur Judson Brown, *One Hundred Years: A History of the Foreign Missionary Work of the Presbyterian Church in the U.S.A., with Some Account of Countries, Peoples and the Policies and Problems of Modern Missions*, Book 1 (New York: Fleming H. Revell, 1936), 811-12.

CHAPTER 7

Insects

As a child brought up on a farm, I quickly became acquainted with the typical bugs in the countryside. We did not have too many animals but enough to attract a number of bothersome insects: flies, ticks, fleas, and mosquitoes were an everyday challenge. My initiation as a warrior against these enemies of hygiene and good health was at six years of age. The small fly swatter my father had made me with a stick and a piece of screen was like a toy. I loved crushing the odious invading insects. The truce put into effect during the winter months was broken in the summer, and I assumed with enthusiasm the noble mission of a crusader to put a definite end to the sucking and pestering creatures. I became an expert in pest control. What we suffered later, however, during our years spent in Chiapas, surpassed anything I could have imagined and rendered ineffective all of my warrior skills. There were such a vast number of insects ready to make our lives miserable that it is impossible to mention all of them.

In Chiapas fleas seemed to multiply more in the cold country than in the tropical heat. We first met these ornery little fellows in missionary Harry Phillips' house in Jalapa, Veracruz. There we spent our first three months of Mexican residence in language study. Until we were able to rent a house, we lived with the Phillips family in their two-story home. Fleas were so numerous in the second floor bedroom assigned to us that our mutual, life-long custom of kneeling at our bedside for prayer, came to an abrupt halt. In San Cristóbal de Las Casas, one could see fleas hopping onto our daughter Joy's bobby socks as she worked in the kitchen. A common practice was to spread pine needles on the church floor to give it a festive appearance. But that was also useful, since the tar in the needles trapped the fleas. When dry, the needles were swept onto the patio and burned, temporarily reducing the number of fleas. The itch produced by fleas crawling over one's body was a minor irritant compared to some other bugs. "Don't scratch the bites" was the warning to all newcomers.

The children's friends came in to play every afternoon. Playing with a blanket (*rebozos*) was a sure way to transfer lice, so parents examined their children's hair and clothing constantly. We often heard the saying: "Comitán de los piojos y San Cristóbal de las pulgas" (Comitán of the lice and San Cristóbal of the fleas). Other small and annoying bugs were the *chaquistes* (gnats). There were seasons of the year when the air was filled with very tiny gnats capable of transferring pink eye from one child to another. One avoided working outdoors just to avoid these insufferable thorns in the flesh. I recall taking a group of young people to a town for a meeting and spraying their legs with the Flit I had brought with me.[1]

There were also *mostacillas*, a tiny version of the tick that lived by the thousands in pastures. We learned to avoid striking bushes with a leg while walking, because in an instant, hundreds would be on us. We got so used to that, that even in the United States, we would avoid touching any clump of grass. Too many of the pesky little things would bring on a fever. Bed bugs were also common. When returning from trips, I was always careful not to throw my trip clothes on the bed, but even so, there was a time when we felt the bites in our bed. We would examine the entire bed every morning and find nothing. One night, I turned on a flashlight and saw some bed bugs scampering up the mosquito net to the wooden frame that supported the net. That was where they slept in the daytime. That frame was thrown out and burnt. A Mexican Christian friend was being bothered so much in her hotel room in Tapachula that she could not sleep. So she began picking the

---

1   *Flit* was the brand name of an insecticide lauched in 1923 which was sprayed with a manual spray pump and mainly intended for killing flies and mosquitoes.

bugs and transferring them to a fruit jar. In the morning, she wanted to humiliate the hotel owner by showing him the large number she had collected. He shook his shoulders and said, "What can I do? I gave you the best room in the hotel." If my hammock ropes were tied to the beams of a Mexican home, the only way of discouraging the descent of the unwelcome bugs, was to tie a kerosene-soaked rag to each arm of the hammock. I could instantly tell a bedbug bite from that of other insects.

It took me some time to be able to identify the *niguas* (jigger flea). This small, almost invisible insect was found under fingernails or toenails, producing a film-covered ball of white eggs the size of a small pea. It was necessary to remove the entire sac in order to destroy all the reproducing eggs. If not removed soon enough, it would deform the nail. One year, I traveled seven days across the state to accompany Bible school students to their homes. While I was traveling, Mabel was busy checking the bodies of our children and removing *niguas*. They were infected because one of the students, the day before our departure, had dug out a *nigua* nest from his toe and had carelessly strewn the tiny eggs onto the patio floor. A florist from Saugatuck, Michigan, was visiting us one day, and we told him about the *nigua*. He said, "Would you look at my toe? I feel as though I may have one of those bugs you described." Sure enough. While we were trying to remove the sack of eggs intact, he almost fainted. Afterward, he said that it was not the pain that bothered him but the thought of something foreign growing in his body.

The *colmoyotes* were also very common. I did not know the English name. Personally, I was never stung by one, but José Coffin seemed to be a favorite target. A mosquito-like bug would lay an egg usually in the back of the neck. A worm developed which would become hairy if left long enough. Coffin would have someone heat a glass bottle and then, placing the opening tightly over the swelling, suck out the worm as the bottle cooled. Something similar was the *filaria*. For a number of years, the coastal mountain area was plagued with this disease which seemingly had no cure. A fly would bite someone in the neck or head, and a ball of tightly wrapped string (*filarial*) would develop to the size of a marble. It affected the eyes, causing a great deal of blindness. All that could be done was to remove the growth surgically. We visited the rural congregations in that infested area with fear and trembling. We were witnesses to the blinding effect of that plague. Like nomads in the desert, it seems to have gone away as silently as it came to Chiapas.

There were other insects to which, somehow, I became accustomed because we had them on our farm in Iowa. In Chiapas, however, cattle ticks were so abundant that cows welcomed birds to pick them off their backs. Horses' ears had to be examined, lest they harbored too many ticks that could produce an infection. From the horse, they transferred to the rider. They would dig into the skin with their prong, and if not discovered, they would grow to the size of a small pea in a matter of days. They especially liked armpits. Unless they were removed carefully, the prong would remain and fester. Often, we tried to burn them with an extinguished wooden match to get them to release their hold. When traveling, our underwear always became stained with spots of blood.

There were other creatures totally unknown to us until we came to Chiapas. Scorpions (*alacranes*) were common. The ornery scorpion has claws to grab hold of a victim and a sharp needle at the tip of its tail, with which it stings its prey with lightning-like speed. We were careful picking up cloths in Tapachula and in Tuxtla Gutiérrez. We would turn our shoes upside down and shake them before inserting a foot. I remember well two particular bites. Early one morning, while it was still dark, I was saddling a horse in Tapachula. The saddle blanket, as I discovered too late, harbored a scorpion. I never saw the thing, but the pain of its quick work was with me for hours. On another occasion, in Tuxtla, I had returned from a trip and, about to take a bath, had slipped on a bathrobe. Suddenly, there was a sting in the pit of my stomach, and as I tried to squash the scorpion with my arm, I received a second sting. A swollen tongue and loss of equilibrium meant that the scorpion had been large and full of venom. Mabe, coming home from church that night, said it took me forever to walk the length of the house to open the door for her. At a presbytery meeting in Tabasco, with a Tabasco minister presiding in the bamboo-walled chapel, we all simultaneously warned him of a large scorpion on the wall in back of him. He paused, turned around, and grabbed the scorpion with his thumb and forefinger and squashed it. We all "oohed" and "aahed" at such a feat.

Another unknown creature to me was the tarantula. This large and hairy spider would circle the hoof of a horse, collecting hair no doubt for nesting. In so doing, it would deposit venom which, unless cauterized soon with caustic lime or potassium permanganate, would start festering, and in time, the hoof would come off. On one trip, I lost two horses simultaneously, two days from home.

Mention should be made of the many different kinds of ants that permanently menaced our house. To protect food from kitchen ants, we suspended a box with wires from the ceiling. Even then, we sometimes had to attach Flit-soaked rags to those wires. The more prevailing and destructive ant was the *arriera* (leaf-cutting ant). An army of these ants could strip an orange tree of its leaves in one night. Leaves of rose bushes seemed to be their favorite food. Each plant had a circular clay trough around it that we tried to keep filled with water. If a twig or a piece of straw fell across the trough, it became a bridge, and what was a leafy rose bush in the evening would be a stripped stalk in the morning. Pouring hose water down the ant tunnel was ineffective. Digging up the nest was difficult because their tunnels ran deep and often under buildings. Chemical sprays helped some, if one kept at it. One effective solution was to pour a flammable liquid down the hole and then explode it with a match, which would send the poisonous fumes deep down into the hidden chambers. There were also huge ant hills in the countryside. In our early years, shortly after the Mexican Revolution (1910-20), there were many tales of plantation owners who would catch fugitive peons and fasten them to stakes in the ant heaps.

This long list of pests and other irritating creatures is not exhaustive, but these examples serve to make it quite clear that Chiapas was the kingdom of these bugs. They were part of our everyday lives. People in the United States, particularly in Iowa and Michigan, complained because they had to fight snow and ice. Take your pick![2]

2   JRK, unpublished personal notes, n.d., in JAH.

CHAPTER 8

Money Matters

Believe it or not, I was burdened with timidity in my early years, partly because of my farm background and partly because a country school teacher had moved me up an entire year, so unfortunately, I was the youngest student in my high school class and possibly in college. My father was a relatively prosperous farmer because of his conservative philosophy and lifestyle. We never spent any money unnecessarily. During my days in high school, and especially during my college days in Holland and later Princeton Theological Seminary, I kept a detailed record of my expenses. I used a small notebook, which I have preserved throughout the years.[1] That training came into play during the forty years I served as treasurer of the Chiapas Mission, where we never ended a year without a considerable surplus in our budget. On a $1,500 salary during our early years, with no perks other than travel and rent, we managed to save money each year for the future educational needs of our children.[2]

---

[1]   These documents are in JAH.
[2]   JRK to DDM, April 29, 1988, in JAH.

In our administration of the mission, we kept a detailed account of our expenses and demanded the same on the part of those whose travel and salaries we subsidized. The most delicate and painful task each year was to determine at presbytery meetings how much the mission would contribute to each pastor's and each worker's support. To encourage self support, the amount had to be kept to a minimum. I am surprised that with such a sensitive responsibility, there were not more hassles and ill feelings. What a relief it was when that pressure was reduced once the church became self supporting!

The Tapachula church and school property was one big headache. Before coming to Chiapas, Mr. Coffin had worked with the Northern Presbyterian Mission, who handed out money generously. When we arrived in Tapachula, he assumed that the Reformed Church would do the same. For some time since July 1919, the congregation had rented a room on the corner of Avenida Hidalgo (4th Avenida Sur) and 4th Calle Poniente. The congregation, under the leadership of José Coffin and Genaro de la Rosa, decided to buy this property with the intention of building a church. The property belonged to the widow Juana María Sinclair, but the members did not have enough money to close the deal. Coffin, De la Rosa, and missionary Newell J. Elliot managed to collect the money. Finally, the site and the house on it were bought. In 1924 they built the first Presbyterian church "Jesucristo el Salvador."[3]

Two problems occurred at this point. One had to do with the title of the property, which was in Coffin's name. In those years, religious institutions or organizations were not allowed to hold property. The legality of civil societies holding property, as became possible much later, was not yet known. Property titles had to be under private persons. Therefore, it was Coffin who held the title of the property. Members of the church, however, believed this property belonged to the church. In addition, without our consent and as we were looking for our board's support to fund the project, Coffin bought more property, on the corner of which stood the little wooden chapel of the Tapachula congregation. He did this, in fact, to enlarge Mrs. Coffin's private day-school. The problem was that in those years, the leftist government forced the closure of all church-supported schools, and Coffin's school was considered as such. When, after months of correspondence, the board finally authorized me to pay the cost, there had to be added to that sum the outlandish amount of interest Coffin had paid while we sought approval. Again the newly acquired property was placed in Coffin's

---

[3]   Esponda, *El presbiterianismo en Chiapas*, 178.

name. But church members claimed that the funds had originally been offered to them. When the government claimed ownership to the portion of the site occupied by the school, the church was limited to a small corner of the land José Coffin had bought. This was the primary reason for the loss of half the membership, who saw Coffin's residence and the school occupying and using most of the property while the congregation was limited to the meeting chapel. I expressed to Coffin my disagreement, and he suggested that to solve the problem, I become a naturalized Mexican citizen in order to hold title to the property.

Later, as Mexican laws were passed that all church property should be turned over to the government, the necessity of keeping this property safe was not comprehended by the church membership. Regretfully, more than half the congregation left because of this and other conflicts. When we later built the large new church, the land was given to the government (assigning the church as user of it), a considerable portion was set aside for the parsonage, and the rest was sold to avoid further intrigues and get the necessary resources for construction. In this way, with the passage of time, when it was evident that there would be absolutely no possibility of reopening the private school of the Coffins, and when the church was long in need of an enlarged new building, I assured Coffin that there would be no mission aid in constructing the church until the land now in surplus was sold. Grudgingly, he complied, and I proceeded to build the new church and manse. It was a difficult predicament on which our inexperienced board never took any firm stand.

We had a more difficult time—even painful—with Mr. Coffin's salary. The churches contributed very little to his salary, so his family relied on the mission check. He, however, as a Tabasco native, loved to spend months in that state meddling uninvited in other ministers' fields when he was paid for working in Chiapas. Year after year, I would complain in presbytery meetings and set limits to the time he could be out of Chiapas, to which they would agree, but they never risked Mr. Coffin's wrath by demanding compliance. Finding no other way, I took the drastic step of reducing his salary for all excess time off the field, even though I knew that Mrs. Coffin and her children, who had moved to Mexico City, relied heavily on that income. Naturally, the presbytery and the synod, in whose eyes the great Mr. Coffin could not be in error, complained, but to no avail. Even Chuck Bennett of Mission Aviation Fellowship, who worked in Tabasco and was privy to only one side of the difficulty, made a passing swipe at my conduct in a booklet he wrote.

The assistance of a board secretary to carry the onus of these decisions would have been welcome.[4] But this never happened.

Both Mabel and I were well learned in choosing a very simple lifestyle. For some, it could have been more than frugality—maybe stinginess. But for us, it was the right way of being good stewards of what the Lord gave us to serve him. Mabel was an excellent and efficient housekeeper. She never threw away any leftovers. When we lived in a rented house in San Cristóbal de Las Casas, because we were teaching in the Bible school located there, we used to have three or four laying chickens in a small enclosure in our back patio. Mabel fed them vegetable scraps from her food preparation, potato and carrot peelings, and in return, we received fresh eggs. These chickens had been given to us as gifts from appreciative people in the churches we visited.[5]

I see now that sometimes I was too frugal. On many occasions, I went to Tuxtla to buy a small box of oatmeal only to return home a bit frustrated. I used to tell Mabel how the price had gone up five centavos in the store where we usually bought the oatmeal. And then I had to go to three other stores before I could find one at the old price five centavos cheaper. I recognize now that issues like this probably were too much. But I have been very thrifty all my life and kept account of all my expenditures, even the most insignificant. I remember having a tablet in our house in Tuxtla in which I had recorded all my expenditures for the office, including one pencil for five cents and a notebook for ten cents![6]

Sometimes my frugality was painful for those I loved most, particularly my children. I recognize the stern discipline I imposed on them, including the use of money. We lived on a very limited income, and despite the fact that our colonial house in Tuxtla Gutiérrez was nice, we had two maids at our service, and later even a new car, I never gave my eldest son Roger even a few centavos of spending money. People around us may have considered us wealthy, but I never gave Roger any money to buy a comic book, a candy, or even enjoy a movie. With regret, I remember him on a Saturday, more than once, asking timidly if he could go to the movies, and my answer was always "No." And if he dared to ask "Why?" my logical answer was, "Because I said so." Of course, it was not so much because of the cost but because I did not want my children to participate in an activity that was considered by most believers as "worldly."[7]

---

[4]   JRK, "Some of This and Some of That," unpublished manuscript, n.d., 11-12, in JAH.
[5]   Helen C. Hofman, interview with author, Holland, Michigan, April 8, 2014, in JAH.
[6]   Ibid.
[7]   Roger D. Kempers, "My Other Life: Memories of a Childhood in Chiapas," unpublished document, n.d., 31-32, in JAH.

As to the national ministers, things were not much better for them in terms of the compensation they received from the mission and the churches. The ministry had never been a popular profession in Mexico. When a missionary crossed the border into Mexico, he lost his halo. The Mexican pastor had never even worn a halo. He did not wear a clerical collar or a gown or a stole and was rarely called "reverend." There was even a time when the government said that since a pastor had no useful profession in society, he could be jailed as a vagabond, and he was sometimes set to work laying cobblestones in the hot sun. That mistreatment passed, but his salary was still minimal. He received none of the perks the American pastor was guaranteed. He had to support his family, pay for their education, and somehow save money for medical emergencies. If his shoes wore out tramping to the twenty-five or more congregations he was responsible for, besides his own church, then he stood the expense for new footwear.[8]

In Chiapas, Mabel and I learned that the work of the Lord does not rest on the amount of money that we have at our disposal but on the "immeasurable greatness of his power for us who believe, according to the working of his great power" (Ephesians 1:19).

[8]   JRK, "Reformed Church Women's Triennial," unpublished manuscript (July 18, 1991), 3, in JAH.

CHAPTER 9

Preaching by Laypeople

One of my favorite childhood games was to play church worship service. Being the third in line of nine siblings, I enjoyed the privilege of having a rather large audience. I played the preacher in imitation of our pastor at First Reformed Church, in Sioux Center, Iowa, the congregation of my family. Later, I saw my own children doing the same; it seems that this is a favorite game of children raised in Christian homes. We, however, took this performance very seriously, even when, at the farm, we sometimes had a mixed congregation with either a dog, cat, goose, or turkey interrupting the liturgy. Nevertheless, all of us (including the animals) had this in common: we were truly worshiping God, and we were all lay people (or animals).

During the first years of our ministry, there was little organization, travel was difficult, and groups were small. All of the missionaries were taught responsibility, and because of the daily testimony of the faithful, believers and groups multiplied. A salaried colporteur traveled the trails selling Bibles. No other workers received any remuneration. The miracle of God's grace was that with only the preaching of untaught lay members and with occasional pastoral or missionary visits, sometimes fewer than once a year, these groups retained their devotional and missionary spirit.

Unable to administer the sacraments because of my foreign nationality, I limited my ministry to preach and counsel in the churches, to print and distribute literature, and to teach in institutes to train lay leaders. Many of the first ministers in the state were taught by me. The others were able to attend Bible school in San Cristóbal or the seminary in Mexico City.

Though Coffin and I used the same methods in the early days, as time went by, there was an increasing difference of opinion on policy. The vast Chiapas area, the increasing number of churches, and the demand for pastoral care cried out to heaven for the introduction of other ministers into the state. This was something José Coffin rejected tenaciously, even after Rev. Ezequiel Lango and Rev. Isidro Estrella came to Chiapas, and Genaro de la Rosa was ordained. The growing church demanded Sunday schools, Christian Endeavor Societies, and Women's Societies, all of which we missionaries slowly introduced in spite of constant criticism and sometimes resistance. When at last the mission's ideal of a presbytery in Chiapas was realized, in spite of the obdurate opposition from the mother Presbytery of the Gulf, Coffin moved to Tabasco to remain with the old presbytery, and we were granted more freedom to organize the work in Chiapas.

Six more native-born ministers (Rev. Genaro de la Rosa was also a Chiapas son) were ordained in those years. There were thirteen consistories, a Christian Endeavor Union, and the Union of Women's Societies, which met in annual conventions. These were high points of inspiration and instruction every year. When the ninth annual meeting of the Presbytery of Chiapas was held in Tapachula in 1958, reports showed a church membership of twelve thousand. The churches continued to grow tremendously in the following years.[1]

The key to the increase in the number of believers and churches planted was the active participation of lay people in the task of the proclamation of the gospel. It would have been impossible for us to do all the preaching and teaching throughout the state of Chiapas. We could and did, however, perform one key ministry that helped to expand the number of people involved in ministry—training lay leaders. From the beginning of our mission, I knew that our greatest need was for the training of national ministers and preachers. Accordingly, the first training school for chaplains (lay preachers and teachers) was held

---

[1]   JRK, "How the Gospel Came to Chiapas," 4-6.

in Tapachula in 1927, with classes in the church, as the law demanded. A lean-to on the chapel patio became a dormitory and our veranda, the dining room. We had so much to learn ourselves. In their culture, these men scooped food from enamel plates with tortillas, yet we gave them dinnerware, both china and silver. A glass of water at knife tip was a novelty, and each man reserved his for the accepted after-meal mouth cleansing and swishing on the ground—in this case the cement floor. After the first dinner, water was excluded from meal service. Regional institutes soon followed, with the missionary traveling to teach the men in their own localities. The next step toward a more permanent school would be taken four years later.

In 1931 Dr. Gustavus A. Watermulder, who once said that, if he were younger, he would choose Chiapas for his field, satisfied our continual longing for help and visited us. With his keen and sympathetic understanding of the situation, he encouraged us in our growing desire to move inland toward our original goal of reaching out to the indigenous population. Following his advice, we returned in April to Tuxtla Gutiérrez, where we had previously enjoyed the warm reception of believers who pled with us to either live among them or provide another minister. At that time, Mabel and I were just two. But now we had a three-year-old son and a six-month-old daughter traveling the long day's train trip with us from Tapachula to Jalisco (now Arriaga), after which we had to jounce eleven hours by car the next day over the hundred-mile oxcart road to the Zoque Maya town, at the foot of the peak of Mount Mactzumactzá (The stone of eleven stars). We hastened as quickly as possible to Tuxtla, because once the June rains began, we were confined without exit for six months.

In Tuxtla the Bible Institute opened in 1932, with students housed in the brick-floored veranda at one end of the old Spanish colonial house, which was our rented home. School costs were cut to a minimum by building partitions and the humblest of furniture out of packing boxes and by maintaining a common family/school kitchen and laundry. Through the years, a great many men and boys, both Maya and *mestizo*, lived within those adobe walls, some as full-time Bible school students; some enrolled in public school morning classes, with afternoons and evenings free for Bible study; and some attending high school and college.[2] Two of the men became active pastors in Chiapas; several were elders, chaplains, and workers in the churches; some as

---

[2]   *Mestizo* means "mixed," and describes a person of mixed blood, more specifically a person of mixed European and indigenous American ancestry.

teachers, influenced their communities with Christian witness; and three were ministers outside the state.

Lay evangelists played a key role in the process of bringing Chiapas to Christ. One of them was Mr. Matuda, a Japanese rancher. He was converted in Japan. When he moved to Mexico, he tried to practice his faith, but he did not preach it. One day, Jeremías Cruz, a Roman Catholic of his acquaintance, asked him, "How is it that you never try to trick your workmen but always pay the full amount due?" Matuda answered, "Because, although I could deceive them, I cannot deceive God. They cannot figure accounts, but I can, and they must be exact." "But we have our God, too," answered Jeremías. "Yes, you have gods but in your churches. My God lives here," said Matuda pointing to his heart.

That was the beginning of Matuda's evangelistic work. Jeremías bought a Bible and was converted, and slowly others began to come. Sunday after Sunday, Mr. Matuda held a Bible class in his home. By 1935 the group had an attendance of sixteen adults. He taught his converts not only the Bible but also courtesy. They greeted one another following the Japanese fashion. He helped them to avoid the despicable Mexican custom of borrowing money and working out the debt later, guiding them to earn money before spending it. He trained them to eat at tables instead of on the ground around the open fire. He also tried to help them build more permanent homes and simple furniture. Truly, this was an ideal piece of voluntary work carried out by a lay evangelist.

Colporteurs have always been the most outstanding of all the laypersons proclaiming the gospel in Chiapas. Beside the fact that they had pioneered the work in the state, they also proved to be courageous and persistent in their labor of letting the Word of God be known. By the 1950s, Zenón Cueto, a veteran colporteur, continued to distribute many Bibles, although his radius of activity was now limited by his age. All but one of the lay workers who were active in those years graduated from our Bible school. Their names will remain in my memory forever: Gamaliel Hernández, who assisted his brother Margarito Hernández; Joaquín Jiménez in Laguna Abajo; Genaro Méndez in the Tuxtla field; Silvino Vidal in Cacahoatán; Juan Trujillo in the Ch'ol territory; and Enrique Cruz, a Bible school graduate who did his secondary school work in preparation for seminary entrance. Many others came later, but these men were the pioneers.

With opposition so strong and sin so prevalent, it was necessary for all Chiapas believers to make a complete break with the past. Some would consider their attitude toward liquor, dancing, and smoking as

Faithful colporteur Zenon Cueto
begins another adventure
of Bible distribution

puritanic. It was vital, however, that the new converts were different
in life and behavior from the unbeliever. Our enemies were the first to
criticize when so-called believers yielded to worldly appetites. A changed
life and missionary zeal went hand in hand, so the Chiapas missionaries
used the slogan: "Every Christian a convert; every convert a missionary."

Another notable feature to which much of the progress of the
church in Chiapas must be attributed was the activity and commitment
of the lay Christians, both men and women. On Sunday mornings, more
than a hundred church services were held simultaneously—and there
were only nine ordained men in the state at that time! Believers were
free and had opportunities to exercise their gifts and use their talents
in the service of the Lord. Some of them participated by preaching
and teaching the Word, others by joining forces to build a church, to
cook for special occasions, and to host the small congregations in their
homes. Hospitality was a vital part of ministry. In rural areas, there were
no inns or restaurants, and though people sometimes shut the door to
lay workers, ministers and missionaries were never refused lodging or
food in all their travels up and down the state.[3]

---

[3]   Ibid., 8-10.

CHAPTER 10

Education and Information

Education and the free flow of information have always constituted a significant part of the Protestant body of principles. Reformed people inherited these ideals from John Calvin and his wise teachings taken from scripture and illuminated by the Holy Spirit. Education and information, particularly through the printed page, have also been an important aspect of our ministry in Chiapas. Mabel and I had learned this in childhood. I remember when I was nine years old in my elementary school, how much these two elements were sown into my mind and heart, with the insistence that they were foundational to a truly free society. Even at that early age, I understood that the only way to real democracy rested on sound education and a free press.

Interestingly, in Mexico, in the very troublesome framework of the transitional years between the nineteenth and twentieth centuries, Presbyterians were of the same conviction and became deeply committed to these two ideals, rendering in this way the best service to the republic. An expression of this contribution was the founding of the magazine *El Faro*, the official organ of the National Presbyterian Church in Mexico, first published in 1885. It soon became the evangelical periodical with the largest number of copies printed. It had a distribution that reached several other countries in Latin America and also the United States, Spain, and Portugal. In the beginning, it was a monthly publication; from 1886 on, it was semi-monthly; and in 1909, it became a weekly. The Mexican participation in its administration and production was significant. Regular collaborators in the Presbyterian mission were men like Arcadio Morales, Plutarco Arellano, Pedro Aguirre, Abraham Franco, Leandro Garza Mora, Miguel Z. Garza, and José Coffin. All of them were well educated and experienced leaders.

In a time when illiteracy was prevalent, these Mexican Presbyterians had access to various levels of education and information and were useful in diffusing their faith through these means. *El Faro* became the most important organ of evangelical reflection and proclamation of the gospel in the complex years of the Porfiriato (the dictatorial and liberal regime of Porfirio Díaz, 1876-1911). Publication of *El Faro* continued, with its valuable resource of information from churches, Sunday sermons, moral advice, and reports of national and international events. Its editorials extended beyond doctrinal and ecclesiastical issues. Without any particular political inclination, the periodical offered substantial interpretations of the rich and complex Mexican reality, particularly during the Porfiriato.[1]

Later, in spite of its dictatorial character, the administration of President Plutarco Elías Calles (1924-28) was inclined to favor public schools, particularly in rural contexts. Since revolutionary days, Mexico had established between six and seven thousand such schools. Calles was spoken of as "the Apostle of Rural Schools." When by February 1931, Dr. Gustavus A. Watermulder, of the Board of Domestic Missions, paid a visit of several days to Mexico, he was very much impressed with the educational projects of the Department of Public Instruction. He spent a few days with us in Chiapas and was also touched by the extent of the indigenous population without any sort of education. By then, there were eight million native peoples in Mexico, to say nothing of the seven million *mestizos*. In our isolated state of Chiapas, most of our congregations were distinctly indigenous. We had the opportunity to accompany Dr. Watermulder to visit some of them. His report of this experience confirmed our own conviction of the need to bring education and information to the rural communities and especially to the church leaders. He said:

[1]   Penélope Ortega Aguilar, "El *Abogado Cristiano Ilustrado* y *El Faro*: la prensa protestante de la época ante el Porfiriato" (Lic. in History diss., Universidad Nacional Autónoma de México, 2011), 29-31.

There is this danger in our work in Chiapas; we have quite a number of lay chaplains who lead the congregations in the isolated villages. These men are not trained but are devoted, loyal Christians. They need Christian training. Their souls must be fed before they can feed others. What is greatly needed in Chiapas is a Bible school where native leaders may have thorough training. They are the ones who will spread the gospel and lead their own people. And what a marvelous opportunity it is for our church to help train native men to bring the gospel to the 450,000 people of the state of Chiapas.[2]

I have learned through the many years of my missionary experience in Chiapas the importance of the development of church leaders through apprenticeship. The leaders of most of our churches in the state were those laymen who had worked their way up in the local congregations through an informal kind of apprenticeship system. They often began as ushers; then they sold scriptures and tracts as colporteurs. They might next serve as Sunday school teachers, then as deacons or elders, and finally as assistant pastors, often in small, newly formed congregations. Finally, when these men were forty or fifty years of age, they might become full pastors of a church. Then even with full ministerial responsibilities for a large congregation, they might continue to earn a living at some secular job, while giving all their spare time to the church. In other cases, they could become full-time workers for the church, with some economic assistance from our mission. The obvious advantage of this type of program was that neophytes were not turned loose on congregations before they were seasoned by experience in a number of roles in church life. Moreover, by the selective process, only those with real leadership ability tended to rise to the top.[3]

Education and information are important, but they should not be the focus of a missionary project. Evangelization is more significant than information, and planting churches is more necessary than building schools. The primary purpose of mission schools is Christian education. Some denominations may have schools where the religious emphasis is forbidden, as was the case in Mexico during our years of service there. But that is not the church's work nor the proper way to use mission funds. In 1940 the Mission Board of the Northern Presbyterian

---

[2]   Women's Board of Domestic Missions (WBDM), "Education in Mexico," *The Christian Intelligencer* (April 8, 1931), 211.

[3]   Eugene A. Nida, *Understanding Latin Americans: With Special Reference to Religious Values and Movements* (Pasadena, CA: William Carey Library, 1974), 139-40.

Church sent a deputation to visit their Latin American fields, and they closed well-established schools with expensive equipment, because those schools no longer had a clear religious emphasis. If education is to be along materialistic lines, Mexico does it pretty well—too well. This is so because the country is educating the youth away from a belief in God, in spite of the chaos which materialism has brought upon us all.

The same is true with medicine and medical training. One cannot practice medicine in Mexico without being licensed by the country. Practically the only way such a license can be obtained is by studying medicine in Mexico. As a church, we can do little along the lines of medical missions except to support the work of national Christian doctors. Mexican Christian Presbyterian doctors and nurses organized themselves to carry on Christian work under the catchy theme, "The Ministry of Medicine."

It would be interesting to learn whether Japan learned more from Western teachers in American mission schools in that country or from sending students to the United States for specialized training. The practice of exchanging students was a fine custom and apparently efficient. Educating Latin Americans in the United States, however, does not always create goodwill. Some of the most rabid "Gringo-haters" I know were educated in the United States. Much depends on their associations and the treatment accorded them by their fellow students.[4]

Education and information play a significant role as integral parts of the missionary responsibility of the church. But they are not the primary focus. Evangelization continues to be the most important responsibility of any missionary enterprise, not only in Latin America but also around the world.

---

[4]   JRK, "The Call of Mexican Youth," *The Intelligencer-Leader* (November 13, 1942), 17.

CHAPTER 11

The Mexican Revolution

In the year 1910, when I was ten years old and experiencing personal revolutions of my own, the country where the Lord was preparing me to go as witness to the gospel of Jesus Christ was also undergoing a revolution. This revolution, however, had lasting implications for the history of a nation and extended its impact on the entire continent and even the world. It became one of the most powerful revolutions in the history of humankind.

The survival of feudal vestiges characterized the structure of Mexican society. The economic system was oriented more to a medieval past than to the expectancies of a bright progressive future, as promised by the intellectual positivistic elites in the city of Mexico. The traditional structures were especially glaring in the area of labor relations. There was, however, some variation in labor conditions from region to region. In 1910 forced labor and outright slavery, as well as older forms of debt peonage, were characteristic of the South (the states of Yucatán, Tabasco, Chiapas, and parts of Oaxaca and Veracruz). The rubber, coffee, tobacco, henequen, and sugar plantations of this region depended heavily on the forced labor of political deportees, captured indigenous rebels, and contract workers kidnapped or lured to work in the tropics by a variety of devices.

An ample spectrum of political, economic, and social circumstances summed up a growing discontent in the nation. The depression of 1906 and 1907, which spread from the United States to Mexico, caused a wave of bankruptcies, layoffs, and wage cuts. At the same time, the crop failures of 1907-10 provoked a dramatic rise in the price of staples like corn and beans. By 1910 Mexico's internal conflicts had reached an explosive stage. Strikes, agrarian unrest, agitation of middle-class reformers, disaffection of some great landowners and capitalists, all reflected the disintegration of the dictatorship's social base. Despite its superficial stability and posh splendor, the regime of President Porfirio Díaz was rotten from top to bottom. Events proved that only a slight push was needed to send it toppling to the ground.[1]

It is impossible to grasp the depth of this unique event without a clear understanding of the "Mexican Revolution." It was a fruitful concept, fertilized as it was by association with other great progressive watersheds such as the French Revolution and the more recent Bolshevik Revolution in Russia. The concept of revolution implied an irrevocable break with a corrupt past and a consequent opening to a better future. Accordingly, the progressive technocracy, which was the Porfiriato, had to be caricatured as a reactionary *ancien* régime, which had sold out the noble ideals of Benito Juárez and La Reforma to the greed of proforeign aristocrats and an obscurantist Roman Catholic Church.

More positively, the idea of revolution obliged an aspiring Mexican ruling class, for the first time since independence, to create the idea of a nation which would unite the people behind a common identity. The Mexican Revolution was to recover the heritage of the Aztecs and the Maya, which had been perverted for so long by Spain and her champions before and after independence. In this respect, the new order was anti-Spanish and anticlerical. Now the true Mexican identity would be forged from the fusion of indigenous and Spanish traditions. The day of the *mestizo* and the native had arrived. They could also find a dignified place as full citizens in a new Mexico that was taking shape.

The Revolution was converted into the ultimate source of the government's authority. In effect, appeals to the spirit of the Revolution could function as a transcendent approval of political power, a modern equivalent of the divine will which had theoretically underwritten the

---

1   Benjamin Keen, *A History of Latin America*, 4th ed. (Boston: Houghton Mifflin, 1992), 219-20.

decrees of the Catholic monarchy. The state thereby acquired a mystique which the illiterate multitudes found easier to sympathize with than such bloodless liberal abstractions as the "sovereignty of the people." But to achieve a monopoly of legitimacy that would rival that of the Catholic monarchy, the new rulers had to convert the Revolution into a permanent reality. Authority could not be vested for too long in any one person, for this would dissipate the mystique that legitimized the state. The Revolution had to be a self-perpetuating and impersonal process. In practice, this meant that the problem of legitimate succession had to be solved—a problem that all previous Mexican rulers had eluded. Even so, a self-perpetuating, one-party state, legitimized by a transcendent Revolution, was to take a further decade of bloody struggle to create.[2]

My personal growth was not as painful as was the maturation of Mexico as a modern nation. I was still playing as a child and beginning to assume responsibilities as a young person when Mexico was going through the pangs of giving birth to a new society. Nobody was excluded from these pains. This also involved the small evangelical community scattered throughout the extended national territory. In fact, the General Synod of the National Presbyterian Church in Mexico could not hold a meeting for a period of five years (1912-17) due to the instability created by the Revolution. The Mexican Revolution, however, was not initially antievangelical. For instance, President Venustiano Carranza, who led the republic from 1917 to 1920, showed an interest in their schools. But evangelicals suffered in the general turmoil prevailing in the nation. Many young students preparing for the ministry had to assume responsibilities in the struggle, as did some pastors. Communications became almost impossible, and travel was quite dangerous. Meetings of local congregations and presbyteries were cancelled or not regularly convened. Even inside the communities of faith, the membership was politically divided, and difficulties multiplied. To worsen the situation, the Cincinnati Plan (see chapter 16) weakened the work of the various denominations involved, despite the opposition of most of the national leadership. Nevertheless, evangelical churches grew. The total membership in 1916 was more than twenty thousand, and in 1946, it was over two hundred thousand.

When the Revolution burst upon the country, evangelicals took it as a sign that God was calling them to increased activity. For North American Missions Boards, however, conditions worsened. Whereas in

2   Edwin Williamson, *The Penguin History of Latin America* (London: Allen Lane-The Penguin Press, 1992), 391-92.

1910 there were three hundred missionaries in Mexico, by 1916 threats to life and property had reduced that number to thirty. Many buildings were destroyed, and believers scattered in all directions.[3] The United States invasion of the port of Veracruz in 1914 did not help at all in improving the public image of the missionaries coming from the north, who were taken as part and parcel of the same imperialistic intervention. Nevertheless, for believers, opposition and even persecution resulted in a significant stimulus to their faith and commitment. This was particularly true in Chiapas.

At the national level, the Presbyterian work was maturing and advancing with a dynamic rhythm. The General Synod, founded July 8, 1901, had made great progress in ten years. It commemorated the independence of Mexico with a special event, recognized the National Association of Sunday Schools, began to publish the *Fanal* for Sunday school teachers, and continued to sponsor the seminary under the leadership of William Wallace. When I was ten years of age, I didn't even know there was a country by the name of Mexico, and even less that there was such a remote region called Chiapas. The events that were taking place in this corner of the world, however, became very significant when Mabel and I ended up ministering in the name of Jesus to its people.

3   J. Edwin Orr, *Evangelical Awakenings in Latin America* (Minneapolis, MN: Bethany Fellowship, 1978), 110.

CHAPTER 12

Rivalry for Power

When I was eleven years of age, I had my first "boxing" experience at school. I was a rather quiet and meek boy but with a strong sense of justice. I learned this from my parents, and throughout my life, I have lived by this principle, and at times, I saw that justice was upheld. Bullying is not a new idea; somehow it was part of our everyday experience at school in those days. There was one student in particular who felt the need to demonstrate to everybody else that he was stronger and in control, and one day, he targeted one of my closest friends as the object of his teasing and mortification. During a break one day, he told my friend, "After school, I'll wait for you, and beat you until you cry." I heard the menace, and that was the drop that made the glass overflow. Coming out of school, I ran to protect my friend, and gathering courage from somewhere, I told him, "If you dare to touch him, I'll blow your face!" Never again did this bullying champion challenge anybody else.

Human life is a permanent sequence of "bullying." In the end, whether it is in politics, business, or any other human relationship, it is an issue of rivalry for power. Nowhere in life is this feature more evident than in the political sphere, where power comes from the top and is mediated to society through a pyramidal structure or governmental hierarchy. Such a power system can only regard opposition as treason. Basically, in a system in which "error has no rights," there can be neither a two-party system nor "a loyal opposition." To even tolerate opposition is regarded as a sign of weakness and a failure of leadership.[1] Mexico has been an example of this political authoritarianism in action, and Chiapas was no exception to the rule.

In 1911 important farmers and ranchers of San Cristóbal de Las Casas, in alliance with the natives of the highlands of Chiapas, organized an insurrection against the dominance of Tuxtla Gutiérrez that lasted for two months. They wanted to recover the power represented in holding the capital of the state. The various municipalities took sides. Comitán backed the Tuxtlecos (inhabitants of Tuxtla Gutiérrez), and Chiapa de Corzo backed the Coletos (inhabitants of San Cristóbal de Las Casas), with the result that the capital remained with Tuxtla Gutiérrez, and a great and long-lasting rancor developed between the two municipalities. Interestingly, when we arrived in Chiapas fifteen years later, this competition and rivalry was still in existence, and regretfully, was reflected even in the attitudes of the churches of both cities.

All these difficulties were closely related to the conflict created in the country during the aftermath of the Mexican Revolution. The hopes and promises of the hard-fought Revolution were soon swallowed up by ambition, greed, and leftist ideology and practices. One antireligious decree followed another. The agrarians killed and plundered and with government support took land from titled owners. Businesses all had syndicates with oppressive and confiscatory regulations. The government took over private enterprise but later tried to return it to the private sector. The prosperity promised to the masses went to the few. The peacock quickly lost its lustrous tail.

Although there was religious repression throughout Mexico, the state of Tabasco exceeded all in severity under Governor Tomás Garrido Canaval, an avowed atheist. Ministers and priests were expelled from the state. Many church buildings were leveled. Laymen caught doing religious work were sentenced to days of laying cobblestones in the hot city streets.

Officials in Chiapas did not wish to be outdone by those of the neighboring states. No one who professed any religious faith could hold a government position or teach in a public school. Copying Tabasco, teachers and all other government employees were forced to bring

---

[1]   Nida, *Understanding Latin Americans*, 22.

their household images or statues of saints to the public square, where a bonfire consumed the heap. It was whispered that most people had brought the least valuable "saints" and hidden the more prized ones. All churches were closed. When it was suggested that the government be more lenient with the Protestant clergy, which had always been wholeheartedly supportive of the Revolution, someone cried out, "No, ¡parejo para todos!" (Treat everyone alike). The mail could not be used for sending religious propaganda, but somehow the sending of my church *Boletín* (later to be *El Despertador*) was never interrupted.

Many of our churches had already been closed, often because of the zealous revolutionary spirit of school teachers. The Tuxtla church in 1935 was granted permission to celebrate the ever-popular Christmas program, on condition that we invite public officials. We complied, but halfway into the program, with the church packed wall to wall, enjoying what it heard and saw, young Red Shirts walked boldly in with a new order: stop immediately and turn over the church key to the authorities. We hurriedly threw the rented folding chairs over a wall into a neighbor's yard. Six of us shouldered our piano used for the occasion and carried it nonstop to our house four blocks away. The next day, one of the carriers could not straighten his back and continued to suffer from the strain. But we were able to save Mabel's piano from destruction! Services, however, were suspended for a time. Vigilance was so strict and limitations so numerous, that one could only visit people personally. We were disappointed to tears (as was my mother when she heard the story). But we remembered the words of the veteran missionary, Harry Phillips, "Remember, God loves his church more than we do."

One day, I rode to Tecpatán. As soon as I arrived at the home of a believer, where I was to spend the night, a written order came from the town hall. I was to present myself immediately. With no undue haste, I went and was greeted sternly with a demand that I identify myself. It so happened that after that night with the believers in Tecpatán, I had planned to continue travel to Finca La Blanca, whose owner, Dr. Sturgis, an American dentist, had recently died. His widow, living in the United States, had entrusted me with her power of attorney. Identifying myself as such, although I had no proof with me, the hostile attitude changed instantly to offers of assistance. I asked for hay for my horse and a guide for the mountain trail the next day.

Paradoxically, during the Revolution, Dr. Sturgis was forced to carry the family sewing machine on his back wherever the troops marched. His wife was so abused by the colonel that, once safe in the United States, she vowed never to return to Mexico. The seven years we knew Dr. Sturgis in Chiapas, his wife was not with him. The remnants of the buildings of Finca La Blanca and the coffee fields were used to house a Christian Guatemalan family, whose head had been active in politics. He had been imprisoned, and after escaping from jail successfully, he crossed the border into Mexico. There, at considerable risk, we befriended him and his family, who followed later. The little curly-headed boy who had played with our children grew up to be a leader in sports, a man outstanding in Christian education and evangelism in Guatemala. Ownership of the plantation was lost to the strong and dangerous agrarians who took over titled properties for their use.[2] I remember this particular case as an illustration of the kinds of difficulties believers had to face during the long years of the Revolution and in the years that followed.

The major political difficulty created by the Revolution was the constant change of leadership. This was nothing more than a shifting of responsibility among the members of the same ruling class. This meant that the Revolution and its aftermath were little more than a *coups d'état* or a changing of the guard. The *caudillos* had changed, but the essentially feudal system had remained intact. Even with such changes, there were certain fascinating and often tragic failures. One strong leader did not want to complete projects begun by his predecessor. This would be giving too much credit to the ousted leader, and it might also reflect on the creative leadership of the new incumbent. Therefore, everything started by a former regime was wiped out, and a new beginning was made.[3]

Regretfully, this same pattern could be observed occasionally in the rivalry of power that occurred among the churches, their leaders, and in the governance of the denomination in the state. Of all these contradictions, the one that affected me most was my rivalry with José Coffin. Although he and I had the same method of ministry, our differing goals brought us into sharp conflict. Coffin was quite content to be the only ordained Presbyterian minister in Chiapas. He would appoint lay chaplains for the new groups and hold elections of elders for the larger congregations. But he was very reluctant to train others for ordination to the ministry. He did, however, eventually approve the ordination of one of his chaplains, Genaro de la Rosa, to assist him in Tapachula and the surrounding area.

As a foreigner, I was prohibited by law to administer the sacraments, but I was allowed to teach and preach. In 1932, Chiapas, following the example of the Federal District, limited the number of clergy to one for every sixty thousand inhabitants. That allowed only

---

[2]   JRK, "Some of This and Some of That," 12-13.
[3]   Nida, *Understanding Latin Americans*, 22-23.

eight or nine men who could officiate in the Catholic and Protestant churches of our state. Fortunately, José Coffin was accepted as one in this limited number together with a Nazarene minister living in the southwest corner of the state. When we realized that our work was scattered over the entire state, with almost impassable mountain roads connecting the villages, the inconveniences of this system became clear. Children often had to wait from one to two years for baptism and candidates for church membership likewise. Church discipline— imperative on the mission field—was equally handicapped.[4] But the most egregious consequence of these restrictions was that a minister could take advantage of his position to accumulate power and influence. Coffin came to be convinced that Chiapas was "his" exclusive field of service and was not willing to share that position with anybody else.

In light of these circumstances, I soon realized that an even greater priority was the training of leaders for the many congregations in Chiapas. Only a year after our arrival, we began to conduct training sessions for the chaplains, with the church building serving as a classroom and dormitory and our home as the dining hall. We also initiated youth work and women's societies with the idea of harvesting potential leaders for the churches. All of these new activities were opposed by Coffin, but they went ahead nonetheless.[5]

Coffin did not want to share his power over the congregations in Chiapas with any intruder into his "kingdom," and his indefatigable ministry had the perpetuation of his memory as its primary goal. In our last year in Chiapas (1965), however, I was teaching a class in the Bible school in San Cristóbal, and somehow I brought up the name of Coffin. I thought I detected a blank look on the faces of the students, so I said, "Surely you all remember José Coffin." They shook their heads. They had no idea who he was. Finally, one student said, "I remember my folks talking about him once." I was stunned! Coffin's name had been synonymous with the Presbyterian Church in Chiapas. He had traveled the state as I did—only at a slower pace. He had baptized children and adults, ordained elders and deacons, and organized churches and missions. He represented the Chiapas church at the annual Presbytery of the Gulf meetings, and he was so highly thought of outside Chiapas, that he was elected the first moderator of the General Assembly when that body was organized. Yet, here in Chiapas, ten years after he left the state, he was almost totally forgotten.[6]

[4]   MVD, "Indian Work in Mexico," *The Christian Intelligencer* (March 15, 1933), 172.
[5]   JSH, "The History of the Chiapas Mission," 5.
[6]   JRK, "Reformed Church Women's Triennial," 3.

CHAPTER 13

Potatoes Twice a Day

I have always known that all farmers kept cows for milk and butter and for domestic use, hens for eggs, and chickens for special Sunday meals. Every farmer, my father included, planted about a quarter acre of potatoes, enough for a year's supply. Today, Iowa farmers ride a powerful tractor and are not bothered with raising chickens, milking cows, and keeping potato patches. They can buy all they need at the supermarket.

I remember planting potatoes in rows when I was twelve years old, later spraying the green plants with Paris green, and then harvesting them. Father plowed the row, and all the kids, me included, got on our knees to fill bushel baskets, empty them in a wagon, and take the product to be stored in a cave or cellar. In the spring, we had to enter that odious enclosure to pluck off all the sprouts from the remaining potatoes, since these had to last until the new fall crop was ready for harvest.

Many years later, I gave a talk at the Women's Spanish Club on the origin of Peruvian potatoes some three to six thousand years ago, their spread to 130 countries, and their wide use today. *National*

Geographic, in some of its excellent articles, confirmed the data I had collected elsewhere and added more information. I studied these articles carefully.

Francisco Pizarro, the conqueror of Peru, and his men, as they marched rough shod, ignorantly and disdainfully over the Andean potato patches, had no idea that someday a one-year world crop of 291 million tons would be worth more than all the gold they had confiscated or mined. Potato consumption overcame superstition, and potato production spread all over Europe, England, Ireland, and North America. Russia came to raise and consume one third of the world's supply. Polish people relied heavily on the nutritive potatoes, as did the Irish. The Netherlands made more money from exporting potatoes than it did from its famous tulips. In the United States, Maine has ceded first place as producer of potatoes to Idaho, with its rich soil in the Snake River area. Potato plantations in Caldwell, Idaho, process one hundred thousand pounds of potatoes every hour, twenty-four hours a day. That's no small industry!

All this reminds me that in Peru, they raise delicious potatoes— some the size of a robin's egg. The Quechua names for their forty-one varieties are vast, many hard to pronounce, and come in all shapes and sizes and colors of the rainbow. Four types of them are raised in the United States. One of the books that I have enjoyed reading is Germán Arciniegas, *Latin America: A Cultural History.* He makes a remark on potatoes that caught my attention.

> The man who orders beefsteak and potatoes in a Paris restaurant and has it served to him surrounded by slices of tomato, eats food entirely unknown to Europeans during the first sixteen centuries of the Christian era. Potatoes and tomatoes came from America. The feat of initiating Europeans to the taste of the potato called for valor, and the men who performed it, such as Parmentier in France, are commemorated as the heroes they were. Today almost everyone eats potatoes. But people in some places cannot yet conceive that any creature save an animal could eat corn. In Italy it is disrespectfully called the "Turkish grain." On the other hand, the whole world enjoys chocolate from the cacao tree, which like corn, originated in America.[1]

Men and women around the world know how to prepare an assortment of potato dishes. But in France, there was a culinary school

[1]   Germán Arciniegas, *Latin America: A Cultural History* (New York: Alfred A. Knopf, 1966), 58.

from which none could graduate until he or she was able to fix at least sixty different potato dishes. Some people do not eat potatoes because they think they will cause weight gain. I consider that to be an unnecessary and unwise sacrifice. Potatoes are not fattening at all. A potato has no more calories than an apple, as much vitamin C as an orange, as much potassium as a banana, and it also provides vitamin B, copper, magnesium, and iron. You will not need Geritol if you eat potatoes![2]

Henry Ford had the idea of obtaining gasoline for his cars from potatoes. He was indeed ahead of his time. The fact is that today you can get twelve hundred gallons of ethyl alcohol from just one acre of potatoes. At fifteen miles to a gallon, this means that you can get eighteen thousand miles to an acre. That is much farther than some of us drive in a year.

Viva la papa! . . . and childhood memories of raising potatoes on a farm in Iowa and eating them twice a day.[3]

---

[2] Geritol is a United States trademarked name for various dietary supplements, past and present.
[3] JRK, "Iowa Club," n.d. and not signed document, probably written in 1981, in JAH.

CHAPTER 14

Beginnings of the Presbyterian Work in Tapachula

The human experience brings great joy when a person closes one stage of life with success and begins the next with hope. In 1913 I received my eighth grade diploma from School District Number Six of Welcome Township, Sioux County, Iowa. The diploma was signed and given at Orange City on May 31, 1913. I was now ready to start high school. I began in Sioux Center, but later, in God's wisdom, my parents sent me to Northwestern Academy, in Orange City.

New beginnings were also occurring at that time in Chiapas. In 1910 there were only six hundred Protestants in the state, half of them Germans and other foreigners. But in 1913, as we have seen, colporteurs from Guatemala distributed scriptures, and converts to evangelicalism in other parts of Mexico returned to their birthplace in the state. A spontaneous folk movement began with congregations springing up all over the state, more especially in the Soconusco area. Although they appealed for help, no missionaries were available to visit them.[1]

The Soconusco region is one of the most beautiful in Chiapas. An old legend says that the ancestors of the people populating that area

---

[1] Orr, *Evangelical Awakenings in Latin America*, 110.

believed that Votan (a Maya mythological god of war), astonished at such natural beauty and wishing to honor the inhabitants of Soconusco, caused a marvelous palace to come forth from the earth, not only with its gardens, apartments, and furniture but also with all kinds of servants ready for the royal mansion. Tapachula, the most important city of that region, was the general headquarters for our mission work in the state of Chiapas. It was the center of a great number of rural congregations. The daily school for girls founded by the Coffins was growing and sowing for the future. Medical work also began by the Coffins was spreading its benefits among the poor. Both were a great aid in our religious work.

Soconusco was also the most important commercial and agricultural region of Chiapas. It was the first region of the state to separate all its Roman Catholic churches from the Vatican. All the churches of this area became the property of the Mexican state and were run by Mexican Catholics (foreign priests were expelled). All over the Soconusco, the Mexican flag could be seen at the altars, and the mass was heard in Spanish instead of Latin. This had all happened since the day that a Mexican priest, with all his officials, took possession of the parochial church in Tapachula and said that, after one hundred years of independence, he was going to place the National flag on the last bulwark of the Spanish dominion in the Soconusco. He predicted the same thing would be done all over the country, as well as all over the Americas.[2]

The jewel of the Soconusco was the city of Tapachula, located at the far south of the region. The name of the town comes from the indigenous Nahuatl word *tlapachol-atl*, which means "flooding water." Since its foundation in colonial times, the city has been an important commercial and cultural center and a strategic point of communication through the International Federal Highway and the National Railroad of Mexico. It has an airport and is the second most important city in Chiapas, after the capital city of Tuxtla Gutiérrez.

The year 1913 was the beginning of the Presbyterian testimony in Tapachula. The number of believers in the area, particularly in this city, multiplied quickly. The strategic location of this small town helped to develop it as a commercial and communications center. Hearing that there were other Presbyterians in Mexico City, they sent word asking for pastoral help. Responding to the request, the Presbyterian leaders in Tabasco decided to send Rev. José Coffin and his wife Luz Otero to

---

[2]   "Chiapas from South to North: Notes of Rev. José Coffin's Missionary Trip," *The Christian Intelligencer* (September 7, 1927), 570.

Calle Zaragoza. Tapachula. Chis. México.

Together with the Coffins, we began our ministry in the city of Tapachula

Tapachula. The Coffins began their work in 1920. Five years later, the Presbyterian center in this city included a chapel, a parsonage, medical work, six primary schools, and a community Red Cross office. José Coffin had organized three additional congregations and was visiting families and groups of believers in eighty-one locations scattered throughout the interior of Chiapas.

The beginnings of the congregation in Tapachula illustrate the way many other churches in Chiapas had begun. On the San Vicente farm, known later as the "Benito Juarez" colony, in the municipality of Cacahoatán, Chiapas, brother Eulalio Ramírez was working as foreman. The boss, Eduardo de la Cerda, observed that Eulalio habitually prayed before eating and asked him if he was evangelical. After his affirmative answer, the boss encouraged him to preach the gospel on his farm to the workers who were drunkards. He wanted to have honest people working for him. Ramírez said that he had no money to buy Bibles and other Christian literature. De la Cerda told him that he would buy those materials in Guatemala. The first convert was José León Coronado, who later became a preacher in the congregation at Tapachula. Josefa Gramajo Ramírez and several others came to faith in Jesus Christ and gathered in the homes of believers.

That group eventually disbanded. The boss wanted to seduce a number of the young girls, who resisted his advances and were forced to leave the farm. They were dispersed, taking the gospel with them and having Tapachula as the center of their worship services. Josefa

Gramajo and her family went to Santa Rita and won people who later became leaders in the church. In Tapachula, the group that remained was enlarged and packed the meeting room. They soon felt the need of a pastor and began to pray for the Lord to provide one. A colored woman of the congregation went to Veracruz and talked with the pastor of the church in that city. Soon afterward, two men were sent to visit the faraway town of Tapachula: Rev. José Coffin and missionary Newell J. Elliott. When they got into the church building, which was packed with people, they perceived an ambience of reverence to the point that nobody responded to their greetings. Greeting people inside the church was against their concept of reverence. Coffin and Elliott were dubious about the doctrinal convictions of that group, but they relaxed when they saw a Bible and the Constitution of the Presbyterian Church on a small desk at the front. The original small group at San Vicente met on Saturdays and had some Adventist influences. But with the orientation of the newly arrived leaders, they affirmed a Presbyterian faith.[3] This was the first congregation Mabel and I met when we arrived there in 1926.

---

[3]   "Datos históricos de la Iglesia Presbiteriana de Tapachula, Chiapas," n.d., not signed document, in JAH.

CHAPTER 15

First World War

When I was fourteen, in my peaceful and predictable little world of Sioux Center, when I was starting my secondary school but before going to Northwestern Academy, nothing disturbed the harmony of most people. The provincial mood and isolation from the rest of the world was enough to keep everybody insulated from the cares of the world. In July of that year, however, nobody could escape the news coming from Europe of the beginning of what was later called the Great War. In no country did the masses desire war or know much about the events that led up to it. But even in Iowa, we came to know that war was a possibility. Everybody talked about it and hoped it could be averted. That is why, to the last moment, we believed that it would soon be over.

Yet, when it came, the majority of people in every country, including ours, and even in my little town—after a moment's hesitation—supported the war with enthusiasm. It was easy for us to believe that this war was different from any other, and in this view, we were confirmed by the official propaganda that also reached us. The war had scarcely begun, and we were discussing it in classrooms and cloisters. Most of us felt that this was our patriotic duty; it was a war of self defense against sinister and aggressive enemies. This was even more so when the United States got involved in the conflict in April 1917. In the beginning, this enthusiasm was all the greater, because we believed that this war would soon end in the defeat of our enemies. These optimistic hopes were soon dispelled. In all, the war lasted for four years, took the lives of some 8.5 million people, and left about twenty-one million wounded.

Meanwhile, in Mexico, the Great War added tension to the turmoil already caused by the Mexican Revolution, which began in 1910. Mexico was going through conflicts other than those which were tearing Europe apart. The Mexican revolt somehow spilled over into the United States, which is why our country in 1915 sent an army into Mexico led by John Pershing. So Mexico was indirectly involved in the world conflict. In early 1917, Germany was expecting to be soon at war with the United States. The German foreign minister Arthur Zimmermann tried to secretly arrange for Mexico to declare war on its northern neighbor, if the United States decided to oppose the European power. In return Germany would send money and weapons to help the Mexicans recover territories taken from them by the Americans, like Texas, New Mexico, and Arizona. The scheme was discovered, and President Venustiano Carranza declined to make any arrangement with the German Empire. Nevertheless, Mexico benefited in some respects from the war, due to the greater demand for oil and other mineral resources by the European powers, particularly Germany.

To understand the political, social, and economic situation of Mexico during the years of the Great War, it is necessary to take into account both the endemic conflict with the United States and the development of the Mexican Revolution. As to the first, the war brought up old rivalries and intensified the xenophobia of Mexicans against the *gringos*. Porfirio Díaz is supposed to have exclaimed: "Pobre México, tan lejos de Dios, y tan cerca de los Estados Unidos!" (Poor Mexico, so far from God, and so near to the United States).[1] This sentence eloquently summarizes the traumatic relationship of Mexico with her northern neighbor. The increased anti-Yankee mood which developed during these years had enormous consequences on the strategic decisions made by the North American Boards of Foreign Missions in Mexico and the proclamation of the gospel by foreign missionaries. In fact, our own ministry, through forty-five years in Mexico, was deeply impacted by these circumstances.

---

[1]   George Pendle, *A History of Latin America* (London: Penguin Books, 1990), 164.

As to the second, Mexico experienced an unending violent revolution and a civil war. In those years, this nation was involved in the internal total war represented by the Mexican Revolution, which was turning the country upside down. This transformation process went far toward destroying the social structure based on large-scale landholding, as did the revolutionary movements in eastern Europe after the First World War. But the toll was high. To the political, social, and economic changes was added a deep cultural reorientation and a movement toward integration that brought to prominence the native heritage. This process involved a social revolution through which depressed classes and isolated peoples moved toward full citizenship. In this sense, the Revolution set in motion both a social revolution and what has been termed "the reconquest of Mexico by the Indian." The result was not only to alter the class structure but also to change racial and cultural values, until it was no longer a source of prestige to be "European" but rather to call oneself "Indian" was an expression of pride. The impact of the new self image, which the Revolution brought to the people of northern and central Mexico, did not stop there. In time, it penetrated the isolated and remote land of Chiapas.

In Chiapas the population was composed of three main elements: Maya, *mestizo*, and some European. The small European overlay consisted of the descendants of European conquerors and later, immigrants (Germans in the Soconusco). The natives in Chiapas had been barely touched by European ways; they were isolated from national life and oppressed mostly by the *mestizo*. The numerous native populations in Chiapas continued to live within the structure of their traditional, geographically isolated communal culture and work as peasant-laborers, often in a state of quasi serfdom, on the large estates and plantations. The course of the Revolution and the policies of its leaders veered in different directions from time to time, accelerating or slowing the process of land distribution, intensifying or relaxing the antagonism to foreign investors, becoming anticlerical or tolerating the Roman Catholic Church. But these policies, with the best of popular methods and intent, never reached the majority of natives in Chiapas.

As for the *mestizos*, and especially for the Maya, another deeper and more radical revolution was necessary, the revolution produced in the lives of people when they come to Jesus Christ, receiving him as Savior, recognizing him as Lord, and obeying him as King. This was the revolution that later we wanted to bring to Chiapas and that we proclaimed under our goal of "Chiapas para Cristo."

CHAPTER 16

The Cincinnati Plan

American denominationalism had devastating consequences in Mexico. By the end of the nineteenth century, there were six Protestant denominations working in the Mexican republic, with eleven different missions. There was competition in the occupation of the territory and great confusion on the part of believers who could not tell the difference between one tradition and another.

In the hopes of improving this situation and bringing about a wiser distribution of forces, a conference of representatives of the boards and missionaries was held in Cincinnati, Ohio, in 1914, which resulted in an agreement on a union press, a periodical, a bookstore, a union theological seminary, and a church for Americans—all in Mexico City. There was also a redistribution of territory between the missions of the Congregationalists, the Presbyterians, Northern and Southern Methodists, and the Disciples of Christ and Friends. The other denominations did not participate in the plan. In accordance with this agreement, our Presbyterian Mission withdrew from northern Mexico and from the states of Michoacán and Guerrero on the west coast, giving up much of the mission's oldest and most securely established work. In return, the mission was assigned the states of Oaxaca, Veracruz, Chiapas (taken over by the Reformed Church in America Mission in 1925), Tabasco, Campeche, Yucatán, and the territory of Quintana Roo and retained its old work in the Federal District and Mexico City. This total territory represented one-fifth of the entire area of Mexico and made the mission responsible for the evangelization of one-quarter of its inhabitants.[1]

The political situation of Mexico in those years (1910-17) was disastrous. After assassinating Francisco I. Madero, Victoriano Huerta took control of the country but had to face military uprisings led by Venustiano Carranza, Francisco Villa, and Emiliano Zapata that shocked the nation. The Mexican Revolution was consuming in fire and blood not only the political parties in conflict but also the economy of Mexico. More and more the ministry of foreign missionaries, particularly those coming from the United States, was becoming difficult. This situation forced some American missionaries to return to their country. This included the Presbyterians that departed *en masse*. In New York, the board was convinced that there was no future for the Presbyterian missionary work in Mexico unless they joined forces with other denominations in a common plan.

From June 30 to July 1, 1914, in Cincinnati, Ohio, delegates of the six denominations gathered to discuss the issue under the leadership of Robert Speer (northern Presbyterian) and William F. Oldham (Methodist bishop). The territorial division of the missionary work was discussed seriously, without any sort of consultation with the national churches. On the other hand, some boards, whose missionary work had been deeply affected by the Mexican Revolution, saw the agreements as even more pernicious to their interests. In this way, a plan to save the supposedly paralyzed missionary work in Mexico, ended up killing it. The reaction against the Cincinnati Plan by some of the national churches was even stronger. Mexicans, already embedded in the typical nationalistic mood of the Revolution, rejected the Cincinnati Plan as an imperialistic and abusive strategy by foreign boards, in total ignorance of the real condition of the churches in Mexico.

For many Mexican Presbyterian leaders, the plan, right from its inception, fell to tactical and practical mistakes. Those who designed the plan had a wrong view of the church in Mexico. It is true that political and economic turmoil had caused much uncertainty as to

[1]   Gonzalo Báez-Camargo and Kenneth G. Grubb, *Religion in the Republic of Mexico* (London: World Dominion Press, 1935), 138.

the future of the work. But the seed of the gospel was well planted in the country, and despite the fact that railroads were destroyed, factories dismantled, sugar plantations burned, churches destroyed, and congregations scattered, the Christian testimony continued to be strong. Besides, Mexico was not an experimental laboratory where the experts in missiology in the United States could run their tests, not considering the fact that by then the National General Presbytery had already been organized. These national leaders were not taken into consideration at the time these decisions were made. There were no Mexican representatives either in Cincinnati or later during the application of the plan in Mexico.

According to the designers of the plan, the strategy of missions in Mexico was not defined in Mexico but in the United States by the boards of foreign missions of the denominations working in this country: Presbyterians, Methodists, Baptists, Congregationalists, and Disciples of Christ and Friends. The anti-American attitude of the Mexicans was not taken into consideration. Neither did the designers pay attention to the fact that, because of the Revolution and later the Constitution of 1917, most Mexicans considered it their right to dissent on what seemed unfair to them and to lead their own work in Mexico. Above all, it remained a fact that the territorial distribution, which was the most disturbing decision in the Cincinnati Plan, was not balanced and followed foreign interests more than national convenience. Some American missionaries of different denominations resisted the plan, but the rejection of the national ministers and churches was even more radical.

The national Presbyterian allegiances of the Mexicans were not taken into account in the creation of the Cincinnati Plan. National ministers were asked to leave their churches if the congregation was assigned to another denomination, with all the inconveniences that this caused in terms of family, work, and relationships, not to mention the forced change in doctrine and ecclesiology. Among the nationally recognized and most distinguished Presbyterian ministers who opposed the plan were José Coffin, Plutarco Arellano, Arcadio Morales, Leandro G. Mora, Eleazar Z. Pérez, Carmen A. Gutiérrez, Plácido López, Antonio G. Alvarez, and Pedro Rodríguez. It was clear to the Mexicans that the plan had serious tactical and practical mistakes.[2]

These are some of the reasons why the Cincinnati Plan did not always operate smoothly. Long-established denominational lines

---

[2]   Joel Martínez López, *Orígenes del presbiterianismo en México* (Matamoros, Tamaulipas: n.p., 1972), 205-12.

were not easily obliterated, and the independent Mexican churches were not satisfied with some features of the plan, as the actions of the National Presbyterian Church and most of its leaders illustrated. What some Protestant leaders in other parts of the world considered a good example that represented the triumph of cooperative Christian work over that of the old-time sectarian program was taken as a major loss for the advance of the Kingdom and a great headache. In fact, in Mexico, the Cincinnati Plan was known as Plan de Asesinato (The killing plan).

In spite of the numerous and formidable obstacles formed by the Cincinnati Plan, together with the politically hostile environment created by the Mexican Revolution, Protestantism appears to have been firmly established during those years. A report from the Mexican National Presbyterian Church of 1935 listed 584 churches, 1,203 congregations, 259 ordained ministers, 205 lay workers, 44,113 communicants (one to every 375 of the population in that year), 39,802 Sunday school scholars, and a Protestant community of 89,750.[3]

---

[3]   Báez-Camargo and Grubb, *Religion in the Republic of Mexico*, 138.

CHAPTER 17

How It All Began

On more than one occasion, I have asked myself, "What if my folks had not transferred me from the Sioux Center High School to Northwestern Academy in Orange City?" That move had enormous consequences on the course of my life. That was the juncture the Lord used to call me to his service. On a weeknight in the early months of 1915, as a young lad of fifteen, I was sitting in the main auditorium of the First Reformed Church in Orange City, Iowa, listening to Mrs. Walter C. Roe, missionary to Native Americans, who had done some travel in Central America and in Mexico. She was a fluent and enthusiastic speaker, and she mentioned the "millions of unsaved Indians living south of our border." That was the seed which the Holy Spirit planted in my heart and which slowly and quietly developed.[1]

My devout Christian parents had dedicated me in my infancy to the Lord's ministry. The influence of that home in the cornfields of Sioux Center, Iowa, so strongly Christ centered, and of my godly

---

[1] JRK, "How It All Began," unpublished document, n.d., 1, in JAH. See also, JRK, "Strength through Weakness," unpublished document, n.d., in JAH.

grandfather, saw results when I finally became Rev. John R. Kempers. After graduating from Hope College, I spent a year in Coopersville, Michigan, serving as a high school principal. This experience helped me to develop my teaching skills. My call, however, was to serve the Lord on the mission field and particularly among the natives. Because I didn't want to be an ordinary pastor preaching twice on Sunday and visiting people during the week, in the fall of 1922, I attended Princeton Theological Seminary. I did it in the hope that something would turn up which would be different.[2] In fact, I chose Princeton and not Western Seminary or New Brunswick Seminary, because by then, I already had in mind to serve the Lord on the mission field in Latin America. That choice was providential because later the prestige of being a Princeton graduate would be a valuable asset in Mexico. Princeton University awarded me my master's degree in 1925, at the same time the seminary conferred on me the ThB.[3]

For my first summer of work after a year of studies at Princeton, I applied to the Women's Board of Domestic Missions of the Reformed Church in America. I traveled up the Hudson River to preach at the Schodack Landing Reformed Church, and I spent that summer there. The following summer, I was assigned to the Comanche Mission station in Lawton, Oklahoma. Rev. Richard Harper was the pioneer missionary in charge of the ministry to the Native Americans. He was an excellent teacher of missions and later a dear friend of mine. His wife died of cancer that summer. After the funeral, he was given an extended vacation, and I was left in charge of the work. I carried on the established work diligently but routinely. Mr. Harper was favorably impressed that a young seminary student could handle the job.[4] He was so surprised and pleased with my handling of the Comanche and Apache ministry in his absence that his letters to the Board of Missions were full of praise. It was this support and recommendation which led to our appointment to the Chiapas Mission a few years later.[5]

I, however, was not impressed with the missionary work taking place among Native Americans, and although I dismissed this mission work from my future service, I did not give up hope that something might turn up in Latin America. I conversed with Latin American missionaries who were on furlough at Princeton, but none of them

---

[2]   JRK, "How It All Began," 1.
[3]   From a brochure published by the Board of Domestic Missions of the Reformed Church in America, in JAH.
[4]   JRK, "How It All Began," 1.
[5]   JRK, "Strength through Weakness."

seemed enthusiastic. I was unaware that three of the men of the preceding class were ready to go to Mexico under the Presbyterian Board. Why I didn't apply, I do not know, but it was providential. God had prepared other plans.

During my senior year, there were two calls from Reformed churches in the East which I held in reserve. Then, unexpectedly, a telegram arrived from the Women's Board of Domestic Missions of the Reformed Church. I remember each one of the words of that telegram: "Don't commit yourself to anything until you hear from us."

It turned out that they were dickering with the Presbyterian Board of Foreign Missions to take responsibility for the evangelization of the state of Chiapas in Mexico. In 1917 the Cincinnati Plan, hailed by the ecumenically minded boards as an ideal plan and simultaneously denounced by the denominationally minded churches in Mexico, had assigned the entire southeastern part of Mexico to the Northern Presbyterians. Because of the high-quality indigenous missionary work done in the United States by the Reformed Church, the Presbyterians agreed to turn over the responsibility for Chiapas. A committee of the Women's and Men's Boards of Domestic Missions traveled to Tapachula, Chiapas, to make arrangements with Rev. Harry Phillips, a Presbyterian missionary residing in Jalapa, Veracruz, and Rev. José Coffin working in Tapachula and a member of the Presbytery of the Gulf of Mexico. Although at first hostile to the Reformed Church, of which he had never heard, Coffin was impressed by the women of the committee traveling all the way to Tapachula, one of whom had the Presbyterian name of Knox. What also impressed him was that I was graduating from Princeton, to him the most famous and prestigious Presbyterian seminary.

I was never informed of what the arrangement was between Coffin and our boards. The Presbytery of the Gulf criticized him for making the arrangement single handedly, and they never knew just what the details of the arrangement were. The salary agreement was made directly between the board and Mr. Coffin, without consulting the presbytery, and his salary was mailed directly to him, as was money for expenses. This continued until I insisted that all funds should pass through the Reformed Church in America mission treasury.

Soon after receiving the telegram from the board, I was asked to go to New York City to meet with a committee. The project was presented, and they asked me if I would be their first missionary to Mexico. With great enthusiasm, I gave a positive answer to their question. Once I left the building, it began to dawn on me what I had agreed to. I walked from

Twenty-Second Street to Forty-Second Street on Broadway oblivious to everything around me. There I met a friend, and we went to a movie, which I sat through but did not see. When I told Mabe, who was in Michigan, I received a Ruth-like answer: I will go where you go; your people will be my people.

The remarkable thing in all this was that the board had no way of knowing of my interest in Latin America, and I had no idea that they were contemplating work there. Our denomination was very reluctant to go into new fields. It turned out that Dr. Richard Harper, with whom I had worked before in missions to Native Americans, had persuaded the board to commission me. God's timing was perfect, and there were the necessary contacts for this all to work out.[6]

It is amazing how the Lord works. He is the Master Player who moves the pieces on the chessboard according to his eternal purposes in Jesus Christ and following a strategy he has treasured in his heart and mind throughout eternity. How great it is to serve in the hands of our Master, knowing that every move in our lives is in response to his will.

---

[6]   JRK, "How It All Began," 1-2.

CHAPTER 18

The Panama Congress

I had three major preoccupations at the age of sixteen: sports, girls, and Latin— in that order. I had a passion for running and for basketball, a healthy attraction to girls, and an insatiable interest in Latin. My academic obligations at Northwestern Academy and my participation in the life and ministry of First Reformed Church in Sioux Center, gave me opportunites to invest my time and energy in these areas of interest. Of course, a lot of cooperation from my friends was necessary to accomplish my goals with these three aspirations. It is always like that in life. There are no Robinson Crusoes able to achieve goals by themselves without assistance from others. In life, we all need each other and mutual cooperation to achieve our dreams.

The work of the Kingdom is exactly the same. Cooperation is fundamental to accomplishing the work of the Lord. The first important step toward securing missionary cooperation in Mexico was taken during the World Missionary Congress, which met in Edinburgh in 1910. Missions in Roman Catholic lands did not fall under the purview of that congress, but a number of the delegates met each day and began to plan for a special gathering to consider this work. The Foreign Missions Conference of the United States and Canada planned a conference of representative workers which met in New York in 1913. At this time, a small continuation committee was named which, in time, grew into a larger one with representatives from some thirty boards and societies working in Latin America. Working with a corresponding committee in Europe, this committee issued a call for a deliberative congress on Christian work in Latin America, which convened in Panama in February 1916. Dr. Leandro Garza Mora attended the conclave representing the Mexican Presbyterians. In the Panama congress, he opposed the Cincinnati Plan as a wrong strategy for the development of the evangelical testimony in Mexico.

Immediately on its adjournment, a permanent committee on cooperation was organized, and it was largely due to their efforts that the work of cooperation between Christian ministries moved forward to such an unusual degree. Its functions were altogether consultative and advisory, and its endeavor was to serve the boards and the missionaries through the coordination of missionary work and the outlining of future plans. They came to agreement on primary regional responsibility in a number of countries, and with this limitation of fields and responsibilities, the various boards and missions were able to do more extensive work than would otherwise be possible.

In Mexico, for example, the boards so allocated their forces by means of this delimitation of territorial responsibility that the whole republic could be cared for with no overlapping of missionary funds or workers; whereas, formerly, many of these boards worked in the same centers, and a large part of the country was deprived of evangelical services. Various publication houses were combined into a union printing press; the denominational periodicals were united to form a single weekly publication, which ministered to all the evangelical groups; seven of the missions were united to form Union Theological Seminary; and schools and other forms of service were planned under cooperative auspices.[1]

This work of cooperation was thought to prove that the most compelling force to bring Christian workers together was not uniformity of belief or creed but rather the burden of a common task, and it was this unusual situation that would challenge the service of young people who were looking for a place in which to invest their lives, who were more interested in setting forth a great and common cause than in the

[1]   Webster E. Browning, *New Days in Latin America* (New York: Missionary Education Movement of the United States and Canada, 1925), 188-90.

strengthening of denominational fences. Close cooperation was a great idea, but in the field, it didn't render the expected results. Team play is important, as is strategy. Particularly in Chiapas, when we later came to serve, this was the case. You can gather together the best of intentions, but if you don't have an effective strategy to do the work, you will lose the war. In the end, the good ideas and initiatives taken at the Panama Congress were of little or no effect in our missionary work in Chiapas.

Somehow, the prevailing political conditions in Mexico and the governmental oversight in Chiapas prevented the organization of the work of each denomination and even more any attempt to carry out cooperative projects. From 1916 to 1920, Carranza was in power in Mexico. The 1917 Constitution, as will be seen later, provided for the complete separation of church and state. Article 3, however, abolished religious education, while Article 130 set limits to religious worship and prohibited clerical interference in political matters. Had the Constitution of 1917 been rigorously implemented, the wars that destroyed the Porfiriato (the dictatorial regime of President Porfirio Díaz) could have ushered in a genuine social revolution. But the 1917 document did not lead to a transfer of power between classes; it marked instead the eventual accession to national government of new land-owning elites from the North. During his term of office as president (1917-20), Carranza failed to evolve into a strong national leader.[2]

Nevertheless, in spite of the many difficulties presented by both the national and state political conditions, the work of the Kingdom continued to increase. In 1918 José Coronado and Jesús Martínez arrived in the small town of Mazapa de Madero from Tapachula. They organized large group meetings on Saturday evenings, with many people coming to the Lord. Meanwhile, in Tapachula, the local congregation rented the property on Fourth Avenue South and Fourth Calle Poniente Nº 36. With pride and courage they placed a sign in the front of the building: Iglesia Presbiteriana Jesucristo el Salvador (Jesus Christ the Savior Presbyterian Church). The Great War in Europe was coming to an end, and in Mexico, the Revolution was creating all sorts of difficulties. But the work of the people of God was growing as believers took every opportunity to spread the gospel.

---

[2]   Williamson, *The Penguin History of Latin America*, 388-89.

CHAPTER 19

The Mexican Constitution

The difficulties that the pioneer American missionaries had to contend with in Mexico were for the most part the same as those encountered by Protestant missionaries in other parts of Latin America. Most missionaries—Mabel and myself included—suffered isolation, loneliness, and the hardships of itinerating by oxcart or on horseback over almost impassable roads. To all this was added the hostility of Roman Catholic priests who, in the period of their domination of the government, brought sixty Mexican Protestants to a martyr's death and incited occasional mobs, such as that at Acapulco in 1875, which caused the death of thirteen Mexican Protestants and the injury of more than twenty others.

When I was graduating from Northwestern Classical Academy in Orange City, Iowa, receiving my diploma on June 18, 1917, after excelling in oratorical contests, and Mabel was about to begin her studies at Hope College in Holland, Michigan, the most serious difficulty in Mexico involved restrictions on religious liberty imposed by the government. The Presbyterian testimony in Chiapas suffered delicate handicaps during these years immediately after the consecration of the Mexican Constitution of 1917. One of those was that the public meetings of the believers in Tapachula were suspended. To the legal oppression, an unexpected circumstance was added on October 27—an epidemic of Spanish influenza that took many lives. The brethren, however, survived both plagues and soon obtained a house where they could hold their worship services. In 1918 they rented a room on a site occupied today by the Presbyterian Church Jesucristo el Salvador. By July 1919, the group had grown to seventy-two people and continued its development. With the arrival of José Coffin, this congregation was consolidated and affirmed in the Presbyterian faith until the church was organized in 1922.[1]

The climate of religious restrictions created by the new Constitution of 1917, however, continued to oppress the proclamation of the gospel. Americans who believed in the separation of church and state were naturally sympathetic with the effort of any people to free themselves from the yoke of a dictatorial ecclesiastical hierarchy, which had been the case with the Roman Catholic Church for centuries. They appreciated the force of the public statement given later, on November 5, 1935, by the Mexican minister of the interior, Silvano Barba González: "The Church, through spiritual conquest, came to exercise political hegemony and seized economic control of the country to such an extent that it owned at least four-fifths of the property, with lamentable consequences to the immense majority of inhabitants, whose material improvement was systematically sacrificed on the altars of constant promises of life hereafter."[2]

Fair-minded Americans recognized the importance of many of the reforms which the Mexican government had inaugurated. There were a few positive measures taken, such as the breaking up of vast estates, thus making it possible for tenants to acquire land of their own; the provision of educational facilities for rural as well as urban dwellers; the improvement of roads; and various other measures for the benefit of common people. American friends of Mexico were particularly gratified when Article 24 of the revised 1917 Constitution stipulated that "Every man is free to profess the religion of his choice and to practice the rituals, devotions, or acts of the respective creed in the churches or in his home, provided they do not constitute a crime or an offense punishable by law."[3]

---

[1]   Esponda, *El presbiterianismo en Chiapas*, 168-71.
[2]   Quoted in Brown, *One Hundred Years*, 812.
[3]   Quoted in ibid., 813.

Unfortunately, this liberal provision was practically nullified by other articles which drastically strengthened stipulations in the former Constitution designed to limit the political power of the Roman Catholic Church and to exclude foreign priests from positions of leadership in Mexican churches. These provisions were not strictly enforced for several years, but in July 1926, President Calles pronounced that his government intended to enforce them. In January 1927, priests were required to register with the government, and all church properties were expropriated, made the property of the State, and permitted to operate only under regulations prescribed by the government under committees of trustees composed of laymen. The Roman Catholic archbishop and bishops, under orders from the Vatican, strenuously protested and, when their protest was not heeded, directed their members and priests to resort to strikes and to refuse to register in accordance with the law. When the government retaliated by refusing to allow priests who were not registered to discharge their duties, the archbishop closed the churches.

In 1929 a modification was agreed upon: the ecclesiastical authorities could name the priests who would register the church properties and, in July 1930, public services were resumed. In 1931, however, following radical action by several of the state governments regarding the number of priests who might serve a given proportion of the population, the federal government issued regulations restricting the number of priests and ministers in the Federal District to one of each denomination for every fifty thousand inhabitants of the district, and to twenty-five in Mexico City, with churches in the same proportion, and no priest was permitted to preach outside of his own church. The remainder of the churches might remain open if properly registered by civilian committees, but no priest might conduct services in them. Since there were two hundred Roman Catholic churches and over four hundred priests in Mexico City alone, the effect of this law can only be imagined.

When the Roman Catholic archbishop failed to comply with the demand to name the required number of priests to be authorized to officiate in Mexico, the government, on May 31, 1932, closed every church in the federal district. The archbishop himself could not preach, neither could any Roman Catholic bishop, nor the bishops of the Mexican Methodist and Protestant Episcopal churches. Mexican Protestant ministers who were not registered pastors of a given church might act as laymen, as long as they did not discharge any of the functions connected with the ministry, such as administering the sacraments or pronouncing the benediction. Conditions similar to those in Mexico City prevailed in the states of Chihuahua, Veracruz, Yucatán, Tabasco, Tamaulipas, and Chiapas. In Tabasco, no religious service was permitted for over ten years, and no minister of religion was allowed to reside there. During and after the administration of President Calles, the law excluding foreign clergymen was more rigorously enforced. Ordained Protestant missionaries, however, were allowed to enter the country if they promised to confine themselves to activities open to laymen.[4] In 1925 Mabel and I were the last American missionaries allowed to enter the country as such.

On the other side, it is worth noting that it was in 1991, after more than seventy years of official hostility, the Mexican government put an end to church restraints. Legislators completed constitutional changes that gave legal recognition to religious institutions and allowed parochial education for the first time since the Mexican Revolution. The measures, culminating a three-year reconciliation process between church and state under President Carlos Salinas de Gortari, were overwhelmingly approved by the lower house of Congress on December 18, 1991.

The measures applied equally to all faiths but were intended primarily to end the conflict between the government and the Catholic Church. The new laws also restored the clergy's rights to vote and criticize the government; legalized the presence of foreign priests, ministers, and missionaries; and forced religious officials to pay income tax. The new legal framework ushered in a new era of competition between the Catholic Church and Protestant churches. In this arena, evangelical churches have won the day, since they have been growing steadily with amazing numbers, particularly in Chiapas.

The modification of just five constitutional articles that dealt with religious matters closed a void between the laws passed by triumphant but insecure revolutionaries and the realities of a nation rushing to modernize and integrate its economy with the rest of the world. It was a gap that until now had been filled largely by myth and legends of a distrustful nationalism. Despite the formal ban on the public display of faith that was imposed for so many years, the fact is that millions of Mexicans have testified to their Christian faith, and the gospel has found its place in the hearts of multitudes, and the restrictions, although not being enforced at the time, were officially lifted in 1991.[5]

[4]   Ibid., 813-14.
[5]   Tim Golden, "Mexico Ending Church Restraints after 70 Years of Official Hostility," *New York Times* (December 20, 1991), A1, A6.

CHAPTER 20

Opposition and Obstacles

The early testimony to the gospel in Mexico had to face three grave dangers. On one side, there were the difficulties that arose from an exaggerated nationalism. It is reasonable that patriotism should be expected in every citizen, and people who habitually find nothing but cause for discontent in the institutions of their own land are hardly to be envied. An insistence on national rights is a legitimate sentiment, and even more so in developing nations which are facing a firm struggle for commercial progress or political stability. But nationalism is apt to degenerate into a parochial jingoism. As such, it is a very old disease, and lest we should give ourselves airs on the subject, it is well to be reminded that there have been periods in the history of many nations characterized by the attitude of vulgar and ignorant contempt for foreigners, absurd pride, and sheer pugnacity and acquisitiveness. And this is exactly what happened in Mexico in the decades following the Mexican Revolution.

When carried to extremes, nationalism is capable of dealing a very dangerous blow to missionary work. It is, in fact, a far more dangerous enemy than any other. Nationalism is definitely hostile to such a broad conception of the social order as represented by Christianity. In its acute form, it substitutes a new-fangled religion of blood and race for the old paths of faith and piety. The rigid and centralized control maintained by a nationalist government is highly averse to the existence of voluntary organizations, such as evangelical churches. Even the Roman Catholic Church in Mexico has found its activities seriously limited by nationalism. This control has been centered in the State, which takes care that the community counts for very little; the State, not God, must be "all in all."[1]

Two weeks after we arrived in Mexico, Plutarco Elías Calles, the president, put into effect a law prohibiting any foreigner from officiating in any church in Mexico. Many Spanish priests had to return to Spain. We were the last people to enter Mexico as "foreign missionaries." This meant that those who were pastors of churches had to turn these over to Mexicans. What many had interpreted as a terrible blow to missions, however, was in reality the best thing that could have happened. It instantaneously turned the church in Mexico into a self-governing entity. Usually this was a step missionaries put off too long, creating friction.[2]

The second major hindrance to the proclamation of the gospel in Mexico has been the Roman Catholic Church. In spite of the determination of the State to control the church, at the level of the populace, the church has continued to exert a profound influence. The War of Independence in 1810 freed Mexico from Spain but not from the power of the Roman Catholic Church. In 1850 Benito Juárez had promulgated the reform laws curtailing the church, but it was difficult to enforce these decrees. The hierarchy, the priests, and many of the laity were reactionary. In the Revolution of 1910, again the church sided with land owners and conservatives. Year by year, anticlerical hostility built up.[3]

Despite enormous limitations and the lack of political power, the Roman Catholic Church was strong enough to resist penetration of the gospel brought by evangelical missionaries. In certain places, this opposition turned into open persecution with tragic results. The spirit of the Inquisition did not fade with the advance of modernism. Many bishops and priests belonged to the obscurantist type, and they labored hard to keep the traditions of their predecessors of colonial times. Few

[1]   Kenneth G. Grubb, *An Advancing Church in Latin America* (London: World Dominion Press, 1936), 56-58.
[2]   JRK, "How It All Began," 4.
[3]   Ibid.

native-born men of superior character and training entered the ranks of the clergy, and recruits from the lower classes of society were readily influenced by their foreign ecclesiastical superiors, particularly those from Spain. A vengeful and intolerant spirit remained strong, especially among the priests of foreign birth.[4]

A third major hindrance to the advance of the Christian gospel as proclaimed by evangelical churches was the development of an anti-Christian ideology. Agnosticism and atheism grew as the country moved toward leftist political convictions. This process occurred from the Mexican Revolution on, but particularly during the 1930s. This anti-Christian spirit increased as the country turned more and more nationalistic and socialistic during those years. In 1934 I wrote:

> The Mexican government has gone socialistic, striving for some vague ideal not as yet defined by anyone. It is the kind of socialism, however, where the leaders ride about in large cars and are salting away property and cash. Along with this kind of socialism, we have rationalism. The two make a good team, so the story of Russia and Mexico tells us. At first, the priests were done with. Then the Catholic churches were closed. Recently the images of saints have been and still are being burned. And now the Protestants, who as a market woman said, "have neither priests nor saints," have to be interfered with.[5]

All church properties had to be turned over to the government. No priest or minister had the right to vote. It was illegal to send religious literature through the mail. It was also illegal to hold religious services anywhere but in an authorized church. All our churches started by way of worship in private homes. By 1935 the atheistic movement was at its height, and our churches were closed for a time. During those years, I always had someone on the platform with me while I was preaching, supposedly an official in charge of the program. No one ever interfered, and when I learned that people in Tuxtla Gutiérrez considered that I was the pastor of the local church and did not complain, I worked more openly.[6]

The combination of these factors resulted in serious restrictions on religious practices, which thereby severely limited the evangelical

---

[4]   Webster E. Browning, *Roman Christianity in Latin America* (New York: Fleming H. Revell, 1924), 52-53.

[5]   JRK to "Dear friends," Dec. 27, 1934, in JAH.

[6]   JRK, "How It All Began," 4.

testimony. These circumstances affected three fields: ministry, education, and property. As already indicated, in Mexico, for many years, no foreigner could be a religious minister. The country was no longer a free region insofar as the entry and activity of foreign missionaries was concerned. On the other hand, the national ministry was restricted numerically and subject to special laws of registration. About three hundred licensed ministers for each religion were permitted in Mexico by 1935, with a population of seventeen million inhabitants. Evangelical denominations were considered separate religions, and each could nominally have enough ministers to lead the congregations. These congregations, however, were very small, as was the number of those trained for the ministry.

Ecclesiastical properties in Mexico belonged, through all these years, to the State which had closed a number of churches. Those which were still in use were conceded by the authorities for this purpose, and no service involving an act of worship could be held outside a registered building. A law approved in August 1935, extended the definition to other types of buildings. Some evangelical properties could no longer be put to any profitable use.

The educational issue was also a grave one; it was a battlefield for decades. Have parents or religious and voluntary groups the right to determine how the hearts—let alone the minds—of children are going to be swayed, or not? Mexico answered by substituting "socialist" education for the "lay" education formerly required. At the same time, the existence of private schools, in particular those directly or indirectly controlled by religious bodies, were forbidden. Article 3 of the Mexican Constitution by 1935 said that education given by the State may be socialist, and besides excluding all religious doctrine, it should fight fanaticism and prejudice. For this purpose, the school would organize its teaching and activities to instill in the minds of the youth a dogma of the universe and society. Additionally, only the State could give primary, secondary, and normal education. Under these conditions, the continuance of Christian teaching in any kind of school was almost impossible.[7]

The measures taken, in fact, were less important than the tendency they illustrated. There was a subtle evolutionary preconception that, in religious matters, the survival would be of the fittest. Religious groups should be content with fighting for survival. Under these circumstances, the traditional missiological strategies were not effective. A new

---

[7]   Grubb, *An Advancing Church in Latin America*, 58-63.

approach was necessary to spread the gospel, increase the number of believers, and fulfill the Christian mission. In Chiapas, we could develop this new strategy with success, and probably this is the reason for the explosive growth of the church in the decades that followed.

CHAPTER 21

First Missionary Visit

President Alvaro Obregón marked the years from 1920 to 1924 with authoritarianism as the primary characteristic of his administration. During Obregón's term of office, some of the foundations of the new "revolutionary" system were laid. In effect, what Obregón and his "revolutionary family" were setting up was a capitalistic system under the corporate direction of the State. The system was fundamentally ambiguous and one with which the Mexican state has had to wrestle ever since. The official rhetoric and ideology were nationalistic and socialistic, as was dictated by the notion of the liberating Revolution. But economic realities were not qualitatively different from those of the Porfiriato: capitalist development financed by the export of raw materials and foreign capital investments.[1]

This authoritarian mood was typical of José Coffin, the first Presbyterian pastoral agent to work in Chiapas. Coffin represented the third avenue for the coming of the Protestant testimony into Chiapas, the one that entered from the North, from the neighboring state of

---

[1]   Williamson, *The Penguin History of Latin America*, 392-93.

José Coffin and his wife responded
to the Macedonian call
from remote Chiapas

Tabasco. We called it "the Kentucky Connection" because of its origin of immigrants coming to Mexico from Kentucky, far away in the United States. This region of southeastern Mexico had received the gospel as a result of the American Civil War. Five Confederate soldiers from Kentucky, who preferred exile to Yankee rule, had traveled south for over two thousand miles to the coastal plains of Tabasco. They carved ranches out of the tropical jungle and married young Mexican women. Their leader was Johnny Green, whose sons became influential political leaders. Johnny Green's son Carlos was elected governor of Tabasco in 1917. It was, however, a turbulent and violent time in Mexican politics, and two years later, he was forced out of office. When he attempted to regain the office in 1924, he and his brother were killed by their political opposition.[2]

In God's providence, another one of the men from Kentucky was Joseph Coffin. He and his Mexican wife had to wait over ten years for the birth of their first son, whom they named José and dedicated to the Lord's service. José Coffin was of a strong Presbyterian conviction and early in his youth was sent to the Presbyterian Seminary in Mexico City, where he married an educated and dedicated young woman, Luz Otero. After his graduation, José and his wife returned in 1905 to serve

[2]   JSH, "The History of the Chiapas Mission," 2.

in remote Tabasco. They set up a primary school in Paraíso, and José began his pastoral and evangelistic work. With his ministry, dedicated and focused, the Presbyterian Church in Tabasco grew and was well organized. He joined two veteran Mexican ministers who were serving several Presbyterian congregations in Tabasco. These two experienced pastors, along with three ministers from the Yucatán Peninsula, formed the Presbytery of the Gulf of Mexico in 1896.[3]

A Presbyterian missionary named Sutherland and the two Tabascan ministers had already penetrated into the jungles of northern Chiapas, finding some response in some isolated ranches and villages, and since March 21, 1919, José Coffin had been involved in their work.[4] In 1920 Coffin accompanied the Tabascan minister, Rev. Eligio Granados, on a trip into Chiapas. Their preaching in the village of Tumbalá was rewarded by a large number of converts, including both Mexican ranchers and Ch'ol native laborers. They immediately baptized all of them and promised to visit them again. Six years elapsed before that promise was fulfilled.[5]

It was, however, in this year of 1920 that José Coffin did his first pastoral circuit in the region. This was in response to a kind of Macedonian call. Hearing that there were other Presbyterians in Mexico City, believers in the city of Tapachula sent word to them asking for pastoral help. Responding to the request, the Presbyterian leaders in Tabasco decided to send José Coffin and his wife to that town. Coming from Veracruz, they arrived at Tapachula, where there was a group of believers not totally of a Presbyterian conviction. Coffin worked hard to gather as many as possible of these sheep already evangelized but without a shepherd. He was the only national Presbyterian minister in Chiapas until 1937 when Rev. Ezequiel Lango was called to serve as pastor.

After José Coffin organized the church in Tapachula on May 16, 1920, he traveled to the northeast to visit the small congregation that was already in existence in Mazapa. For them, it was a very exciting experience since Coffin was the first pastor to come to the group. His best contribution there was to organize the church on June 6, which has been known since then as the Presbyterian Church of the Holy Spirit. By that time, the congregation had some two hundred members, including children. As a member of the Gulf of Mexico Presbytery,

---

[3] Ibid.
[4] José Coffin, "La última visita del Rev. Señor Elliott a Chiapas," *El Faro* (October 1923): 10.
[5] JSH, "The History of the Chiapas Mission," 2.

Coffin appointed elders and organized the consistory linking the congregation to the mentioned presbytery.[6] The first evangelical church building in Mazapa was built on a site donated by Pablo de la Cruz.

The decade began not only with great triumphs in the faith but also with increasing opposition both by the Roman Catholic Church and the political authorities. Nevertheless, there was success in Bible distribution, and the Mexican believers met these circumstances with a powerful movement of prayer and intercession. Evangelicals of all denominations participated with enthusiasm and commitment. In the city and in the country, there was persistent prayer. Believers understood well that evangelization is impossible without intensive prayer. Besides, the problems confronting the small groups of believers were many.

The southernmost state of the Mexican Union, Chiapas, was 92 percent illiterate in the 1920s, 80 percent of its inhabitants being pure-blooded Maya, a majority of whom could not speak Spanish. San Cristóbal de Las Casas, at eight thousand feet, with fourteen thousand people, was served by a score of Roman Catholic churches and priests. This city had been the seat of Bartolomé de Las Casas, and the religious life seemed much superior to that of nearby communities. The city, however, was full of idols. Its religion was a mixture of Catholic popular religiosity with indigenous pagan practices. When José Coffin, a Mexican pastor of *gringo* blood, came from Tabasco to Chiapas to investigate, he found a field ripe for harvest.[7] In a single month, he baptized more than four hundred adults. He settled down in Tapachula, but the congregations here and there used elected elders to conduct their services.[8]

Under the leadership of Coffin, the believers in the southern tip of Chiapas multiplied quickly, including the group in Tapachula, the commercial and communications center of the area. In five years, the Presbyterian center in Tapachula included a chapel, a parsonage, medical work, six primary schools, and a community Red Cross office (founded by Coffin). By then Coffin had organized three additional congregations and was visiting families and groups of believers in eighty-one locations scattered throughout the interior of Chiapas. The heavy workload prompted them to request missionary help from the Presbyterian Mission Board, but the board responded that they were

---

[6]   Esponda, *El presbiterianismo en Chiapas*, 37-38.
[7]   *Gringo* is a foreigner in Spain or Latin America especially when of English or American origin. The word is often used disparagingly.
[8]   Orr, *Evangelical Awakenings in Latin America*, 110.

already overextended. The Presbyterian Mission Board did, however, invite the Reformed Church in America to provide a missionary for Chiapas, in accordance with the agreements signed with the Cincinnati Plan. The Board of Foreign Missions of the Reformed Church responded that they were also already overextended. In spite of these human limitations, the Lord had other plans.

When the Reformed Church Women's Board of Domestic Missions heard of the ministry opportunity, it accepted the challenge. The women justified their beginning a ministry in this foreign land by saying that, since most of the Chiapas people were natives, the board's participation would be an extension of its mission work among Native Americans.[9] Praised be the name of the Lord that his plans through this board came to fruition so that Mabel and I could become a significant part of them.

---

[9]   JSH, "The History of the Chiapas Mission," 3.

CHAPTER 22

Springtime Love

After salvation, the most extraordinary gift that I received from God was Mabe. What a marvelous blessing she has been in my life! We have always been in love with each other. We grew and matured in our shared love. Through the many years we spent together—most of our lives!—expressions of our love spiced our conversations. I called her "Mabe," "my dear *esposita*," "mommie," "my mate," "*Pascarita*," "honey," "dear," "my love," "sweetheart mine," and "my own dear girl." When addressing me, she called herself "your own," and I was "Kemp" for her and her "dearest." Words of love were interchanged through the many letters we wrote for two years before our marriage. The post office was the arbiter of our communication of love, since for most of our young relationship, we were separated because of study and ministry.

Before we came to know each other, we were total strangers. She was a redhead, and I a handsome (so she said) brunet. Our eyes first met across a crowded room, and both of us knew at that moment that our lives were designed by God to walk together. We first saw each other on a Sunday afternoon, in the fall of her freshman year at Hope College. Her sister Lillian had asked her, "Mabel, will you be home Sunday to

Courtship in a canoe on Lake Macatawa in Holland, Michigan
(*courtesy Joy Fuder*)

help entertain when Chris brings his roommate Kemp?" That "Kemp" was me. Lillian and Mrs. Walvoord's nephew arranged our first meeting. And there it happened. What was it—a voice, a glance, an aura, something entirely intangible and soulful—that moved each one of us to think, "This person I like"? What mysterious and divine impulse is the one that compels you to say with certainty to another human being, "I love you"? While outsiders exclaim, "What did she ever see in him?" or "Why did he ever marry her?" The two hearts braided by these feelings can only say to one another "I love you. I love you."

On the night of Mabel's graduation from high school, a favorite teacher of hers sang an all-but-forgotten song in her full contralto voice. It was a song Mabel liked and sang to me in our budding friendship as we sat one day overlooking Lake Michigan. Imperfectly, I recall some phrases of its lilt and lyrics:

> I bring you heart's ease and roses . . .
> For love is sweetest in springtime,
> And flowers to lovers belong . . .
> But the love that is best
> Is the love that will last
> When the flowers of spring time are gone . . .
> And the love that is best
> Is the love that has lived
> When the springtime of life has fled.

Who can explain the amazing expansion of this love that comes with marriage! It grows nurtured by the daily experiences of partnering in the shared experience of living together. I still remember my first letter to Mabel after we got married. I wrote it from Santa Lucrecia as I was traveling to Puerto Mexico, in my long adventure with José Coffin crossing Chiapas in 1926. "Dear honey bunch. [This is] my first letter to you since we have been married. Just a little note it is going to be but chuck full of my love to you. . . . I'm going to like this trip for a while at least. If only my girl were with me! . . . Be a brave and happy girl. I will write as often as I can get letters mailed, but they may reach you after my return. Just one long drink of the nectar of your lips and a good tight hug! Your lover boy."[1] My second letter to Mabel was written from Comalcalco, Tabasco, during the long trip. It was also expressive of my passion for her:

> Honey, yesterday was the longest day I've spent in I don't know how many years. I couldn't sleep. My paper and envelopes were out in the country, and all the while I was dreaming and longing for you dear. How happy we have been these last months just loving and loving. Time goes fast, and we are happy when we are together. And so we always will be. And when we have a house of our own designing, with a garden and flowers and a little larger family and our work systematized, oh, girly, but we'll love and be happy. Just come close now, dear, and I'll kiss you again on every spot where I kissed you the night before I left. I wish I had a picture of you with me, but I haven't. Your husband. Kemp.[2]

This missionary travel to Tabasco and then crossing through the state of Chiapas from north to south took us almost two months. This was a time of trial for our love. But our love came out of the test refined and even more precious. I kept telling Mabe: "Be a brave little girl for just a few days more, and I'll come. How many many times I have pictured and dreamed of our first embrace. But it's going to come. If God will keep us well, it will be soon, dear." And I continued to ask her: "Pray much for your boy and love him and be happy. How he loves you, and how lonely and unhappy he is when separated from his very own. How soon you have come to mean more to me even than my parents. I love you, Mabe."[3]

[1] JRK to MVD, n.d. (July 1926), in JAH.
[2] JRK to MVD, n.d. (July 1926), in JAH.
[3] JRK to MVD, August 26, 1926, in JAH.

In our case, love matured to encircle, first a son, then a daughter, a second son, and after seven years, another daughter. What a miracle! Love multiplied throughout the years as our children met their mates, and our family grew. We came to have a family of four noble sons and four lovely daughters! How much delight we have found in each of them! How proud we are of them all! And the blessing continued to multiply with the grandchildren who have stretched this love twelve more times! The wave grew even wider when some of them continued to make their choice of a mate for their lives.

Love is perfect and perfectible. It is so especially when the source of that love is God's unique love. A good marriage is possible only when God is recognized as supreme, when he is consulted continually, and his will obeyed. There were those who said of us who had come this far on life's road, "Now they're going downhill." Not so! We continue to travel the King's Highway, and that always leads up! Nor is it true that we go into the sunset. Our faces are turned in eager anticipation of seeing the great sunrise of our Lord's glory.[4]

---

[4]   MVD, "Thoughts on Our Golden Wedding Anniversary," 1-2, in JAH.

CHAPTER 23

Different Races

My graduation from Hope College with my baccalaureate degree (bachelor of arts) in 1921 was followed by a year as principal and teacher in the public high school of Coopersville, Michigan. At Hope I was a four-year-letter man in long-distance running. At Coopersville I coached the basketball and baseball teams. I took great delight in all sports, but I excelled in running. I was featured on the cover of the *Banner*, the magazine published by the Christian Reformed Church. The photo shows two competing runners at the starting line of the Hope College relay, the official about to shoot off the gun, and a young lad looking down the street. The race was on Eighth Street, the main street in Holland, a cobblestone street with the Interurban tracks running down the middle (see p. 113).[1]

Meanwhile, in Mexico, another race was taking place, and it was not exactly athletic. Since 1921 Mexico had been engaged in the constructive stages of a revolution, the belligerent phase of which began in 1910. The result was that the old order had largely passed away, and

---

[1] *The Banner* (June 25, 1976), 1-2, in JAH; photo taken May 15, 1920.

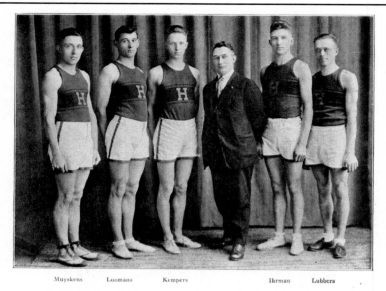

Muyskens   Loomans   Kempers   Ihrman   Lubbers

**Running cross country at Hope College prepared
me for the rugged trails of Chiapas**

both the status of religious practice and the social condition of the masses had been profoundly affected. This race, however, was through an obstacle course of sorts. In 1920, Álvaro Obregón, one of Venusiano Carranza's allies who had plotted against him, became president. His government managed to accommodate all of the elements of Mexican society, except the most reactionary clergy and landlords. As a result, he was able to successfully catalyze social liberalization, particularly in curbing the role of the Catholic Church, improving education, and taking steps toward instituting women's civil rights.

Consolidation of the Revolution was the focus of Obregón's administration. His was the first in a series of strong central governments led by former generals of the revolutionary armies that governed Mexico. Most Mexican presidents complied with the constitutional provision mandating a single six-year term (*sexenio*) with no reelection. Ineligible for reelection, Obregón chose his interior minister, Plutarco Elías Calles, as his successor. This race in Mexico was taking place as I ran my race through the streets of Holland, totally oblivious to these circumstances unfolding on my future mission field.

The same kind of political race was concentrating the attention of the powerful elites in Chiapas. The competitors for the state government were the same as those at the national level: *revolucionarios* and conservatives representing the powerful dominant families of Tuxtla

At the starting line of a relay race. I was set to run with determination and stamina

Gutiérrez and San Cristóbal de Las Casas. In November 1920, Tiburcio Fernández Ruíz, a revolutionary, was elected governor of Chiapas and remained the strong man in the state. He was for the Plan de Agua Prieta that put an end to a short but bloody civil war, taking sides with Álvaro Obregón against his rival Venusiano Carranza. In February 1921, the present Constitution of the state was promulgated. In 1921 and the years following, important institutions were organized in Chiapas, such as the Partido Socialista Chiapaneco, the Confederación Socialista de Trabajadores de Chiapas, the Unión de Partidos Revolucionarios (Revolutionary National Party), the Cámara de Comercio of Chiapas, and the Unión Regional Ganadera of Chiapas. All of these institutions played a significant role in the political and economic life of the state by the time of our arrival in the region.[2]

This political race in Chiapas, however, had no winner. The political triumph of the Revolution did not rectify the social condition of the Chiapanecans. Most of them continued to be subject to the rhythms of life as determined by the production cycles of the principal products of the state: corn, coffee, sugar, and cotton, the raising of cattle, and the exploitation of wood. Most of the population of Chiapas remained totally unaware of the struggles for political power. The demographic increase of the population, however, was a more important factor in the social life of the state. The numbers were doubled during these years. This provoked an increase of economic pressure, in particular on the

[2]   Zebadúa, *Breve historia de Chiapas*, 145-47, 176.

indigenous communities in the highlands. The insufficient availability of cultivable lands provoked the voluntary or forced migration of a good number of peasants to work as hired servants or peons for the coffee plantation owners in the Soconusco region, the bosses of the rubber tree plantations in the north, the timber dealers in the Lancandon jungle, or the cattle ranchers in the central valley.[3]

There was, however, another race going on in Chiapas in those years, a more glorious and transcendent race—the race for souls. That race required the bold investment of time and energy to bring people to a saving knowledge of Jesus Christ. This endeavor was unique, because it was not the work of any foreign missionary or movement but largely the work of the people themselves. Rev. Newell J. Elliott, a missionary sent by the Board of Foreign Missions of the Presbyterian Church in the United States had general supervision over the state. He had planned the development of the field and worked out the guiding principles for the growth of the church, but his home was in Orizaba, in the state of Veracruz, three-and-a-half days distant by rail, and with his responsibilities in that section of Mexico, he had obviously not been able to keep in close personal contact with the small and scattered congregations in Chiapas.

The real local runner there was Rev. José Coffin, the son of a Scottish father and a Mexican mother, a man of striking and pleasing personality who combined the creative fire of the Latin with the staunch persistence of the Scots. His primary method of reaching the goal in this more glorious race was direct personal work by and among the people. At first, people were sent to explore a certain district, then colporteurs with Bibles began their work, and later teachers of catechism were sent. This was done in a district which was called a "mission," and the work was carried out by native missionaries who held meetings in homes, until the time came for the establishment of a church group and the designation of a room or a building as the chapel.

In those years, new believers had to pass through a six-month period of probation, and when this period was over, those whose lives reflected Christ's teachings were received as full members of the church. The congregation was considered a unit of the larger community of the church as a whole in Chiapas. In this way, by this year 1921, seventy-two groups, large and small, had been formed, including four large church centers, twenty-three "chapels," twenty-four "missions," and twelve "missionary fields of action," with a total communicant membership

---

[3]   Ibid., 148.

of about eight hundred and with more than two thousand candidates waiting for admission. This same year, four hundred children were baptized, and two hundred people were admitted to full membership. With the exception of Coffin, whose salary was paid by the Presbyterian mission, two-thirds of all of the leaders in the church were volunteers. There was no current subsidy from the mission, aside from a small sum for the travel expenses of Coffin, nor had the mission thus far invested any money for property.

This race for the Kingdom of God was a true obstacle race; opposition and persecution were no minor threats. Alvino López, a church member who lived near Tapachula, was threatened with death if he should continue to hold to the Protestant faith. One night, he was shot and killed in an ambush as he opened the door of his home. A memorial service was held by that little congregation of twenty people. Afterward, traveling on horseback, they gathered at the Tapachula chapel and took a solemn oath with uplifted hands to be true to the Protestant faith, to preach the gospel, and in memory of their fallen comrade, to win others to Christ. They kept this pledge, and in the months that followed, in the face of persecution and threat of death, they brought 132 individuals to Christ. Such a spirit of victory is invincible and later, during our days in Tapachula, we saw abundant evidence of its many triumphs.[4]

From a different perspective, this race for the imperishable wreath was not as though beating the air. The race in Chiapas was exceptional because it was practical, and the runners kept themselves focused, with their eyes set on the goal. Their efforts were invested in developing Christian communities, which through ownership and cultivation of the land would become independent and self-supporting. By then, they had already organized agricultural colonies, one of them named Eisleben in honor of Martin Luther, which, numbering sixty-two families, had purchased one thousand acres of land and was going forward successfully in this practical experiment. There was a pavilion built, with uprights of natural saplings and roofed with coconut palm leaves. The colony was rich in the production of a wide variety of fruits and vegetables.

The triumphant race of the church in Chiapas was accompanied through the years with the singing of a hymn that was very popular in all the Spanish-speaking communities:

---

[4]   W. Reginald Wheeler, "The Challenge of the Church in Chiapas," *The Christian Intelligencer* (September 23, 1925), 596-97.

Trabajad, trabajad, somos siervos de Dios;
Seguiremos la senda que el Maestro trazó;
Renovando las fuerzas con bienes que da,
El deber que nos toca, cumplido será.

To the work, to the work, we are servants of God,
Let us follow the path that the Master has trod;
Renewing our strength with the blessings He gives,
The work that is given to us will be done.[5]

5   Ibid.

CHAPTER 24

Toward a Doctrinal Definition

In 1919 José Coffin began visiting Chiapas. He was a member of the Presbytery of the Gulf of Mexico and was sent by the Synod of Mexico. As a result of the work he carried out on his many travels throughout the state, a number of churches were organized. The work expanded and grew in impressive numbers, but in doctrinal terms, the faith of those believers was rather shallow. Syncretism prevailed, and doctrinal confusion grew like a plague. Some believers were inclined toward Adventism, emphasizing a legalistic observation of the Sabbath; Jehovah's Witnesses prevailed in some areas; other people were attracted to the doctrine of the Nazarene or various other denominations; most believers probably continued to treasure their old beliefs and practices proper of the unique fusion of Roman Catholicism with indigenous idolatry and animism.

Coffin was very doctrinally conservative, a hard shell and old-fashioned Presbyterian who would not make any concessions in the field of his personal convictions. He was fond of calling himself "Juan Presbiteriano."[1] His orthodoxy sometimes defeated his orthopraxis and

---

[1]   José Coffin, "Carta abierta del mexicano Juan Presbiteriano a su tocayo el ruso lván Ortho Doxis," *El Faro* (July 1932): 10.

put in danger the results of his intensive efforts to proclaim the gospel. But in those early years in Chiapas and particularly in Tapachula, where he began to serve in 1920, his insistence on teaching sound doctrine proved to be adequate and necessary. In his zeal, he systematically taught the biblical doctrines of the Presbyterian Church. In his first letter to the Board of Domestic Missions, he described very accurately the spiritual context of his work in Chiapas.

> Our membership is among every class of people, not only those who live in the hot coastal countries at sea level but also those who live at an altitude of twelve thousand feet. With the exception of the members of the church at the capital [Tuxtla Gutiérrez], these believers are all new converts, who have been won by personal work. During the first few years after conversion, we try to ground all the believers in the fundamentals of our faith. We use the Shorter Catechism and Bible in all the churches and Sunday schools. We are gradually introducing the International Sunday school lessons, where the churches are best prepared. It is our custom to thoroughly train all in the doctrines of our church.[2]

Coffin was a man 100 percent committed to evangelization. His goal was truly to bring to salvation as many people as possible. He manifested the same spirit of the apostle Paul when he said, "I have become all things to all people, that I might by all means save some." His conviction on this was very strong. He once said, "We feel that our work has one end only, namely, to bring men and women to a saving knowledge of Christ. We believe strongly that evangelism is the primary object in any field, and all other effort must be conducted in such a way that it will lead to the same end."[3]

This evangelistic fervor was not without problems and frustrations. The intensity in the proclamation of the good news at the beginning was not followed by a deepening of the faith through a persistent process of discipleship. The results soon became apparent. A number of those who had already embraced the doctrines and practices of the Adventists left the Tapachula group. Coffin intensified his indoctrination enterprise, particularly through Sunday school classes on the Ten Commandments. But those who left did not return.

Wide-spread illiteracy was a major obstacle in the process of discipleship, so it was necessary to organize an elementary school,

[2]   Luz Otero de Coffin and José Coffin, "Rev. José Coffin of Chiapas Sends Greetings to the Reformed Church," *The Christian Inteligencer* (September 16, 1925), 584.
[3]   Ibid.

of which Coffin was the director and his wife the teacher. She was a graduate from Normal School of San Ángel in Mexico City. Other sisters helped as teachers. The strategy of combining both ministries—the Sunday school and the elementary school—was successful in bringing the whole congregation into a Presbyterian understanding of the Christian faith.[4]

As Coffin was struggling himself to secure a solid Presbyterian theological standing in the scattered groups of believers in Chiapas, I was trying to do the same, starting my theological studies at Princeton Theological Seminary in New Jersey.

[4] Esponda, *El presbiterianismo en Chiapas*, 171-72.

CHAPTER 25

Education in Chiapas

Mexico had never established a strong public education system. The custom was for the wealthy to send their children abroad for education; others maintained private schools for their children. At the time we were ready to travel as missionaries to Chiapas, there was nearly 80 percent illiteracy among the people as a whole. Even along the railroads, there were villages that had either no schools or utterly neglected schools. In the uplands—the mountainous region and the vast jungle region beyond the reach of mail and telegraph—schooling had been and was still practically nonexistent.

Schools in the rural sections of the country often consisted of a palm- or bamboo-thatched, one-room hut—in the villages, adobe was used. Into this one room, pupils of all ages were crowded. Books—when there were any—were hopelessly inappropriate to the pupils' needs, and the teachers lacked training. There were exceptions, of course. In some of the major cities and larger towns in Mexico, splendidly built and well-equipped schools might be found, with a teaching force of exceptional ability and ideals. But that was not the case in Chiapas, even in the capital of the state.

Mothers were also ignorant of the necessity of the most basic hygiene, and the same vast rural areas that lacked the ministry of schools were also without the benefit of sanitation, doctors, hospitals, and the medical knowledge that so greatly alleviates the sufferings of mankind—especially children. A tragic proportion of little children died victims of utter ignorance.

During the 1920s, however, education and culture were promoted intensively in order to propagate the new revolutionary vision of Mexico. It was said that Dr. Manuel Gaimo, who had received part of his scientific training at Columbia University, had developed a wonderful source of a new creative impulse and culture suited to the instincts and needs and within the grasp of the people of that region. This project consisted partly in teaching them not only the three Rs but also the beautiful arts and crafts of weaving, embroidery, ceramics, leather, and metal work. These individual crafts were taught following the order of the gorgeous objects of this character uncovered by the archeological excavations in many areas of Mexico and particularly in Chiapas. Dr. Gaimo was then subsecretary of education in the Elías Calles government.[1]

The great initiator of cultural nationalism, however, was José Vasconcelos, Álvaro Obregón's minister of education, who believed that the future lay in the formation of a "cosmic race" created from the eventual fusion of all the ethnic groups in the Americas. It was this belief that provided the inspiration for the tremendous effort in the early 1920s to rehabilitate the indigenous people and the *mestizo* in the cultural self image of Mexico. This campaign was undoubtedly one of the triumphs of the Revolution. It represented the earliest and the most enduring attempt to overcome racial divisions, which had been the worst legacy of the Spanish Conquest, and to forge a coherent sense of national identity. Mexico's political stability in the twentieth century was due in no small degree to the success of this policy to incorporate the native heritage into the idea of the nation.

Vasconcelos—"the *caudillo* of culture," as he was called—promoted literacy among the rural masses. Schools were built, libraries founded, and cadres of young volunteers sent out to teach in the villages and towns. This campaign was accompanied by extensive official patronage of indigenous arts and crafts as a means of fostering pride in the achievements of the people. After Vasconcelos' resignation in 1924, the cultural and educational policies of the state focused on the more narrow political aim of liberating the peasantry from the grip of the

---

[1]   Edith H. Allen, "Understanding Mexico," *The Christian Intelligencer* (August 19, 1925), 520.

Mabel stands next to Mrs. Coffin, who established
this school in Tapachula

Church, and this secularization was to lead to a renewal of violence in
the deeply religious Mexican countryside.[2]

Somehow the emphasis on education by the Mexican government
represented an opportunity for the National Presbyterian Church.
In Chiapas, before we arrived, Mr. Coffin had established six schools,
the largest of which was in Tapachula, with Mrs. Coffin as principal.
That school had 121 pupils enrolled by the year 1925. Although it was
primarily a school for girls, they did accept boys. Plans were developed
to open a separate school for the boys and also to have it grow into
a kind of "work-your-way" industrial school. There were also fourteen
small agricultural colonies exclusively for families of believers, where
boys and men were taught how to farm and girls and women how to
develop Christian homes. Mr. Coffin also created the Bible Institute
for the preparation of men called to ministry. This was in response
to the fact that, if the Chiapaneco students left the region to study
somewhere else, they might be lost for the regional work; they may not
return to where the conditions were so undeveloped. Coffin expected
to enlarge this part of the work, because that was the only center in the
state preparing Christian workers. By 1925 there were four students in
the institute, and six were on the waiting list. The last ones were not
accepted because of lack of equipment and teachers.[3]

[2]   Williamson, *The Penguin History of Latin America*, 393-94.
[3]   Coffin, "Rev. José Coffin of Chiapas Sends Greetings," 585.

CHAPTER 26

Thinking about the Unknown

By the end of 1923 and the first few months of 1924, Mabel and I were seriously thinking about going to Chiapas, Mexico, to serve as missionaries to the natives in that region. At that time, however, we did not have the slightest notion of what Chiapas was all about. Mabel did some research only to learn that practically nothing about the place was written in English. *Terry's Mexico* was somewhat authoritative and said the area was 70,524 square kilometers, which meant that we would have a mission field equal to half the state of Michigan or more than three times the state of New Jersey.[1] We were told that Chiapas was 16 degrees north of the equator, but the temperatures varied all the way from the equator's heat to the cold of Canada due to the altitudes. The land was well watered and marvelously productive. There were many ruins of the ancient indigenous civilizations, since Chiapas happened to be almost at the center of the region where these civilizations lived. Transportation could be by rail to the coastal cities or towns and then inland by horse or mule.

[1]   T. Philip Terry, *Terry's Mexico: Handbook for Travellers*, 2nd ed. (Boston and New York: Houghton Mifflin, 1911), 563-69.

The rugged hills of Chiapas made travel and communication very difficult

The approximate population of Chiapas according to Mr. Terry was 360,599. Eighty percent of these were pure-blood, indigenous people. To the east, there was a primitive indigenous tribe—the Linguas (later we learned they were known as the Lacandones)—who still used the bow and arrow. No Christian worker had ever been among them. We would have to use Spanish and the many other indigenous languages. *Terry's Mexico* affirmed that there were about fourteen distinct indigenous tribes in the state, each with its own language. But some of Terry's statements were less than plausible, for instance, his curious assertion that some of these natives (who mixed as little as possible with the whites) were able to communicate telepathically across hundreds of miles, employing a sort of native, wireless telegraphy, whose secrets were guarded from all outsiders.[2]

If we were ignorant of the facts and the conditions in Chiapas, those who were about to send us were no better informed. When the Board of Foreign Missions of the Presbyterian Church in the United States and later the Board of Foreign Missions of the Reformed Church in America declined the invitation of the National Presbyterian Church in Mexico to send missionaries to help Mr. Coffin in Chiapas, it was the Reformed Church Women's Board of Domestic Missions who assumed the responsibility.

[2]   Ibid., 565.

The Men's Board of Domestic Missions agreed to join them in considering this opportunity. An investigation (exploration) committee of four made the long trip from New York to Tapachula in February 1925. The trip included a long cruise from New York to Veracruz and a slow train trip to the southern tip of Chiapas. The committee was formed by Edith H. Allen (Mrs. John S. Allen) and Ada Quinby Knox (Mrs. Taber Knox) of the Women's Board and Rev. Gerrit Watermulder and Rev. Henry Sluyter of the Men's Board. They conferred with members of the Presbyterian Mission and with the pastor in Tapachula, Rev. José Coffin. Their report back in New York was decisive on the actions taken by the board and particularly in their decision to invite me to go to Mexico. Of great impact was Mrs. Allen's bold challenge. The Chiapas Mission many years later gave her the title, "The Mother of the Chiapas Mission"; they marveled at her quick understanding of the situation in Mexico, her grasp of details, and her personal interest in Mabel and me and the Mexican workers.[3] Upon her return to the United States, she wrote a report of their trip and their visit with the Coffins, including this sentence which gave a blueprint for the future work in Chiapas:

> Shall the Reformed Church in America come to the help of this noble servant of the Master and send preachers, medical workers, and such native helpers as may be, to some well-chosen and equipped Reformed Church Mission center in Chiapas, to be associated with the Presbyterian forces there in bringing Chiapas into that fellowship of Christ through which in his own time, it will itself be able to achieve entirely, not only its own Christian ministry but also send gospel messengers to Indians of other more remote sections of South America where millions wait the gospel of a Savior's love and healing?

She answered her question with an enthusiastic shout:

> The Domestic Boards have said "Yes" to this call from Over the Border, and some in our churches by their gifts have also said "Yes." A noble, young son of the church and recent graduate of Princeton, with his prospective bride, have answered "Here am I, send me,"— and they are going, and we are going—all of us— through prayer and love and gifts, for the Reformed Church in

---

[3] Board of Domestic Missions, "Chiapas for Christ" (July 1958), 4-5.

Mrs. Ada Quinby Knox made such an impression on the Coffins
that they named a park after her

America does not put its hand to the plow and hesitate—it does not fail. Yes, in Christ's name and in his power we are coming to help you, brother Indians of Chiapas! We are coming, honored brother, José Coffin, and all other lovers of the Master there whose names we know not yet. Blessed, heavenly Father, lead Thou us on, that Thy will may have its way with us for Chiapas and all the great work to which Domestic Missions is called.[4]

Although the Reformed Church in America was infused with a growing consensus and enthusiasm for the idea of sending missionaries to Mexico, in Chiapas, José Coffin, himself an ardent Presbyterian, was not too pleased when he heard that instead of missionaries from the Presbyterian Church, he was being offered aid from the Reformed Church in America, which he suspected as being much too liberal. But his concern was eased when he learned that one of the women on the investigative committee had the hallowed name of Knox. The Coffins were so impressed by her, that they named the playground of their school in Tapachula, "Ada Park."[5] The missionary zeal, the unrestricted support, the conscientious prayers, and the budgetary provisions to support the work were manifested with generosity. There was, however, a total lack of information, orientation,

4   Edith H. Allen, "Seen and Felt in Mexico," *The Christian Intelligencer* (June 3, 1925), 341.
5   JSH, "The History of the Chiapas Mission," 3.

and preparation of those who were sent, that is, Mabel and myself. Even later, when in December 1925, fresh out of seminary, newly ordained, and recently married, I was sent with my bride by the board to Chiapas to open a new missionary field, the only directive was: "Find out what can be done. We don't know anything about it."[6] And there we went.

By the middle of 1924, things had begun to take shape, at least in terms of the organization of the polity arrangements. By then, different parts of Mexico had been allotted to different denominations for missionary work, and the southern part was under the Presbyterian Church in the United States. They, however, had no missionaries in the state of Chiapas, and so our church (Reformed Church in America) was asked to take over that state. There would be no Dutch Reformed Church in Mexico, but our missionaries would counsel and train and assist the natives to evangelize like the Reformed Church missionaries in India, China, and Japan were doing, so that in time, the natives might be able to take care of the work. At the time, Mabel and I believed that goal would take a long time, because as far as we knew, the people were nearly all illiterate, and it would be many years before they could properly manage the work.

A committee had been organized to make the necessary arrangements with the Presbyterian Church in the United States and the church in Mexico and also to get a general idea of Chiapas. But that general idea of Chiapas did not reach us before we started our trip to Mexico. All we knew by this time was that there was a man, whose father was a Scot and his mother a Mexican, who had been for some years quietly working in a small coastal city and had trained some native workers. Our work was supposed to be in harmony with his work, although in a different locality. At that time, we thought that we would probably go inland.

We were to be the first white people to go, and we were asked to study the field and the people and, if possible, open the way for a larger mission. Those who had been there found that the people were very receptive to religion, but at that time, they were wandering about without any definite religion. The Mexican Presbyterian church, however, wanted only conservative missionaries to work in the field, and we thought we qualified in this regard.

By then, the most pressing question for us was, "How do we happen to be going?" If we cared to go into that venture, both of us

---

6   JRK, "After Sixty Years: A Look at the Beginnings," unpublished and unsigned document, probably written by JRK, n.d., in JAH.

knew our particular sides of the story. For me, all this began way back in my childhood. A prominent preacher was often heard to tell of his sitting, as a young boy, in the balcony of the old First Reformed Church in Orange City, Iowa, listening to a sermon that led him to dedicate his life to the ministry. Well, in that same church, years earlier, I, as an academy student, sat and heard an eloquent appeal to work among the natives south of the border made by Mrs. Walter C. Roe. A seed was planted in my young mind that later was to influence my choice of seminary and my acceptance of a summer assignment with the Comanche-Apache Mission in Lawton, Oklahoma, under the direction of Dr. Richard Harper.[7]

So for me, my missionary call somehow had to do with my time at Princeton and then my serving the Native Americans in Oklahoma. Later we received the news of the plans of the Reformed Church, and those plans began to materialize just at my graduation. It was the providence of God, as we used to call it.[8]

Also unknown to us was the political situation in Mexico. Starting in 1924, Obregón's protégé, Plutarco Elías Calles, began to develop what came to be known as the Maximato. Over the next ten years, Calles would make a fair bid to become the new strongman of Mexico. There were two obstacles in his way: the provisions of the 1917 Constitution and the ideological authority of the Catholic Church. Because both proved insuperable, Calles was forced to institutionalize the power of the new revolutionary elite in a national party, formulating rules for the presidential succession which would preserve oligarchic government behind a democratic façade. The result has been called the Maximato (a word modeled on Porfiriato).

Calles's presidency was overshadowed by the massive insurrection of the Catholic peasantry known as the War of the Cristeros, with their battle cry: "¡Viva Cristo Rey!" (Long live Christ the King). Rural Mexico—especially the central and western regions—was overwhelmingly Catholic, and attempts by the anticlerical *caudillos* from the north to replace church education with secular schooling created serious disaffection among the peasants. The immediate cause of the war was a dispute between Calles and the bishops over a law passed in 1926, which enforced and extended the religious restrictions of the 1917 Constitution. The Catholic hierarchy responded by suspending all church services throughout the country. Coming on top of virulent,

[7]   Ibid.
[8]   MVD, "Chiapas, Mexico," unsigned and unpublished document, n.d., in JAH.

antireligious propaganda, which included setting up a compliant rival Roman Catholic church, this threat to the very existence of religious life outraged Catholics. In the west-central states of Jalisco, Michoacán, Guanajuato, Colima, and Zacatecas, there were large uprisings of peasants.

Calles's hard line toward the church was intended partly to strengthen his authority at home while he was involved in a nationalist confrontation with the United States over oil rights. Severe repressive measures—such as the gunning down of unarmed *campesinos*, scorched-earth tactics against their lands, and the forced relocation of indigenous communities—failed to subdue the Catholic peasant guerrillas. A year later, their numbers had risen to some thirty-five thousand, with thousands more sympathizers, and by 1929, there were about fifty thousand. The armed forces appeared unable to crush the rebels.[9] Most of Mexico was set on fire with these confrontations, and in 1924, as we were preparing to go into this tumultuous country, Mabel and I had no clue about any of this.

---

[9]   Williamson, *The Penguin History of Latin America*, 395.

CHAPTER 27

The Call to Chiapas

As expressed before, we went to Chiapas very much under a Macedonian call. But instead of receiving the divine call through a young man in Troas, I heard God's voice through a pious woman when I was finishing my studies at Princeton Theological Seminary. In 1924 Mrs. Edith A. Allen, corresponding secretary of the Women's Board of Domestic Missions, wrote me a letter disclosing a project under advance consideration by the board. It had to do with the opening of a work somewhere, sometime, across our southern border and suggested a possible commission to be their missionary in this venture. "I hope you will never have cause for regretting if you decide to accept," she wrote me later. Had I been allowed a telescopic view of the trail ahead—long years without reinforcements, lone decisions, exasperating government restrictions, and the wall of opposition within the church itself which had to be hurdled before advancement could be made—would I have accepted?

On the other hand, the time I spent in the summer of 1923 serving Native Americans in Lawton, Oklahoma, was truly preparation for this ministry in Latin America. I remember writing my dear Mabel the following lines on July 28, 1923:

> Dear Mabel Mine:
>
> My home is broken up, and so it's a lonely boy who is writing you this night. Monday or Tuesday the Harpers will leave for vacation, and so I may not see a white face around here until the ladies come back on the twenty-fifth of August. Oh, there are lots of white people up town and near here, but all these buildings here will have one lone occupant. I am going to move into the parsonage so I can answer phone calls. . . .
>
> In a letter I typed for Mr. Harper today, he told the Board: "In my absence Mr. Kempers will carry on the work, pushing ahead with Camp Meeting plans. He has done so splendidly this summer that I am not at all worried in leaving the field in his care. He is most earnest in his work and conservative in judgment and action." Now, you know, I don't quote that in any lengthy way but I just want you to know because I am sure you appreciate other people's opinions of me. . . .
>
> How things have changed since I left Princeton. I came out here expecting to be a flunky and then they made a preacher out of me. Now they all leave me and give me two churches with about two hundred and twenty-five natives (225 members but many more non-Christians) scattered over a field of seventy by thirty miles about. I like responsibility tho, don't I? Only five weeks of it.[1]

With my fiancée's quick acquiescence and confirmation of my convictions, I knew that the project to go to Mexico had begun to take shape. This was the opening I had been seeking. Now I was ready to commit myself without reserve to life on a rugged frontier. Mabel and I were of one heart and mind on this, and we never regretted that decision.

The Reformed Church in America had no work in Latin America. When I was about to graduate from Princeton, I received several invitations to pastorates in the United States. Suddenly, as I have already mentioned, there came a telegram: "Do not commit yourself to anything until you hear from us." The two Boards of Domestic Missions (Women's and Men's) of the Reformed Church were making arrangements to start a venture into southern Mexico, and their search for a missionary candidate had led them to me. Dr. Harper liked what he had seen of my work with the Native Americans in Oklahoma and strongly recommended me. The fact that I had not applied for work in

---

[1]   JRK to MVD, July 28, 1923, in JAH.

Mexico under the Presbyterian Church in the United States, to which three seminary friends were assigned the previous year, nor in Colombia or Brazil, was surely the Lord's doing. When yearning, opportunity, and timing in this Reformed Church undertaking converged, there was evidence of divine calling. This gave assurance in the difficult years ahead that mine had not been a foolhardy choice but a Spirit-led decision. If the Lord had sent me together with my wife, then only the Lord could recall us.[2]

We were soon informed that Mexico had a church known as the National Presbyterian Church of Mexico, somewhat like the Church of Christ in Japan at that time. There were also a number of American missionaries in various parts of the country. American churches engaged in missionary work in Mexico in 1918—Presbyterians North and South, Methodists, Disciples of Christ, and Congregationalists—signed what was known as the Cincinnati Plan (the agreement was made in Cincinnati). The Baptists declined to join them. The plan divided the entire country of Mexico, with the exception of the Federal District, for missionary purposes. The Southern Presbyterians, long active in the northeast, moved to the Michoacán-Guerrero area in the southwest, leaving their churches to become Methodist. The Methodists moved out of Oaxaca, turning that over to the Northern Presbyterians. There was to be one seminary, the Seminario Unido, and one church publication, *El Mundo Cristiano*. Presbyterian pastors in the north, however, refused to leave their churches, stating, "If the missions will no longer support us, our people will, and if our people won't, we will support the churches." After some years, the Presbyterians again began to publish their own paper, *El Faro*, and then reopened their own seminary. The ecumenical efforts backfired, and for the rest of our years in Mexico, the words "Cincinnati Plan" and "ecumenical" would set people's teeth on edge. Because the Presbyterian Boards would not renounce the plan, there was always disagreement between the nationals and the missionaries and their boards.

The plan, however, did have one favorable result. The Northern Presbyterians, who were assigned the states of Veracruz, Oaxaca, Chiapas, Tabasco, Campeche, Yucatán, and the territory of Quintana Roo, which cover the entire southeast of the country, had neither staff nor funds to evangelize that entire vast region. When the Reformed Church in America, in response to the active pleading of the missionaries to the Native Americans (Mrs. Walter C. Roe, Gerrit Watermulder, and

2   Ibid.

Leonard Legters), was looking for a field beyond the United States border, the Northern Presbyterians agreed to yield responsibility for the evangelization of Chiapas to our denomination.

The Women's Board of Domestic Missions was the agency of the Reformed Church that took the initiative to conduct work among Native Americans. But realizing that in Mexico the woman's place was still in the home, the women, in their wisdom, invited the Men's Board of Domestic Missions to join them in the venture. A joint committee from the two was to meet monthly to administer the field. The arrangement was frustrating and ineffective, a handicap that was finally overcome when the boards were united as the Board of North American Missions. Eighteen years passed, however, before the first visit of a board secretary to the field in Chiapas.

CHAPTER 28

Letters of Love and Commitment

During the months of separation due to my studies at Princeton Theological Seminary, Mabel and I fostered our relationship through letters. Our correspondence was packed with expressions of our love and commitment to each other. But mostly, we were very busy working out our plan to serve the Lord in a foreign land. In fact, things precipitated with such speed that we had almost no time to process the details. We made some of the most important decisions of our lives in these letters.

On Friday, January 31, 1925, Mabel wrote me a letter that I kept with me to read again and again:

Dearest One,

I have been thinking so much of our work there [Mexico], of our pioneering together, and it is real, it is becoming. . . . You said just recently that the Board's willingness to send us would be our call—and, dear, I do think it is so, too.

I wonder just what you expected me to answer you. I believe you had enough faith in me to expect me to answer as I did. But, honey, you did give me chances to creep out—and change my mind. And then I have wondered if, when you had read an

Beautiful Mabel, anticipating our marriage and life (*courtesy Joy Fuder*)

answer opposing the plan, you would really feel satisfied that my judgment was the better. For, love of me, would you give up what you called your call, and do what I wanted you to do? I should know, I suppose, what you would have chosen, me or your work there. But, honey, I fear I don't know you well enough for that. It seems that it would be right to choose your work for Christ. But I wonder which it would have been.

There is one thing that worries me most of all about being down there, and that is sickness there. I have seen so little sickness of any kind at home that if you should be ill, dear, I would be hopelessly incompetent. The thought of your lying sick and needing help, when there would be only I, your girl-wife, to care for you, well, that scares me. And then there is this, our having children there, away from medical attention and the care and association of people of our kind. But all that is a foolish worry—maybe so—but I am a baby about seeing people in pain and in feeling it, I think. I think right now I see that point of hardship because I haven't been feeling well the last couple of days. That was on my mind much the night before last, 'cause being ill, I couldn't sleep, and then I had your letter to think about. And so all together—the darkness and the pain, and the thinking, thinking in the night—made me a bit of a baby. Do you know what picture came before my eyes constantly? The scene in "The Marriage Cheat" that we saw together in Chicago. There before

I was deeply in love with Mabel
(*courtesy Joy Fuder*)

me was the picture of that woman suffering alone there with only that helpless native woman to help her. But, then, there was the man she loved and who loved her! And there will be for me my man—whom I will be loving always and who will love me much! And then there is this—which happiness she didn't have—the man who will be there to give me joy will be and is in my dream picture, the own father of the tiny one that will be ours. And so that worry, like all the others, is lightened by the thought of your nearness and dearness. Dear, do you see how much I love you?

There will not be any message from you in the morning. Will you be thinking much of me just the same? I know you will though, Kemp, and in the afternoon you will have my special. . . .

Now, good night, dear. My note became rather elongated, but you don't care! Just yours I am. Mabel.[1]

By March I was deeply involved with my studies at Princeton, trying to complete my degree. We were totally convinced that the Lord wanted us to serve him in Mexico. But there were many other important things that had to be resolved before a final move: my ordination to ministry, our wedding, and the definition by the Women's Domestic Board of Missions of a specific call to a specific missionary project. All these important matters were the subject of many letters that went in different directions, particularly from Michigan to New Jersey and vice-

[1]   MVD to JRK, Jan. 31, 1925, in JAH.

versa. On March 12, I wrote my Mabe, updating her on how things were moving along and my expectations.

My Pascarita,

Thinking and wondering about our summer and our wedding! It is quite a problem. The middle of the summer would make it inconvenient. . . . September first or at least the beginning of September was the date set by the Board, although their findings on their present trip [to Chiapas] may alter matters somewhat. I have tried twice to get those medical questionaries so that we might know whether we are fit to go, but I can't seem to get them. It is rather provoking, because if doctors should discover something to prevent our going, I ought to be looking for a church here. Then, too, I have been keeping the Muitzeskill people [Dutch Reformed Church at Muitzeskill] waiting. I can't tell them we are going to Mexico, because we don't know, and so the weeks have gone by, and Muitzeskill is not getting a pastor for the summer or for next year.

Something perplexes me even more than the date of our wedding and that is where we are going to spend the summer. Your folks will want you to be at home, and they have a right to wish that. And my folks will want me home, and they surely have a right to that after all my wanderings these last years. And I do want to be at home for a few months, and you want to be at home for a time, and we want to be in each other's homes, and our folks will want us in the respective homes, so what on earth can we do! Then, too, I would like to go to some summer school for six weeks to study Spanish if there is a school offering a six-week course.

All of these need not be solved immediately, and I am sure it will work itself out some way. . . . I wish we could be married early because it would be much better for us to live together for a while, to get used to each other, before being separated from civilization so completely. There is absolutely no possibility of a day in June? You must not be inconvenienced though, in any way, because this must be a happy wedding and a pretty wedding.

Yes, dear, I realize that a church wedding is out of the question, not because of expense but because there is no church with which we are affiliated of the size that would be expedient, appropriate or pleasant. No, Mabel, my dream wasn't a large expensive wedding—far from it—but I have long wished for a simple church wedding.[2]

[2]   JRK to MVD, March 12, 1925, in JAH.

As to my dedication to ministry, I had my service of ordination at First Reformed Church, Sioux Center, Iowa, on June 25. On Friday night, June 26, I wrote my beloved Mabe:

> My dear Pascarita,
>
> You wished you could have been at the services last night, but it was nearly all in Dutch, and it lasted two hours and twenty minutes! It would have been real nice to have you there, but I fear it would have been somewhat tiresome for you. The church was quite filled, and everything went well. Polly sang "My Creed" quite nicely. (That would have been a good part of the program for my girl!) But I thought of you a lot, dear. After the services Jo [Johanna?] and Harriet and I sat on the porch here and talked until nearly twelve. And there, too, you should have been. Such a beautiful evening it was.[3]

We were thinking all the time of our future and our ministry in Mexico. I remember the night after my ordination to the ministry, I had a chance to meet somebody that reminded me of the challenge we were facing of learning Spanish, a rather complicated language. I have always considered certain experiences to be signals sent by the Lord to mark our way, and I understood my meeting with this man to be such. I immediately shared with Mabel the experience, knowing that she was of the same mind as I.

> Tonight, I walked toward town, and a carpenter asked me whether I was the man who was ordained last night. Then he started to ask questions on Mexico and its languages. He deplored the fact that the early history of the Americas is not known and talked much on the beauty of the Spanish language. He never studied the language but just the names he remembered from history and geography. To find an old carpenter—as Dutch as they make them—appreciative of musical terms in languages made me stay and talk on, so we went over the Dutch writers and their remarkable works. He could quote passages from Kuyper and Bavinck, passages that are especially beautiful and rich in meaning. Titles of books mean a lot to him, too. Isn't that remarkable to find an old carpenter with a taste for real literature like that?[4]

Ah, those days of enchantment and magic, of poetry and love, of dreams and expectations! My excitement for our future ministry in

[3]   JRK to MVD, June 26, 1925, in JAH.
[4]   Ibid.

Mexico and my love and commitment to Mabel went hand in hand. In fact, even today, I think that the Lord cultivated these passions together in my heart with an eternal purpose. I continued my letter to Mabe:

> But then I walked on in the beautiful night and how lonely it was and is. Truly, love is a beautiful thing because it always is strongest when surroundings are beautiful. But love is sad too because it is strong when we are in such a mood. Sometimes we find a note of sadness in things that are beautiful and often beauty in what is sad. But always, we want to go on and on looking for beauty even as this old carpenter, and we will find it, I know, first in our love and then in our life and among the people to whom we are going.
>
> My Pascarita, you are going to marry a man who loves you with his whole self and completely. Goodnight dear. Your Kemp.[5]

---

5   Ibid.

CHAPTER 29

Letters of Support and Encouragement

There is nothing more reassuring than a letter received in due time. Words of encouragement written by relatives and friends hearten the spirit and strengthen the will to go for the impossible and attempt the challenging. What a wondrous power pervades timely words when they are spoken with love! How true is the Word when it says that "the tongue of the righteous is choice silver." Yes, "A word fitly spoken is like apples of gold in a setting of silver."[1] For Mabel and me, this was our experience through the remarkable year of 1925, as we were preparing to go to Mexico.

As I was approaching the completion of my studies at Princeton, there were two very important issues that I had to resolve which held enormous consequences for my life and ministry. First, I wanted to marry Mabel Van Dyke, my one and only love; second, I had to define my ministry and where I would serve the Lord. These two decisions, which normally require a good amount of time and reflection, descended upon me almost in a matter of weeks. I had to think about them, pray a lot, and constantly consult with the Lord, but also I had to discuss

[1]   Proverbs 10:20; 25:11.

143

At Princeton Seminary, I waited for the Lord to open
a door to Mexico (*courtesy Joy Fuder*)

these issues with my love, her parents, my parents, my church, and
those who were inviting me to be a missionary in a foreign land. Many
letters circulated expressing my feelings, convictions, and even doubts.
Line after line of correspondence went through the mail in those very
busy days of 1925.

I do not remember the date now, but by June, I had sent a letter
to Mr. and Mrs. Van Dyke asking their permission to both marry Mabel
and take her to Mexico. I thought it necessary to have their approval
and blessing since she was only twenty-three years of age and had never
gone outside of Michigan. So I wrote the following:

> You have for some time been acquainted with the hope which
> Mabel and I have had that a way might open up for us to work
> among Central or South American people. This is a hope which
> for me at least is by no means new but had its beginning some
> nine years ago. Always, it has been vague and like a far distant
> possibility, but in recent years the Woman's Board of our own
> Reformed Church has realized the great need and opportunity of
> just such work, and with their plans coming to a head just as I am
> finishing my Seminary work, it does seem very evident that God
> is working out his own program.
>
> But there is another thread woven into all of this and
> that is the love Mabel and I have for each other. This you have

watched develop and this I have been very bold to assume went with your approval. Mabel has for some time wished to and has been willing to go where I felt my life would count for most and recently she has faced a rather definite proposition and is as eager to undertake it as I am.

That proposition is the rather unexpected news, which came from the Woman's Board of Domestic Missions, that they will be prepared to send us as their first workers to some territory in lower Mexico bordering Central America—a region inhabited by as many as 50,000 Indians and many more Spanish speaking peoples and all of these without a church and without the Christ.

The details have not been worked out, but they are waiting for our answer as to whether we are ready to undertake the work. Mabel and I are, so far as our own minds go, entirely willing and eager, but we are taking no action until and unless we have your consent and that of my folks.

I recall the remark made last Christmas by Mrs. Van Dyke, that she hoped we would not be going for a year at least, and it did seem as tho [though] the Board would not be ready for at least that period of time. But now, they say they are ready to send us on the first of September of this year.

The length of the term is at present set at five years, but I am hoping to get them to make the first term 3 yrs [years] and from then on, five years. The Board promises to supply a fee of [$]1,500 annually plus all traveling expenses, and house rent I presume. In the near future, additional workers may be sent.

But my question as to your consent to our going involves another question which I regret to find necessary to ask by letter. Had this sudden change in the Board's plans not arisen, there would have been an occasion for a personal interview, no doubt. The question concerns your approval of our engagement and our wish to be married during this next summer. Our love for each other we know to be true and lasting and to me Mabel means all that any woman could possibly mean to a man.[2]

Finally, with their approval and the blessing of my parents, we got married on August 13, 1925. Once together in matrimony, our first challenge was our shared commitment to serve the Lord in Latin America. We concentrated our prayers and interest in the possibility

---

[2]   JRK to Christina and William E. Van Dyke, n.d., in JAH.

of going to Mexico under the invitation of the Women's Board of Domestic Missions. We were also worried not only about the specific place of service and our commission but also about our support and the material means to carry it out. In fact, our sustenance has never been a motive of preoccupation for us throughout our ministry, but it was the preoccupation of our parents, particularly mine. My father felt responsible for this, and he did his best to motivate our church, First Reformed Church in Sioux Center, to have a share in the burden. In those days close to our departure, he sent a number of letters to our place in New York City, informing me about the involvement of the church in our missionary adventure.

> In regard to the support of a second missionary by our church, I can say this: when the Deacons went around for the ministers' salary last fall, they also asked what they thought of supporting a second missionary.[3] About half were really willing. But some of the others, and especially some of the renters, thought they had load enough the way it was. So the Dominie thought of raising it among the more well to do in our church.[4] And so, at the congregational meeting, [he] made a fine speech asking for their approval to do so. But some in the church were not sure that the church as a whole would want to support one, that they made a motion and demanded a vote. Dominie tried to prevent this. But [he] could not convince them. As he only wanted their approval, the vote was 63 yes, 68 no. Then, they made a motion to vote the approval of De's [Dominie's] plan which carried Big. Then, someone asked if that excluded anyone, and the answer was given them that anyone who desired could join in. He is trying to get pledges for one year first. De [Dominie] has not asked very many yet. But claims he is meeting with good success. [I] will write the outcome later. The congregation has accepted the budget for minister salary: Poppen, De [Dominie], De Pree and Poor Fund all in one. But we had nearly an empty treasury at present. But the Deacons will put it high enough so they will have some on hand next fall which will make it easier.[5]

Another letter by my father, written from Sioux Center, Iowa, when we had just arrived in the field, also expresses his concern and

---

3   The Reformed Church in Sioux Center, Iowa, already supported a missionary, Rev. Alvin Poppen.
4   Term used in the United States for a minister or pastor of the Dutch Reformed Church.
5   John Kempers (JK) to JRK, n.d. (November 28, 1925, according to the postmark on envelope), in JAH.

preoccupation for our sustenance. This attitude of his was very encouraging, for I understood it to be an expression of his deep love for me and his support of my vocation. On this occasion he wrote:

> Saturday morning.
> All the children here had planned a surprise on Mamie on her birthday, and it worked 100%. . . . One more thing and I must close for this time. Yesterday, after prayer meeting, a meeting was to be held of those who were willing to contribute to your salary. As Dominie had rec'd [received] a telegram a few days ago to wire back what our church had done in regard to your salary as they saw a possible other opening, so he wired back that a meeting would be held Friday. I told De [Dominie] that I would not be there so they could talk more freely. The meeting turned out fine. They did not have quite enough pledges yet. But decided to go ahead and pledge your salary for a year. So they wired the Board last night yet. De claims he is so busy; otherwise, he would have seen more people. He has been working on a longer period than one year, and some were willing to pledge longer, others rather go year by year. A little more work; otherwise it is the same. I have not seen the hit [*sic*] yet. But at least two pledges of 100.00 each, quite a few 50.00 each, and some 25.00 and so on. It is nearly always this way. If you want some money, you got to go after it, at least in our church. Quite a few ask how you are getting along. Now as they are going to support you, it seems to me that it would be a good thing to write a letter describing somewhat your trip and welcome over there, how things look, what you are doing, etc.: a suggestion. So a letter can do a twofold purpose if you address it to our church and sent it to De. Then, he could read it in church and have it published in our town paper, or have extracts of it read in church. People are eager for some news. . . . So spend a little time in writing. It will repay. Even Mabel's little writing in *The Christian Intelligencer* was eagerly read. Hoping you will enjoy your work and that the Lord may bless you folks and also your work. And that you may enjoy good health. Greetings from us all. Pa.[6]

There was a letter written about the time Mable and I embarked to sail to Mexico, which was very encouraging to us. Mrs. Taber Knox was part of the company of four (two women and two men) who had

---

6   JK to JRK, n.d., in JAH.

gone to Chiapas very much in the fashion of the twelve spies sent by Moses "to explore the land." On December 2, 1925, the day previous to our sailing to Mexico, Mrs. Taber Knox sent us a beautiful letter.

Dear Mr. and Mrs. Kempers:

I am looking forward with very great pleasure to the hour of your sailing for Mexico tomorrow! It will be very like the day our delegation sailed on the same vessel, on Feb. 19th of this year. Your sailing is like the fruition of our dream. You certainly are going out with a host of deeply interested and loyal friends behind you who will keep you in loving remembrance and follow you with their prayers. I am glad that you can go first to Jalapa where, with Mr. and Mrs. Phillips, you will get a clear understanding of the Mexican work, under most favorable conditions and a grasp of the language it would be difficult to acquire in the States.

My own trip to Tapachula, with all that came firsthand on such a journey, has filled my heart with a deep desire to bring the needs home to as many as possible of our church people, and I have welcomed the privilege of speaking of the work in a large number of conferences this fall and in very many individual societies. Everywhere, the interest has been marked, and at the close of one address, one Society pledged $500 to carry on this work. I know you will be glad to know of every increase of interest.

I have everywhere urged constant prayer, as well as gifts, and I am fully assured that you will both be very earnestly remembered in prayer by a very large number of devoted Christians both East and West. Your earnestness and consecration has been a source of much joy and thanksgiving not only to our Board members but also to many others.

The privations and handicaps will, I am sure, appear as nothing when you find how responsive these long-neglected people are. I know you will be very deeply impressed, as I was, with the courtesy and innate refinement of the people. It will be a delicate task to reach them, but sympathetic interest, tact, and Christian love and grace will certainly win the day; and I almost covet your great opportunity of entering this new untried field of service and helping to put the stamp of Christ upon these precious souls. Be well assured dear Mr. and Mrs. Kempers that I will follow you constantly with keenest interest and prayers. Sometime when opportunity offers, I would enjoy hearing from you.

I am bringing a few sweets and salted nuts and a few apples, grown in our Warwick parish, which I hope you will enjoy. I sent them in preference to other fruit, thinking you would like them as I do. A loving good-bye as you go forth on your great Christian mission. I wish for you a favorable journey and a very wonderful presence of him in whose name and for whose sake you have dedicated your lives.

Your sincere friend,
Ada Quinby Knox (Mrs. Taber).[7]

[7]   Ada Quinby Knox to JRK, Dec. 2, 1925, in JAH.

CHAPTER 30

New Experiences

The year of 1925 had an abundance of new and exciting experiences. The first part of the year flew past. I graduated from Princeton Theological Seminary of the Presbyterian Church on May 12, 1925, with a master of divinity degree. Later, on July 16, I received my master of arts degree from Princeton University.[1] On June 25, I was given my certificate of ordination at Sioux Center, Iowa, as a minister of the Reformed Church in America and was admitted to the Classis of West Sioux. A few days before, on June 17, I had received a certificate of licensure by the classis at Sioux Center.[2]

On the Thursday evening of August 13, at six o'clock, Mabel and I made our solemn covenant of love before God to spend the rest of our lives together. The wedding ceremony took place at Beechwood Reformed Church in Holland, Michigan.[3] That night she was extremely beautiful. Her blue eyes were shining with joy, and I was enchanted by the cut of her hair—*la garçonne*—which was very much in fashion in

---

[1] Original diplomas, in JAH.
[2] Original certificates, in JAH.
[3] Wedding card of invitation, in JAH.

Our beautiful wedding, with sister Lillian and brother Bert at our side
(*courtesy Joy Fuder*)

those days. Attending us were Lillian Van Dyke (her sister) and Bert Kempers (my brother), with Dorothy Ann Van Dyke serving as flower girl, and Rev. James M. Martin, the senior pastor of Third Reformed Church, officiating.[4]

The weeks prior to our wedding were frantic with preparations. On June 27, I wrote my Mabe in Holland from Sioux Center, telling her:

> Honey, finally, I am sending you the number of invitations there ought to be for my people. We have decided to cut it down to a minimum by not sending any to the numberless cousins excepting perhaps Ray Lubbers if he is in Holland and Rev. Wyngaarden in Grand Rapids. The total of invitations that would mean for grandparents, aunts, uncles, and brothers and sisters is twenty-three but possibly twenty-five to make sure. And the announcements will be seven as a minimum.
>
> As I thought, the folks will want to give some sort of a reception but they will have cards made here to send to cousins and uncles as well. As far as I know, there will only be eight of my relatives who can come. That is eight as a maximum besides my

---

4   David W. Kempers' presentation on the occasion of his parents' golden wedding anniversary (August 15, 1975), JAH.

folks and Jo [Johanna?], which means that there will be quite a bit of room for your relatives. You are a lucky one to be marrying a faraway man. One thing to counterbalance all the months of separation it has cost us.[5]

Immediately after our wedding, we began preparations for our departure to Chiapas, the most remote corner of Mexico. In September we studied Spanish at the Berlitz School in New York and attended classes at the National Bible Institute, where we had a room until departure for Mexico, via Ward Line Steamer. The board had suggested boat travel because the research committee had visited Mexico that way. The travel plan was to go from New York to Veracruz in Mexico. Veracruz was near Jalapa, where the Phillipses (Harry A. and Ellen Pratt Ramsay), American Presbyterian missionaries, resided. There were no entrance restrictions at the time, although we did have a little mix-up with our freight, since we had not made the proper application to get these admitted for free. We were on our own, and good advice was hard to get.[6] In fact, we had no idea of the place to which we were going, of legal regulations, or of thousands of other details.

We had been invited by the Board of the Women's Domestic Missions of the Reformed Church in Flatbush, New York, to be the pioneer missionaries of the church to an underdeveloped and unknown field in southern Mexico. At the November 1925 commissioning service just prior to our departure, Mabel sang a soprano solo entitled, "I'll go where you want me to go, dear Lord." It beautifully expressed the complete surrender of her will to follow God's direction and her total partnership with me in the Chiapas Mission. In fact, both of us were committing ourselves to the unknown, but we were willing to go, knowing that God would be with us.

---

5   JRK to MVD, June 27, 1925, in JAH.
6   JRK, "How It All Began," 2.

CHAPTER 31

Sailing to Our Destiny

The week before our departure to Mexico, we were scheduled to speak to a Christian Endeavor Society in New York, and although at the time, our hearts were not in it, it was a beneficial meeting. We spoke with a man who had just come from Tapachula, Chiapas, where José Coffin lived. This gentleman had owned (farm) businesses in Tapachula but lost most of them when US troops entered Mexico to get Pancho Villa, and Mexican natives destroyed farms in retaliation.

On this occasion, we also met Mr. Mason C. Alcott, president of the Hudson River Day Boat Line, who knew Mexico and South America and was a big gun. He took an interest in us and entertained us over lunch at his club in lower Manhattan. After the meal, Mr. Alcott drove us around in his big car driven, of course, by a chauffeur and introduced us to some high-up officers of different Atlantic boat lines. He had heard Mabel sing at the Christian Endeavor meeting and was impressed. Mabel had learned the hymns of the Reformed Church on her father's knees and sang in grade school, high school, college, and in church choirs, often doing solo work. Mr. Alcott wondered whether Mabel would have a piano in Chiapas; it seemed doubtful to him. Just as

Sailing with faith and courage into an unknown future

we got out of the car, he spoke of it, and Mabel said we hoped someday to have a piano. "Well," he said, "I'll tell you what I can do. I can get you a 'baby organ' if you can take it with you." I said that would be fine if we could take it along.

No more was said, and because he seemed forgetful, we thought no more of it. On the morning we sailed, he and his wife came through the rain with a real fine Bilhorn folding organ and a sturdy canvas bag with fruit and other supplies.[1] That folding organ, which surprised Mabel on that rainy morning of our departure, was later carried on the backs of mules and men to homes and rustic churches in Chiapas. In fact, for some thirty years, Mabel was the only Protestant church organist in the state of Chiapas. She began choir work and organized the short-term music institutes to teach new Christmas and Easter songs simultaneously to delegates from many area congregations. The day we boarded the ship, Mr. Alcott, however, not only brought to us the promised folding organ but also introduced us to the officers of the boat. Such a man! And if we had not spoken in the Christian Endeavor Society, we would never have known him. He said that, had he known us before, he would have given us a free boat trip up the Hudson to Albany and back.

The week of our departure from New York was filled with surprises. On Monday, we had our board luncheon, at which an even dozen were present. That was our official farewell which took place at a marvelous club! On Tuesday noon, as I have already mentioned, Mr. Alcott invited

[1]   Ibid.

us to lunch at a club of his. He had also invited Dr. Samuel Guy Inman, a very prominent man in the missionary world, and a Mr. Jenks, who had traveled Mexico and South America in the mining industry. A piece of pie cost thirty-five cents, so you can imagine what the meal cost. It cost Mabel and me five cents each to get down there, but that was all.

Our trip to Mexico started on Wednesday, December 2, 1925, and extended to December 12, when we landed in Veracruz, Mexico. The departure was delayed for a couple of days due to bad weather. I have kept the memory of this unique trip in my mind in the form of a diary.

Wednesday 2: Mrs. Knox of the board was there to see us off and had a big bundle of apples and candy and nuts. Mary Van Brunt, who took us to that high-priced eating place, was also there and gave me two books costing five dollars and two dollars and presented Mabel with some fine flowers. People from Holland had sent flowers to our room by telegraph, and Miss Kendall had a big box full of little boxes which were marked and were to be opened as we went along on our trip. Then we were given letters and telegrams with good wishes. The night before, we were in a room at National Bible Institute with three Hopeites and Miss Zwemer from Holland (later on the board) with a cake and ice cream. We packed until one o'clock the next morning.

Thursday 3: Early in the morning, somebody came down, and he and Mabel took one trunk in a taxi, and I another. We were to sail at 11:00 a.m., but the sea was rough, so we lay at anchor until 6:30 the next morning. Our steamship was a bit delayed due to a storm that kept her pier bound.

Friday 4: On a rainy Friday morning, we left the port of New York on our steamer *Mexico*, heading to our missionary field in Mexico. The rain was heavy, but the trip could not be delayed any more. In the end, the vessel was put to sea and turned south toward the country whose name she bore. With her cargo of freight and passengers headed for Havana, Progreso, and Veracruz, this was a routine run. But for us, alert at the porthole of state room thirty-eight, it was the passageway to our life's missionary adventure, albeit beset with sea sickness.

As we left the port of New York, the fun began! We sat up to see the lights of New York and the Statue of Liberty for a last time and went back to sleep. When they called for breakfast, I got up, but the waves were kicking up somewhat, so I had to vomit. I tried twice to get up, but we stayed in bed until three o'clock in the afternoon. They brought us something to eat, but we could not keep it down. From three o'clock until nine o'clock that evening, we sat still on deck and had a sandwich and a few olives. Then we made a beeline to get flat in bed. One had to be either out on deck in the cool air or flat.

Saturday 5 and Sunday 6: The next morning was calm; we ate breakfast and enjoyed the morning. At noon, it got rougher, and foolishly, we went into the dining room to eat. That threw us off for the rest of the day. We did not eat a thing until Sunday morning breakfast, which was served on deck, as well as Sunday dinner. It was calm all day, so we read. At night we ate inside again. During the day, we saw a big fish. We didn't know whether it was a big shark or a baby whale. Only three of us saw it, so we can't prove anything. It was about fifteen feet long. The weekend flew quickly as we tried to adjust to a totally new experience for us both. We had never before sailed the high seas!

Monday 7: That morning we had breakfast inside. Of course we didn't wear any overcoats by then. Some people wore summer dresses. Mabel wore her rose dress (flannel) with short sleeves. It had been raining a good deal, but that day, the sun was with us and all was beautiful. Through the morning, we were sitting on deck in our steamer chairs viewing the coast of Florida and discussing if we were in front of Palm Beach or Miami. Anyhow, it was a land covered with trees and buildings and a sandy beach. There were large hotels every once in a while. The boat, however, was not very impressive. It was much like a Lake Michigan boat, only larger but with no orchestra and no gymnasium, like some boats had. Most unusual was the smell of burning oil, which was strongest at the end where our stateroom was.

Tuesday 8: After sailing past the palm-fringed shore of Florida, we made a stop in Havana, Cuba. That gave us our first view of a Spanish-speaking people. Now we were in the beautiful and quiet Caribbean city of Havana, with its gorgeous boulevards, the *Malecón* (sea wall), and its exquisite buildings designed after European models. We had our early breakfast, which was delicious and abundant. We sat at the table with the ship's doctor who had missionary brothers and was therefore very interested in our project. At that early hour, we saw the most stunning sunrise we have ever seen. The sun was projecting its light on a beautiful harbor, packed with all sorts of vessels and boats. The grass was as green as in late June and the air like a July morning. The old harbor, where Commodore Dewey and the battleship *Maine* made history, was before our eyes, and we could not believe that we were looking at the scene of this episode of American history.

Havana was great fun. Before we could get permission to disembark, row boats with cigars and bottles and candies came alongside, with a rope to throw any of these products to those who would buy, with a basket at the end. The streets were all very narrow. They were about sixteen feet or less and mostly one-way streets, down which the

We enjoyed our cruise to Cuba, and then we were on to Mexico
(*courtesy Joy Fuder*)

autos went. Most of the streets had two names: the name given by the government and the old name the people used. The buildings were of Spanish and French architecture, and some had façades of carved stones with beautiful balconies. The fronts were open, so there were no doors to worry about. For some reason, flies were not a bother. The people seemed to live in back of the stores and upstairs, so you could see many stairways and painted glass. Behind the stores, there were yards with palm trees, fruit trees, and abundant green grass.

Everybody chatted in Spanish, though we found a few English-speaking people. We ventured to have a haircut for fifty cents each. In New York, it was sixty cents for men and seventy-five cents or a dollar for women. We saved money on haircuts but lost money when it came to eating an American lunch at noon, for which we had to pay $1.70. We spent the rest of the day walking around the town. We sat in the park and watched people go by. We were surprised with the diversity of people around us. There were Chinese carrying baskets on their heads and Cubans selling things. There were all sorts of poorly and thinly dressed people sitting in the park for a while, taking a nap. The poor people wore a sort of tennis shoe in white or blue. Some wore bedroom slippers, and some were barefooted. Because of the heat, we did not see any socks. The school boys struck us as funny. They wore knickerbockers and little coats, but they all seemed to have such thin legs and big heads, on top of which, they wore an adult-size American straw hat.

Wednesday 9 and Thursday 10: We spent these two days walking around Old Havana to discover its secrets and hidden treasures. The trees on the sidewalks and in the parks were palm, cactus, and other tropical varieties. There were flowers everywhere. The air was heavy and hot just like in a greenhouse. The blocks were short, so there were many corners, and on almost every corner, there was a saloon or bar (*café*). Liquor was present everywhere, and we could see no end to the bottles and the smell of alcohol and tobacco. And yet, we didn't see a single drunk. Instead of the heavy American dray horse, they had little donkeys to transport their goods. My father would have liked it there, because there were no taxi-like cars! There were plenty of taxis, but they resembled other cars, and instead of hearing the usual "Taxi!," they came around and said "I've got a nice car." Nice car? We didn't want to ride though, so we bought a thirty-cent map and walked all day. In the evening, we were glad to get on the boat again and on the water where it was cool.

Because we left New York late in the previous week and rode in a fog for a time, we arrived in Havana a day later than planned. Nevertheless, we had enough time to visit the city and marvel at its beauty. We also spent time making friends on board. There were some nice American people on board and some nice Mexicans, and many others, but not a big crowd at all. Some were going for a visit, some on business. The board members told us to be careful because Mexicans, they said, were born thieves. But others who had lived there for years said one would be safer there than in the United States. Wise counselors disagreed.

These comments did not help us too much. In fact, we were worried about our stuff. Our freight, all we possessed, was on board. If this ship went down or our property was stolen, we were broke. We also wondered how we would get through customs with all our silverware and silver dishes—perhaps quite readily—but we were totally inexperienced in these matters, and nobody had given us the simplest piece of advice. We were pioneers for the board and had to discover and prepare the way. We realized that the board surely could not help us if anything unexpected happened.

They surely had the best food on this boat, the very finest imaginable, and all kinds of it: fruit, ice-cream, nuts, dates, grapes, raisins, figs, celery, olives, salads, vegetables, cheese, and so forth. All this was better than we were able to afford in New York . . . and it was all part of the ticket (chicken, turkey, beef, lamb, pork, fish, and more). There was also all kinds of liquor, if one wanted it. Coffee, however, was strong enough for us. Coffee, tea, orange juice, and sodas were plentiful and free.[2]

Friday 11: We continued our navigation until we arrived at Progreso, our first point on Mexican land, lying becalmed for a day in this shallow harbor in Yucatán. We, however, remained still four miles from land because there was no harbor in Progreso. So they anchored the steamer, and smaller boats came to get the passengers and freight. Sharks were plentiful here, and they swam around looking for food. If someone fell overboard, he would be out of luck. We tried to stay as quiet as possible and held each other's hands.

In the morning, we watched them unload in Progreso. Boxes marked "This side up" were generally upside down because they could not read English. Packages marked "Handle with care" were banged around as much as any other. We got nervous just watching them, because we expected every box to break. Besides, it seemed to us on board that this boat could have made the trip at least one or two days quicker. We realized that we should take the train on our return trip to save time, although it surely was much nicer on board a ship than on a dirty, dusty train. Nor have we ever lived in such high class for so long a time. Food was plentiful; read and sleep and eat and dream was all we did. But one must remember to limit oneself.

While passengers and cargo were unloaded, we walked off the boat into a festive crowd in the streets of the port. But the throng of excited Mexicans waving flags on that day was not a welcoming party for newly arrived American missionaries. On the contrary, the festivities were in honor of the patron saint of Mexico—the Virgin of Guadalupe—whose legendary exploits are celebrated by Roman Catholics nationwide. And it was to these people and this country that we had come to serve with the good news of a risen Savior and to build a new church in an ancient land.[3]

Saturday 12: After crossing the Campeche Bay, we finally arrived at our destination, the city port of Veracruz, on the Gulf of Mexico. While waiting at the rail before disembarking, we heard our names called by someone on the pier. It was a complete surprise for us. The board secretary had wired Rev. Rosales asking him to meet us. He was there waiting for us with his hired man who got our baggage through. He engaged a taxi, and we were on our way to a hotel on the square, where he had secured a reservation for the best room for the *Americanos*

[2] JRK to JK, n.d., in JAH.
[3] JRK to JK, Dec. 11, 1925, in JAH.

ricos (rich Americans). At the hotel, we had a large room full of too-bright sun, two double beds, a bathroom, and a living room. Pastor Rosales had arranged it all. The following nights, we stayed in cheaper rooms. We were scheduled to stay there until Monday morning and then go to Jalapa. At two o'clock that afternoon, he showed us the city. We had been warned not to eat this and that, so we practically starved as we watched others eat plates full of delicious food.[4]

We spent several days in the port of Veracruz, in the midst of the festivities honoring the Guadalupe. We were shown the Presbyterian work in the city, basically a small wooden church with broken windows and a medical dispensary. What a disappointment after sightseeing in New York City! We felt, however, that it was a miracle of the Lord that we were already in Mexico. He led us to come to Mexico now and not to wait until after one last Christmas in the United States with our parents and relatives. When we presented our passports to the Mexican immigration officials, they glanced at mine which openly declared, "Occupation—Protestant minister," and waved us on. Just two weeks later, legislation was passed that prohibited all foreign ministers and priests from entering Mexico. Authorities expelled hundreds of them but at the same time allowed some ministers and priests already in Mexico, like us, to remain. The only limitation imposed on us was that we were stripped of our right to officiate in pastoral capacity and particularly to administer the sacraments.

---

[4]   JRK to JK, Dec. 12, 1925, in JAH. See also JRK, "How It All Began," 2.

CHAPTER 32

Adjusting to an Old World

After a few days at the port city of Veracruz, we moved to Jalapa (state of Veracruz), fewer than seventy miles away. There we spent the first three months of 1926. The train ride to Jalapa was thrilling. Venders calling *"Hay papaya, hay papaya!"* The heavy-laden orange trees and banana stalks which could almost be reached from the train's windows were all so new to us as the train wound its way up the mountains to Jalapa.

The Phillipses (Harry A. and Ellen Pratt Ramsay) were at a mission meeting in Oaxaca, but the church pastor, Pedro V. García, was at the train station, and he arranged for carriers for our heavy trunks and suitcases. When I saw some men lifting our heavy steamer trunk onto another man's back, I ran to warn them of its weight, but that man carried that trunk two miles uphill and then climbed to the second floor with it.

Leonor, the maid, was at home; she assigned us to a room and served meals we were not afraid to eat. The Phillipses helped us find the furnished home of an American who would be away for a few months. Arrangements were made for language study with a teacher who knew no English whatsoever. The Ainleys (Charles H., Jr. and Vera E. Wolfe) and the Schaumbergs (Ludwig C. and Lillie H. Schrader), Presbyterian missionaries, also resided in Jalapa for some time, so we were blessed with American fellowship while we adjusted to Mexican living. We had a social evening once a week with fellow missionaries.

After our time in Jalapa, we moved to Mexico City to learn the Spanish language. On the way, we visited Puebla, where we were shown the hospital, the Methodist Boys School and the Girls School. In Puebla there was a necessary transfer from one railroad station to another. When I got the trunks to the second station, I was told I would not be able to check them until just before train time the next morning. The solution was to rent a small room in a hotel near the station to store the trunks that night. All night, I worried whether I would find them there in the morning. By then we had been told so many stories about crime in Mexico that we were very scared. Our fears, however, were more the result of our ignorance, than of the facts themselves. Throughout our many years on the mission field, we learned how to deal with irrational fears, which can have devastating results on the work of a missionary in a foreign land.

In Mexico City, we found a room in Ayuntamiento, a downtown neighborhood. The place had a bedroom with the use of a kitchen, shared with others. There we found a teacher who knew a lot of English. We got to know the missionaries living in the city, and Mabel sang in the choir of Union Church. Our purpose in spending that season in Mexico City was to continue learning Spanish. By that time, we were very anxious about going as soon as possible to our field of service in Chiapas. Chiapas, however, was not just around the corner. Travel by rail was a three-day-long marathon, with a two-night endurance test as the open car windows and doors let in swirling dust along with the breeze and unrelenting heat by day and chilly air at night. It is necessary to see this long pilgrimage on a map to understand the true extent of its tortured winding.

As we were leaving for Chiapas, I found *cargadores* (porters) on the street to carry our trunks, a barrel of dishes, a cedar chest, and some other baggage to the San Lázaro railroad station. Thinking that I would be able to walk faster than they carrying the load, I let them start out first. But when I headed for the station, I could find them nowhere. After a long wait at the station with plans to check for our things in the thieves market the next morning, the men appeared. They had gone to the wrong station—Buena Vista—in the opposite direction. There was no extra charge for the extra miles, but it was now too late to check the express, so again I went through the procedure of renting a room for the night. That was the Mexico City of another age, where young men carried your baggage, and you walked to train stations.[1]

We started our trip to Chiapas in Mexico City, with the train zig zagging across the country, first to the Gulf port of Veracruz, then down across the Isthmus of Tehuantepec to the Pacific, and finally eastward along the coast to the tropical town of Tapachula near the Guatemalan border. We arrived in Tapachula at midnight. It was pretty dark since there was no electricity in the town in those days. At the railroad station, we were welcomed by Rev. José Coffin and his family.[2] We arrived at our final destination on *5 de Mayo* (May 5) the day of the celebration of the independence of Mexico. Everybody was enjoying a great *fiesta*, and we were suffering great weariness. That night, at the small local congregation, brother Genaro de la Rosa conducted the service as a lay preacher. We were taken to a hotel via a little street car with a gasoline motor. Next morning, the Coffins sent over a basket of large mangoes. We had not yet learned to appreciate their flavor. We did not dare to give them to anyone, fearing the recipient might be friends of the Coffins, so we threw them over fences on our morning walk.

Mr. Coffin had found a new little house for rent which he thought would be just right for us. We took one look and decided it was fit for a chicken coop, not a home. He was disappointed, and we walked the streets several mornings looking for a house. In the end, we had to settle in the house Coffin had found, which was quite spartan and required considerable adaptations. Immediately, I set to work putting on screen doors, screening the entire corridor and building a lattice fence to separate our patio from that of the neighbors. I also built some furniture. Brother Genaro would help in any way he could in these projects.

I bought a bed spring which we rested on a trunk at one end and two chairs at the other end. Mrs. Coffin helped Mabel make a *pabellón* (mosquito net). There was good cedar lumber available, so I made a dining room table, a bookcase, and a writing desk, and we were in business. When we had all our books on the shelves, a visitor asked whether they were all Bibles. For the local believers, there was no need to read other books.[3] The formal dining area belied the primitive kitchen. Of course, there were no electrical appliances and certainly no

---

[1]   Ibid., 3.
[2]   DDM, "John and Mabel Kempers: Pioneers of the Faith," 10.
[3]   JRK, "How It All Began," 3-4.

refrigeration until the 1950s. Nevertheless, Mabel managed to make our simple home into a palace. Her dinner table was always graced with an arrangement of flowers, often of daisies or whatever was economical to purchase. She always used placemats and cloth napkins in sterling silver napkin holders, engraved with our names. Mabel was an excellent cook. She boiled water for drinking and stored it. She always made a dessert for the main meal, often a boiled pudding or some native fruit prepared in a tasty manner. Rarely, however, did she use the oven for cooking or baking. Mabel was very frugal and never threw away any leftovers. In later years, I was amazed when I saw her put a teaspoon of scrambled eggs in a small container and place it in the refrigerator to use later in a soup. She would also clean the pan where rice had been cooked with a bit of water and place the water and grains of rice gleaned from it into a small bottle in the refrigerator to be used in a soup for another meal.[4]

In the days that followed, I decided to postpone any attempt to move inland to indigenous areas, although the original plan had been to settle there and evangelize monolingual tribal people. The uneasy political situation called for prudent and cautious action. Mabel was soon teaching English at Mrs. Coffin's day school; I had classes in gymnastic exercises and later introduced basketball to as many people as I could. With time, we had an all-girls team.

The first few weeks in Tapachula were intensive and demanding. There were so many new things to which we had to adapt. We began to make trips on horseback, with horses the brethren provided, to Mediomonte, Eisleben, and Cacahoatán. We used extensively the only train line available to go to Suchiate and Huixtla. Coffin and I went to San Francisco, inland from Escuintla. A little girl from there came to help Mabel in the house and to attend school. She was no doubt the slowest girl we had ever lived with, but at least Mabel was not alone later during the two-month exploratory trip that Coffin and I had made.[5]

[4]   Helen C. Hofman, interview with author, April 8, 2014.
[5]   JRK, "How It All Began," 4.

CHAPTER 33

Arrival in Chiapas

At last we were in Chiapas—our dream! After a long trip, we were finally in the place where we knew the Lord had sent us to serve him. Mabel and I had succeeded on the last lap of our trip to the little-known, undeveloped, unevangelized state of Chiapas in southwestern Mexico. We had a tiresome ride in a day coach with the dust of the dry season swirling through open windows, mixed with engine smoke and the sound of music. Marimbas were playing patriotic music at the stations celebrating Cinco de Mayo, a national holiday. Through a strange coincidence, it was on the morning of another Cinco de Mayo, forty years later that we left Chiapas to begin our work in the seminary in Mexico City.[1]

The name of the state comes from a word of Nahuatl origin, *tepechiapan*, which means "water under the hill" (from the Nahuatl *tepetl*, hill or mountain; *chi*, under; *atl*, water, bread, river, place). The official name of the state is Estado Libre y Soberano de Chiapas Free and Sovereign State of Chiapas), and it is one of the thirty-one states

---

[1]   JRK, "Reformed Church Women's Triennial," 1.

The city of Tapachula was proud of its modern trolley cars

that configure the thirty-two federative entities of Mexico. Located in the far southwest corner, it became the nineteenth state of Mexico in September 14, 1824, after a popular plebiscite, since during colonial times it was part of the Captaincy General of Guatemala. Later we learned that it was the most gorgeous region of Mexico, because of its scenery, and one of the most inviting, because of the treasures of world history contained there.

In the nineteenth century, there were great controversies as to the location of the seat of political power in the state. On the one side, the city of San Cristóbal de Las Casas claimed that right because it had been the historic capital since the days of the Spanish conquest. On the other side, there was Tuxtla Gutiérrez, which, due to its better location in the center of the territory, argued that it was a better option for a capital city. As usual in Mexico, this led to a civil war between the two factions. Finally the conflict was resolved in 1892, when Governor José Emilio Rabasa Estebanell definitively transferred political power to the city of Tuxtla Gutiérrez.

At the time of our arrival in Chiapas, when the government took restrictive measures prohibiting foreigners of any faith to administer the sacraments in Mexico, we were forced to serve with a very low profile. This was the reason why, right from the beginning, we had to take a secondary roll in the development of our mission. Besides, we desperately needed to learn Spanish to be able to carry out our commission.

The town of Tapachula is located in the extreme southern region of the Mexican coast of the Pacific known as Soconusco. This is also a name of Nahuatl background, *shokonoshko*, which means "place of sour prickly pears." When we arrived, the city had a population of about thirty thousand, and the municipal president was Humberto Elorza. The city was the most important business and cultural center in both southern Mexico and northwest Guatemala, since it was located just twenty-nine miles from the border. Most of its economic importance had come since the late nineteenth century with the establishment of coffee plantations. This agricultural production began a history of migration into the area which has continued ever since. Because of these factors, the city was known as the "pearl of the Soconusco."

When we arrived in Tapachula, everything looked gorgeous to us, even Mr. José Coffin. We were very much impressed with the gentleman with an almost aristocratic aspect who had already made history with his pioneering missionary work in the state. His wife, Luz Otero, also fascinated us with her polished manners and excellent level of education. They were at the railroad station to welcome us with Mexican courtesy, and in the following days, they introduced us to life in that corner of the state. A few months later, Mr. Coffin invited me to make the already-mentioned exploratory trip with him.[2] But this is a story that deserves its own narration. Meanwhile, Mabel and I tried to get acquainted with the hot and dusty city.

At that time of overflowing idealism and enthusiasm, everything looked beautiful, curious, and original with a unique enchantment. We went to the central plaza which was surrounded by new and beautiful buildings. The historic center was marked by a large, tree-lined plaza called Parque Miguel Hidalgo. The center of this plaza contained an octagon kiosk with Baroque ironwork with some Moorish influence. Parque Miguel Hidalgo was the center of the city surrounded by the old municipal palace, the Perez Portal, and the Teatro al Aire Libre (Open Air Theater), which often had marimba concerts. The San Agustín Roman Catholic parish church, dated from the eighteenth century, was established to honor Augustine, the patron saint of the city. It is a simple construction with a red Spanish tile roof, supported by wood beams. The façade is a simple Neoclassical style, with six Ionic order columns, three on each side of the entrance, joined by false arches. The top of the façade has two bell towers. This design was based on the Teopisca church. Later in 1958, shortly after the Tapachula diocese was established, the church became a cathedral.

[2]   Ibid.

We joined the Coffins, Chaplain Genaro de la Rosa, and
colporteur Carlos Fernando in Tapachula

The building that later was known as Casa de la Cultura, one of
the most emblematic in Tapachula, was built in 1929 as the municipal
palace, when the city was prosperous because of the surrounding coffee
plantations. Although the style is Art Deco, the façade is decorated with
Oaxacan style fretwork, images of Aztec warriors, and stylized serpents,
along with the Mexican national and state coats of arms.

Something that caught our attention during our first year in the
city was its popular festivities. Never in our young lives had we seen
anything like it. Major annual events included the Chinese New Year,
the festivities of San Benito, the Feria Tapachula, and the celebrations
in honor of San Agustín, Jesús de la Buena Esperanza, and San Miguel.
After the Spanish conquest, Tapachula was part of the Soconusco
region, known for its then profitable production of cacao. The city
became the capital of the Soconusco region in 1794. It was officially
declared a town in 1813. The current municipality at our arrival was
created in 1915, with Tapachula as the governing entity. It was declared
the provisional capital of Chiapas by forces loyal to the revolutionary
leader Victoriano Huerta in 1924, just a few months before our arrival.
Later, in 1929, the first air route was established, connecting the city
with Tuxtla Gutiérrez and Mexico City.

As Mabel and I began to take short trips in the region around
the city, we discovered its main ecosystems and most scenic places.

They included low growth rainforest, medium growth rainforest, and holm oak and pine forests. Many of these forest areas were suffering overexploitation with significant loss of both plant and animal life. The most difficult thing for us to accept was the climate. The temperature ranged from very hot in the low coastal areas to temperate in the higher elevations. There was a small area with a cold climate in part of the Tacaná volcano, but that place was not fit for living. The climate in the city was hot and humid most of the year. It was one of the rainiest areas in the world, with an annual rainfall of about four meters, drained by a number of rivers and streams that flowed from the Sierra Madre of Chiapas over the coastal plain to the Pacific Ocean. The main rivers were the Huehuetán, the Coatán, and the Cuilco that I crossed hundreds of times on my missionary pilgrimages. The rainy season occurred from June to September, and during those months, it was almost impossible to leave the city, since the few roads open were flooded or impassible because of mud.

Daily life in Tapachula was remarkable for us in the beginning, in spite of the hot, humid, and dusty environment in which we were submerged. We soon came to appreciate the "cooling off" time of the day. As sunset brought the air temperature down, families came out of their houses to sit on small benches on the sidewalk. Men riding their horses in the evening enjoyed the sound of the clapping hoofs of their mounts on the cobblestones, and when passing in front of these families, they took off their *charro* hats, saying "Buenas tardes" (Good evening). It was a noble gesture. A walk downtown and especially to the central park was a must for most families, who found in this free entertainment and an opportunity to socialize.

The streets became even noisier during the celebration of the *todos los santos y los fieles difuntos* (day of all saints and deceased faithful). On the evenings of November 1 and 2, children came out to the streets to ask for pumpkin preserves or money. They went from door to door singing:

¡*Ayote tía!*	Ayote lady!
Ángeles somos	We are angels
Del cielo bajamos	Descended from heaven
Pedimos ayote	We ask for ayote
Para que comamos.	For us to eat.

If people gave the children sweets or money, the children thanked them shouting "¡Que viva la tía!" (Long live the lady). If they did not receive anything, they would shout "¡Que muera la tía!" (Let the lady die) and run away.

Birthdays and anniversaries were also noisy celebrations. The house of the person honored was decorated with an arch made with bamboo and flounces and decorations made with China paper of many colors. These decorations were hung on the door of the house as people sang *mañanitas* (Mexican folk songs), accompanied with an incredible amount of rockets. All this was an indication that somebody was celebrating a birthday or an anniversary, and free food and drinks were ready to enjoy inside the house.

San Agustín fair in August was a very special celebration. The central park, Miguel Hidalgo, very close to our house, was packed with small kiosks. On the streets Octava Norte and Tercera Poniente, in front of the majestic municipal palace and the church of San Agustín, there were installed the little horses, the wheel of fortune, and the flying chairs, which were the delight of both children and adults. On August 28, during the festivity in honor of Saint Augustín, the patron of the city of Tapachula, special events took place, such as a processional with the image of the saint. Lots of people made a pilgrimage from the many towns outside the city. Mabel and I were thrilled in admiration with the cultural richness of these festivities. It was really a new world for us, and we immediately fell in love with it.

CHAPTER 34

Yankee Go Home!

The framework of evangelical work in Latin America had changed greatly since the Congress of Panama in 1916. World War I and its aftermath created the need to reexamine missions strategies. Christian forces endeavoring to carry out programs of brotherly service might consider facing the task with a renewed commitment to unity. It was decided, therefore, to hold at Montevideo in April 1925, the Congress on Christian Work in South America. The Committee on Cooperation in Latin America laid careful plans for this congress several years in advance. And although this congress had South America as its focus, its deliberations and conclusions were of significant importance to us since we were just establishing our ministry in Chiapas.

This congress was imperative due to the challenging new situations in most of the countries in the southern continent. Those conditions, however, were very similar to the ones we were facing in Mexico and particularly in Chiapas. The remark was made that the nations had grown stronger economically and politically. New social movements had arisen that marked a renewed interest by the common people in the development of their countries. In many places, women were inspired and came out of isolation to take part in solving their nation's problems. Educational forces had taken on new life. Governments were reorganizing their school systems, which made necessary an evaluation and realignment of the work of mission schools. New health movements were demanding leadership.

The Congress of Montevideo was preceded by a long and intensive study of existing conditions, under the direction of twelve commissions, with members on the field and in the United States. The subjects under study included a survey of unoccupied fields, indigenous peoples, education, evangelism, social movements, the health ministry, the church in the community, religious education, literature, missionary relationships, special religious problems, and the problem of cooperation and unity.[1] All these issues were part of the Christian testimony in South America, but the deliberations were quite stimulating for us when we read them in light of our own challenges in Chiapas.

Nevertheless, most of the conclusions of the Congress of Montevideo were disconnected from the political and ideological reality of Mexico. In more specific terms, the good ideas shared in the South American enclave were inapplicable in a context ruled by the entrenched Mexican anti-Americanism. Any missionary project sponsored and implemented by American missionaries was seen as American imperialism. Before any evaluation of the task in question, rejection was felt and applied.

This kind of prejudice and presupposition, however, was understandable. The frequent interventions of the United States in Latin America were incontestable arguments. In many parts of Latin America, economic penetration and political interference became inseparable. Together they added up to Yankee imperialism on a wide scale, and for millions of citizens in the southern countries, the United States became known as the Colossus of the North, ready to impose its will by force whenever the occasion arose.

A brief summary of the most important of these armed interventions will give some idea of their scope. From 1899 to 1933, Nicaragua was virtually a protectorate of the United States, and for more than twenty of those years, Nicaragua was under US military occupation. Aid was given to a rebellion in Panama, and that province was "taken" from Colombia in 1903. The Dominican Republic was under absolute United States control between 1905 and 1924 and was

---

[1]   Browning, *New Days in Latin America*, 192-94.

occupied by marines for ten years. Haiti was under military occupation from 1915 to 1934. Between 1907 and 1925, there were six armed interventions in Honduras. Mexico was invaded several times between 1846 and 1916, including the bombardment and occupation of Veracruz in 1914, and the punitive expedition of more than ten thousand men sent into Mexico under General Pershing, who chased Pancho Villa for several months across the country while World War I was raging in Europe. Many other Latin American nations were coerced by only slightly less violent means. The Mexican writer Luis Quintanilla in his book, *A Latin American Speaks*, mentions a total of sixty United States interventions in fifty years.[2]

American imperialism in Mexico created bitterness, not so much toward the American way of life and the benefits of its comfort and technology but to America's continued attempts to grasp territory and exploit its economically weaker neighbor.

President Woodrow Wilson, during the time of President Huerta, helped to reinforce the impression the Mexicans had of American foreign policies. This was the beginning of a new era in the relations between the United States and Latin America: the "moral" principle had been invoked, and recognition was being withheld from a *de facto* Latin American government as a measure of coercion against that government. President Wilson later clarified the issue when he stated in conversation that it was his intention "to teach these Latin American republics to elect good men."

The general consensus at the time seemed to be that Huerta was not a "good man." Most of his own countrymen now admit that he was an inveterate drunkard, a murderer, a ruthless tyrant who had no respect for constitutional law, an upholder of the feudal policy of the Porfirio Díaz regime. No sooner had he attained power than he filled the jails with political prisoners, having dozens of them shot. He surrounded the halls of Congress, declared that body dissolved, and imprisoned 110 Mexican deputies. Revolution broke out against Huerta almost immediately under Carranza, Obregón, Calles, Villa, and other leaders.

The fuse of violent reaction against Wilson's policy of "watchful waiting" was lit by the so-called "Tampico flag incident." A group of American soldiers had landed in a forbidden area in Tampico (Tamaulipas); they were arrested by the Mexican authorities, held for half an hour, and then released. A formal apology was given to the American commander. The Mexican official who had ordered the arrest

---

[2]   Quoted in John A. Crow, *The Epic of Latin America*, 4th ed. (Berkeley: University of California Press, 1992), 686-87.

was punished, and a salute was ordered to be given to the American flag. The American admiral demanded that the salute consist of twenty-one guns. The Mexicans balked at making such a tremendous concession, for a twenty-one-gun salute is given only after the gravest of outrages, and Huerta, who had already tendered his personal apologies, along with those of the commandant, attempted to excuse his government from the indignity. The Americans were adamant. As further persuasion, ten warships were promptly dispatched to Tampico with a regiment of marines. Huerta now offered to place the matter before The Hague Tribunal. When this offer brought a negative response, he agreed to have the twenty-one-gun salute fired, provided the Americans fired their twenty-one-gun return volley at the same time. Otherwise, he said, he was afraid that the salute might not be returned at all, and his government would thus be humiliated.

The argument was still going on when it was learned in Washington that a German vessel, the *Ypiranga*, was nearing Veracruz with a load of munitions for the Huerta government. The government of the United States, now determined to bring about the fall of Huerta, decided to block the arrival of this aid, and President Wilson wired the American forces to take Veracruz at once. Despite strong Mexican opposition, a landing was made, and after considerable fighting, the city was captured. Seventeen American soldiers were killed and about two hundred Mexicans, including several women and children, lost their lives in the storming of Veracruz. The only fact that the Mexicans could see was that Mexico's sovereignty was violated.

The capture of Mexico's main port cut off a fourth of that country's imports and made the survival of the Huerta regime impossible. Mexico City was taken by the revolutionists, and Carranza became president. He was promptly assassinated, and the revolution continued. By this time, the United States had become involved in World War I, and Mexico became a secondary issue. Naturally, feelings in the country continued to be bitterly anti-American.[3]

In spite of these historical circumstances, Mabel and I did not feel menaced or rejected by anybody in Chiapas. In the 1970s, it was commonly thought that the work of American missionaries was over because of the anti-Yankee sentiment of most missionary fields around the world. I never agreed with this evaluation. Many Latin American people used to say "Yankee go home!" And we took it seriously and obeyed that command: in Chiapas we were at home—Chiapas was our home!

[3]   Ibid., 689-91.

CHAPTER 35

First Missionary Adventure

As I said before, a few months after Mabel's and my arrival in Tapachula, Coffin invited me to take an exploratory trip with him. We would enter Chiapas from the north by way of Tabasco and then work our way south across the state back to our homes in Tapachula. When I said goodbye to Mabel, I fully expected to be back in two weeks, but two full months passed before I saw her again. No one in his right mind would plan to be away from home on the day of his first wedding anniversary. But this is what happened. Mabel was alone in Tapachula.

That night, I tried to sleep in a rope hammock stretched out across a small corn crib in northern Chiapas, with a pack of noisy rats for company; they robbed the owner of his corn and me of my sleep. There were no trains or planes or automobiles in Tabasco or in northern Chiapas in those days. In Tabasco, with its many rivers, most travel was by dugout canoe or riverboat. In Chiapas, one rode a horse or a mule up and down the steep mountain trails and across unbridged rivers. After six changes of mounts and guides in our crossing through Chiapas, we returned to Tapachula.

We launched from Palenque in northern Chiapas and began our journey into uncharted territory. The adventure included, at no cost, swarms of gnats and generous bites of all sorts of insects. We slept in the comfort of our hammocks (with a mosquito net well tucked in to keep out thirsty insects) or on beds of plank benches, trunks, or floors. We ate what was available in the places we stopped—whether much or little—with only a large spoon or often without cutlery of any kind.

There was, however, a magnificent compensation to all of this. We could gaze at beautiful sunsets; observe an amazing variety of trees, vegetation, and flowers in the heart of the jungle; and marvel at rainbow-colored butterflies and birds like nothing I had ever seen before. On the other hand, we also saw neglected, despised natives, suffering all manner of disease for lack of medical help. We came upon the burned ruins of ranches, deserted since the Mexican Revolution (1910-20), and we saw the hopelessness of people living and dying without the gospel.

Although I was to make scores of similar trips in the years to come, the exciting novelty of the sights and sounds of people and the landscape called for a sixteen-page description of everything unusual we encountered during those two trying months. The small groups of Bible-reading believers we encountered would be incorporated into the church later. The last lines of the account or report that I sent to the board afterward contained these words: "Two months to cross the state. When will we ever cover it?"

The parting words of the board secretary in New York were, "Find out what can be done down there. We don't know anything about it." My suggestion was that, due to the size of the field (half the size of Iowa), the lack of transportation, the dominant Roman Catholic opposition, the restrictive atheistic government regulations, and the small number of North American missionaries, it seemed the best strategy would be to train as many Chiapas men as possible for the ministry to evangelize that vast field.

It took eighteen years before we could find a way to get additional missionaries into the country. Several were commissioned throughout the years, and each contributed much in his or her own way. Much was done in many places. Considerable work was carried out in evangelization, education, and medicine on the indigenous fields, the only places where these things were possible or allowed. Youth work was my delight. Mabel initiated and developed women's ministries. There was much translation work of hymns and study material. Wycliffe translators lived among the natives and made New Testament translations for the different language groups. Our own people—missionaries sent by the Reformed Church—were diligently translating the Old Testament and other portions of scripture for the larger language groups.

There was much construction of church buildings with the missionary serving as architect and builder. And there was much evangelistic work by missionaries, especially before the ordination of Chiapas pastors. Throughout the years, we kept telling the churches in the United States about these long, horseback tours throughout the state. A young man introducing me before the sermon in the Tapachula church one night said, "This man knows Chiapas better than any of us. He knows it like the palm of his hand."

All that work by the missionaries was helpful and much appreciated by the Chiapas church people, who showed their gratitude with scrolls, citations, parchments, silver platters, gold medals, and hand-woven skirts and blouses. But all that work was really only *coitán* (a word heard only in Chiapas, probably of indigenous origin). When a merchant throws an extra handful of corn or beans or rice into the purchaser's container, it is *coitán*. Our nearest English equivalent would be "bonus."[1]

During those many years of missionary service, Mabel and I witnessed the power of God to save, to heal, and to set people free in marvelous ways. And it all started during those two months of suffering, sacrifice, and sighs for each other. The morning Coffin and I left Villahermosa, Tabasco, to enter Chiapas, we were in a dugout canoe along with Mr. Luis Schaumburg, the Presbyterian missionary in Tabasco, and Rev. Salomón Díaz, the Presbyterian pastor. They were headed for a church meeting and planned to drop us off at the juncture with the mighty Usumacinta River, up which we were to travel to reach Chiapas. As we moved along on the quiet Grijalva River, Mr. Schaumburg suddenly said, "Do you men realize that if someone who doesn't like us were to upset this canoe, there would not be a single minister or missionary in all of Chiapas or Tabasco?"[2]

How true was the Lord Jesus when he said, "Very truly, I tell you, unless a grain of wheat falls into the earth and dies, it remains just a single grain; but if it dies, it bears much fruit" (John 12.24). I have seen these words fulfilled in amazing ways through the forty-five years of our missionary venture in Chiapas. After our retirement, we received report after report telling us that there were dozens of ordained men in active

---

[1]   JRK, "Reformed Church Women's Triennial," 1-2.
[2]   Ibid., 2.

ministry in the state. These reports were enough to make us jump out of our seats with a "Praise the Lord!" and an "Alleluia!" These numbers would not seem large in the United States, because American believers are used to big seminary enrollments and multiple ministries in their churches, but to us, those dozens sounded like a thousand, really like a "great a cloud of witnesses" (Hebrews 12:1).

CHAPTER 36

Discovering Tabasco

Upon receipt of a telegram from Coffin, who was attending a synod session at Toluca near Mexico City, I left Tapachula by train to meet him at Puerto Mexico (state of Veracruz), as we had arranged. Our plan was to enter the state of Chiapas from the north by way of Tabasco and make our way somehow southward back to Tapachula, the town of our residence in those days in 1926.

From the very beginning, I was assured it would all be done in Mexican fashion, for at the appointed hour of three on the morning of the thirteenth of July, I was at the station with baggage and magic lantern to await the train which had only thirty miles to come. Yet it arrived four hours late. Four hours to observe the always interesting people at a Mexican train station, as well as the changing colors of the eastern sky above the peak of the nearby volcano Tacana. At seven o'clock that morning, however, we were off on the first lap of the trip, a twenty-five-hour train ride. All that day, we crossed rivers where women did their washing on stones, wading into the water, wearing only a large cloth tucked about the waist, their dresses on the banks of the rivers. We passed by fields or patches of corn, some in "good standing," others likewise standing but stripped altogether by swarms of locusts that had devastated whole regions of southeastern Mexico at that time.

On we went, skirting the Pacific Ocean and passing through dense tropical vegetation that wound about the many varieties of trees. In my youthful eagerness, I asked for the names of these trees, but before long, I discovered there was no end to them. Because of its varying altitudes, Chiapas contains almost every kind of tree that exists, from pine, cedar, mahogany, and oak down to rubber, *ceiba*, dyewood, and mangrove. There are shrubs from which blueing, soap, flavors, and medicines are extracted and others which produce every fruit of the tropical and temperate zones. Chiapas was one of the richest states in the republic of Mexico, but because of the lack of training and the lack of transportation, people lived in extreme poverty.

After a night's sleep on a wooden bench in an almost empty car, I arrived at Puerto Mexico, where Coffin met me and took me to a hotel. There the canvas cot was a bit more comfortable than the bench of the previous night. The church there was completely upset since the chaplain had just left his wife and run off with another woman. The evening service helped to restore calm, and in spite of his vociferous protests, a child was baptized.

A launch was to leave the morning of the fifteenth of July to Santa Ana, and I, still too much of an American, was ready to board it at four in the morning—the hour that had been set. From four o'clock in the morning until seven, I sat with my coffee and with swarms of mosquitoes and admired a beautifully colored, tropical sunrise over the water. Finally, we were off at seven o'clock, having lost the cool part of the day and now riding three hours under a blazing sun in an open launch. We arrived at Tonalá at eleven and were told we would not leave until the next morning. I really did not mind it, since Tonalá was as beautiful an example of a South Sea island village as one could picture. The beach was strewn with dugouts, and fishing nets were hung out to dry. Farther back were the bamboo huts beneath the stately waving palms; grown folks and children, pigs and chickens quietly moved about, seemingly unreal.

I tried fishing with long lines and large hooks with a boy who traveled with us to his home in Tabasco. Although we could see the great big fish leaping out of the water, a crab-like animal called *jaiba* managed to get all of our bait. With nothing left to tempt the fish, we walked over to the Gulf and took a swim in salt water. That relaxed me and helped me to sleep that night. Sleeping, however, in our hammocks in a newly built store or *tienda*, with all doors and openings closed, the intense heat gave me a lot of discomfort. Nevertheless, we again were up at four o'clock in the morning. At seven o'clock, we were at Santa Ana, once a place where large steamers anchored to load the mahogany for which Tabasco was famous. By then, the town, which was no more than some bamboo huts that stood without shelter in the hot sun amid pestholes that bred mosquitoes, was a center for malaria and revolutions. Never had I been in a more disagreeable village, among a more bandit-like people.

A man who was taking some provisions to his inland store in a dugout *cayuco* (canoe) offered us a ride. At twelve noon, we piled on top of beer boxes and other freight and were off. Two natives were rowing with one oar each and the owner polling from the rear where the water was not too deep. Occasionally, there was a mild breeze, and at such intervals, the sails were raised, and we glided along more swiftly. With a sudden change of wind, the sail shifted, shoving the owner of the cargo into the lake. It was funny at the time, but try to imagine an intelligent, supposedly friendly person, later telling others, it all happened because we were Protestant ministers. That entire day and all of the next, we were out on the water in this canoe under the blistering sun. I had to wear my sunglasses from morning until night, and a big straw hat served well to keep the sun from reaching my face from above, but the reflection of the sun on the water burned my skin to a crisp.

The mosquitoes began to attack as we pulled in toward shore to pass the night with some locals. As fast as I could move, I put up my hammock and *pabellón* (a mosquito net made to fit the hammock) and dove in. Coffin, more immune to the sting of the mosquito, passed slices of bread with sardines and strong coffee under the *pabellón* with quick actions, so as not to admit mosquitoes that swarmed by the millions.

The following noon, we drew up to shore again and had a dinner of tamales of new corn, tortillas, and a most delicious roasted fish named *sargo*. These lagoons also contained many kinds of *camarón* (shrimp), the fishing of which was the only means of livelihood of the people of Santa Ana and of those few who lived along the shore. The lakes also contained much *agua mala* (bad water), an amphibious waxy vegetable-fish that gives *vómito* (vomit) to bathers who happen to touch it. Here I had the novel experience of dipping my hand over the side of the dugout, pulling up several oysters, and eating them raw. In one place, dead oysters almost bridged the lake, which was about two miles wide. Although, like all the waters of Tabasco, these lakes were said to contain many sharks and alligators, I saw only the *tonina* (dolphin), a fish the size of a horse said to be the friend of the sailor. It kept away the sharks, preventing their eating an unfortunate man who might be thrown into those waters. Some twenty *tonina* followed us for miles.

At sundown, we entered the Santa Ana River and rowed upward. It was a quiet river, lined with dense vegetation, with multicolored birds sweeping about, parrots flying in pairs, fishing birds that dove beneath the water and remained there for several minutes, and all the lesser kinds of richly colored birds of the tropics. As day, however, changed into night, mosquitoes became active again. I buried myself beneath my covering as much as possible until a rainstorm overtook us. It was decided best to stop at a house along the river, where we were protected from the rain but not from the mosquitoes that swarmed and mutilated us. Unable to endure it any longer, I found my way back to the dugout and crawled under the heavy tarpaulin which was used to protect the cargo. There I waited until we moved on to the ranch, or what was left of the ranch, El Golpe.

All that night, mosquitoes kept entering my net, and I was unable to detect their mode of entry. In the morning, however, a man called my attention to a small opening that some of the thousands of mosquitoes had detected. With the buzzing of the mosquitoes about the net, the crunching of big hogs as they ate the pieces of food and bone left on the floor, and the presence of a brood of chicks under a mosquito net next to mine, there was little chance for pleasant dreams. Early in the morning, I heard alligators flopping into the water and the rhythmic sound of the oars as the boys took the boat back to Santa Ana.

We had sent word of our coming to the ranch Asunción, the old home of Coffin and still the home of his sister's family and of his mother. While we waited for them to come with horses, we spent most of the morning under our mosquito nets, occasionally venturing forth to drink coconut water from fresh coconuts or to eat guava. It was not until noon that we realized this was Sunday; we traveled twenty-seven miles to Coffin's ranch that afternoon.

This whole region was the center of twelve years of revolutions, and during that time, the Coffin ranch was burned three times. Before the revolutions, it was peopled mostly by men who had come from the United States, like Coffin's father, leaving the country because the South had lost in its war for independence, even though the emigrants themselves were opposed to slavery. With a vow never to return to the United States, they bought land in Tabasco and made fortunes shipping mahogany and raising cattle and horses. Large ranches like the southern plantations were built, and everything spelled progress and activity, until the revolution came with its accompanying savagery.

Every village and every ranch was burned to the ground. Of all the construction at the Coffins' ranch, only the mahogany beams of the chapel remained. Over four hundred head of cattle and as many fine horses were confiscated for war purposes. Coffin's father came from Kentucky and spent much of his time raising a fine breed of horses.

When we arrived at the ranch on July 18, 1926, two years had passed since the last fighting. The people who remained were in a small way trying to rebuild their homes, but because of the swift growth of vegetation in hot regions, their property again had the semblance of a wilderness.

The following day, we turned Monday into Sunday and had services throughout the day. The meetings were announced by the blowing of a cow's horn (*cuerno*) in place of a bell. People came on foot from their distant homes, carrying guns as protection against snakes and other animals. Only a week before our arrival, two boys had been killed by poisonous snakes. Coffin's aged mother, a Mexican, was too ill to attend the worship services. With true pioneer blood, she had refused to leave the ranch to come and live in Tapachula in a good home with Coffin and found her only happiness in trying to rebuild the ranch which was destroyed. His sister, Doña Margarita, was known throughout the entire region as a fearsome woman. She could use both gun and pistol and had no sense of fear. The federal soldiers at one time threatened to tie her to a horse's tail and drag her to Comalcalco, a town a half-day's journey distant, for having nursed two wounded rebels. Without a sign of fear, I dare say without a sensation of fear, she stood before them and said she was ready if they thought it honorable and just.

The next day, July 20, on our way to Comalcalco, we stopped at the village Aldama to rest. Once a thriving center of that region, it was burned so that not a house remained. When we arrived, it was becoming again a thatched-roofed hamlet, while in its cemetery, there were crosses marking the graves of many generals—American and Mexican. In my understanding, they died in vain in those senseless revolutions that caused so much destruction and killing.

At night, we arrived in Comalcalco having finished our journey through this most unpleasant territory. The cocoa and coffee plantations, the birds, and the moaning—roaring, rather—of monkeys in the woods gave the region a romantic touch, but the clouds of mosquitoes, the *chaquistes*, the sandflies, and sleeping with dogs and pigs and lousy chickens was like being in hell. Although I was to endure all of these pests for the remainder of those long months, they made my life so miserable during that first week in Tabasco that I shall always shun that state. Thankfully, they were not that serious in Chiapas, our field. There we were in civilization, where a few trucks rattled down the cobblestones and a telegraph office gave me the opportunity to send a wire to Mabel and the Coffins in Tapachula.[1]

[1]   JRK, "Chiapas, Mexico," unpublished document, n.d., 1-3, in JAH.

CHAPTER 37

From Comalcalco to Palenque

We arrived in Comalcalco on July 21, 1926. We went to the home of one of the Tapachula school boys, which gave us the opportunity to visit the Maya ruins on this ranch, ruins which were almost completely unfamiliar to me. Unlike the other ancient ruins of Mexico, these were constructed of brick because of the lack of stone in Tabasco. Someone has ventured the opinion that from here, the ancients (many believe before the time of Christ) relayed messages by a chain of pyramids to the central city of Palenque, in Chiapas. At the evening prayer meeting in that church—the fruit of years of missionary labors—I spoke a few words. Coffin went to Paraíso to have the mahogany planks of his old school taken apart and shipped to Tapachula to be used in Mrs. Coffin's school. For the next two days, I rested while Coffin went back over the trail we had covered to some groups of believers in a place where for some ten years no minister had entered.

Comalcalco, like all towns in Tabasco, was being taxed to death. Business was at a standstill. All day long, merchants stood in their stores more or less surprised if someone entered to make a purchase. The latest event was the levying of a tax of ten pesos (five dollars) per month on all advertising signs merchants had in their stores. Down came the signs, and the only signs that remained were on the post office and the telegraph office, which were government buildings. In spite of it all, the people seemed happy, and their laughter and merriment, as they called to each other across the street, seemed good to me after living in Tapachula where all is business-like and New Yorkish in its serious aspect.

By autobus, I left early for Paraíso, arriving in spite of the terribly rough road, in a little more than an hour. The regular fare was one peso, but I, being a *gringo* (American), had to pay three. The mode of travel from there to Villahermosa was by boat—a little motorboat pulling a large scow or *chalana* (a large, flat-bottomed boat). A short time before this, Luis Schaumburg, the Presbyterian missionary of the state of Tabasco, had come down from Villahermosa in this same boat—which was the only one, by the way. In crossing the current, the rope slacked, and the sudden jerk tipped the motor, sending it to the bottom and drowning the motorman. When Schaumburg wanted to make the return trip, he was told that he could not enter the boat, not even when he offered to pay three times the regular fare. The owner, a Roman Catholic of superstitious type, blamed him, a *cura protestante* (Protestant priest), for the accident on the previous trip. I was told of this, and people doubted whether I would be allowed to make the trip. Not being known and talking as little as possible, I was on board when they started off.

It was a beautiful afternoon as we chugged slowly up the river, which was fairly choked with drifting water plants that die when they reach salt water. We rode all day, and the evening brought a beautiful sunset we watched through the tall coconut palms. The romantic part of the trip, however, passed with the sunset. The mosquitoes came once more! My bed was a trunk altogether too small for my dimensions, and somehow my mosquito net, not fitting a trunk, could not keep the insects out that night—at least not all of them. Also, since none of the others had nets, they slapped and stamped and cussed and talked all night, thus keeping me awake. Twice on this trip, we had run onto sand bars, and twice the engine had to be repaired, which made my heart fairly stand still lest the *padre protestante* (Protestant father) be singled out as the Jonah of the trip. I slept about an hour in the morning though, and with the new day came the sight of buildings in the capital of Tabasco: Villahermosa. One of the boys from the church also made the trip, and he took me to the Schaumburgs' home, where I parked bag and baggage until Coffin's arrival on the next boat trip, nine days later.

From July 25 to August 3, I was hosted in the home of the Schaumburgs. There I was royally entertained. It was a week of rest, reading, and conversation. One of the large rooms of their house served as a church, and there were services almost every night. Whereas in Chiapas the gospel seemed to appeal to and taken root most firmly among the poorer people, in Tabasco, the more well-to-do people were found in the churches.

On August 4, the day after Coffin's arrival, a boat was to leave for Monte Cristo. In the evening, Coffin conducted a service, baptizing the children of a Dutch family, seven in number. The father, Mr. De Witt, was the manager of a banana company in Villahermosa. In Tabasco they had the custom of having *compadres* (godfathers) at baptisms, and one of the little girls asked me to stand up with her at her baptism. At ten o'clock that evening, with Schaumburg and Salomón Díaz, the native minister of Tabasco, we made our trip across town to the coast. Had newspaper reporters been on hand, they might have written an interesting news article. It would have been sensational news for the Roman Catholics: the departure of four Protestant ministers, the only four in the states of Chiapas and Tabasco.

We slept on the floor of the boat that night, arriving in Frontera early the next morning where we called on Protestant families and had a consistory meeting in the afternoon. Because of government opposition, it was decided to close the church for a time and hold group meetings from house to house. The chaplain was willing to continue paying the taxes he was required to pay for preaching out of his own savings. With tears in his eyes, after a brief prayer, he said he was ready to die if need be, but wished to keep the church open. Though we admired his faith and faithfulness, we too preferred to keep the church open.

A night's ride on the same boat brought us to Jonuta, where we stopped long enough for me to run over to look at a pyramid of the ancient Mayas. At this stop, Schaumburg and Díaz took a *cayuco* (dugout canoe) up another river, while we went on up the Usumacinta, the third largest river in the Western Hemisphere, the Amazon and the River Plate of South America being larger. Traveling all day up that great river brought us at night to the town of Monte Cristo, where we obtained permission to put up our hammocks in a restaurant or boarding room.

Early on the morning of August 7, Coffin was out looking for horses. Trying to economize, however, caused us a day of suffering. Although the road was good, it was a path over a plain country that might have been Texas or a part of Oklahoma or Arizona, and it took us all day to ride the thirty-six miles. I had a cruel saddle, and my horse was never meant to be ridden. He had a good appearance but an awful stride. At five o'clock that afternoon, a rain overtook us, and after dark, in crossing a ravine without a bridge, the pack animal—a cripple—was unable to make the slippery grade and rolled down the embankment, cargo and all. Though the poor creature thought he was dying, by the light of our flashlights, we took off the cargo by cutting the ropes and soon had the animal reloaded, albeit somewhat worse in appearance because of the mud. Coffin too, leading his horse, slipped to a wet seat in the mud. At eight o'clock, we arrived in the little town of Palenque, passing the soldiers who were supposed to guard the entrance to the town but were apparently asleep. The store owned by an American was already closed at that hour, and although a caretaker slept within, he refused to answer our calls. We therefore slept on the cement porch; the others slept on the floor, but I preferred my hammock, even though it was in a precarious position, resulting in the only fall from my hammock on that trip.

Six miles from the little town, there were the famous Palenque ruins. Archeologists have crossed seas to study these ruins, and we considered ourselves most fortunate to be near enough to make a visit to them. We speak of the riddle of the Sphinx, but the ruins of Palenque hold a secret equally hidden. Who built these structures that have weathered the wind and the earthquakes of thousands of years? From whence came those huge stones that were used in all the buildings? What people had a civilization so advanced as to have artists who could mix colors that remain intact in that humid region for all these centuries? What primitive people had sculptors who could carve the figures of their leaders into stone with perfect proportions? Civilizations have come and gone, but these ruins endure. Vandals have carried away riches from the sepulchers of kings, yet for ages these ruins have remained untouched. Today, however, the government keeps them guarded. In the Palacio de las Leyes (Palace of the Laws), there are three huge stone tablets arranged symmetrically on symmetrical walls in this symmetrical building, on which are hieroglyphics, probably their code of laws, which archeologists have spent years trying to decipher. Books—long books—have been written by scientists on Palenque. But always these writers must close with the admission that their writings are only an hypothesis, a personal judgment, and that no one can speak with certainty. It is the opinion of some, that these were erected before the time of the Mayas and that they are as old as the pyramids of Egypt, remnants of a civilization that has been completely wiped out, leaving only some seemingly indestructible buildings and tablets with undecipherable hieroglyphics.[1]

A German scientist was making a study of the ruins at the time of our visit. He was the only member of a large delegation of scientists sent from Mexico City who arrived. The others, in their trip across Chiapas, had fallen out by the wayside because there was no "beer on ice." Too many inconveniences in other words. After a swim in the canals dug by these ancients, where the kings of old once bathed, and a splendid meal at the house of the guard, we hurried back to the town of Palenque, arriving just before the afternoon rain.[2]

---

[1]   The Ch'ol people of modern times are direct descendants of that great Maya civilization. Hieroglyphics in the Palenque ruins can now be read by anthropologists, and when they are read, present-day Ch'ols can understand what is being read.

[2]   JRK, "Chiapas, Mexico," unpublished document, n.d., 3-5, in JAH.

CHAPTER 38

The Chiapas Crossing

We acquired a new set of horses in the little town of Palenque, and we were off early in the morning of August 9 for Salto de Agua. One cannot use horses of the plains in the mountains, and so, at regular intervals, we had to go through the trying ordeal of renting horses. The owner of these horses was having trouble with his wife and was very suspicious of the lunch she had sent with him. A bit of poison in one's food was an easy and much-used method of getting rid of undesirables in parts of Chiapas. After traveling some distance, the scoundrel offered it to Coffin who, contrary to his usual custom, declined to share it with him. Later on, the man did risk eating it.

That night, we stopped at a miserable halfway house owned by some Doña Linda. Having no *pabellón* (mosquito net), the man who owned the horses could not sleep, and so he talked with the family long into the night. During his conversation, he told the woman of the house that he had been suspicious of his food. Mexicans are commended for their courtesy, but in all parts one meets people, whether in trains or in hotels, who are absolutely inconsiderate of others who try to sleep. Not only did he annoy us by talking all night, but he kept swinging his

An Indian guide leads the pack horse and José Coffin across the river

hammock, back and forth, bumping into Coffin with each swing. In the United States, one would put up with such a fellow for about five minutes. Here, not a word is said. It is not prudent, and it is not safe. On any road of Mexico, one may encounter a cross marking the place where an argument took place, and right or wrong, one was the loser.

The following day, we had intended to get an early start, but when the man went out to feed the horses, he reported that my mule was gone. He had run off, pole and all. We found the pole not far from there, and nine miles toward Palenque, the man found the mule beneath some lemon trees headed home. The trip from where we were to Salto de Agua was tiring. More than half-a-dozen times, we had to dismount to have our horses cross muddy creeks, which the seasonal rains had made almost impassable. At each of these stops, all the cargo had to be unloaded, carried across, and reloaded until the next creek. Twice, we had to unsaddle and stash our cargo and saddles in the dugouts. Incidentally, at the narrower river I crossed that day, the horses got a much needed bath.

We were told that from Palenque to Salto de Agua, we would find an automobile road kept by an oil company. The road was just about a mile long. Before the revolutions, this road was well kept by the ranch owners, mostly Americans. Of all the ranches in operation in 1926, now only the land and the names remained, names such as Iowa, San Francisco, and Philadelphia. Every building had been burned, and the revolutionaries had left it a wasteland.

Boisterous neighbors kept us awake again in Salto de Agua—hog buyers on one side of us and, on the other, a woman closing the day

Sometimes there was a canoe to assist in the crossing

with her family and their Roman Catholic prayers much louder than we thought necessary. There were some Protestant families in Salto de Agua, but somehow they never trusted us. The group had had trouble, and one woman, tired of it all, had left town for her ranch, where she started a little congregation all by herself and was holding weekly services. Unfortunately, we were unable to visit her on this trip.

After much waiting, we finally secured mules suitable for the trip from Salto de Agua to Yajalón, over roads which ranked among the worst. At seven in the morning, on the thirteenth of August— Mabel's and my first wedding anniversary—Coffin and I left Salto de Agua, passing through an oil camp to a higher altitude. All at once, we turned off down a steep hill. Probably a horse could get down that steep, muddy hill alive, but I preferred to ride a good mule. So steep and muddy was the trail that my mule would turn sideways to brace himself at regular intervals. We had breakfast at the ranch Chival (Place of Many Goats), where the owner of the mules lived. With more crossing of mud holes and climbing and descending of rocky mountains, we arrived in a driving rain at a little village called Trinidad. There we slept in a granary, where besides the stuffy smell, there were just hundreds of rats. What a contrast. A year ago was the first night of our honeymoon!

Practically all of the next day, we climbed up and up, over rocky, unkept roads, roads that for twenty years had not been repaired, and with each rainy season, they became practically impassible. At eleven o'clock that morning, we stopped at the ranch El Porvenir. Of all the

We never knew what we would meet on the trail

meals good and bad that I had had on the road, this particular meal, prepared in about fifteen minutes, seemed to me the best: fresh juicy fried meat; plenty of eggs; real, tasty tortillas; and coffee. That may not sound like a banquet now, but this was our breakfast at eleven o'clock in the morning after swinging about on a saddle for four hours in a steady climb.

At various intervals, we met natives or other boys driving pigs to Salto de Agua, a very difficult task of many days, since the roads were narrow, muddy lanes through the woods. With a herd of fifty pigs, it was easy for some to disappear, but they had to be accounted for. Then, too, "pigs are pigs," whether they are American or Mexican. The ranch Triunfo was located on this road—the most complete and best organized *finca* (farm) in the state. It was a regular village with small houses for the workmen, the manager's dwelling, a store, shops, and a church. Thousands of pesos had been spent in the making of an automobile road from the ranch to the river for shipping purposes but alas the revolutions again and what has come after them!

Just before the afternoon rains, we arrived at Tumbalá, way up in the clouds, where the night was cold—very cold. At eleven that night, with their meager clothing drenched, a group of natives arrived—men, women, and children—carrying cargo on their backs. They did not ask for shelter; they simply spread a large leaf they had found somewhere along the road upon the floor of the porch and slept in that cold air. In the morning, they resumed their journey. Ch'ol Maya these were, dirty and primitive, wearing their native clothes or even just a cloth.

Tumbalá was the highest point in that region, and in a conspicuous place stood what was left of an old Catholic monastery, built in the sixteenth century. The roof had disappeared, and vegetation grew upon the walls and towers, but still these well-built, five-foot-tall walls stood intact. The church was used as a sheep corral. Nearby was a cave where the natives worshiped Carranza. They refused to believe that he had died, believing that he would come again. One wondered how much they ever did know of Carranza. They fought for him at least.

From Tumbalá, one could see the plains of Tabasco miles and miles away, and the people told us that on a clear night, one could always see light beyond the plains, possibly the lights of Frontera on the coast. At 6:30 a.m. the next day, we began our last lap to Yajalón. Some roads were bad, but this one was the very worst. Uneven, ugly rocks were surrounded by deep mud, not on a level but either ascent or descent. The worst stretch was known as El Paso del Diablo (Devil's Pass). My mule was getting terribly self confident, but I trusted him because he had not slipped once. Trying to maneuver around a wet rock, however, he slipped, and fearing that my leg might get caught under him, I threw myself from the saddle, which was also slipping, and landed in a mud hole of yellow clay. Through most of the pass, we had to dismount and lead our mules.

Hidalgo was a purely indigenous village with a halfbreed at its head, a village of thatched huts lying deep in a valley completely surrounded by mountains. Here we had to cross a river with a raging current. With much shouting and throwing of sticks, the horses were induced to swim across; we, however, were taken across by natives on a raft of three big logs tied together. They paddled upstream some distance, then with strenuous polling, crossed the current, and finally, they polled upstream again, their course forming a "Z." In indigenous villages, one cannot buy food, so we had to live on sardines and bread that day. After us, some natives crossed on the raft, and it was interesting to see some of them bury their heads in cargo or clothes so as not to see the water, while others jeered at them for their cowardice.

In the early afternoon, we caught our first glimpse of Yajalón lying in the far distance below us, reaching it after more than an hour ride. Beautiful Yajalón! High, green mountains surrounded her, not unbroken but irregular to give a stunning effect. A river ran along the side of the town making a pleasing sound, because of the many rocks in it. The town was quiet and garden like. Children walked to and from school, locals in native garb scooted along or idly stood in someone's door with expressionless faces. Some carried cargoes, others loaded mules for the long trip to Salto de Agua.

As the early Christians had warned Paul not to go up to Jerusalem, so were we warned by evangelicals not to enter this region. The reason for their fear dated back to 1922. Rev. Granados, the native minister at Villahermosa at that time, took his daughter with him to sing, and he had planned public meetings in Yajalón and other towns in that region. Holding public meetings in nonevangelical regions in Chiapas and other states was merely inviting trouble and did more harm than good. At the evening meeting in Chilón, nine miles from Yajalón, Dr. Smelling, a German doctor of the *fincas* in the neighborhood, came to lend his assistance. Just as the meeting had begun, the town bully pounded the door for entrance. He had refused to interfere with the Protestants because he had learned to respect them in Guatemala. But he was drunk, and his companions had told him that the minister had spoken insultingly of his father. Aroused by this, he went to the place of the meeting, and when Dr. Smelling opened the door, he shot the doctor through his abdomen. Forgetting himself and believing he was dying, the doctor seized the young man, grabbed his pistol, and shot him in the forehead, killing him. The doctor recovered and was later acquitted, but Protestantism received a blow. The people were up in arms, and the father of the young man began to seek vengeance. The father failed in his attempts to kill Rev. Granados, who died in Campeche about a year after the event. Nevertheless, the evangelical testimony had a setback which was not easy to overcome.

For this reason, we traveled in that territory without telling some of our guides the purpose of our visit. At Yajalón, we were taken to a house where, as our guide said, men of note generally lodged. The man who lived in the house was named Jesús Rico (Rich Jesus). The following day, the Protestants were quite shocked to hear of our staying in this house, since it belonged to the priest, and the room we were sleeping in was the priest's room when he visited that town. More than that, the cot I was sleeping on was the priest's cot, and what I imagined to be an ornamental doll hanging over my head was his saint. The saint, however, bothered me less than the noise of the rats at night. We were somewhat anxious though, because the priest was expected any day, and he might make things unpleasant for the lady who had offered us the room.

Our stay was rather prolonged due to the usual difficulty of securing horses, but neither did we care to show any sign of fear by changing to a room at a Protestant friend's house. Before leaving

Yajalón with mules the local evangelicals had rented for us, most of the people knew we were *padres Protestantes*, but rather than showing any fanatical tendencies, they seemed to think that our stay in this house was a good joke. I thought they might have been a bit sorry the priest did not arrive during our visit. These far-off places craved for a little out-of-the-ordinary adventure. Some of the natives had been told that a prophet was to come soon. One day, I overheard some of them who stood watching me through the window say, "There he is! There he is!"

On August 18, we were at Chilón, the scene of the shooting previously mentioned. We stopped at the very house where the shooting had occurred and visited the three Protestant families in that town. One dear old lady still had some old tracts and copies of *El Faro*, which she had jealously guarded in her fight during the Revolution. The night was spent in an indigenous village bearing a bad reputation and with no food to be bought. But we warmed some of the food the Yajalón people had given us, and we were off bright and early the next morning. We arrived at Ocosingo early, but we decided to stop for the night since the next place suitable for lodging was too far distant.

Had we been warned of the disease raging at Ocosingo, we might have avoided the town, taking the San Cristóbal road to Comitán. But since this was considered the better road, we chose it. Without any warning or premonition, the sickness struck me with a bang. At seven o'clock that evening, we went to sleep in our hammocks, which we had hung in a corridor. At nine o'clock, my stomach began troubling me with a resultant vomiting and diarrhea. At midnight, I was too weak to get up, and at four o'clock in the morning, cramps were seizing both of my legs. Three days from a telegraph station, a ten-day ride from Mabel in Tapachula, and lying in an uncomfortable hammock! When morning came on August 20, they looked around and finally found a storeroom in a house across the street that could be fitted up for me. Between Coffin and our guide, I walked to that room with one eye closed because I was seeing everything double. What a storeroom it was—a bed of solid boards with no mattress or pillow, not a window in the room, and instead of the customary aroma of sick-room flowers, the nauseating odor of *aguardiente* (firewater, strong liquor). But it was more comfortable than being outdoors in a hammock, surrounded by people talking about the many who had recently died of this malady.

By the providence of God, there happened to be a doctor in the town, a Polish American who called about five times that day. He gave me the best of care, and Coffin was more attentive than a nurse. The servants of the family—it was the town president's house—heeded our every request, and the family was most sympathetic. They spent the day in the Catholic Church presiding at a wedding, leaving the keys of the house to Protestants. Thanks to the doctor's pills, the following morning, I was feeling somewhat better, and the cot did not seem quite as hard. I even managed to eat some egg and oatmeal at intervals throughout the day and drink some juice made from the oranges that grew just outside the door.

Nevertheless, I had my doubts as to how a day's riding would agree with me. But anxious to get nearer home, I got into the saddle and at intervals that day stretched out on the ground to rest, arriving at San Carlos that night, happy to find a board cot upon which to sleep.[1]

CHAPTER 39

Back Home

The pace was a little faster the next day when we left San Carlos and moved to Comitán. With a mountain chain to climb, I suffered a sharp pain in my abdomen all that day and the next, until in Comitán we entered civilization once more. There in a hotel, we again had board cots but now with the additional luxury of mattresses, pillows, and sheets. For two days, we had journeyed through pine country, miles and miles of giant pines with "cold country" flowers beneath. It is interesting to travel from lower to higher altitudes, passing through places where the trees of the tropics stand side by side with oak and pine. For the next four days, we buried ourselves in this hotel, sleeping, reading, and—unexpectedly—dieting. Coffin had had trouble with his stomach since leaving Ocosingo and was to live eighteen days on a liquid diet to recover from dysentery. These four days of rest in the hotel, however, brought me back to health, and before moving on to Cajcam, a small village outside of Comitán, I was again eating heartily, enjoying the apples, peaches, and figs of Comitán.

Cajcam was peopled mostly by evangelicals. What a Sunday it was for us, we who had met only a few Protestants since leaving

201

Villahermosa! In the course of two days, there were fifteen baptisms, fifteen confessions of faith, and three marriages. (Those who were married by the state, upon joining the church, were again married by the church.) On Sunday night, Coffin did not feel well enough to preach, so I showed the views of the Old Testament and of the life of Christ with the magic lantern that had been such heavy cargo over all these muddy roads in the north of the state. The final baptisms were on Monday morning when the *adioses* (goodbyes) were said, and we were off, accompanied by several people from the village—women and children included—for almost a mile. There, the final *abrazos* (hugs) were given.

After a stop for prayers at the one Christian home at Independencia, we went on to Zapaluta for a night's lodging. About a mile from town, we crossed a muddy creek. The familiar path, however, was treacherous, and the horses would have sunk down dangerously deep had we taken it, so we worked to find a better crossing. Finally on the other side of the creek, we decided to wait for the pack animal lest he find a muddy grave. We waited an hour and then decided that Coffin and one of the boys accompanying us should go on to Zapaluta and arrange for food for the horses and for a room, while the other boy and I waited. We were assured and reassured that there was no other road to town, but after waiting two more hours, we were notified that the pack animal had arrived in town just after Coffin, having taken another road. For three hours, we had waited out in the damp and now in the dark, and finally in a pouring rain, we entered the town. After a baptism at the home of a Christian family, we were ready for sleep.

It was a four-day journey from Zapaluta to Mazapa, traveling at our rate. At Salvador and at Nonal, we slept in corridors, which means sleeping outside but under a roof. There was no food to be bought at these places, so I lived on eggs and oatmeal which one of the boys had prepared. He was assigned to do the cooking, while the other boy attended to the horses. In Mexico, like all people of the upper class, ministers were not supposed to do anything suggestive of menial work and were respected more—by the very servants themselves—if they did not. It was far more difficult to watch somebody slowly saddling a horse or roping baggage than to do it yourself, and often I transgressed, when I was in a special hurry, only to be reprimanded. It was so in all Latin American countries.

Before reaching Nonal, we had to cross several miles of muddy swamp with quicksand, which became very hazardous during the rainy season. We were, however, fortunate to be crossing before the heavy rains of the year. For several days, we had been asking travelers we met about the height of a certain river—or rather two of them. Most of them told us the rivers were high. It took us an hour to cross one of the rivers. The pack horse was afraid, so the load had to be put on one of the larger horses, which necessitated considerable crossing and recrossing. The current was especially strong, and this with the many stones made it very perilous. Often mules lost their footing when the water was high and were carried down the river. A little later, we met a man who had entrusted the crossing of his cargo to boys, only to have it all, including five hundred pesos, go down with the current.

On September 2, we spent the night at Río Blanco. That night had a touch of comedy. There was no food to buy at the ranch, so we produced a can of sardines and asked a lady to fry beans with these, using the oil of the sardines in place of the missing lard. Coffin was still on a diet, but I found the combination especially good, leaving most of it, however, for the boys. Upon questioning them later as to the taste of the beans, they rather protested and informed us there had been no beans. The servant girl of the lady of the house had decided that the family should breakfast on them. *Frijoles con sardinas* (beans with sardines) was a good joke until the end of the trip.

We had traveled many roads—steep and treacherous—roads that only the best of mules could cross. But as dangerous roads go, perhaps none was more dangerous than the one from Río Blanco to Mazapa. I had gone to bed many a night only to dream of slipping down some muddy grade or over some cliff. But this road was almost entirely a narrow ledge cut out of the mountainside, often with a clear drop of three hundred or more feet. The rest of it was a steep slope of hundreds of feet, where perhaps some trees might stop a person should part of the ledge give way or a passing pack mule "hog the trail." I was riding a mare who would not follow a path and whose romantic nature felt the call of the abyss seemingly, for she always chose the side of the path nearest the drop. All day long, I had to pull the reins to keep her from committing suicide and taking me with her. After prayers with the Amatenango believers, a few hours more of riding brought us to Mazapa.

Mazapa, I dare say, was the most famous missionary outpost in all of Mexico. It was a Maya town, where within a few years, practically all of the inhabitants had accepted Christ and gone out establishing missions in the surrounding country. Cachequels they were called, and the story of their past is remarkable.[1] Their original city was in the

---

[1]   The Kaqchikel (also called Kachiquel) are one of the *indigenous Maya peoples* of the midwestern highlands in *Guatemala*. The name was formerly spelled in various other ways, including Cakchiquel, Kakchiquel, Caqchikel, and Cachiquel.

mountains, and the Catholics had them put up an immense church which was soon destroyed by an earthquake. The town was moved to a lower elevation, and when the new church was finished, the river flooded and carried away the church and the town, leaving only a mango tree and a palm tree to mark the site of Pueblo Viejo (old town). When the town was built on its present site, plans were made for a new church, but it took several years to complete the project with help from Catholics from a neighboring town. The gospel message had come to this religious people very early. A Protestant chapel went up, and nearly all the people became believers. The village president was an officer of the church, and the school teacher once studied for the ministry with Coffin.

On Saturday, September 4, we rested in the pastor's house, a house built for visiting ministers or missionaries. In the afternoon, I went out to see the town, only to have my walk cut short by border guards who asked for my passport. We were near the Guatemala border, and I, being a stranger, had to be identified. I had an idea that the proprietor of the saloon, near which they were standing, was responsible for that, wishing to have a little fun at my expense. My passport was in Tapachula, but one of the border guards accompanied me to see some papers I hoped might serve as substitutes. Upon seeing Coffin, however, whom he recognized, all was well. A prisoner with a clear conscience I had been.

Coffin's health had worsened, so he could not attend services on Sunday. Over 150 of these natives had packed the little chapel, and although I could not preach, I did try to give them a message after the morning sermon. Mazapa was down on the river level. High up in the mountains to the east lay the homes of Tuixcum, and on a still higher central peak stood the white chapel of Tuixcum. From five o'clock until seven that evening, we had services there. It was only a two-hour climb from Mazapa, yet most of it was next to perpendicular into oak and finally into pine country. Again, the missionary spoke, and after the meeting followed the others down the steep trail to the house where he was to sleep. Down we went in utter darkness, I trusting that the man ahead of me knew the trail and that the mule would keep the path.

The floor of the house was strewn with pine needles; the lamp was a pile of burning *ocote* (pine heavy with sap). While the women prepared a tasty chicken, some fifteen men sat around the cabin listening to my broken Spanish. I ate alone—as people of distinction did!—but I did not sleep alone. The morning light explained the heavy breathing I had sensed during the night. The floor was strewn with members of the family and others who, having rolled into their *sarapes* (blankets) had slept on the dirt floor. The morning was beautiful, and I did not remember ever seeing a region quite like Tuixcum. There were cabins set at distant intervals with patches of corn here and there. Though the mountain ridges were as far as three miles apart, one's voice would carry from one to the other, either salutations or the frequent, "Hay ganado en la milpa!" (There are cows in the cornfield). People who lived on a little patch of corn could not afford to have either their own or others' cattle enter their fields.

At Mazapa, I found Coffin up. He had slept during the night and thought he could continue the journey. The people had prayed much for him, and on the previous night, when all others had said good night, Gerónimo came back alone with his violin. Slipping into the room, he had played hymn after hymn while tears ran down his face. As quietly as he had entered, he left. Later, a woman came who asked if she might say a prayer, after which she too went out into the night leaving Coffin to sleep—a much-needed sleep, a sleep which came in answer to their prayers.

Gerónimo was at one time a down-and-outer, as we speak of them at home, with debts all over and drinking himself deeper into debt. He was converted, and someone told him that believers did not play violins or accordions. He sold these to friends of his, and it was not until long after, on a visit to Tapachula, that he was assured by Coffin that the violin was fine for church music. In Tapachula, he began an immediate search. They asked $150 pesos for a violin, but he secured one in Motozintla for $29 pesos, and since that time, he has played in the church and in missions.

We got a very late start that morning, partly because people were slow in preparing the mules, but mostly because so many natives had come to bid us farewell that our little service continued on and on. Six miles from Mazapa lay Motozintla, a good-sized town with a congregation that was old and small. It seemed a difficult missionary center. All of the people had heard the gospel, but they had not accepted it. A man, once posing as a believer, ended up forbidding his wife and children to go to services. An indigenous woman was struck in the face, drawing blood, just a month previous to our visit for refuting a statement made at a washing place that the Protestants were the cause of the present oppression of the Catholics.

The mules had to be shod, and once more, the eternal *mañana* (morning) of Mexico kept us waiting and waiting until it was no longer wise to try to reach the next stopping place. One may ask why not camp out in the open as we did at home, but this, one must remember, was the land of the pistol and the knife, and since the revolutions, such a practice had not been safe. We had traveled only six miles that day, but after an afternoon service and a look about the town, we went to bed there. Getting to bed, however, took various attempts since others came at various hours to greet the ministers.

So anxious was I to reach home the next night that I slept little for fear I might oversleep. Before two o'clock in the morning, I was up and about getting the baggage ready and seeing that breakfast and the mules were ready. A three-hour climb brought us high up on the top of the Pam Ridge where one looks down upon the clouds below. This is the dividing line of Chiapas: the rivers down one side flowing into the Pacific, the others toward the Atlantic. It was so cold that our fingers actually felt numb. One can hardly believe that so near the equator there are cold places, but a three-thousand-foot difference in altitude also makes a difference in temperature. After one has successfully climbed a mountain, there follows the descent. After that slow process had been completed, we began to figure out the miles and the remaining hours before train time at Huixtla.

We knew it was impossible at that pace to reach the train on time. Although Coffin's stomach pained him, we increased our pace. On and on we went, eating as we rode, taking advantage of every little stretch of road that was good and then losing precious time crossing rivers and mud holes so treacherous that mules with cargo got stuck in them. At two o'clock that afternoon, the rain started, and it continued until six o'clock that evening. Being forced to dismount at times, our feet were caked with mud. In crossing rivers, we were splashed with water in spite of our *capas de hule* (rubber capes); we were quite well soaked and were to remain that way until one o'clock the next morning. At six o'clock that evening, we neared Huixtla, stopping for a cup of hot coffee and for prayers at a believer's house on the roadside.

Nearby was a bandit center, Tuzantán, as I learned afterward. A suspicious, hatless character came down the muddy road, and I slowed a bit being rather far ahead of Coffin. When the man reached me, he asked where my companions were. "Right behind me," I replied, which was more nearly true than I was sure of. "Oh," was all he said and went on. Had I been traveling alone, my watch and money would have been gone, no doubt. Just before dark, we reached Huixtla, only to learn that the train would be hours late, but after a service and a little sleep, we heard the train whistle. A real train with a whistle and things we had not seen or heard since leaving Puerto Mexico two months earlier! How the sight did thrill us!

In less than three hours, I was knocking at the door of our home in Tapachula. Home again with knives and forks and spoons and with soft pillows and sheets and a soft bed with a bed spring, which on this trip, I had known only at the Schaumburgs' home in Villahermosa. I was now back home, with two months of mail—letters and papers and magazines! We had been away from the world of newspapers for so long, and of course there were no magazines inland. I received one letter from Mabel at Villahermosa and a number of wires when we reached telegraph stations. We had crossed one state to enter our state and then in turn crossed our state from north to south. Our trip was meant to be one of exploration to find out where there were believers and to locate centers for missionary work. Though the north of the state had been neglected and therefore was populated by a different type of people, there were groups of believers. They were already breaking down the wall of opposition, so that Catholics could no longer look upon Protestants as devils, and we could travel all these days without being harmed. My final lesson after experiencing this long crossing was to think that, if it took us two months to cross the state, how then could we ever cover it with the gospel?[2]

---

[2]   JRK, "Chiapas, Mexico," unpublished document, n.d., 9-12, in JAH.

CHAPTER 40

Biblical and Theological Training

I made my first attempts at teaching in Spanish during our second year in Chiapas. Chaplains from the Tapachula area were invited for several weeks of study. Classes were held in the church, as required by law, and meals were served in our home. Every time I asked a question of an elderly man in my class, he would give me the same answer, "That I haven't learned yet." Another man told me privately that I was using many words they did not understand. Was I transliterating, or did these theological terms need more explanation?

We were able to squeeze in one more institute our first term. After our return from furlough, we arranged for a month of studies in Mazapa. That was the first two-day trip on horseback with Mabel, and little Roger had his first mountain-climbing ride, sitting in front of me on a seat I had built on the pommel. Similar classes were held when I traveled alone on other occasions.

Soon after we settled in Tuxtla Gutiérrez, male students selected by their consistories arrived to live on one end of our large veranda, where I gave them daily teaching during the rainy season when I could not travel the state. Without any protests, our family cook and the

In Tapachula, I offered further training to the chaplains
of the congregations

house and laundry servant took on the extra work. A heavy piece of iron hanging at the kitchen door clanged to call the boys to pick up their plates of food. They returned the dishes washed.

In this way part of my time was devoted to training chaplains for the local churches. Each of the ninety groups we had in 1936 was led by one of their number, except on such occasions when colporteurs, missionaries, or pastors could visit them. Since the majority of the groups were composed of the humbler class, there was a woeful lack of educated leadership. It was to better prepare these chaplains for their work that classes were held each year in our home in Tuxtla Gutiérrez.

Unfortunately, because of family responsibilities, many could not attend, and there was always the danger of training someone who might drift away and use his acquired knowledge for personal gain. Candidates for the school needed to be approved by their consistories. This eliminated several candidates, and for those who did come, a certain number were mentally unable to profit enough from the studies in order to warrant a longer stay. We also had to keep the number down so as not to draw the attention of the government. In 1936 we had three advanced students and one selected beginner at the opening of classes, and there were a few more who were interested in joining later on. Members of the Tuxtla church quite often came to listen to courses that were especially interesting.[1]

---

[1]   JRK, "Mexico after Ten Years," *The Intelligencer-Leader* (April 15, 1936), 12.

Staying in our home in Tuxtla was an opportunity
for education for these young men

Of those students, two plus Genaro de la Rosa, who had studied in our Tapachula days, were ordained. Two others, Nehemías García and Daniel Aguilar, were sent to the seminary in Mexico City for three years of study. It was these five who, once ordained, became the nucleus of our long-coveted Presbytery of Chiapas. Now we could break away from the Presbytery of the Gulf, which had been a weight around our necks. Coffin, a Tabasco-born leader and loyal to that presbytery, had fought us all the way, and when we prevailed, he remained with that presbytery and moved back to Tabasco, his native state. He had an outstanding physique and an attractive personality, which made him the immediate focus of attention in any group. All I knew of missions strategy, I had learned from him. Sadly, in his later years, he was such a negative, antidevelopment influence, that we were all relieved when he left voluntarily. Among other things, he was not convinced of the strategic importance of training nationals for leadership to help the work grow and mature. Most likely this negative attitude was due to the fact that he could not suffer competition in what he considered to be *his* field.

Once organized, the Chiapas Presbytery assigned Daniel Aguilar and Rev. Garold Van Engen to Bible school work in San Cristóbal de Las Casas, a move which freed me up for full-time pastoral work in Tuxtla and its congregations and for evangelistic travel around the state. During Van Engen furloughs, we would reside in their house in San Cristóbal and manage the school. At other times, when increased enrollment demanded additional classes, we rented an extra home in San Cristóbal and joined the teaching staff, commuting to Tuxtla by Jeep every weekend for church work and preaching. Early two-hour trips, winding around 521 turns in the highway, would bring us back to San Cristóbal by Monday for the 8:00 a.m. classes.

When a few of the Tzeltal leaders wanted to go to Guatemala for Bible training, they met the objection of the presbytery, which then appointed Mabel and me to arrange for their lodging and to teach them in Tuxtla. Classes were held on our veranda, until the cold-country men found the Tuxtla heat unbearable and we moved to San Cristóbal, where the institute room at that time was vacant. Francisco Gómez left the class suddenly and unexpectedly but never divulged why or what his problem was. He rejoined later, when courses which included the native students were added to the Bible school and Mabel and I joined the staff. After a while, it was my privilege, in the presence of some three thousand Tzeltal Christians, to "give the charge" at the ordination service of this outstanding native leader. In time, all three of the indigenous men we were assigned to teach in Tuxtla were ordained.

After all of our children had left to continue their education in the United States, Mabel, having finished home teaching, was appointed by the presbytery as director of Women's Work in Chiapas. She traveled frequently with me now as I visited churches in different parts of the state. Bible institutes and boys schools were familiar to this culture, but there was no special training for girls. A few girls had lived in our home and were taught private classes for short periods of time, but more work in this area was needed. A girls Bible school would have been too revolutionary at the time, so Mabel, as the director of Women's Work, invited churches to select dedicated girls and entrust them to our care for a month of concentrated teaching. We called the classes "Curso Breve para Señoritas" (Short courses for girls). A series of three of these were held in successive years: two in San Cristóbal and one in Tapachula during public school vacation time. In each session, graduates from the Girls Bible School in Mexico City helped to teach and manage the institute.

After our transfer to Mexico City in 1965, Garold and Ruth Van Engen continued these very worthwhile classes for several years, a program that we had hoped might pave the way for a formal girls Bible school. Some years later, in the late 1970s and early 1980s, the Union of Women's Societies of Chiapas formed the Mabel and Ruth Bible School for Women, named after Mabel Kempers and Ruth Van Engen. Jean Van

These students of the Bible school in San Cristóbal became
strong leaders in the church

Engen helped with its beginning as a member of the school's board of
directors. Both she and Charles taught in the school. After Charles and
Jean returned to the United States in 1985, Gene and Arlene Meerdink
continued to supervise and teach in the well-organized Mabel and
Ruth School located by then in Berriozabal, near Tuxtla Gutiérrez, and
housed in their own distinct building. It may be that our innovative
experiment was a first step in that direction.

Together with biblical and theological ministry training, Mabel
and I gave special attention to the introduction of music into the
liturgy of the churches and to the development of musical skills in
the leaders. For years the only church member in Chiapas who could
accompany hymns on an instrument was my Mabe. The folding Bilhorn
portable organ, presented to her as she was about to board the ship on
the rainy morning of our departure from New York, by the gentleman
Mr. Mason C. Alcott, president of the Hudson River Day Line, was for
many years the only available instrument for church worship. For us, it
was a God-sent gift. Transported on mules or on the backs of willing
church members, the organ accompanied the singing in meetings at
all altitudes and in all climates. The movement of Mabel's fingers as
the organ produced the notes was watched with fascination by curious
children. A few larger organs and pianos have been obtained by city
churches, and capable musicians have been trained since then. But my
Mabe and her Bilhorn were pioneers.

For Mabel, teaching Bible school classes for young
women was a delightful task

Mabel also played a unique role in training musicians in many local congregations and in introducing new hymns and songs for their use in the liturgy. Because Christmas programs brought out large crowds with open hearts, there was a need for skillful music and meaninful songs. Mabel could translate songs from English to Spanish, but how could one person teach these songs to the ever-multiplying number of congregations seeking help? The idea came to us of inviting delegates from each of the congregations in the Tapachula area for a week of special training in the city church, so that these singers could in turn teach the people in their congregations. The Tapachula consistory acquiesced, and while Mabel by constant repetition had the delegates learn each song, I, working with Doña Goya, an able Mexican cook, was busy seeing that food was served to these enthusiastic young people.

One year, Sam and Helen Hofman, on their way to Guatemala, stopped in Tapachula long enough to help Mabel with the teaching. When we hear those tunes today, we can still hear Sam's voice as he taught those songs. The students were so determined to learn the songs correctly that they would continue to practice during the evening hours and even during breaks. It amazes us how correctly those songs are still being sung today by those who learned them and passed them on to others. After we left Chiapas, Ruth Van Engen and Arlene Meerdink taught similar concentrated training sessions for Christmas and Easter.[2]

---

[2]   JRK, "Some of This and Some of That," 6-8.

CHAPTER 41

Sunday Schools

During our first three-year term, living in Tapachula, we attended a few of the Red Cross meetings José Coffin held in the kiosk on the school patio. He had taken an active part in the Red Cross work during the Revolution while living in Tabasco. He understood the need for medical work in Chiapas and was exploring ways to meet this need. The city entrusted the care of the tuberculosis and leprosy patients to the evangelical church, and the Christian community under the leadership of José Coffin was instrumental in the development of the lazaretto for those suffering from tuberculosis in Tapachula.

This lazaretto (quarantine station) had a long history. In October 1917, the inhabitants of Tapachula suffered an epidemic that left many families destroyed and numerous orphans. The epidemic was known as the Spanish influenza. The church temporarily suspended its worship services and focused on assisting the ill the best they could. Many years later, in 1924, according to the information in the minutes of the church, the leaders planned to build a small clinic to serve those with health conditions and to be the location of the Red Cross in the city. Dr. José E. Monjaraz was in town, and he worshipped with the church throughout the year. With his help and orientation, and the hard work of the congregation under the leadership of Coffin, they built the planned ward. A number of believers received training in first aid, vaccination, and infirmary from Dr. Monjaraz and Rev. Coffin. The lazaretto was built in an abandoned area, and it served as a means to develop positive relationships with the community and earned the respect and consideration of the city authorities. Once the sanitary crisis was over, the place was given to the city government and continued to be the location of the Red Cross in Tapachula. When we arrived, the only thing remaining was the program of the Red Cross led by Coffin, which consisted mostly of some regular meetings. We found these meetings to be an absolute waste of our time.

Strangely enough, there was no Sunday school ministry in the churches, so we asked permission from the consistory to teach the children on Sunday afternoons. Permission was granted, and soon older people were attending as well, requiring multiple classes. When the rainy season commenced, the daily afternoon downpour made attendance difficult. We requested and received permission to meet before the morning church service. Attendance grew, and before long, the Sunday school took over the entire morning. Preaching was reduced to the Sunday evening service. In this way, a full-blown Sunday school program evolved slowly, gradually taking over allotted morning time and replacing the worship service. Most of the Sunday school teachers in Tapachula were women.

Because the pastor and the missionary family lived in Tapachula, that church served as a model, and before long, all the congregations and churches of Chiapas were using Sunday mornings for concentrated Sunday school Bible instruction. The Tuixcum church was an exception, possibly because it was too cold there to have evening preaching services. In the coming years, a few churches in Chiapas would follow this example and squeeze in a noon preaching service after the Sunday school session.[1]

Interestingly, the first Maya churches among the Ch'ol and Tzeltal people did not follow this model slavishly. For years their Sunday school teachers were men, since few women could read or write. The classes consisted only of prayer, followed by scripture reading and an explanation of the passage. As the literacy rate increased in many areas, older Tzeltal girls, with instruction and help from missionary wives, were allowed to teach children's classes with the aid of flannelgraph

---

[1]   JRK, "Some of This and Some of That," 5.

lessons to illustrate the scripture lesson. These lessons fascinated adults as well as children.[2]

It is necessary to take into account that any religious activity organized on Sundays faced lots of difficulties in Mexico in those years. To begin with, under the existing government school regulations at that time, Sunday was not observed as a day of rest. Instead, it became a day on which to have regular excursions and picnics—an extra day for the tired teachers to fill in certain practical points in their curriculum. It was discouraging to try to train children that Sunday was a sacred day, when they were accustomed to seeing it desecrated. Truly, if it were up to humans to strike the vital spark in the hearts of the lost, how impossible it would be!

Sometimes when we were too dependent on human strength, it seemed that no amount of headway could be made, that no impression was being made, even after weeks and months of concentrated effort. But it was evident that our good God was planning and directing and doing the miraculous all the time, claiming his own in his own way. The very futility of trying to do things alone was mightily impressed on any person who worked in these surroundings and conditions. And certainly, if our purpose was to establish merely an improved social order—and some thought it should be—Christian missionaries would give up the strain and effort and go in for something easier and more popular.

We, however, were convinced of the importance of Bible teaching and Christian discipleship. We certainly had seen the power of the Word of God to convict of sin and to bring people to new life in Jesus Christ. Throughout the years, we had collected hundreds of testimonies on the power of Bible teaching and instruction. I remember one day when we called on an old man who had a Bible which had been given to him years ago and had recently begun to attend our services. We sat there in the one-room home, surrounded by huge pieces of leather, half-worked sandals, a long work table, and the heavy smell of tanned leather. Our daughter Kathleen Joy was four years old and occupied a small homemade wicker chair, our host a leather-covered *butaca* (reclining chair), and Mabel an unpainted "straight" chair. When we remarked about his continued absence from church, he went out to the little lean-to porch, brought in his worn Bible, and putting on spectacles, which from long use had become twisted and bent, he showed us just

---

[2]   Dorothy Dickens Meyerink, *Ministry among the Maya: A Missionary Memoir*, Historical Series no. 72 (Grand Rapids: Eerdmans, 2011), 90.

how far he had progressed in his lone Bible study. "When I finish the whole book," he explained, "I shall return to church services to get some pointers on obscure passages."

I tell this incident, not only to demonstrate local color but also to recall the power of God's Word to attract the human mind and soul and to inspire one to speak of his discovery to his friends. Through this man, a family consisting of father, mother, daughter, and grandson, had come to know the gospel; they were fairly regular church-goers and had joined the Christian Endeavor Society. Another interesting case was a little old Maya woman who had also become interested in spiritual truth through the personal work of this old white-haired man. But, as happened in this case, the friends brought to Christ often became more devote Christians than the one instrumental in their enlightenment.[3]

---

[3]   MVD, "A Letter from Mrs. J. R. Kempers," *The Intelligencer-Leader* (November 28, 1934), 12-13.

CHAPTER 42

Christ's Army on the Offensive

When Peter struck in defense of his Master, he was told to put away his sword. That was not the proper weapon for Kingdom purposes. The early church won its unparalleled victory over mighty Rome, which laughed at the despised Nazarenes, without so much as hacking off an ear. In many lands, the church is again called to fight as the adversary puts forth another herculean effort to overthrow it. Those who ask "What can we do? Is there anything that can be done?" forget that it was under circumstances such as these that the early church grew. And what tremendous strides it made in those days!

During our many years of service in Chiapas, there were countless people in Mexico who wanted to break the power of the Roman Catholic priests and make sure they did not regain it. It is not my purpose here to discuss the reasons for this. The reasons are quite evident to anyone who knows, even slightly, the history of Mexico. There were also others who wanted to eradicate entirely all belief in God, and such was the avowed purpose of the Revolutionary Party, which was in control of the country during those years. On their official paper, the purpose of the Revolutionary Party was clear: "The concept of 'God' must be banished as false, erroneous, and unfounded, because it brings with it the belittlement of the spirit and the moral valor of the human social group, creating in it a sense of inferiority for the development of its own strength, because of expecting everything from a divinity entirely absurd and fallacious."[1]

We had, of course, no fear that this group would succeed in its efforts to destroy our Christian testimony. If Russia, after all of her systematic, anti-God propaganda, in which she spared neither expense nor cruelty, had to admit failure, then the sporadic and tepid efforts in Mexico would win only those who found it convenient to deny God. Like the devout Catholic teacher who had to answer the child's greeting, "No hay Dios, maestra" (There is no God, teacher) with a "Sí, niño, no hay Dios" (Yes, child, there is no God), lest she lose her position, so the vast majority of those in public office were religious at heart.

We did not fear the future. God is on his throne. As the Psalmist says, "He who sits in the heavens laughs." A social revolution such as the one that had been going on in Mexico for decades was bound to go to extremes. But time and calmer reasoning would expose faulty judgment; and time proved that we were right. The gospel increased in Mexico, and particularly in Chiapas, in record ways compared to the rest of Latin America.

We did not in any way, however, minimize the seriousness of the curtailments in religious work to which we in Mexico had been subjected. I had in a file a series of newspaper clippings over the course of several years which told of the closing of churches in one state, the limiting of the number of priests in another, and the banishing of all clergymen from yonder, and so the relentless march went forward like removing chessmen from further play. In some states, all churches and places of public worship were closed, and ministers were not allowed to exercise their profession in any form. In other states, churches were open but without the participation of pastors either in the churches or in the homes. In other states, the professional taxes levied against the ministers were so high as to become prohibitive. There could be no evangelical schools anywhere in the country, so that all children might receive socialist and antireligious instruction in the state and federal schools. Bible schools and seminaries were against the law. Church periodicals and religious literature were denied the use of the mail system, and in 1935, for example, there were in Veracruz ten thousand pesos worth of Bibles which were held up by customs officers.

---

[1]   Quoted in JRK, "Christ's Army on the Offensive in Mexico," *The Intelligencer-Leader* (June 5, 1935), 5.

That was not a rosy picture, so we did not wish to judge too harshly those who in a tone of despair asked, "What can they do in Chiapas?" Long years of free use of church buildings and formal meetings had led most of us to feel, perhaps, too dependent on these. More people in Chiapas had become interested in the gospel during these days of opposition and persecution than during any previous year that we had spent in Mexico. There was more actual missionary work being done in these times of testing than at any former time. Sometimes missionaries become burdened with institutions and organizations that leave very little time for actual evangelistic work. An elder of a certain elite American church, criticizing the preaching of a visiting minister, asked, "What do you think this church is, a Rescue Mission?" In Chiapas, a renewed emphasis had been put on the "rescue" aspect, which to our mind was the primary purpose of missionary work.

The believers in Chiapas had a sense of the importance of winning others to Christ, although some, while rejoicing when there were new gains, left the work to others. As a rule, the newer converts were the most active missionaries, but all over the state, believers took the Great Commission in earnest. Through the years, as a natural reaction to opposition, the Tapachula and Tuxtla Gutiérrez churches in particular had taken on new missionary zeal. Under the auspices of the Tapachula Christian Endeavor Society, groups were sent out to chapels on the coffee plantations or in the villages, benefitting both those who went out and those who were visited.

In Tuxtla we formed a missionary society. But we had no officers; we took no minutes; there were no collections and certainly no speeches. Membership was limited to a small number of men and women who had been invited because of their activity in personal evangelism. We made a chart listing the names of people in the vicinity who were interested in the gospel or who were at least willing to listen. We discussed those people and planned who was to visit them during the week. We added new names to the list and discussed methods of approach, and we spent time in prayer for those on the list and for ourselves.

Other individuals were inspired by this new enthusiasm and undertook work on their own initiative. One elder ordered thirty-five pesos worth of "Select Portions of Scripture" and distributed them for free. Thirty-five pesos was a sacrificial sum for a man of his means. He also ordered a shipment of Bibles and sold them, devoting every other week to that work. To do so, he had to leave his farm in the care of his wife and children during his absence.

We attended church in Tapachula one morning and noted the absence of a particular deacon. After the evening service, he told us of his visit to the jail that morning, where he had obtained permission to distribute tracts and give a message. No one told him to do this; no one knew about it, and as exceptional as such work was under the restrictions we were facing at that time, he spoke of it as though it were an ordinary event. One young convert ministered through personal outreach in Escuintla and neighboring towns, the likes of which, for sheer valor and amazing results, we had not seen there before. Another young native, while ridiculed by unbelievers, voluntarily spent twelve days cutting a trail up a wild mountain so that missionaries and colporteurs could visit a new group interested in the gospel.

By 1935 there seemed to be a lull in antireligious activity. We believed this was due partly to the attention drawn upon this phase of Mexico's program by the American senator William E. Borah's resolution, and no doubt the undercurrent of political unrest at that time had much to do with it. Senator Borah of Idaho carried on an investigation into the Mexican persecution of religion. He supported many New Deal measures and was an expert on foreign affairs. He became known for his pro-Soviet views, favoring recognition of the Soviet Union by the United States, and was also in favor of the Mexican Revolution and the way Mexico was managing its internal affairs.

Fortunately the antireligious laws were not all strictly enforced. Some religious literature continued to reach its destination; our five hundred monthly bulletins were sent out regularly. Sunday school literature concealed in special wrappers reached us. Catholic priests and some Protestant ministers baptized in homes in forbidden territory. Our colporteurs continued their work. Only seven Protestant churches in the state had been closed by 1935, and in nearly all of these places, people were having services in their homes. In Tuxtla we were quietly using our church, even though at Christmas there was a verbal order by a low-level official to suspend our work. That year we celebrated Mother's Day in a religious way on our veranda with a large crowd present.

For a time, a group of Christian workers in Mexico City (pastors, laymen, and earnest women of several denominations) met weekly. But in view of the critical times, at the noon hour, they gathered daily for prayer that God would protect and guide his people and awaken in them a greater zeal and consecration. Mexican Christians kept themselves in constant prayer. We knew, too, that in the home churches, a great many earnest prayers had been sent heavenward, and we believed these prayers were being answered in God's own way. In the midst of opposition and many limitations throughout our many years of missionary service in Chiapas, we have seen Christ's army on the offensive.[2]

[2]   Ibid.

CHAPTER 43

A Blessing and a Curse

The year of 1928 began with the most blessed of all blessings from the Lord. On February 29, our first son, Roger Dyke Kempers, was born at the American Hospital in Puebla. The hospital was affiliated with the Methodist Church. We had hoped to go to Guatemala for Roger's birth but discovered that our passports had expired, and so we were forced to go to Puebla. We went a month early, rented a room with access to a kitchen, and did a thorough review of our Spanish grammar while waiting. The doctor kept Mabel in the hospital for fifteen days. They did things differently in those days, but he also knew that we would be making the long and difficult trip back to Tapachula. During her stay in the hospital, I made a trip to Mexico City, and while there, I saw the film *The King of Kings*. We had tried for years to rent or buy this film, but someone had a contract, and until that expired, no one else could show the film in Mexico. We eventually had three copies in circulation in Chiapas, and it was shown hundreds and hundreds of times.[1]

Mabel's firstborn was quite a challenge for her. If it is difficult for an American woman to care for a newborn with access to lots of

[1]   JRK, "How It All Began," 5.

Mabel and I displaying our
firstborn son in front of our
humble Tapachula home

resources, at least in urban centers, try to imagine how it was for this young mother, just twenty-six years old, under primitive and stressful conditions.

Commitment to family, however, was another value to which Mabel was deeply devoted. Her love for me expressed in her letters and in our intimate conversations continued throughout our life together. She was equally dedicated and loving to our children in her role of mother as teacher. There was nothing slip shod or casual about her home schooling, starting with Roger and continuing with the other three children that the Lord gave us. After eight years of her teaching, our children were very well prepared academically and ready to take on the challenge of high school in the United States.[2] This strong woman raised and educated these children without depending on any infrastructure or the benefit of a pediatrician.

After the arrival of our firstborn son, the year 1928 was filled with a series of difficulties and contradictions. In June the Synod of Mexico met in Tapachula. That brought Rev. and Mrs. James M. Martin (pastor of Third Reformed Church in Holland, Mabel's home church) as representatives of the Reformed Church in America to our place as guests. We also had the blessing of hosting Rev. Paul Burgess and our great friends William Cameron Townsend and Leonard L. Legters from Guatemala, who in 1934 founded Wycliffe Bible Translators. They and Rev. Ludwig (Luis) C. Schaumberg all ate their meals in our home. The

[2]   JSH, "Mabel Kempers's Eulogy," 4, in JAH.

Our missionary friends in Puebla were delighted
with the arrival of baby Roger

sessions of the synod were bellicose because, even though by then the Mexican ministers were in charge of the churches, there was still much antimissionary feeling on the part of some. In Chiapas we never had this kind of trouble.

Many of the local Tapachula church members were fed up with Coffin, especially concerning the property issue already explained, so they sent a petition to the Presbytery of the Gulf of Mexico, which met just prior to the synod. They lacked a spokesperson, so their petition went nowhere. Some became Jehovah's Witnesses, some formed a Baptist group, and a larger number organized a Mutual Society.[3]

The year ended with the most horrible death of all deaths. In July of that year, the elected president Álvaro Obregón was assassinated, felled by the bullets of an ultra-Catholic fanatic, it is believed. Governor Tomas Garrido of the Mexican state of Tabasco decreed vengeance. All churches in that state of Mexico were ordered closed. The delegates to the synod read the news while traveling back home by train.[4] Garrido believed that Catholicism shut workers into a cage of fear, terrorizing them with the threat of eternal fire. For freedom to come to Tabasco, said Garrido, religion must go, and he kicked it out, decapitating saints,

[3]   JRK, "How It All Began," 5.
[4]   Ibid.

wrecking churches, yanking crosses out of cemeteries, forcing priests to marry, and renaming all the places which were named after saints. The state capital, San Juan Bautista, became Villahermosa. And in a solemn ceremony, he had a stud bull named "Bishop" and a donkey named "Pope." He well deserved his nickname, the "Priest Eater."[5]

[5]   Eduardo Galeano, *Memory of Fire*, vol. 3, *Century of the Wind* (New York: Pantheon Books, 1988), 73.

CHAPTER 44

Youth Work

The real charm of our missionary work was in our association with young people and in witnessing their spiritual growth. It is true that in Chiapas, early Protestant work had not attracted to any extent the youth of the state. In most of our various stations, the congregations had few actively interested young men and women. But in those places where young people had come into the life of the church, there were some fine, exemplary Christian lives to encourage us and to give life to the local congregations. And this occurred in a state—a country, in fact— where Protestantism was a comparatively new and unpopular idea and where Christian youth could potentially encounter persecution. Given these circumstances, it was not difficult to understand their hesitancy to respond or indeed their reluctance to even enter a Protestant church. At school they had to withstand the ridicule of both teachers and fellow students. The real wonder is that with no Christian background, little home training, and in an environment contrary to their beliefs, any were able to hold fast to their new faith.[1]

---

[1]   JRK, "Mexican Young People I Know," *The Christian Intelligencer* (September 1, 1933), 477.

It was during our first term in Chiapas that Mabel organized a society for young church girls for social and religious purposes. Knowing how skeptical José Coffin was of youth work, we were puzzled that he permitted that group to organize, unless it was because his own daughter, Maggie, was a member and could report any deviations from what he would approve. He considered young people's and children's work to be a menace to his control of the mission work. With this senseless attitude, he was risking the future of the church. The church in Tapachula held a Wednesday evening meeting called "Christian Endeavor." But, led and directed by older people, it was little different from the Sunday evening preaching service. Certainly, it was not a youth gathering.

We transferred to Tuxtla Gutiérrez in 1931, and during our second term, we became associated with a remnant of the church which started there in the early twentieth century. Elder Simón García showed us a Christian Endeavor pledge card he had signed in 1904. The Revolution of 1910 meant a hiatus in church activity there and in neighboring Ocozocoautla, called "Coita." The group in Coita, which had been stronger than that in Tuxtla, never recovered. A descendant of a member, however, became a one-term governor of the state, with no anti-Protestant bias.

In Tuxtla, after the Revolution, Simón García gathered former members of the church to hold meetings as a Christian Endeavor Society. What seemed incomprehensible to us was that Dr. José E. Monjaraz, a military man stationed in Tuxtla, who took an active interest in the church, and who, in later years, was a national leader in Christian Endeavor work, did nothing to correct the anomaly of having Christian Endeavor officers direct the church. After participating in the Tuxtla church for a while, Mabel was elected to be president of the society and discovered that, according to their way of thinking, she was to run the church and oversee the church building campaign. We set to work to write a new constitution for the local society and to emphasize continually that the Christian Endeavor Society was an organization of the church and did not govern the church. We stressed that Christian Endeavor was meant for the youth, although older people could attend. This caused some hard feelings, because some of the elderly claimed we were shutting them out of the church. That society with its enthusiastic young membership became a model for all the other societies.

We were in fact fascinated and satisfied with the achievements in young people's and children's work. By 1933 the Christian Endeavor Society was reorganized but not without some qualms and misgivings

Conferences for Christian Endeavor leaders were exciting
and encouraging events

and—inevitably—a few offended past members. It was crucial, however, to make it a distinct group, something belonging to the young people, instead of a general congregational gathering, as was the case in Tapachula under Coffin. With the enthusiastic backing of the young people themselves, the change was a profitable one, and new life was evident.

The same was true with regard to the children. What had previously been a general Sunday afternoon meeting for all the children of the church was transformed into a Junior Christian Endeavor, with happy results. It was remarkable that there was such interest and commendable attendance in a town whose custom it was to spend Sunday afternoons in the streets. It indicated a sincerity of purpose on the part of the twenty boys and girls and a healthy home influence. We had high hopes that in a few years, the elders of this group would become a real asset to the elder society and to the church in general. And we were more than pleased with the results.

In March 1933, the kindergarten class was formed when the young children were culled out of the Sunday group. A short table and low benches raised interest immediately, and we enjoyed Thursday afternoons, learning children's hymns, Bible stories, Bible texts, and each week doing some colorful crayon work. Twelve children were enrolled right from the beginning, all either children of church members or living with believing families. With Mabel, who was very much involved

With Roger and Kathleen in attendance,
Mabel teaches a Sunday school class

in all of these initiatives, we were all convinced that we were working for the future of God's kingdom and his church.[2]

Later when we were residing in San Cristóbal, I wrote Alfonso Marín, who was in Tuxtla Gutiérrez, and suggested the idea of holding a convention of delegates from the Christian Endeavor Societies. He had been thinking along similar lines, and so by correspondence, we created a program, made hospitality arrangements, and invited the different societies to send their delegates. The delegates from San Cristóbal traveled with me by car, and in 1943, with great enthusiasm, we organized a union and celebrated the first of many conventions which grew year by year in quality and size as churches and societies multiplied and as travel and communications became easier. Remarkably, the Union of Christian Endeavor Societies was organized before the Constitution of the Presbytery of Chiapas (organized in 1949).

A particular secretary of the Presbytery of the Gulf who had been ousted from his church in Yajalón by an unsatisfied congregation blamed me for his dismissal. To get even, he accused me of "violating church rules" in organizing the union without official approval. Throughout the years, however, the Chiapas endeavorers honored me with plaques and certificates for doing what this Maya with an inferiority complex was trying to have me censored for.[3]

[2]   MVD, "Indian Work in Mexico," 172.
[3]   JRK, "Some of This and Some of That," 6.

I determined that I would accept the tributes of the Union of Christian Endeavor Societies only if Alfonso Marín was recognized as cofounder. He was a man of outstanding character and one of the most influential leaders in the church in Tuxtla Gutiérrez. He was a successful businessman in Tuxtla who had an auto machine shop and an auto parts business. He served for many years as a deacon in the church and often taught stewardship. He and Garold Van Engen, in the mid-1960s, founded and developed the first Union of Societies of Deacons in Chiapas—the first in the National Presbyterial Church in Mexico and possibly the first in Latin America. Alfonso's daughter-in-law, wife of his youngest son, Carlos, was the first director of the Mabel and Ruth Bible School of Women that began in the building in San Cristóbal. That large house had once been the Van Engens' home.[4]

---

[4]   Information provided by Charles Van Engen, email, July 18, 2014.

CHAPTER 45

First Furlough

With the coming storm of the Depression and chronic political turmoil on the rise, Mexico was inundated with uncertainties about the future. The year 1929 saw the organization of the National Revolutionary Party (Partido Nacional Revolucionario), and although they held power for decades, this party never brought the country to a place of real growth and development.

Thanks to the Lord, we were scheduled to have our first furlough after four years of exhausting missionary service. At last our furlough had come! We took the train to Laredo, and when we saw the American flag flying there, it brought tears to our eyes. American food was unbelievable! We spent our furlough at the homes of the Kempers and Van Dykes, visiting a lot of churches. We went to Sioux Center, Iowa, and Holland, Michigan, during the time from December 1928 to July 1929. We made our trip mostly by train, with the intention of spending as much time as possible with our parents and relatives, but we also did a good deal of speaking in the churches. Christmas in Holland was magical for us, sharing special services at Third Reformed Church with William and Christine Van Dyke and their children Russell, Lillian,

Milton, Edmonia, and Ed. We had a number of furloughs throughout the years, about one every three years, but this first one had a special significance.

Finally our furlough was over, and we had to return to Mexico. The Reifsnyders (Bancroft and Vera G. Brewer) from Mexico City had informed us that if I didn't return to Mexico within six months, I would not be allowed to return. I was scheduled to speak at General Synod, but I left for the border, arriving the day before my six months expired. The immigration official, seeing that I was a missionary, said the time limit was too nearly expired. They put me in a taxi and returned me to the American side of the river. I wired Bancroft Reifsnyder in Mexico City telling him of my predicament. I asked him to please make a complaint to the immigration officials. The order that came through read, "If he can prove that he applied for readmission before the six months was up, let him in." I immediately made the request, and they gave me an extension of six months. I could have returned to Holland, trusting I would now have another six months, but I decided to go all the way to Mexico City and obtain some written document from the immigration office. They said that was unnecessary, but upon my insistence, they made out some documents. With that I returned to Holland to wait until my brother Bert, a medical doctor, and my sister-in-law Harriet were ready to go down with us. There was no guarantee that Bert would be able to practice medicine without a license or that he would be able to obtain a license, but we thought it might be worth a try.[1]

After a lot of planning and dreaming, my brother Bert and his wife, Harriet Heneveld, joined us on our return to Tapachula. Like a large safari caravan, we finally arrived at the border entry at Laredo. The immigration agent at the border this time just happened to be the same man who tried to refuse my previous entry. This time he objected because I was listed as a minister in his records. But when I pulled out the letter I had from immigration headquarters, he suddenly became very cooperative.

In those days, we took with us trunk loads of supplies for the three-year stay; there was so little available in Mexico in the way of clothes, toys, and equipment. An inspector opened all the trunks and boxes and took out everything that looked new and unused. We had made arrangements with an American customs broker to handle Bert's furniture (which included some of ours). He saw what was going on, so remarked to the head inspector that we were staying a long time

[1]   JRK, "How It All Began," 5.

and were not planning to sell those things. The headman signaled the inspector with a move of the hand, and he had to put everything back into the trunks.

We traveled on a Pullman train. The milk in the diner was sour, and when we arrived in Mexico City, Roger was running a fever. Since Bert was new to Mexico, we called in a Mexico City doctor who was not nearly as alarmed as we were. After a few nights' stay in downtown hotels, we were able to rent a large house in Coyoacán on the corner of Abasolo and Paris Streets for one hundred pesos a month. Once we had Bert and Harriet settled in there for language study, Mabel and I and the baby went on to Chiapas. I still marvel at how we were able to get bags and trunks from depots to hotels to Coyoacán. The fleas were so bad in their house that Bert and Harriet had to find other living quarters before long.

As for us, the first day back in Tapachula, I walked down a street and saw a large vacant house whose floors were being scrubbed. We rented that property. Again the Lord had a house ready when we needed it, as he always did throughout all of our years in Mexico.[2]

---

[2]   Ibid., 6.

CHAPTER 46

Bert and Harriet Kempers

After some months of language study in Mexico City, from five to seven hours a day, Bert and Harriet moved to Puebla in early December 1929 for more study of the people, customs, possibilities, and details of medical work. In Puebla, Bert could observe and work in the American Hospital, having been invited by Dr. Meadows, who was in charge of the hospital. In this way, Bert was able to learn Spanish medical terms, observe tropical diseases, and learn how to work with the native people. Bert and Harriet were treated most courteously by other missionaries in Mexico City who did everything possible to help them and to make them feel at home.[1] Bert took some field trips with a Mexican minister, and Harriet played her violin in the Baptist church services. What perplexed them both was being refused communion by the closed-communion Southern Baptists.

When they joined us in Tapachula, we built an extra bedroom on the large veranda, and half of the study became the medical office. Meals we had together. Bert was a well-qualified medical doctor and

---

[1]   "Our Missionaries in Chiapas, Mexico," *The Christian Intelligencer* (December 4, 1929), 773.

I introduced my brother Bert to Chiapas

Harriet an equally gifted partner in ministry. They had been called by the Lord to begin a medical ministry in Chiapas, and they would have made an excellent contribution to the mission work.

For the next ten weeks, I took my brother on some long trips over the trails to show him how desperate the health needs of the people were. The first long trip on horseback started in Tuxtla, where we bought three horses. We had too much baggage, so our extra horse gave out in the Yajalón area. We sold him for fifteen pesos, sight unseen in the region. In Comitán we bought a young mule that might have killed himself the first day running away with the baggage, but I held on to the rope as we dashed down a steep cactus-covered hill. Bert had a horse that fell frequently. Once this horse dumped his rider into a river, ruining a camera and a bag of fresh crackers. Quite often, after our all-day ride, when we showed slides for believers in the evening, they would want to continue singing, while we wanted to get to sleep to prepare for an early start the next morning.[2]

On June 4, 1930, we started another long trip. The coming of the Kempers brothers was eagerly awaited by the various groups of native Maya who had become Christians and who faithfully held services, even though they had no permanent pastor to minister to them. The first unpleasant episode of this trip, however, took place right at the outset. While saddling the horses in the dark, a large scorpion, which

[2]   JRK, "How It All Began," 6.

had hid in the saddle bags, stung my thumb. Though we had killed dozens of them, this was the first time I had been stung. A tourniquet and "Curatina" used externally and internally prevented any after effects, but the pain continued until noon. Usually one's tongue swells and becomes numb, and the arms become very sore. Rain had made the roads exceedingly slippery, and fording streams was difficult, but we finally reached Nazaret, where we held an evening service. After the service, several more families arrived, so we found another Bible passage and started all over again. We slept in the chapel that night.

About a mile from Huixtla, a terrific rain descended upon us, and even with the protection of our rubber capes, it was not pleasant riding. But the youngsters in Huixtla, stripped of all their clothing, were playing in the streets and thoroughly enjoying this impromptu shower-bath. There were so many sick people in this village that we had no time for a preaching service.

We crossed the Huixtla River, my horse being almost swept away in the swift current, and went on to Santa Rita. We had to climb a steep mountain for five hours. In Santa Rita, almost all of the people were afflicted with a fly- and mosquito-carried disease that had spread throughout the entire district. The affliction consisted of a thread-like worm tightly wound in a ball that was generally found under the scalp. The victim's eyes were invariably affected, and there were some cases of total blindness. There was no cure or prevention for this disease, although the removal of the worm was a simple operation and relieved the eyes. My brother performed several such operations, and we had a worship service that night.

On June 7, we were at Armenia, one league from Santa Rita, where our guide for the day joined us. From there on, the road was only a path connecting some *fincas* or plantations. Three men had been killed earlier by bandits on this road, and given that we were often taken for plantation owners carrying money, we were very thankful when we reached the plantation La Esmeralda. This American-owned plantation was managed by a German count who was married to a Protestant Mexican. Count Bernstoff had set aside one of the ranch houses for a chapel, and here we had services on Saturday and twice on Sunday, as well as Sunday school. Our guide presented himself as a candidate for church membership.

On Monday morning, with a new guide, we set out again, passing through several plantations where believers were at work in the fields. We reached Zapaluta at three o'clock in the afternoon. This was another crossroads through the woods, but it was more like a path of the Lacandonians than a road. Frequently our machete was called into service to open up the path. Two or three families who lived in Zapaluta were recent arrivals from Mazapa who were trying to make homes in the wilderness with all the hardships and charm of pioneer life. Their coffee was a drink made from ground corn, and the rest of the meal was boiled corn made into a *tamalito*.

On June 11, we arrived in San Francisco, the location of one of our oldest congregations. Everyone afflicted with the same disease as in Santa Rita came to receive assistance from Bert. We had a service that night and another in the morning before leaving. Our next move took us first up into the clouds to sheep country and huge fir trees and then down to Motozintla and Mazapa at river level. We spent Sunday in Mazapa, which meant teaching Sunday school and preaching in the morning. We had planned to leave after dinner, but then in a last-minute rush, the patients began to come. A downpour had started, so we stayed and showed slides that evening.

From here on, the journey became very arduous. Bert was ill due to poor food; the rain came down in torrents, and the horses finally gave out from exhaustion. Both my brother and I, however, kept on until the last of June, visiting a different station every day, preaching or teaching Sunday school, showing slides, and administering medical treatment. In twenty-one days, we had visited as many stations, and only twice were we obliged to stay overnight with unbelievers. My long-cherished dream was fulfilled, to serve the Lord together with my brother in an essential mission. This dream, however, would not last long.[3]

Bert and Harriet were eager to serve in Chiapas. But the Mexican Medical Society successfully lobbied the government to prohibit foreign doctors from doing medical work in Mexico. The closing of this door and the forced return of Bert and Harriet to the United States was a huge disappointment for all of us and especially for me.[4]

Our most serious concern, however, was Harriet's health. After returning from our trips in the region, Harriet became sick with dysentery. She kept getting worse, so we called in a local doctor with more experience in tropical diseases. Unfortunately, he recommended the same treatment that Bert had been using all along. So Bert decided the only thing to do was to take Harriet to the hospital in Guatemala, to a higher and more healthful altitude. We were making preparations for

---

[3]   WBMD, "A Missionary Journey in Chiapas," *The Christian Intelligencer* (October 15, 1930), 674.

[4]   JSH, "The History of the Chiapas Mission," 6.

a train trip with an overnight delay at the border, when Mr. Coffin came by and said that he had just heard that a plane was coming through that day. So we rushed to get their *salida* (exit) papers (the required documents to leave the country) and dashed to the airport in a taxi. The plane landed before we arrived, but its departure was delayed while the necessary paper work was taken care of.

Bert was having Harriet sip occasionally from a prepared glass of laudanum in water to dull her pain. Just before leaving the house, she decided not to let this go to waste, so she drank it all. On the plane, she passed out. Bert in desperation could revive her only with smelling salts. Harriet made a gradual recovery in Guatemala, while Bert returned to Chiapas to make a rainy-season horseback trip with me, visiting all the congregations along the coast and inland along the border. We traveled for one month, with a deluge every afternoon making the muddy trails almost impassable in some stretches.[5]

Years later, Bert recollected the adventure of those days: "We slept in the most awful places and climbed over mountains, crossing rivers, and one time we were caught in a downpour. The horses sunk into the mud up to their knees."[6] I was so happy to share all these experiences with my brother. On one trip, we bought a "wild-eyed, belligerent mule" in Comitán to replace a worn-out pack horse. Bert later remembered that I had thought we could tame him with a solid load, and we did. Several times, however, as the load shifted, the mule bucked until objects were scattered all over, and twice he bolted and nearly caused us to lose our footing on the narrow ledge. We had other close calls, and even now we remember—usually at night—how fortunate we were to have escaped alive.[7]

Sometime later, Bert returned to Guatemala, and he notified us that due to Harriet's health, and because he would never be licensed in Mexico, they had decided to return to the United States. That was a discouraging blow to us. Our reply was, "If you don't wish to stay, we will carry on alone." And we did, for the next many years, in spite of growing difficulties, especially due to the World Depression.[8]

For the next five years (1929-34), the Maximato proper, President Plutarco Elías Calles, remained the strong man of Mexico, ruling through token presidents. As the World Depression began to affect the Mexican economy, and production fell, the rule of the shadowy *jefe*

5   JRK, "How It All Began," 6-7.
6   Bert Kempers (BK) to JSH, Jan. 24, 1990, in JAH.
7   BK to JSH, March 12, 1989, in JAH.
8   JRK, "How It All Began," 7.

máximo (top chief) became more repressive. Anticlericalism flourished once more, and fascist-style fanatics terrorized Catholics and contrived to rekindle the Cristero Rebellion, when Calles passed extreme anti-Catholic laws that were brutally enforced by church-burning gunmen. The threat to the Roman Catholic Church was very serious, but it also endangered the testimony of evangelicals. The troubles in Tabasco were too close to us in neighboring Chiapas. These atrocities provided the setting for Graham Greene's novel *The Power and the Glory*.[9]

[9]   Williamson, *The Penguin History of Latin America*, 396.

CHAPTER 47

Great Depression and Persecution

The Great Depression dramatically exposed the vulnerability of the neocolonial, monocultural economy of Mexico. The area's foreign markets collapsed, and the price of Mexico's raw materials and foodstuffs fell much more sharply than those of the manufactured goods it had to import. The country's unfavorable balance of trade necessitated exchange controls and other trade restrictions which encouraged the growth of industries to produce goods formerly supplied through importation. The international economic instability, which caused a virtual suspension of imports of manufactured goods, gave further stimulus to the movement for a timid Mexican process of light industrialization. This was, however, too far from the Chiapanecan reality, which continued to be submerged in a rather primitive cycle of elemental agricultural exploitation, with masses of people oppressed under a feudal system.

Because of the international economic collapse, our situation in Chiapas was not easy. It was fortunate, however, that we had begun our missionary work in Tapachula, which was probably the richest region in the Soconusco and in all of Chiapas. And although we had much to

243

The birth of Kathleen Joy
brought added joy
to Mabel's life

learn from the experienced Mr. Coffin, it was difficult to work there, since he had complete control of everything. So we considered the possibility of moving inland to be on our own and to decentralize our mission. Our two possibilities were Comitán and Tuxtla Gutiérrez. The board was slow to act but did send Mr. Gustavus A. Watermulder, an experienced missionary among Native Americans, to help us investigate the possibilities. He believed with us that it would be advisable to move after our daughter Kathleen Joy was born in Guatemala City. We followed his advice and moved temporarily to Guatemala City, where I substituted for Rev. Lenn P. Sullenberger for a period of six months while he was on furlough. I preached in the large Central Presbyterian Church, which years later placed a portrait of me in their gallery of pastors.[1]

On September 18, our sweet Kathleen Joy was born. She was a great gift from God to us in this time of scarcity and despair. My heart rejoiced so much upon her arrival, because she was so much like Mabel in her character. I always imagined Mabel to be like Joy when she herself was a girl. Later when our daughter had to leave us to study in the United States, I felt horrible letting her go by herself to a totally strange and new environment. Joy had always been a sweet and shy girl, with a very rich spirit and great gifts from God. Our prayers have always been for the Lord to take care of her and guide her to find a path of peace and grace for her life, and I think he has responded to us with generosity.

[1]   JRK, "How It All Began," 7.

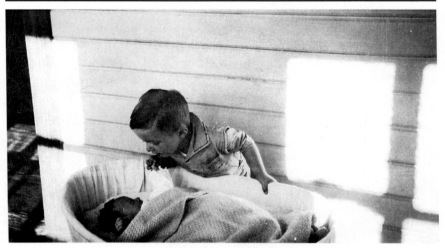

Roger welcomes his sister Kathleen into our family

It was in Guatemala City that Mabel started our guest book. She always exercised her wonderful gift of hospitality which allowed us to entertain a good number of "angels" in our home (Hebrews 13:2). Our guest book is a precious testimony of the diversity of people that honored our dwelling. The first guests signed in on September 16, 1930. Mabel copied this verse on the very cover of the book:

> It is a place where friends
> will come
> the tangled world to flee.
> Brave little nook,
> where peace will bide
> and hospitality.

There was also a glued note saying:

> Guest,
> You are welcome here,
>   be at your ease.
> Get up when you're ready,
>   go to bed when you please.
> Happy to share with you
>   such as we've got—
> the leaks in the roof,

the soup in the pot.
Don't have to thank us
or laugh at our jokes;
sit deep and come often—
     you're one of the folks.[2]

---

[2]   Guests Book, in JAH.

CHAPTER 48

The Gospel in Tuxtla Guriérrez

After six months in Guatemala City, in April 1931, we returned to Tuxtla Gutiérrez, the capital city of the state of Chiapas. We did this to give ourselves more freedom from José Coffin's control in Tapachula. We traveled from Arriaga to Tuxtla in a small car, making the one-hundred-mile trip in the customary time of twelve hours. Our household goods arrived in six days by oxcart, much the worse for the transportation. We secured a large house and immediately set to work to renovate it for our use, with plaster and lumber and screen. This became our happy home, where the children grew up and played with their friends, where boys from other areas came to the Bible school in our home, where the colporteurs had their headquarters, and where Wycliffe translators were introduced to Chiapas. This was the home that became a busy center of missionary activity for the entire state, and as the pastor of the Tuxtla Gutiérrez church, I had many additional responsibilities on my shoulders. The location of our work all over the state called for constant extended horseback tours, leaving my Mabel to educate and bring up the children and to nurse them through their illnesses.[1]

[1] JRK, "How It All Began," 7.

Tuxtla, capital of Chiapas, became our home base

It was rewarding to meet this congregation again and to see the crowd of people that attended our Christian services. Members of the Departments of Finance and Commerce, government employees, army officers, as well as those from more humble callings, all crowded onto the patio. Needless to say, we availed ourselves of the opportunity to draw souls to the feet of Christ, to whom all of this growth was due. Mabel and I had the opportunity to collaborate in the spread of the truth and participate in its growth with enthusiasm. We also began working with groups of believers who had been evangelized nearly thirty years earlier by missionaries from Mexico City.

The Tuxtla congregation developed quickly to the point where they called a Mexican minister, Rev. Ezequiel Lango, from Mexico City to serve them. The work was strengthened by Lango's ministry, and eventually the Presbytery of the Gulf gave him the pastoral responsibility for all of the central area of the state, in spite of Coffin's objections.[2] As for us, we soon began preparations for building a new church at the beginning of the dry season. The land had already been purchased, and money was raised for the new building. We were glad to be part of the Christian testimony of this old and faithful congregation.

Quiet, dreamy Tuxtla Gutiérrez lay in a barren valley about fifteen hundred feet above sea level and about 110 miles from the Pan-American railroad that parallels the Pacific coast. As his bags were being

---

[2]   JSH, "The History of the Chiapas Mission," 6.

After valuable service in Chiapas, Rev. Ezequiel Lango continued his support from Mexico City

tightly strapped to the back of a car in Arriaga, any stranger would have looked forward to a pleasant sightseeing trip. Scarcely would the stranger have left this railroad town, however, when his troubles would begin. Immediately, he would grab the top crossbar of the auto, and if he were able, he would grab the side of the car also, and to these he would cling tensely for ten or twelve hours, until the car would leave the oxcart road and rumble over the cobbled streets of Tuxtla. It is a wonder how any auto could survive repeated trips over that rocky road of potholes. But the Mexican is a born mechanic, and he would soon have the car ready for the return journey.

Eventually arriving at the best hotel, the stranger would probably be given a second story room—a rare thing in Chiapas *pueblos* (towns)—from which vantage point he could overlook the whole town in panoramic view. In all directions, the low, tile-roofed houses formed narrow canyon-like streets. All houses within the block were joined, and instead of front yards, there were solid walls that lined the narrow flagstone sidewalks. The rooms of the relatively humble homes lined one wall, with a covered but open corridor facing the patio. The patio might be a barren, dusty place, where nondescript chickens had scratched away all vegetation and where faded clothes lay scattered about to dry in the sun, or it might be a little flower-filled Eden, rich with the luxuriant foliage and color of tropical plant life. It all depended on the artistic temperament of the occupants.

We noticed a comparatively small number of churches, because at the time of our arrival, there was only the cathedral and two or three other churches. It was because Tuxtla was not of colonial times. There was

These oxen and wagons were the transportation link between
the railroad and Tuxtla, the capital city

not even one Protestant church, though there had been an evangelical congregation here for many years. The believers continued to worship in a rented room in a private home which was very inadequate, and although the use of any place other than a church building for religious services was contrary to law, this irregularity had been overlooked.[3]

It was impossible for us to determine the exact date of the beginning of the evangelical history of Tuxtla Gutiérrez. But from data which had been collected, it was known that this work dated from about the year 1880. At that time, a former bishop of the Catholic Church, José María González, a highly cultured man, began to teach the doctrine of Christ, though in rudimentary form, and it was at that time that other missionaries arrived. Their sacrificial work, although carried on in a time of much opposition, ignorance, and fanaticism, might surely have been blessed.

About 1890 Manuel Fernández, whose denominational affiliation was unknown to us, began a series of missionary trips to this distant region, so lacking in means of communication. At that time, there were no oxcart roads, much less the railroad which later crossed the state paralleling the Pacific Coast. Fernández came to a region of obscurantism, upon which the Catholic clergy capitalized, inspiring the people to fanaticism. But he soon won the esteem of the Tuxtla authorities, and because of this esteem, the clergy were afraid to do violence to his person. Most of the Bibles, testaments, and literature distributed by him, however, were burned. Some of the literature had the desired effect, and some pamphlets survived, like those kept by

---

[3]   JRK, "New Work in Mexico," *The Christian Intelligencer* (September 23, 1931), 602.

A special treat in Tuxtla was playing on the neighbor's tennis court

brother Manuel García, which were given by Fernández to his father Simón García. In time, he left Tuxtla, not to be heard from again.

At intervals, others arrived who distributed portions of scripture. In the year 1900, Rev. Edwin McDonald, of the Presbyterian Mission, formally established this work. This indefatigable missionary worked with such zeal that by 1903, he had succeeded in arranging regular services, having secured the necessary room and furniture. Of the twenty or twenty-five members who had formed this nascent congregation, a majority had already gone on to answer roll call before the King Supreme when we arrived. At the same time that Mr. McDonald started this congregation, he also established the Bank of Chiapas. Some of the most distinguished bankers in the region were taught by him. Mrs. McDonald was an excellent pianist and rendered valuable service in the this ministry.

When the McDonalds left, Francisco Rodríguez took charge of the work and founded the Christian Endeavor Society, Mensajeros de Dios (Messengers of God). This society continued to be active for decades. During his stay, Adelaido Petriz and Simón García carried on evangelistic work in the nearby villages, which resulted in the establishment of two congregations, one in Ocozocoautla and the other in Suchiapa. The former dissolved when the believers moved to Tuxtla, and the latter was destroyed by a proselyting sect. After Rodríguez left, the congregation, for a long time, was without a pastor, but believers always had the cooperation of the consecrated Arcadio Morales, pastor of the Presbyterian Church in Mexico City for fifty years. The congregation also received a number of visits from Dr. Isaac Boyce, of the Presbyterian Mission.

In May 1911, Dr. Dilly came to take charge of the work, but he died shortly thereafter in a neighboring village. He was followed by Rev. David Verdusco, whose stay was also short. Then the Revolution came, necessitating the temporary closing of the church until 1920, when Rev. José Coffin arrived. Coffin's labor bore fruit throughout the state. The congregation in Tuxtla held her pastor of many years in high esteem; through sun and rain, he had many times crossed the difficult mountain roads to spread the glorious gospel, whose maxims might be the basic principle of all morality. By the time of our arrival, the Presbyterian Church enjoyed high prestige in the city and was an important factor in drawing people from the vices of alcoholism and sin to a new life in Christ.[4]

The original plan in 1925 was that the Chiapas missionaries should locate in Tuxtla, but because of the religious disturbances and opposition at the time Mabel and I entered the country, it was thought unwise to move so far inland. Consequently, we remained in cosmopolitan Tapachula with its railroad infrastructure. Then in order to spread our staff over a larger area, and also because of the unbearable heat and unhealthy environment of Tapachula, in April 1931, we with our books and some furniture traveled up the rocky road of potholes previously described to make a home in Tuxtla. Seeing the city for the first time and comparing it with Tapachula, we were happily impressed with the numerous parks and open spaces where youngsters were either flying kites or with ball and club were learning the American *beisbol* instead of idly standing in groups on street corners.

The congregation, accustomed to only annual or biannual visits from a minister or missionary, had taken on a new enthusiasm. Plans were already underway for the building of a church as soon as the rainy season ended. Some boys were on their way to Tuxtla to be the first students in the Bible institute. One colporteur was coming up from the coast and another from Guatemala to make this their central station. Monthly instead of annual visits were being made to the nearby congregations, and from here, general correspondence as well as Christian literature and bulletins went on their mission throughout the state. Mount Mactzumactzá (The stone of eleven stars), which has looked down upon Tuxtla throughout her history, began to see an active, flourishing Christian congregation in this ancient Zoque village.[5]

[4]   Manuel García, "History of Protestantism in Tuxtla, Chiapas, Mexico," *The Christian Intelligencer* (August 26, 1931), 534.
[5]   JRK, "New Work in Mexico," 603.

CHAPTER 49

The Ministry of the Printed Page

The year 1931 has always been remembered by us as a special year. The effects of the Depression were deeply felt, but we were encouraged with new opportunities to serve the Lord. We moved from Guatemala City to Tuxtla Gutiérrez with Roger and our newborn baby, Kathleen Joy, our *guatemalteca* daughter. In Tuxtla we rented a house at Segunda Avenida Sur N° 4 (later N° 6). It was in this year that we began a program to train national pastors that we called Instituto Bíblico de Chiapas. Our first students came from the small indigenous town of Mazapa de Madero: Julián de la Cruz, Epigmenio Jacob Trigueros, Enrique Hernández, Israel Jacob, and Heriberto López de la Cruz. This institute was later moved to San Cristóbal de Las Casas (1948). We also began to lead the church in Tuxtla and promote the construction of a church on Segunda Avenida Sur.

One of the projects started in this year of 1931, which had enormous consequences in the coming years, was our publications program. In those years, some homes in the United States had far more magazines than they could possibly read. But in Chiapas, the opposite was true. When our mission work began, there was extremely little

Roger and Kathleen enriched
our family (*courtesy Joy Fuder*)

reading material available in Spanish and almost nothing in any of the
six major native languages. But gradually, we managed to overcome
this difficulty. "Necessity is the mother of invention." Due to limited
personnel and the need to communicate the gospel to many who were
hungering for it, I realized early on the power of the printed page.

Step by step, the Reformed Church Mission developed the field
of literature and printed matter by means of the printing press. At the
beginning of our second term on the field, I began mimeographing and
mailing church news and inspirational material in bulletin form to all
of the existing congregations. Besides instruction, this was an effort to
create some sense of unity among the separate and often very distant
groups. As the church extended its reach, the paper grew in importance,
so it was necessary to put it out in printed form.

At first the material to be published was sent to a commercial
printer, but as time went on, it became more and more difficult to get
the printing done promptly and satisfactorily. Commercial printing
eventually became a problem because printers were discouraged from
printing evangelical literature. To solve this problem, in 1948, the
mission purchased a small multigraph machine through the efforts
and goodwill of the Reformed Church in Wichert, Illinois, a church
that faithfully supported Garold and Ruth Van Engen during their
thirty-five years of ministry in Chiapas. By then, the circulation of the
bulletin was just over five hundred. As the number of churches and
missions increased, the number of bulletins increased. It was the aim of

With these five students from Mazapa, I launched the
Chiapas Bible Institute in our Tuxtla home (ca. 1931)

the administrator to send a copy to each family that had accepted the
Lord. The churches sent in their lists, and they were supplied with the
number of copies necessary—for free.

As the number of subscriptions grew, it was evident that the
mission could no longer pay all the expenses; the churches should
assume that responsibility. A promotional letter was distributed, telling
the churches the cost of the paper and suggesting that they cooperate
by sending in their offerings. At first they were reluctant to assume
full support, believing that they could not carry the load. But after a
few years of intensive work, the paper was supported entirely by the
national church.[1]

This, too, was soon outmoded, since our first publication grew
in size and circulation, and the task of printing it consumed too much
time and effort. At this point, in 1954, we began to use a linotype
and press, which Garold Van Engen had obtained and managed. We
changed the name of our publication from *Boletín* to *El Despertador* (The
awakener). This periodical was the result of a real need in the churches.

By presbyterial appointment, it was my privilege to be the editor
of this official organ of the church in Chiapas for some twenty-five

---

[1]   Garold Van Engen, "The Printed Page in Missions," *Charm and Challenge of Chiapas*
(n.d.), 9-11.

years. The circulation increased notably from the original few copies to more than a thousand. The eight-page monthly periodical provided church-related reading materials in the down-to-earth Spanish the people were used to and could understand, in contrast to the Spanish understood only by intellectuals, as used in the National Presbyterian paper *El Faro*. Studies on the what, who, when, and how of baptism appeared in serial form and were later printed in pamphlet size and given national distribution. A second printing generally followed. Very popular were articles on the Bible and church doctrine and interesting news items from the various congregations and believers throughout the state of Chiapas. As the church grew, the circulation of this paper increased, and it was gratifying to see its eager reception by believers in all the different areas.

A number of years before that, the young people of the state had organized their Christian Endeavor Union. Their annual convention, held in the month of January, became a matter of great interest and anticipation on the calendar of the church. Out of this convention came another periodical called *El Esforzador* (The endeavorer), which also had a broad circulation. Like *El Despertador*, this pamphlet carried articles of spiritual interest for young people, news of the various societies throughout the state, and a monthly program of material which could be used by the societies in their weekly meetings.[2]

When Pentecostalism began to make inroads in the state, we produced a series of studies on healings. I had to delay the publication of these studies for a time when some Pentecostal orator was able to hold interdenominational meetings in Tuxtla with professed cures. When he returned some time later for a repeat crusade, the eye glasses and the crutches that people had discarded in their hour of enthusiasm were again in use, and the man could get neither sponsorship nor audience. He had to sell his guitar to raise funds for his trip home. Again the series of *El Despertador* articles was printed in pamphlet form and distributed in Chiapas and in other states. My historical sketch, "How the Gospel Came to Chiapas," had two printings. Other series were very much appreciated by our readers scattered throughout the state.

The well known magazines circulating among congregations of the Reformed Church periodically accepted articles reporting on the work of the Chiapas Mission. The *Christian Intelligencer* (in October 1934 this magazine absorbed Hope College's newspaper the *Leader* and became the *Intelligencer-Leader*), and later (1944) the *Church Herald*,

---

[2]   Ruth Van Engen, "For His Glory," *The Church Herald* (November 9, 1956), 5.

We did a lot of creative writing at our desks in Tuxtla

welcomed missionary material in earlier years, and the board secretaries were always prodding us to provide material for publication. Sometimes, the deadline they set had passed before the request reached us. Copies of many of these articles have been preserved.[3] Mabel, whose gift for writing and command of the English language were well recognized, produced among other writings "The First Rain," "Street Sounds," "A House Remembers," and also the historical booklet *Chiapas para Cristo*. As editor Mabel chose the name *Charm and Challenge of Chiapas* and set the pattern of that continuing publication, later edited by Dorothy Dickens Meyerink.[4]

By the mid-1950s, the ministry of the printed page had begun publishing material for our indigenous believers. We wanted gospel truth to reach the native population, most of whom had no access to written Spanish. Young women with Wycliffe Bible Translators, who lived among the Tzeltals, had begun to compose a small, four-page pamphlet called *Smelelil K'op* (Word of truth). In addition, the translators compiled a hymnbook of over sixty hymns translated into Tzeltal, and they requested our press to publish the hymnbook and the pamphlet. A Ch'ol paper, *I We'el Lac Ch'ulel* (Food for the soul), under the direction of Rev. Albert De Voogd in collaboration with Wycliffe

3   In the JAH.
4   JRK, "Some of This and Some of That," 2-3.

working in the Ch'ol field, was distributed among the believers. The main purpose of the indigenous papers was to instruct believers in the Word. For many years, portions of the New Testament were the only written materials the indigenous believers had. Now that the Tzeltals and the Ch'ol finally had the entire New Testament, there developed a great need for explanation and instruction in all the important truths of the Word.

Along with these periodicals, the press published materials for the correspondence course "La Luz de la Vida" (The light of life) which, for years, Garold Van Engen continued to send out daily to people throughout the state. The press also printed thousands of gospel tracts and a number of other publications.[5] Besides the printing that was done for the presbytery, the mission also cooperated with the Christian Endeavor Union, printing its monthly paper, which had a circulation of nearly three hundred by the end of the 1950s. These were paid for by the Christian Endeavor members. By this time, it was impossible for the mission to reach all the eleven thousand people connected with the church. To visit each group once was a task that required a year's work, and then each group was visited only for a day or two. Therefore, the printed page was a means of keeping them informed and, at the same time, of teaching them the doctrines of the church. Many of the periodicals were read and then destroyed, but we have also seen many of them filed and referred to later for teaching on a particular doctrine that was presented years before.[6] In addition, Garold Van Engen, administrator of the publishing enterprises, also printed the quarterly prayer bulletin that was sent to RCA churches and supporters in the United States. At one point, that involved a mailing of thousands of copies, sent out four times a year.[7]

---

[5]   Van Engen, "For His Glory," 5.
[6]   Van Engen, "The Printed Page in Missions," 11.
[7]   Information provided by Charles Van Engen, email, July 18, 2014.

CHAPTER 50

Education in Mexico

I am convinced that every step of my growth and maturity, as well as the strong foundations of my education from my childhood in Iowa to the days of my youth in New Jersey, were guided by God to grant me the skills and knowledge that I would need throughout the long years of my missionary service. I therefore believe that education plays a significant role in advancing the Kingdom of God. The enemy, regrettably, also believes this and will try anything to thwart educational opportunities, particularly in ministerial training. Uneducated believers will find it difficult to have access to the Bible and Christian literature, and ignorant Christians are the ones most likely to cause all sorts of trouble in the church.

Education was highly touted by Mexican politicians and government officials. Its anti-Christian orientation, however, was a major hindrance in the advance of the gospel. The constitutional provisions regarding education in Mexico were drastic in this regard. Article 3 of the Constitution, after its amendment, provided:

1. Education imparted by the State will be socialistic and furthermore will exclude all religious doctrines and combat

A lot of my teaching occurred outside of the classroom

fanaticism and prejudices, and toward this end, the school will organize its teachings and activities so as to imbue in the young a rational and exact concept of the universe and of social life.

2. Only the State federation, states and municipalities shall impart primary, secondary, or normal education. Authority may be granted to private individuals who desire to impart education in any of these grades but always subject to the following norm: the activities and teachings of private schools must follow, without any exception whatever, the precepts of the first paragraph of this article.[1]

The preamble of a presidential decree issued January 1, 1932, stated that since the law of 1926 did not sufficiently present the conditions that should govern private schools, changes and additions were necessary. It also stated that these new laws did not prevent any person or religious organization from opening a private school, nor were they to cause the closing of any schools then open that had religious tendencies. They were simply intended to define the position of the government insofar as a private secondary education in such schools was concerned, leaving the freedom to open such schools or to attend them. The preamble further stated that, in place of incorporation, the Department of Public Education would offer special examinations to the students of such schools. The following extracts from the decree clearly indicated its trend:

[1]   Quoted in Brown, *One Hundred Years*, 814.

Article 2: The Department of Public Education, through the section on secondary education, will accept as valid the studies made in the official schools of the various states and in the private schools of the Republic and in those educational institutions of equivalent character, whenever each of such institutions shall have filled the following conditions:

They must not be Catholic seminaries or schools for the preparation of

ministers of any religion; they must impart their education on an absolutely lay basis; they must not have been founded nor be directed by religious bodies or by ministers of religion; they must not have any teachers who are ministers of any religion; they must accept the supervision and fill the other requisites which this regulation establishes. . . .

Article 4: When all these requisites have been complied with, the Department of Public Education will concede incorporation of the institution involved into the Federal system of secondary education. . . .

Article 8: Incorporation of State and private schools will only be made for a year at a time and will be cancelled at any time for infraction of any of the conditions. . . .

Article 25: Incorporated schools are at liberty to establish the social activities they desire to establish, but with the condition that in such activities, the lay principle is respected.[2]

In harmony with this decree, the Department of Education issued two regulations. One declared that no primary schools could exist in Mexico that had any relationship, financial or otherwise, with a church. The other stated that no secondary school that taught religion in any form would be recognized by the government. The government apparently intended to proscribe theological training altogether, for it decreed that theological seminaries would be permitted to function only on property that had been nationalized. But the government was unwilling to grant nationalized property to be used for seminary purposes. The decree was not enforced immediately, but it was on the statute books, and it created an exceedingly difficult problem for the education of the future Christian ministry of Mexico.

While these laws were general and applied to Protestants as well as to Roman Catholics, in the early stages of the movement, the laws

---

[2]   Quoted in ibid., 815.

did not seriously hinder Protestant missionary work. Some government officials personally stated to missionaries that the laws were intended to end the domination of the state by the Roman Catholic Church. They were not directed against Protestants, because the government understood that Protestants never interfered in political matters. They also said that, as long as they went on quietly with their work and did not raise issues which would compel officials to act, they were not likely to be interfered with.

The Board of Foreign Missions of the Presbyterian Church in the United States, in actions taken January 18, 1927, and January 21, 1929, authorized the Presbyterian Mission in Mexico to conform to existing laws and regulations, as much as they could, while being faithful to their supreme duty to Christ. In the latter action, the board expressed its "earnest hope that it may be possible to continue the schools" but "that it could not agree to their continuance on any basis which would involve the Mission or the Board in misrepresentation or bad faith."[3]

Since 1932 the government had apparently been motivated not only by opposition to Roman Catholic clericalism in state matters but also by a determination to eliminate all religion. The Ministry of Foreign Affairs had flatly declared: "There is no such thing as religious persecution in Mexico. All inhabitants of the country are free to profess any beliefs they prefer."[4] This was purely "diplomatic." No modern nation, except Soviet Russia, had adopted so radical an attitude toward religion as Mexico. The textbooks published by the Ministry of Education were openly atheistic. Second and third grade primers echoed the text of a Federal District official: "There is no being superior to man. God exists only in the human mind."[5]

Teachers in the government schools in one state were required to sign the following pledge: "I declare that I am an atheist, irreconcilable enemy of the Roman Catholic religion, and that I will use my efforts to destroy the said religion and to do away with all religious profession, and that I am ready to oppose the clergy whenever and wherever it may be necessary."[6] In another state, school teachers had to sign the following statement: "I declare that by all the means in my power, I will fight the Roman Catholic religion and other religions. I declare that I

---

3   Ibid., 815-16.
4   *Weekly News Sheet*, issued by the Publicity Department of the Ministry of Foreign Affairs, February 9, 1935.
5   Quoted in Brown, *One Hundred Years*, 816.
6   Quoted in ibid.

will not take part in private or public in any ceremony of the Catholic Church or any other religion."[7]

In view of the contradictory *ex parte* reports in the American and Mexican press, as to what was actually taking place and the resultant confusion in the public mind, the American Committee on Religious Rights and Minorities, in the summer of 1935, sent to Mexico a commission of three eminent laymen: a Protestant, Philip Marshall Brown, a former professor of international law at Princeton University; a Jew, Carl Sherman, former attorney general of the state of New York; and a Roman Catholic, William Franklin Sands, former secretary of the American Embassy in Mexico City and professor of diplomacy and history in the School of Foreign Service in Washington. This remarkably able and broadly representative commission conducted a thorough investigation and presented its report to the committee in September. After a summary of the historical background of the controversy with the Roman Catholic Church, the deputation stated, as a result of its investigation:

> It is now apparent that the National Revolutionary party which controls the government of Mexico has, with deliberation, embarked upon a programme aimed at the destruction of the Roman Catholic Church and with it the destruction of all religions. This policy can succeed if the National Revolutionary party can accomplish its announced primary purpose to prohibit the teaching of any religion to children in public or other schools, and in its often disavowed but unconcealed purpose to, at first, limit the clergy and the number of churches as to make the influences of the clergy insignificant, and later, wherever possible, to entirely prohibit the existence of churches and clergy.[8]

The deputation proceeded to show that Article 24 of the Mexican Constitution, guaranteeing religious liberty, had been violated by a series of provisions which constituted the undisputed organic law of the land and caused the National Congress and various state legislatures to enact laws which might also be regarded as violative of the said article. After quoting the national and state laws providing for the secularization of all education, the confiscation of church properties, and the restriction or abolition of the clergy, the deputation declared that in more than twelve states of Mexico, all priests had been forced

---

[7]   Quoted in ibid.
[8]   Quoted in ibid., 817.

to cease their ministrations. At the same time, in all states, except for four or five, highly drastic limitations had been placed upon their numbers and functions. All civil rights of free speech, assembly, or political action, such as voting, were denied to the clergy, save in a few states. Finally seminaries had been confiscated, rendering the training of clergy virtually impossible. After a full analysis of these and other facts, the report concluded:

> We have mentioned the more important constitutional provisions and other laws directed primarily at the Roman Catholic Church and its adherents. The Protestants do not suffer from the laws limiting the number of ministers (Mexican), but are definitely concerned with the provisions dealing with education and, to some extent, with the nationalization of church property. . . . Whether some states utilize the laws absolutely to eliminate the Church and the clergy—and others pursue a more liberal policy— whether some schools will have atheistic teaching and others not, the laws are there, giving the government the power to oppress the Church if it wills to do so. Since it is therefore evident that no one can seriously question that these provisions are both anticlerical and subversive of mankind's religious rights, it is pertinent to ascertain whether the State can justify their enactment as essential measures to safeguard its civil powers. Analysis of the form, intent, and effect of the provisions does not permit their justification as mere safeguards of such civil powers. When the result of precautionary laws is that they can and do result in the absolute prohibition of religious teaching to children, the complete closing of churches, the elimination of priests in most of the highly populated areas, and inadequate church and clergy facilities in the remaining territory, there is no longer a reasonable separation of powers, but a complete destructive influence. . . .
>
> Our conclusion is definite and unmistakable. We are convinced that the present Mexican government does not recognize its constitutional obligation which guarantees its citizens freedom to profess the religious beliefs or to practice the devotions of their sects. We also conclude that such government is not according reasonable protection to the organized church bodies, whereby they may maintain their rightful functions in the spiritual leadership and guidance of their respective sects.[9]

---

[9]   Quoted in ibid., 817-18.

How marvelous is God's grace! In the midst of all these governmental measures that so deeply affected education in Mexico, and particularly theological education and ministerial training, in Chiapas we were working hard to prepare leaders for churches. In 1932, the year of the presidential decree preventing any religious organization from training their ministers, Margarito Hernández López studied in our house in Tuxtla Gutiérrez for nine months. That year we also had new arrivals of students from Mazapa: Natalio Bravo, Juan López, and Margarito Bravo. From then on, we were involved in ministerial training and religious education, even after our retirement from Chiapas, when we went to serve as teachers in the Presbyterian Seminary in Mexico City.

CHAPTER 51

Christmas in Chiapas

Fiestas are always in order in Mexico, and Chiapas is truly Mexican in its fondness for festivals. Religious festivals that originated at the time of the Spanish Conquest of Mexico, under the influence of Europeans, became more numerous and remained elaborate. In more recent years, however, festivals seemed to retain very little of their original purpose. Great noise of fireworks, disorderly living, and excessive drinking characterized most of these festivities.

It is generally known that Protestants have but two fiestas—Christmas and Easter—and it was not difficult to attract large crowds when the calendar brought us around to their observance. Because of the Mexicans' innate love for fiestas, the Christmas Eve program became an excellent opportunity to present the message of the gospel to people who, perhaps at no other time of the year, could be induced to enter an evangelical church. Whatever the place of meeting—humble home, church, or open patio—it usually could not accommodate the crowd. Standing room only was full, and the open windows and doors were framed with eager faces. One evening in Tapachula, there were as many people congregated outside in the street as there were squeezed inside.

So much so, that each year, as we approached the Christmas season, intermingled joy was felt in our churches. We were to rejoice in the birth of our Saviour, and we were to witness for him before hundreds of people who might have scant knowledge of his importance to them. In light of what was considered good fiesta form, it is no surprise that one year a leader suggested that for the introductory number of the program, all the children, supplied with whistles and other noisemakers, show their unrestrained jubilation. A tone of dignity and seriousness, however, did manage to pervade the Protestant celebration. There was always at least one sermon, which was strongly evangelistic.

In keeping with the joy of the season, there was a great desire to participate. Mothers came begging for some part for their children. The children themselves wanted to participate, and though the director might try to keep the evening's program within reasonable time limits, it was not unusual for it to continue for three hours or more.

With excitement, our Chiapas churches were looking forward to the happy Noche Buena (Christmas Eve). Lots of letters came from the congregations asking for materials for their programs, and since there was a lack of resources, Mabel and I spent hours at the typewriter making copies of literature we had on hand. Packets of dialogues, poetry, hymns, and readings suitable for our groups were going out in all directions for several weeks, so that in remote parts of the state, the blessed Christmas festival might be kept appropriately.

Up in Yajalón, where the colporteur Salomón Ovando and his wife, doña Corona, were in charge, Christmas Eve preparations began in early October. In Tapachula, don Genaro de la Rosa worked for weeks outlining his program and getting it underway. Smaller congregations in that region were looking to the Tapachula church to help them in their activities. In Tuxtla Gutiérrez, experience had taught us that preparations for Christmas came to a veritable standstill while the city went through the celebration of Guadalupe Day, with more than a week of street fairs in mid-December. So Rev. Ezequiel Lango, active pastor of the congregation, distributed program parts during the first week of November instead of waiting until the teachers came back from their vacations in late November, as had been the custom. By the time that fiesta honoring the country's patron Virgin of Guadalupe took over the life of the city, our program needed to be pretty well prepared.

The local church also went through preparations in nearby Chiapa de Corzo where the Christian group was growing, as well as in Berriozabal. People were sent out each week to help believers in those *pueblos* organize their fiestas, and there were joyous times as they had anticipated. Every year in San Cristóbal de Las Casas, the congregation awaited our arrival to lead them in their preparations and to help in the presentation of the Christmas message. As soon as the rains in the mountain regions above us had run their course for the season and the automobile road was passable, we went up to join our brethren there.[1]

Christmas was always an opportunity to share the good news of the gospel, some years with lots of difficulty but other years with an abundance of peace and joy and goodwill. In some places, the celebration was presented in the afternoon instead of on the eve of Christmas. This was done not merely for a change (one strong characteristic of local fiestas was the strict adherence to tradition) but rather to avoid the tremendous crowds which gathered each year for the Protestant church festival. Besides we had to be cautious of whatever unpleasantry envious, and therefore hostile, onlookers might create under the cover of darkness. Everything—the moderately filled church, the order and attitude of attentiveness, the two short sermons, the simple program in which mostly children partook, the tree aglow with candles and color— combined to make it a fitting tribute to our Lord, in memory of his eternally significant birth.

The same spirit characterized our more private family celebrations of the festivity. Christmas Eve at home was an unforgettable experience. How we enjoyed it! The children, excited about their fir tree (brought down from the mountains), sang Christmas songs, which for us could never be replaced by the Spanish versions, and the more sophisticated voices of the radio singers brought us the old tunes from the United States. We did appreciate the quiet and peace of our family celebration, especially since we did not have to spend another busy evening at church. And then, there was the home dinner. Though there were many American foods that were not available to us in Chiapas, there were still compensations. Roast turkey—so inexpensive in Chiapas—adorned the table, as did California apples brought up from Tapachula, and Mexican-raised walnuts and Mexican chocolates were brought down from Mexico City. Holiday eating in the tropics is apt to be more temperate than in the snowed-in North, and I must admit, it does lack a certain zest.

Of course the house was alive at six o'clock the next morning, and the day continued busy until evening. At ten o'clock on Christmas morning, there was a short service at the church, and after that, we

---

[1] MVD, "Anticipating the 'Noche Buena' in Chiapas," *The Intelligencer-Leader* (December 30, 1938), 11.

We took a family photo in Tuxtla before Roger returned for his final year in high school (*courtesy Joy Fuder*)

had the distribution of *aguinaldos* (Christmas bonuses). The candy committee would make bright boxes of cardboard and fill them with cookies, candies, peanuts, and raisins. Some years, the church provided enough gifts for the entire audience on Christmas Eve. In time, however, that custom changed; so many outsiders arrived on Christmas morning, that the preparations of the committee were not nearly sufficient to provide for everyone. On several occasions, we also had the opportunity to collect a Christmas offering designated for one of our neighboring congregations. To sing "Silent Night" and read Luke 2 with our "family" in the church brought a joy too great to be described. Every such experience made us value more truly the rich blessings that Christmas brought us.[2]

Noche Buena—the good night! For us, Christmas was a simple fiesta in a land of fiestas. We always prayed for this celebration to retain its simplicity and beauty and for the Lord to use this very special occasion to bring many people to a saving knowledge of Jesus Christ.

[2]   MVD, "Christmas in Chiapas, Mexico," *The Intelligencer-Leader* (November 18, 1936), 12.

CHAPTER 52

Daily Life in Tuxtla

Just as there were distinctly Mexican sights and scenes that made vivid impressions when I was a novice in Mexican living, so also there were myriad sounds which, though striking and romantic to the newcomer, soon became just the accepted background for the day's activities. Over the patio walls and from the streets through the always-opened doors they came, and I paid very little heed to them when things took their normal course. But while lying in bed with a fever which attacked our household, including institute students, and with absolutely nothing to do but listen for several days, I became newly aware of all the sounds that wove the pattern of noise in our daily life in a very quiet town.

Long before my street door was opened in the early morning, the voices of tennis players on the courts across the narrow street came to remind me of the wonder of life and health and normal strength, and at that hour, I first became conscious of the footsteps—constant footsteps—on the rough flagged sidewalks —bare feet shuffling, sandals scuffing, high heels clicking, heavy military boots stamping—just twenty feet away at almost ear level. And voices, a day-long babble of voices, came in to me. There were the voices of children at play, for the street was the children's playground, and of shoppers (the city market was but two blocks away) bearing atop their black heads the brightly painted hollowed gourds, piled high with tomatoes, onions, oranges, meat, and chiles. I could hear the voices of soldiers at their headquarters next door and of the school children passing in laughing groups. Voices of girls, boys, women, and men—all selling something which usually could be bought at a better price in the market. There were also voices speaking either Spanish or one of the numerous indigenous dialects. Two old women used to meet at my door, stopping to greet each other in their native tongue, Zoque, a language that was still used by the older generation of native Tuxtlecans. A group of Chamula Maya would pass with their cold country fruits and vegetables for the market, conversing in their unintelligible speech.

Oxcarts rumbled past over the stone pavement, bearing cargoes traveling perhaps to or from the railroad several days away. Then there was the sharp report of a horse's hoofs, as the rider spurred it into a clattering gallop. Unmistakable grunts told me that a very unwilling pig was being led by a rope to the slaughter, or maybe the poor man, or more likely woman, carried the objecting animal in his arms. That was humorous, but the other grunts that followed—human, awful grunts— struck an entirely different note, for they told me that the ragged, dirty woman, who was mute, was doing her daily round of pitiful begging. One might become accustomed to countless sights and sounds which were never a part of his or her upbringing, but I think I shall never become accustomed to these pitiful beggars making their unclean, crippled way from door to door. And I hope I may never cease to offer a prayer of thanksgiving to the God who loves us all for physical fitness.

Then there came an ice cream vendor screaming his long list of flavors as he ran along, balancing dangerously his huge freezer on the flattened crown of his straw hat. I wondered just how many customers he was warding off with his shrill salesmanship. There was also a wheelbarrow which bumped itself into earshot. With that noise, I knew it might be piled with bags of coffee or corn. And then a truck followed at what sounded like a terrific speed, as its every sound slapped the house walls opposite and came resounding back to my listening ear.

And the music! A marimba paused to play a few yards away, and though one does become satiated with that sort of music, its quick rippling notes were like the babbling of a brook. It was beautiful and calming to din-jarred nerves. Then as the rapid hammering of the keys ceased, a clown's voice, distorted through a megaphone, announced the evening's cinema performance. Later in the day, a few short strains of martial music from one or two stray instruments wafted in from the corner. Then another clown reminded us of the sale on the next block. "Cheap! Cheap!" he insisted.

Bang! slammed a car door. And across the way, the doctor revved his motor, followed by the customary horn honking, and he was off on his rounds. For some time, I had been hearing, without really noticing, a spasmodic "pick-pick" directly outside. It was not hard to picture the peon there, sitting in the noon-day sun with his long-bladed machete, cutting away the grass that had dared to grow up among the stones in the shelter of the sidewalk. Perhaps he earned something equal to twenty-five cents (American) for his day's work. At about two o'clock in the afternoon, which is the local dinner hour, I was as relieved of his lazy pickings as he was to go home to his little dark hut for his tortillas, black beans, and chile.

Late in the afternoon, there came a distant noise that brought back memories of a real childhood thrill: the passing of the road scraper, which was always a thing of power and enchantment to us. Here it came that afternoon, first the warning, and then the steamroller rolled over the stones, followed by an excited crowd of screaming children as it lumbered at a snail's pace down the narrow ribbon of street.

Dog fights!—too many to enumerate—barking their way into the general melee of the sounds of a not-very-modern civilization. Most families did not stop at owning just one dog; consequently, dogs ran wild in the streets. They usually were lean and ugly creatures, picking up what they could from boxes or piles awaiting the garbage man and sleeping on the sidewalks, snapping at pedestrians who disturbed their lazy naps.

Babies cried, and other children playing in the dirt furnished a good part of the day's entertainment with their happy laughter or screams of anger. And so throughout the day, to the accompaniment of voices and the never-ceasing footfalls, life slowed down and flowed past my busy street. This was the background of our world, a world only slightly affected by the rush of the outside, a world in which we found our happy work among a people indifferent and satisfied. Every day we prayed the same prayer against the noise that came into our house, "Please, God, that we may serve you in such a way that your voice might be heard above all."[1]

---

[1]   JRK, "Tuxtla Street Sounds," *The Christian Intelligencer* (December 7, 1932), 781.

CHAPTER 53

Construction in Chiapas

Construction was a vital part of my missionary work in Chiapas. The Lord equipped me with the necessary knowledge and practice to do this work responsibly and skillfully. I learned the craft of carpentry and some mechanics on the farm where I was raised. Building and carpentry in particular were natural for me since I inherited the knack from my father and my grandfather. The making of furniture and the adaptation of each home to our needs and for our convenience, long before the days of electric tools, was fun work. In Mexico, masonry, plumbing, and electrical work were done behind closed doors, because educated people lost prestige if they were seen doing hand labor. One does not learn construction skills in seminary; on the mission field, however, these skills can be as useful as sound theology and acceptable hermeneutics. That was precisely my experience in Chiapas.

During our first several years in Tuxtla Gutiérrez, church services were held in rented houses, crowded for lack of space. The church owned a very fine lot in a suitable location, but because they had failed so badly in their attempts to raise funds for church construction, no one wanted to talk or even think about another try. I invited the heads

I carefully measured and marked the foundation for the
Bahtsibiltic Tzeltal church

of families to our home and was amazed at their total lack of interest, until I mentioned that our board might be willing to contribute toward the cost. That sparked some interest, and a committee was named. An architect was consulted, but he came up with a plan entirely unsuitable. So I drew up a plan and built a small wooden model for fund-raising purposes, and we were on our way. A church member carpenter knew in which neighboring villages we could obtain cypress for sills, *sabino* (a willow) for lintels, *chicozapote* for rafters, and cedar for doors and windows. Walls were of local adobe.

In all Mexican construction at that time, walls were held together by four-by-four-inch beams, one meter apart. I figured that the A-frame rafters would push the walls out, and iron tie rods would pull the walls inward, such as I had seen in First Reformed Church in Orange City, Iowa, during my academy days. It made for a much nicer looking church building. But even though the building had withstood any number of earthquakes, I do not believe anyone dared to copy this style of construction. As soon as the walls and roof were completed, we moved in and added doors, windows, platform, floor and wall plaster, and furniture as funds came in over the course of the next ten years.[1]

---

[1]   JRK, "Some of This and Some of That," 3-4.

This construction project was made possible because, as soon as we arrived in Tuxtla, in April 1931, we began to encourage the church to think seriously about a new place of worship. Throughout that year, we launched a campaign called Pro-Templo which succeeded in spite of the fact that in March there had been a heated discussion because some of the brethren wanted to buy a house instead. Finally, under the leadership of Martín López, the congregation voted to build a new church.[2]

This experience was replicated later in Tapachula. The congregation in this city of the Soconusco had been collecting church-building money for years, funds which always disappeared to assist in other needs. No one had any idea of what or how to build. The land on which to build was there, but there was neither leadership nor building plans. The pastor, Genaro de la Rosa, had no vision beyond a simple chapel, and his inability to keep financial records was also quite evident. I therefore prevailed upon the presbytery to move De la Rosa to the Tuxtla Gutiérrez church, without people realizing how or why it happened; this gave me the freedom to work and plan with the Tapachula consistory. I puzzled long and hard over how to position the church and where to have the main entrance. Suddenly the idea came to me to have the entrance where nave and transept would meet. Not long afterward, I found a copy of the *Christian Intelligencer* which showed models of three new churches identical to the idea that had come to me. It purported to be a new and modern style.

Ten official signatures from different governmental entities were patiently sought and obtained with the usual difficulty, and then we learned from the estimate of a building contractor that costs would far exceed what we had estimated. The following Sunday morning, I told the congregation about our predicament and said that we could do one of two things: either tear up the plan and documents obtained and begin from scratch with more modest plans or build until funds ran out and continue building in successive years as the money came in, as we had done in Tuxtla. Like a flash, as I had never seen before, all hands shot into the air and they cried out, "¡Eso queremos!" (That's what we want). Because of high coffee prices, the church was fully completed in just a few years.

Something unfortunate, however, did happen. Because I resided in Tuxtla, I could be in Tapachula only periodically to oversee the work. I therefore entrusted the purchase of roofing timber to a church elder.

---

[2]   Comisión de Historia, *Bodas de Oro*, 10.

We were blessed to minister to the Getsemani Church in Tuxtla

Within a few years, the termites had so eaten the lumber that the roof had to be rebuilt using metal trusses.

There was no cedar lumber available in lengths long enough for benches for that wide of a church. In a Tuxtla Gutiérrez sawmill, I found huge *sabino* logs, which I cut into planks thick and wide and of appropriate length. These were hand-planed by carpenters and shaped to be identical to the Hope College Dimnent Chapel seats. The work took months, and with considerable difficulty, the seat parts were shipped by truck to Arriaga, by train to Tapachula, and then again by truck to the church, where the seats were assembled and varnished. Hope College students contributed to the cost. Those who enjoyed the comfortable seats during the services had no idea of the difficulty in obtaining them.

The Tuzantán church building followed. After my retirement, a member of the church wrote, "Thank you, Dr. Kempers, for building our church the way you did. During the recent earthquake, all of our houses fell to the ground. Now we are building them the way you built the church."

Plans for smaller churches in Pueblo Nuevo, Yajalón, Tectuapán, and Copainalá were accepted, and local people completed the construction without much supervision. We had the stipulation that there would be no help unless there were Sunday school rooms in

Manuel Pinto built over twenty churches, including this one in Corralito
(*courtesy J. Samuel and Helen Hofman*)

addition to the sanctuary. Manuel Pinto, an elder of Las Margaritas church, completed the construction of the Tzeltal Maya churches in Corralito and Bahtsibiltic and the Mazapa church. Occasionally, he deviated from the plan. If I arrived in time, corrections could be made. If not, the mistake was permanent.

For the official approval of the plan for the new church in Mazapa, the government required the signature of a licensed architect. By four-wheel-drive Jeep, accompanied by an architect from Tapachula, I climbed the Cumbre del Pan, which is also the continental divide, and descended into the village of Mazapa. The architect signed our drawings without any modifications. Sometime after our retirement, the RCA Mission Board voted to discontinue giving aid for church construction in Chiapas.[3]

3   JRK, "Some of This and Some of That," 4-5.

CHAPTER 54

Travels

Miguel de Cervantes Saavedra, author of *Don Quixote*, the crown of Spanish literature, said that to walk lands and communicate with diverse peoples makes one wiser. Mabel and I have traveled a lot and have discovered that those who never leave their own land live enslaved by their prejudices. One of God's greatest blessings to us was to have blue skies over our heads and clear paths under our feet. As happens with most travelers, I have seen more things than I can remember, and I remember more things than I have seen. Nevertheless, as Miguel de Unamuno, the great Spanish philosopher, once said, "We have to travel because of topophobia, to escape from each place, not looking for the one where we are going, but escaping from the one we are leaving." Probably, these words describe well my obsession for traveling.

Our various furloughs enabled us to do some significant traveling, particularly back to our homeland. From May to December 1933, we had our second furlough. We went by train to El Paso and then we continued northward to spend most of our time with our parents and visiting the Grand Canyon. The highlight of this furlough was that our son David Warren was born on October 10. Now we were a small

Waiting for the train in torrid Arriaga
(*courtesy J. Samuel and Helen Hofman*)

crowd, and moving from one place to another became more difficult. Nevertheless, during these months, I had 105 speaking engagements.

Our travels to the United States were quite an adventure, with the enormous distance we had to travel over land being our greatest challenge. Travel from Tuxtla Gutiérrez to Laredo, Texas, was a fifteen-hundred-mile trip and then from Laredo to Holland, Michigan, was another sixteen hundred miles. A second challenge to this enormous effort was the financial cost. The total cost of such an expedition was $300—a fortune at that time! As usual, I kept detailed records of our expenses on all these travels.[1] A third challenge had to do with time. I have estimated the days used in our travels outside of Mexico based on the number of exits from the country registered in my Documento Migratorio Único del Inmigrante (Unique Immigrant Migratory Document). From August 12, 1955, to August 2, 1965, the record shows the following:

1955	30 days
1956	1 day
1957	216 days
1959	21 days
1961	236 days
1962	2 days
1963	72 days
1965	122 days

Total: 800 days in ten years.[2]

---

[1]   Records in JAH.
[2]   Documents in JAH.

When there was no road, the Jeep rode the coastal train

A fourth challenge was the horrible condition of most of our means of transportation. We remember the slow, open-windowed, dirty trains along the coast, heading toward Tapachula and the Guatemalan border. I recall the long hours of waiting for the late-arriving trains and the rush to board and find seats in the second-class, half-price cars. Not only did we save money for our limited mission budget, but the Mexican pastors traveled that way, and we had to avoid the appearance of superiority. Food we bought through the open windows at station stops. The *mojarra* (little fish) were always delicious at the station of that same name. Of course, we did run the risk of eating fish which were no longer fresh. The toilets were always filthy, waterless, stopped up, and smelly.

During the dry months, the old Dodges and Fords could manage the one hundred miles of oxcart road in twelve hours from the train station in Arriaga to Tuxtla Gutiérrez. An assistant to the driver would ride on the running board and was responsible for removing rocks from the road, adding water to the radiator as we stopped at streams, and the frequent mending of tires. When traveling alone, I often rode in the mail truck which had a seat in back of the driver for three passengers. There was so little auto traffic in Chiapas as yet that, on nights when Mabel expected my return, she would listen for the sound of the truck as it descended into the Tuxtla valley. Airplane travel was still far ahead in the future.

Horses and mules had become my friends. We had used horses on the farm in my youth, but I had not ridden them. This fact Coffin noticed when he introduced me to Chiapas itinerating together. On one of our first trips, he asked why I mounted from the right side rather

Chiapas roads were very hard on vehicles and passengers

than from the proper left side. I learned, and then I crisscrossed the huge state of Chiapas time and again, usually accompanied. Breakfast I made outdoors—coffee, oatmeal, eggs, and tortillas—using a small Primus stove. Meanwhile, the person with me would feed corn to both the riding and the pack animals. We liked to be in the saddle by five o'clock in the morning and stop at that same hour in the evening, with time to find fodder or pasture for the horses, which was always more difficult than finding a place to hang a hammock or to set up a portable cot. Once I was introduced in one of the city churches as "the man who knows all of Chiapas like the palm of his hand," and this remark was actually quite true.

Horse followed mule or vice versa, one replacing another because poor pasture and hard travel had taken their toll. I have no exact count of the number of animals who entered our service, but I can recall some twenty, like Príncipe, Tec (for Tecpatán where he was purchased), Rosinante, Segundo, Tercero, Subida, Bajada, Canela, Coyote, Azel. The last of them was the fleet-footed Pájaro (bird). On steep climbs, I would dismount and catch the horse's tail for a lift up the rocky climbs. Horses, of their own volition, would stop at the base of a climb for me to dismount. They would do it again, on reaching the crest, so I could remount. I was painfully kicked by some mules, but never thrown. In my presentations to churches in the United States, I often said that, undoubtedly, I was the only minister to have been awarded a doctorate for riding mules—many mules. But praise God for these useful animals,

I bought this horse in Tapachula for a trip to Comitán

which were of such help in our missionary work. May the Lord keep them safe and well served in heaven as the good servants they were!

Later we would enjoy cars and particularly the four-wheel-drive vehicles, such as Jeeps, to ride the rugged terrain. Mission Aviation Fellowship and their planes drastically cut down the time and wear of travel, but they also deprived us of the personal contacts, so necessary for church growth, that we had cultivated going from town to town, enjoying the local hospitality as we traveled with our horses and mules. Alfonso Marín, a Tuxtla deacon, traveled mountain country with me

I encouraged Garold as he repaired the Jeep, and Al made friends with Garold's dog (*courtesy J. Samuel and Helen Hofman*)

on one occasion to instruct believers in church self support. When he returned home before I did, he reported to Mabel his amazement at my ease of living with the country people, eating their food and drinking from badly chipped enamel cups. "Él es más mejicano que yo!" (He is more Mexican than I), he exclaimed in admiration. "If I should ever run for the office of governor, I would want him as my field manager." How well I remember people crying when we would prepare to leave! Likely, it would be a year or two before we could return to some places.

Finally, a fifth challenge had to do with the lodging conditions in most places we visited, particularly in Chiapas. Sleeping quarters might be a shed, a porch, a jail, a school, a chapel, or even a one-room family house, sleeping together with the whole family.[3]

[3]   JRK, "Some of This and Some of That," 10-11.

CHAPTER 55

Church Property

President Lázaro Cárdenas was the godfather of the renewal of the Mexican Revolution during his mandate (1934-40). Having taken the reins of power, Cárdenas worked to regain the revolutionary credibility that Calles had all but destroyed. The centerpiece of his domestic policy was the renewal of agrarian reform. In the first years of his administration, he faced labor unrest over wages and rising unemployment, but under his labor minister, industrial relations tended to favor the trade unions, and the standard of living rose.

Furthermore, the Constitution of 1917 was democratic and liberal, with socialist elements, and this prevented Mexican corporatism from becoming totalitarian. A degree of pluralism had to be tolerated. A free press with little overt censorship, freedom of speech and association, and rival political parties could exist. The official rhetoric under Cárdenas had become tinged with revolutionary socialism, and he liked to make gestures to the international left. Trotsky was granted political asylum in 1937 (he was finally assassinated in Coyoacán in 1940 by Ramón Mercader, a Spanish agent of Stalin), and in 1939, at the end of the Spanish Civil War, thousands of Spanish republicans were allowed to settle in Mexico.

On the other hand, another important objective of the government was to bind and heal the wounds of a traumatized nation. A pragmatic reconciliation with the church was begun under Cárdenas and then reaffirmed by his successor Ávila Camacho, himself a practicing Catholic. But the anticlerical laws of Calles were not repealed. They remained insurance against any interference by the church in matters pertaining to the State.[1]

Nevertheless, the decisions made by the government of Mexico made it irrefutably clear that they were not simply endeavoring to free the country from former ecclesiastical interference in affairs of the State but that they were seeking the abolition of religion itself in much the same way as the Soviet government of Russia was doing at that time. While the Roman Catholic Church was more directly affected because it was the largest religious body in Mexico and the one most closely related to the government in former generations, the laws applied equally to all religious bodies—Protestant as well as Catholic. Judged not by the criticism of opponents but by the enactments of the government itself and the declaration of its own officials, the deliberate purpose was not merely the correction of alleged abuses in any one church but the extirpation of all religion in the country.

There were further confirmations of the government's purpose. The law enacted by the national Congress on December 29, 1934, vested the president with power to legislate on the nationalization of property. Church property had already been regarded as belonging to the State, but no specific law had been promulgated. On September 4, 1935, President Cárdenas exercised the authority given to him by that legislation, promulgating a decree that all churches and any buildings that, since May 1, 1917, had on any occasion been used for public worship were to be considered the property of the nation.

This decree applied not only to churches but also to the residences of bishops, priests, and other church workers and to church schools and the property of corporations and any other institutions intended for religious purposes. This decree was enforced with varying degrees of severity up until more recent times. In some of the states, church buildings were returned to their congregations without interference by the national government, but the law stood on the statute books for decades, one of the harshest and most oppressive antireligious acts ever passed in any land.[2]

---

[1]   Williamson, *The Penguin History of Latin America*, 397-99.
[2]   Brown, *One Hundred Years*, 818.

CHAPTER 56

Church Organization

Years later when we were enjoying our retirement in California, Dr. Charles Van Engen, a former missionary to Chiapas and a very close friend, invited me to visit one of his classes at the School of World Mission of Fuller Theological Seminary in Pasadena, California. I went with pleasure and high expectations. His lecture that day had to do with church government throughout the centuries. Toward the close, he drew on the chalkboard the Chiapas system of church government and organization. He identified an organized church, a congregation, a mission, and a center for evangelism. To my surprise, he asked me if I had designed that plan, and this gave me pause to recollect the history of our ministry's administration.

We as Reformed Church missionaries had been with the evangelical church in Chiapas from its foundation, and we identified wholly with that church. There was not a "we" versus "they" spirit in the work that both missionaries and nationals did together. We worked as a team. Their church was our church. We brought people into the church, and the Mexican pastors baptized them. We prepared people for ministry, and the pastors ordained them. We built churches, and they dedicated them. We prepared special programs for important events, over which they presided. What we contributed materially or intellectually was for the church, so there was not a person's name on it. Any success was everyone's joy; any failure was everyone's sadness.

Van Engen's question, however, compelled me to try to remember who was responsible for the Chiapas system of church government and organization as well as other achievements. Rev. José Coffin was the initiator of the Presbyterian work in Chiapas, and he ordained elders in four of the largest existing Protestant groups and thereby organized these groups into churches. All of the groups in the area became satellite congregations, each with an appointed chaplain responsible for that group and subject to the nearest consistory. The choice of chaplain was determined by one's spiritual life, not oratorical skills.

When Rev. Ezequiel Lango came to work in the northern part of the state of Chiapas, he had already been working for some time among the Maya churches in Yucatán. He brought with him the concept of congregational government by governing officers as opposed to the sole chaplain arrangement. John Beekman, a Wycliffe translator, was eager for some sort of church government in the groups of believing Ch'ols he was working with. He and I agreed on each congregation having a president. A secretary would not be needed since there were no records to keep and because of the unfavorable connotations of that word in political circles at that time. A treasurer was essential as was a preacher. Somehow, this arrangement of congregational government by three people subject to a consistory spread throughout the state, thus ending the chaplain era.

Missions were smaller, unorganized groups visited by missionaries or pastors or laymen of area congregations or churches. Centers for evangelism were places where one or more families had the scriptures or welcomed evangelical conversation and where there was a family willing and brave enough to invite neighbors for a gospel meeting or for the showing of religious slides or films. The hope was that each group would progress to the next category and, ultimately, be organized as a self-governing, self-supporting church.[1]

One of the most significant contributions to the development of the work in Chiapas was the active participation of native workers. By 1936 five of our elderly former students had been called home to rest from their labors, witnessing, no doubt, the efforts of those who remained to carry on. Genaro de la Rosa had studied with us and later took some classes at the seminary in Mexico City. He was our capable

---

[1]   JRK, "Some of This and Some of That," 1.

chaplain at Tapachula and also supervised the nearby missions. Bartolomé Solorzano had grown from a timid boy into a fearless preacher and had charge of the Huixtla church. Margarito Hernández, a full-blooded native, and perhaps the most brilliant student we had, was in charge of the Sunday school and the young people's work in the large Mazapa congregation. With the exception of De la Rosa, these men and some other students were finally ordained, but for many years, they served as lay workers.

There was one indigenous boy, Israel Jacob, whom we took into our home when he was in the third grade. His father, Felipe, had dedicated him to the ministry, and he soon showed the same excellent qualities for which his father was loved and respected. We thought that he would go right on through preparatory school and seminary, but the road was not to be as easy as that. In 1934, while Israel was in Tuxtla Gutiérrez at school, his father died rather suddenly, leaving his mother with five little girls and one other young son. In answer to my question as to who was to take the place of Brother Felipe, the whole congregation rather dramatically answered, "Israel," and with raised hands promised around the open grave to help the family so that Israel might finish his training. But the promise was soon forgotten, and Israel, in spite of our entreaties, decided that he must support his family. We admired him for his resolution but grieved at the thought of having our hopes shattered.

For two years, Israel taught at a country school. Almost invariably, when one of these penniless natives was able to secure a school or government position, he would begin to feel himself too important for fellowship with the rest of the believers and thus was lost to the church. We feared that the same might happen to Israel and prayed for him. Although his own people gave up hope, we kept in touch with him and encouraged him. Finally I received a frank letter in which he stated, Jonah-like, that the teaching profession was not the place for him. We tried to make arrangements for his family, so that he could continue with his studies if he was willing. By then, he was old enough to make his own decisions and to know whether God was calling him to a greater task. Our hopes had long been set on him, and we often felt that if we had been sent to Chiapas only to help him into the ministry, our years would be well spent, and we could, if necessary, give up our work, well satisfied.

Another very significant contribution to the spread of the gospel in Chiapas was the work of the colporteurs. Strangely enough, during the entire period of opposition to religious work, our colporteurs, whose sole purpose was to distribute the Bible, had been relatively unhindered by the authorities. A number of times, they were questioned, but there was always some official to speak a good word for the Bible, even though he was not a believer. One time Salomón Ovando was taken to the police station, and when his turn came to face the chief, this officer called another officer, saying, "You who know something about these things, look over these books." This officer, seeing that the books were Bibles, launched himself into a lengthy speech extolling the Bible. The chief pretended to be working at his desk, but naturally heard what proved to be splendid propaganda for the unrestricted distribution of the scriptures. When the chief officer saw some colored pictures of Bible scenes in the back of a testament, he concluded, "Keep on selling the Bible, but I'd be careful about the pictures, because the government is very much opposed to the sale of 'images.'" Zenon Coeto also had a run in with coast guards, and in spite of upbraiding them for trying to interfere with the distribution of the Word of God while saloons and brothels were being protected, he also was dismissed.

In Tapilula a traveling scissors sharpener interested a number of families in the gospel. Night after night, they met to learn hymns and read the Bible. Some unlettered officials heard of it and, knowing something of the government laws prohibiting religious services in private homes, arrested the male members of the group, keeping them in jail for three days. Each man was fined five pesos and the owner of the house ten, and their Bibles and hymnals were confiscated. Complaints were made to the judge in Copainala, who ordered the officials to return all books and fines. The town authorities replied that the books could easily be returned, but since the money had been spent for municipal purposes, that would be difficult to return. Although the group was thus vindicated and the town officials reprimanded, the fanatical people of the village continued to persecute believers. At times, believers were stoned in the streets, and the children were taken out of school because of pranks played on them by the children of fanatics.[2]

The bravery and courage of these lay evangelists and colporteurs has always been key to the progress of the gospel in Chiapas. Their labors were irreplaceable, and thousands of Christian believers are in eternal debt to their valiant resolve to proclaim the good news in spite of the many dangers and open opposition. The seed they planted with sacrifice and passion prospered in incredible ways. The seed was sown in good soil, and it bore fruit and yielded, "in one case a hundredfold, in another sixty, and in another thirty."[3]

---

[2]   JRK, "Mexico after Ten Years," 12-13.
[3]   Matthew 13:8 (ASV).

CHAPTER 57

Religious Freedom

By 1936 the outlook for religious freedom was not reassuring. On November 5, 1935, President Lázaro Cárdenas, who was inaugurated on December 1, 1934, denied the plea of the Roman Catholic prelates for a modification of the government's policy and declared that the laws regulating religious worship and curbing the religious education of children would be strictly enforced. Kenneth G. Grubb said that of the 4,493 Roman Catholic priests in Mexico in 1926, only 197 of them were permitted to minister or to function in 1936.[1] Clarence E. Neff, of Guadalajara, wrote on January 16, 1936: "To prevent the use of private homes for schools under religious auspices, a law has been passed making any house or other private building in which religious propaganda is carried on liable to confiscation and offering a reward for the denunciation of such property."[2] Under the requirement that all education "shall be socialistic," "excluding all religious doctrine," and that there should be no control or financial aid by any foreign agency, all the schools of the Mission of the Presbyterian Church in the United

---

[1]   Kenneth G. Grubb, quoted in Brown, *One Hundred Years*, 819.
[2]   Clarence E. Neff, letter in *The Christian Century* (February 5, 1936), 15.

States were closed, except the Turner-Hodge School at Merida. Since this mission had no medical work except for an "itinerating clinic," and since foreign clergymen were forbidden by law to conduct public services and administer the sacraments, evangelistic work was largely restricted to lay missionaries and Mexican pastors and evangelists. In these trying circumstances, the mission was wisely endeavoring to adjust its plans to do whatever work was possible under the changed conditions.[3]

We were also forced to change some of our missionary strategies in order to adjust to the restrictions. Fortunately for us, from the very initiation of our work in Chiapas, we had decided not to organize schools or to be involved in an educational program but to turn our attention to the rural areas of the country and do intensive evangelization. We were convinced that it was necessary to focus on the heart-to-heart seeking of souls for Christ, investing directly in the lives of Christians to strengthen and build them up, rather than to depend upon institutions or special programs. Institutions come and go and have a rather uncertain existence, but personal evangelism and genuine friendship are far more powerful and more fruitful for the Kingdom of God. Nurturing personal relationships is more influential than anything else; by this it is possible to truly claim souls for the Savior.

In line with this truly apostolic policy, Mabel and I courageously presented the gospel message to individuals, both *mestizos* and Maya. Particularly encouraging were the relationships that we cultivated with peasants and very poor people in isolated regions. Remarkably, the most impressive piece of evangelistic work in Chiapas was done by lay workers whom we had trained through the years in various programs.

The restrictions on religious freedom resulted ironically in a bold commitment to the work by every dedicated believer. A particularly encouraging characteristic of an otherwise trying situation was the spirit of many of the Christians, especially those of the most humble standing. Secretary S. Franklin Mack, of the Mission Board of the Presbyterian Church in the United States, wrote after his visit to Mexico in 1935:

> Vast numbers of common people, both Protestant and Roman Catholic, have had their zeal for Christ strengthened by opposition. Notable among these are the Christians of the Yucatan. Unable to worship publicly, they have fostered Bible study and prayer

---

[3]   Brown, *One Hundred Years*, 819.

within the home. Limited as to the number of ministers allowed to function, the laity, both adults and young people, have stepped into the breach. They are doing as fine a piece of missionary evangelism as is to be found anywhere in Latin America, and all within the law.[4]

Rev. William A. Ross of the Southern Presbyterian Mission added his testimony:

> We do not recall a time when there was being done a more vital and spiritual work. We are not blind to the conditions which are affecting the work, and we do not know what the future may hold in store; but as we look back over the year which is just closing [1936], the victories of the Cross hold the center. There is beyond a doubt a rising spiritual tide in the churches. This was sensed in the meeting of the Presbyterian Synod in July; it was more keenly felt in the Convention in August, when representatives from all of the Evangelical churches in Mexico met for nearly a week in fellowship and prayer. Again in September, when the women of the Synod of Mexico met in annual gathering, there were clear indications of this rising spiritual tide. Prayer bands are springing up in many places in the country. In the last letter, some matters of church property which had been taken over by authorities in one of the cities were still giving us concern; the Federal Government has ordered these turned back to the Church.[5]

The National Presbyterian Church in Mexico was earnestly grappling with the increased responsibilities forced upon it by government-imposed restrictions on foreign missionaries. The Mexican Protestant ministers were not numerous enough to be affected by the territorial quota fixed by the law, and they displayed a strong spirit of devotion in carrying on the work. The National Presbyterian Church was well organized in an autonomous synod, which was constituted in July 1901. After the withdrawal of Presbyterian missionaries from northern Mexico in 1916, in accordance with the redistribution of territory agreed upon at the Cincinnati Conference of 1914, the Presbyterian churches formed a presbytery which included the churches that had been organized by the Southern Presbyterian Mission and were entirely self supporting.

---

4   Quoted in Brown, *One Hundred Years*, 820.
5   Reported by the International Christian Press and Information Service, February 15, 1936.

The nationalistic spirit that swept over the world after the Great War was as intense in Mexico as in any other land, and it naturally affected the churches and spurred them to demand independence of foreign control from church and State. As American missionaries, just like Americans in other fields of work, we wisely welcomed this demand. We recognized the risks of this demand, but we also realized that this would mean the removal of a great hindrance to the gospel itself: namely, its seemingly foreign character as evidenced by its foreign sources of support and the control of the evangelical enterprise by foreigners. This perception was widely accepted in Mexico, where Catholic propagandists exerted every effort to convince people that the preaching of the gospel was merely a subtle form of infiltration by the American government, with a view to later political control, and that to become a Protestant was really to become a traitor to Mexico. Hence, Mabel and I have always considered that national control of the Protestant enterprise was a positive advantage for the gospel cause.[6]

Dr. John A. Mackay, a well-known and respected authority on Christian work in Latin America was also of this opinion: "The new religious laws in Mexico obliged the evangelical churches to a thoroughgoing nationalization which has been most beneficial for their spiritual life. In 1930 there took place in Mexico City the ordination of the first Mexican bishop of the National Methodist Episcopal Church. In 1931 a suffragan bishop was ordained to guide the destinies of the National Protestant Episcopal Church in the country."[7]

As missionaries of the Reformed Church in America, we too suffered numerous limitations on our religious freedom, but we always tried to see the glass as half full. Unreliable press reports, which fed the mind of the average reader in the United States, commonly associated Mexico with strange and often ludicrous ideas of disorder and backwardness. There was, however, another side to the story, which the American people seldom heard but in which we found strength: that in the midst of the most serious opposition and restrictions, we found our best opportunities to proclaim the gospel of the Kingdom.

In a context characterized by profound changes and challenges, two facts pertaining to the spiritual realm affected our mission. First, strange as it may seem, in view of the press reports that reached the American public during the 1930s, there was an unprecedented interest in religion, not only among the common people but also among

[6]   Brown, *One Hundred* Years, 821.
[7]   John A. Mackay, quoted in ibid.

the educated classes. Second, an open challenge came from certain influential quarters as to the place and function of religion in the life of the individual and in society. As a result, many people seriously questioned some of the fundamental truths of the Christian faith. The real truth and power of the gospel were not known to the great majority of Mexican people, and a good number of them interpreted Christianity with a very limited understanding of its real content and meaning. With these erroneous ideas, there were many who felt justified in rejecting what they thought was the Christian faith, because they found in it many elements which they believed to be opposed to the enlightenment and social progress of the people.

There grew from these two facts the pressing need to present to the Mexican people an objective interpretation of true Christianity. This was the main objective of our mission in Chiapas, and this was the reason why, in the midst of repeated violations of religious freedom, we kept ourselves steady and committed to proclaiming the good news of Jesus Christ. Benito Juárez, the great indigenous president of Mexico, once expressed his hope that Protestantism would become an active force in liberating the Mexican indigenous people from the state of ignorance, superstition, and vice in which they had settled. And later, ex-president Portes Gil, by 1936 the head of the National Revolutionary Party which controlled the government of Mexico, said: "If our children are to become Christians, let that be by seeking the original fountain, the words of the Master which are in the Gospels." Antonio Caso, the leading Mexican philosopher, had sounded this energetic proclamation: "The arms of the Cross are still sufficiently strong to permit us to hang our destinies upon them."[8]

There were many elements in the Mexican condition which were a litmus test of the steadiness and quality of the Protestant work. Those years were a time of trial. But they finally proved to be a time of real and unprecedented opportunity. On the whole, I may say that in the Chiapas Mission, we were not so much concerned about a theoretical recognition of religious liberties, as we were the more practical issue of how to make the best use of the available opportunities to proclaim the lordship of Christ for the spiritual upbuilding of the nation, for the benefit of the people, and for the extension of the true Kingdom of God in Mexico.

[8]   Gonzalo Báez Camargo, "Recent Progress in Mexico," *The Christian Intelligencer* (August 12, 1936), 12-13.

CHAPTER 58

Itinerating in Chiapas

Mabel and I made our first inland trip in Chiapas in 1927, the year Charles Lindbergh flew across the Atlantic. We read about his trip in the newspaper on the train on our return trip. On that occasion, we visited Tuxtla Gutiérrez and San Cristóbal de Las Casas. We were already using slides of the life of Christ with a carbide-burning projector. Our Spanish was still rather novice, but we got to know the people, and they got to know us. Getting to understand each other was a long process which had to be worked out by both parties.

I needed a horse to make trips inland, but when I wrote the board for permission to purchase one, they wired back to put it off. I never knew why. Nevertheless, I bought a horse for one hundred pesos. I traveled by way of Mazapa; from there Miguel Blanco rode with me all the way to Comitán. We visited congregations along the way. One day, we lived entirely on just a *morral* (shoulder bag) of Huisquilar oranges, the sweetest ever. At the night stopover, I had a woman boil drinking water for me. When I drank that water from my canteen the next day, I got a chicken feather in my mouth. In Comitán I was able to sell the horse for one hundred pesos and then go on to Tuxtla by truck,

299

A dugout canoe was a quick and easy way for Mabel to cross a river

giving a series of studies on the life of Christ there, which was much appreciated since the church was having internal troubles—not the first and certainly not the last for Tuxtla.[1]

Itinerating in Chiapas was quite an adventure. Ten years after our first inland trip, I continued to accept the challenge of traveling through the green state. Chiapas, a distinctly mountainous state, in 1937 still had notoriously poor roads. The thirty-seven congregations scattered throughout the state at that time, however, had to be reached somehow, as well as the forty-seven other groups, which for lack of leadership, did not hold services, and the thirty-eight visiting places where there were families friendly to the gospel. Most of the work of itinerating was done on horseback, although oxcarts, automobiles, the train, and even airplanes were sometimes used. Because we had done so much of this type of traveling, that which so impressed us on our first trips—the impossible roads, the rivers that horses had to swim across, sleeping with large families in one-room huts with rodents traveling up and down our hammock rope, having the lady of the house taste the coffee from our cups to test its sweetness—no longer seemed newsworthy. Every long trip, however, brought some new experience, and I wanted to share these adventures with others.

One of these memorable trips was to Tapilula, a *ladino* town, and to Tapalapa, an indigenous village.[2] On the fifth night of our trip

---

[1]   JRK, "How It All Began," 4-5.

[2]   *Ladino* means "cunning," "learned," and in Europe, it described a person of Judeo-Spanish ancestry. In Mexico it refers to a westernized Spanish-speaking indigenous person. Maya used the term *ladinos* to refer to *mestizos*.

My travel companions and I often enjoyed an oatmeal
breakfast on the trail

with colporteur Salomón Ovando, it rained heavily. We were in a high, mountainous region, where the distinction between the dry season and the rainy season was not always clear. Before us, there lay twenty-one miles of travel over trails so steep and rocky in some places that anyone with the slightest regard for his mount would frequently walk. That night, rain and continuous drizzle made our going a decidedly unpleasant task. The poor pack animal had to carry her burden all the way, no matter how deep the mud or how jagged and precipitous the trail.

Ovando had sent a message from Bochil the previous day to announce our expected arrival in Tapilula. For twenty centavos, one could send ten words by telephone to many towns in the state. The obvious advantage of this system over that of the telegraph, was that no trained operator was needed—only someone with a lusty pair of lungs. The fee was readily accepted, but Ovando's message was never delivered. In fact, a line connecting Bochil and Tapilula did not exist at that time.

The gospel took hold first in Tapilula, as I have already mentioned, in about the year 1935. Mr. Montoya, a traveling "mechanic" as he called himself—"scissors-grinder" would perhaps be more accurate—stopped for a few weeks in Tapilula to sharpen tools and mend pots and pans. He was of the Presbyterian faith but a free-lance missionary. For two weeks, he gathered a group of sympathetic listeners around him each night to read the Bible and sing hymns. That was in the days when the antireligious movement was at its peak. As a result, he and

Visiting all the remote groups of believers required extensive travel

the men of each family attending the meetings were incarcerated for three days, fined a good amount of money, and had their Bibles and hymnbooks confiscated. The real persecution, however, was still to come. Encouraged by the official opposition to evangelicals, the people at every opportunity stoned the houses of believers and sometimes even the believers themselves. The children found it impossible to continue in school, and even though life was made miserable for all, their faith increased.

After Mr. Montoya left to journey on, a Russelite (Jehovah's Witness) bookseller happened along and might have ruined everything had we not visited the group soon thereafter. We held no services on that occasion because mobs bent on mischief, gathered at the street corners. But we did become acquainted with all of the families and convinced all but one woman to leave the Russelite literature alone.

Some months later, two of our colporteurs visited there again. On that occasion, one of them preached to the group gathered in a house, and the other, instead of barring doors against the crowd, preached to them outside. The following night, this procedure was repeated with an "exchange" of preachers.

Just a year after my first visit in 1936, I was back in Tapilula. We unloaded our pack animal at don Simón's house. Soon, believers began to step in to greet us, and they brought our hostess an egg or two, a gourd of ground coffee, or a few centavos to help with the entertainment of the "brothers." Then two little boys came to greet us. As they sat on the edge of a cot in the one-room hut, we were told how their father had whipped them and threatened them with expulsion from their homes unless they ceased attending the Protestant meetings. They persisted, however, and finally succeeded in bringing their father too.

There were other new converts, among them a well-to-do family who, because of their social position, had silenced much of the opposition. Our plan to leave the following day was met with convincing objections. Instead, after a morning service, while a full-grown turkey simmered in the pot over the open fireplace and *chile* was being ground into *mole*, several of us went to Yaxhuatán, nine miles distant. There the town president was deeply interested in the gospel but a bit confused after listening to colporteurs of the evangelicals, the Adventists, and the Russelites. We hoped our efforts to explain the different beliefs would help him. Upon our return, we found the turkey well done, the *mole* well-seasoned, the tortillas hot, and the coffee black. We ate at a little table which might have been a miniature piano bench.

There was no one in this group who could teach, but they had been holding "readings" four mornings a week. We outlined a service to follow and tried to show them how they could have more interesting meetings. In time they became a united group because of the common opposition, but we saw signs of contentious natures which might endanger their continued unity. We did not like to leave so fertile a place without a teacher, but each of our stations had to produce its own leader. Frequent visits were needed, but it took four days to reach Tapilula, crossing two mountain ranges, one of 4,000 feet and the other 5,500, and after the crossing of each, the traveler dropped back almost to sea level. Nor did we like to leave poor brother Esteban lying, paralyzed from the hips down, on his rough bunk of slats, without a mattress and with rags rolled into a ball for a pillow. At night, he was frequently prodded with sticks through the open staves of his hut. For five years, he had lain helpless, dependent on his one sister, and he was decidedly discouraged because he could not recover nor earn anything to help, while his appetite, as he said, unfortunately continued.

As a demonstration of Christian love, don Simón and his boy accompanied us twelve miles the next day, leaving us at Pantepec, from where we climbed to Tapalapa. In this quiet little indigenous village lay the ruins of a huge, colonial stone church and convent, the size of which indicated that there must have been thousands of natives living in this region before the cholera epidemic some fifty-four years previous to our arrival. Little Spanish was spoken there, and we could hardly find

I traveled many long miles to encourage isolated Christian families

an egg or a tortilla in the village. While I boiled rice and made coffee on our little Primus stove, which drew an amused crowd of Maya, the colporteur sold them New Testaments and told the gospel story.

To our surprise, there were several natives who knew something about the gospel. One had served as a porter for Coffin for fourteen days, all the way from Tuxtla to Pichucalco. Others had lodged at the home of one of our elders in Tuxtla, and they remembered my visit to Tapalapa four years earlier, with the stereopticon lecture of the life of Christ. They wanted a Bible dictionary, so we suggested their buying one *en cooperativo* (in cooperation). The government used that expression a great deal, so they understood, and the idea appealed to them. We hoped that as the village leaders accepted the gospel, Tapalapa might become another Christian Mazapa.

The fellow traveler who shared our supper and room claimed to be over ninety years old. At that age, he still climbed mountains and was on his way to the next town to cut hair at the fiesta. My mule had tired climbing to Tapalapa, making the last kilometer a few feet at a time, so I dreaded the next morning's four-mile climb. It took us more than two hours, but once on top, the rest of the trip to Copainala was descent, and I could ride again. The old barber, wheezing a good bit, made the climb also, carrying his pack. The natives had a shortcut straight up the mountain, which they called the "ladder" but which no *ladino* had tried to climb. They said that in places, it was necessary to pull yourself up by grasping notches in the smooth rock. Some had slipped and been dashed to the bottom.

As we reached the spot where the "ladder" joined the main trail, a Maya and his son, each carrying a pack, had just made the perilous climb. Even some native women took this short way to save time, although of time they did have plenty. When we left this place, we thought that some day, we would want to visit Tapalapa again. Whether we should try to climb the ladder, I did not know, but we hoped that many of these native friends would someday learn to walk the road we try to follow.[3]

3   JRK, "Itinerating in Chiapas," *The Christian Intelligencer* (April 9, 1937), 7-8.

CHAPTER 59

The 1937 Chevrolet

It is amazing how time flies. Before we realized it, we were making preparations for our third furlough in the United States. We made plans to be out of Chiapas from July 1937 to July 1938. The novelty of this trip was that we were to drive a brand new 1937 Chevrolet. This machine had been purchased by Lillian Van Dyke in Grand Rapids for some $630. She and a Zeeland school teacher drove in over the just-opened Pan-American Highway, all the way to Mexico City. There Mabel and I met with those two courageous ladies and our (then) three children; that meant seven passengers and our baggage, including trunks, all in the shiny automobile. As if this were not enough, I spotted a two-wheeled trailer with a steel frame. I had a blacksmith make attachments to fasten it to the frame of the car. Then I bought lumber and made a box to attach to the frame, so we could hit the road fully loaded. The Taylors (Rev. Norman W. and Geraldine Ely), missionaries living in San Ángel, provided the yard space and the saw and hammer to complete my project.

In Laredo I secured a driver's license in just fifteen minutes! Lillian and her friend headed home by train, and we turned west to visit my brother Bert, a physician in Albuquerque, New Mexico. Later, somewhere in Nebraska, we came suddenly upon a bridge four inches higher than the road. The car managed to jump, but the little wheels of the trailer snapped off. Fortunately, an empty truck came along, and we threw baggage and trailer into that and headed for the town we had just passed, where some welding took care of matters.

After visiting in Sioux Center with my people, we were on the road again. This time, we headed for St. Louis to visit a brother and his wife in government service there. At noon, in Hamburg, Iowa, driving along at a moderate pace, I noticed an oncoming car slowing down for a pothole, followed at rapid pace by a car which ran up the first car's bumper and toppled onto our engine. Lillian, fortunately, had taken out car insurance, but it did not cover our hotel bill.

On our way to New Brunswick, our final destination and the location of our furlough home, while passing by Harrisburg, Pennsylvania, one of the little wheels on the trailer suddenly snapped off and rolled across the highway. We unloaded the trailer and found some very considerate farm people who entertained the family while I drove into Harrisburg. Somehow I found a welding shop with the foreman still there after closing time. Had I arrived five minutes later, we would have had to wait over the weekend to fix the trailer.

We had a wonderful time in New Brunswick and continued to enjoy the new car. I made innumerable preaching visits to as many churches as possible talking about our work in Chiapas. People were thrilled with the stories I shared and appalled with the challenges I issued. I stayed for an extended period of time at Rutgers University in New Brunswick, an enriching academic center. I used this year of 1938 as a sabbatical to study. For Mabel and the children, this was also an exceptional time of refreshment and enjoying new things. Life in the big city was for them like being in heaven, taking advantage of all the amenities offered in an urban setting.

When it was time to return to Mexico, I realized that we had driven that trailer from Mexico City to Laredo, to Albuquerque, and all the way to New Brunswick without a trailer license. When I inquired about the New Jersey fee, I decided it was cheaper to send the trunks and trailer to Holland, Michigan, by freight. There we obtained the license for a fee of only two dollars. Having done this, we headed south, back to Chiapas. The Pan-American Highway in Mexico ended in Veracruz, so we faced the problem of shipping the car to Arriaga, Chiapas, to avoid driving the almost impossible crossroad through the Isthmus of Tehuantepec. No freight cars were available, so I asked the Veracruz church pastor

The road between Tuxtla and San Cristóbal was a rugged
challenge for any vehicle

to have some layman in his church see to the shipping. The car arrived eventually, and the 1937 Chevrolet had traveled comfortably, suffering only the dust of the road.

Some might ask if such an automobile was a luxury in the rather primitive land of Chiapas. It really was, but at the same time, it became an indispensable tool for doing mission work. The six-hour trip to San Cristóbal from Tuxtla Gutiérrez was made time and again without any mechanical problems whatsoever, in spite of the condition of that mountain road. Berriozabal could be visited easily, as well as Cintalapa, Suchiapa, and Chiapa de Corzo. Twice I shipped the car on a flatcar to Veracruz, riding as a caretaker passenger. From the nearest town to Veracruz, I would wire Mabel and the children to take the passenger train to the port city on the Gulf.

There were reports that the Anza brothers (car dealers) had made the first overland trip from Mexico City to Tuxtla Gutiérrez. To avoid the shipping delays, Ken Weathers, with some mechanical knowledge, and I decided to give it a try. The dirt road led toward the ocean from Arriaga and then swung right, eventually crossing the railway tracks. Our main fear was the sequence of bridgeless rivers, but we managed them that first day and spent the night sleeping in the car near the sugar plantation before reaching Juchitán. I do not remember whether we had a team of oxen pull us across the wide Tehuantepec River or whether we made it on our own. (On later trips, when the water was deep, we had to use oxen.) Once we had crossed the river safely, the hazardous part was completed, so we removed our caps and said a word of thanksgiving. We crawled under the dusty car several times to locate a disturbing noise. Later, working on the patio of the Wycliffe building, I discovered a broken spring leaf, which I then replaced.

Winding over the makeshift roads across Oaxaca and climbing the mountain ridge, we detected a slight engine problem. We reached Oaxaca City late on the second night. We had a good bath and slept in a hotel and, forgoing an early start, decided to have the carburetor looked at in a garage. It turned out to be time and money wasted. From Mexico City, I drove to Veracruz to meet the family coming in by train, and on the steep climb from Orizaba, I realized that the occasional miss in the engine was due to the fuel pump. If Ken and I would have installed the spare that I carried in the glove compartment, we would have saved ourselves a lot of concern.

In my humble opinion, only a Chevrolet could survive the mechanical demands of traversing the rugged territory of Chiapas and suffer the frequent marathons to which I submitted this dependable machine. Worry, however, about gas rationing and the lack of tires in the United States by 1942 led me to foolishly sell the car to Mr. Farson, an American war dodger who was running a Christian printing press. For furlough use, I purchased a used Hudson, which gave us considerable trouble and not because of the shortage of gasoline. It was several years before I could buy a replacement car in Tuxtla. Meanwhile, Mr. Farson was driving my indestructible 1937 Chevrolet in comfort.[1]

---

[1]   JRK to DDM, Aug. 25, 1989, in JAH.

CHAPTER 60

Early Work among the Ch'ols and the Tzetals

On March 25, 1939, J. Santiago González summoned a meeting that took place the following day in the town Estrella de Belén, with twenty-three people attending. The townspeople praised God and were informed of the favorable disposition of the Presbytery of the Gulf of Mexico to promote the Christian testimony in their region. By April 2, after they had prepared their meeting place, twenty-eight people gathered for a worship service, and local leaders were appointed by a vote of those present. González kept himself coming and going from Yajalón to the ranch of Amador González as worship services, Sunday school, catechism, and literacy courses were developed. On average, thirty people participated in these activities.

On April 25, González, accompanied by Salomón Díaz, went to Guallaza (a Tzeltal colony). They gave a presentation using a *lámpara* (slide projector) and explained the images in the native language. The people were captivated. Similar activities of Christian testimony using the magic *lámpara* were shared through May in Hidalgo, Tumbalá, Giralda, Estrella de Belén, and in some places using the facilities of the Salon Municipal (city hall). The only limitation to these courageous

311

I assisted the Ch'ol believers in choosing a church location

initiatives was that the *carburo* (fuel) that fed the *lámpara* was exhausted, and they could not continue to use this extraordinary instrument.[1]

By July 1935, the local government had confiscated some forty *láminas* (sheets of zinc roofing) destined for the construction of a church building, used them to roof the city hall, and never replaced them.[2] Nevertheless by the end of May 1939, local believers had bought a site in Tumbalá and were saving some money to build a chapel from the sixty cents to two pesos they were collecting in their weekly offerings.[3] Coincidently it was in 1939 that the first church building in San Cristóbal de Las Casas was also built on the site of Mariano Arista (Ejército Nacional) N° 35.

Christian stewardship has always been a major issue among the natives. They had no cash and found it very difficult to place money in the offering plate. I suggested brother González might try a system that worked pretty well in Yucatán. In addition to teaching the doctrine of Christian stewardship and encouraging believers to be faithful with their offerings, there was something very practical that they could do. I called it *la hectária del Señor* (the Lord's hectare). The idea was to set apart a piece of land that would be cultivated by all the believers, and the product would belong to the church. Supervision and organization

[1]   J. Santiago González (JSG), report to JRK on the work of evangelization among the Ch'ols and Tzeltal during March 25 through May 28, 1939, in JAH.
[2]   JSG to JRK, Oct. 11, 1939, in JAH. See Esponda, *El presbiterianismo en Chiapas*, 56.
[3]   JSG to JRK, May 29, 1939, in JAH.

were demanded for everybody to participate in the work. A sound administration, likewise, was indispensable.[4]

As to the Christian identity of the new converts among the Ch'ol and Tzeltal, it was consistently maturing. By the end of this year of 1939, Christians there had organized a board for protection and mutual help. They were also recognized by other locals as a unique group of people with distinctive ideals and were not forced to contribute money for Catholic religious festivals.[5]

The restoration of the *láminas* was not my primary focus at that time. My goal was to avoid conflict with the local government. In fact, by December 1940, the local belivers had managed to get the blessed *láminas*; they were expecting to get the wood in January of 1941 and start construction in February.[6] I was continually thrilled with the enthusiasm of these people. With almost no resources, they managed to build their chapel in about a year. The chapel was dedicated on March 7, 1943, with an attendance of more than three hundred.[7] Interestingly by March 28, the colony in Allende dedicated their chapel with an attendance of 150, not counting children. On March 21, J. Santiago González (Chanti), Ezequiel Lango, and Emilio led a worship service in Tzeltal and Ch'ol in Agua Azul, one of the most beautiful places in the world.[8]

In October 1939, however, I was more preoccupied with the Christmas celebration among the natives in Tumbalá. The traditional way we celebrated in the Spanish-speaking communities would not work with them. My suggestion was to have some short stories and a lot of hymns, which were so inviting to them. All of this, of course, should be done in their own language.[9] The most important event during this month, however, was on October 9, when we had the organization in Tuxtla of the Church El Divino Redentor (The Divine Redeemer) and the first full-time Mexican pastor installed, Ezequiel Lango, from Mexico City.

As I look back on that year of 1939, it is with deep appreciation of God's amazing grace, manifested in small beginnings that bloomed with extraordinary results. In fact, by the end of the 1930s, evangelical Christianity in Mexico claimed more than a hundred thousand

4   JRK to JSG, June 17, 1941, in JAH.
5   JSG to JRK, Oct. 11, 1939, in JAH.
6   JSG to JRK, Dec. 2, 1940, in JAH.
7   JSG, report to JRK, March 1943, in JAH.
8   Ibid.
9   JRK to JSG, Oct. 16, 1939, in JAH.

members and adherents, and its influence was far greater than its numerical strength suggested.[10] From fifty thousand in 1936, the total number enrolled in Mexican evangelical churches advanced to a quarter of a million by 1946.[11]

This growth was also true with regard to the advance of the gospel among the Maya tribes. Early in 1940, a group of native brothers went to Bascán with the idea of finding a place there to organize a colony of five families, all of them Christians, and expand the testimony in the region.[12] The testimony also extended to Allende, where numerous people were won to Christ and were ready to be baptized. The whole region was ripe to receive the gospel. I remember brother Santiago González telling me that the Ch'ols had been won for the Kingdom, and those with the most savage reputation were the first to accept the Lord.[13]

Various workers contributed to the Christian testimony among the Ch'ols. One of them was Isidro Estrella, who arrived in Yajalón in June 1943, with the purpose of learning their language to be able to preach in Ch'ol.[14] I was very impressed with his commitment to this end. He said: "Both my wife and I are in the hands of God and ready to move to Yajalón, Chiapas."[15] We instructed him to dedicate at least half of his time to the work among the Ch'ols. They lived in distant and isolated *rancherías* (hamlets). I urged him to get a horse to travel to these people and to train some of them to have services in their own place, since some had to walk eight *leguas* (leagues) to come to the place of worship.[16] I was also concerned that the Ch'ols have trained leaders. I asked Estrella to organize some short courses of no more than two weeks for the best qualified among them to become lay workers in the groups of the *rancherías*.[17]

[10]   Orr, *Evangelical Awakenings in Latin America*, 111.
[11]   Ibid., 114.
[12]   JSG, report to JRK on the work of evangelization, February 1940, in JAH.
[13]   JSG to JRK, Dec. 2, 1940, in JAH.
[14]   JRK to JSG, June 22, 1943, in JAH.
[15]   Isidro Estrella (IE) to JRK, May 26, 1943, in JAH.
[16]   JRK to IE, June 22, 1943, in JAH.
[17]   JRK to IE, Oct. 12, 1943, in JAH.

CHAPTER 61

A Trip to a Presbytery Meeting

"¿Ya vino?" (Has he arrived yet). "What do you suppose may have detained him?" These and similar questions referred to the expected arrival of Genaro de la Rosa, the Tapachula lay preacher whom we were awaiting in San Cristóbal de Las Casas. On that particular week of May 1940, we had switched the regular Monday night prayer meeting to Tuesday so that the Las Casas congregation might meet the young man who was on his way to the presbytery meeting to be ordained to the ministry—the first Chiapas-born believer to be so consecrated.

It turned out that De la Rosa, upon leaving the train at Arriaga, had boarded a bus to start the journey inland but had forgotten to get his saddle from the express office. Returning for this, he lost a day, which meant that he did not have a chance to speak to the Las Casas believers, for we had to depart immediately after his arrival on Wednesday. It also meant that we could not stop to have an evening meeting in Chilón, three nights later, as we had planned.

With De la Rosa came an elder of the Tapachula congregation to make sure that, once their leader was ordained, some other church would not take him away from them. I had two saddle horses and a pack mule ready, but there was no time to find an extra horse for the elder, so he and De la Rosa decided to take turns walking and riding. While Mabel served them a late dinner, Arnulfo—my guide on all of that season's trips—and I saddled the horses and tied the pack. In less than an hour, the four of us were on the road—horses and men full of energy and conversation.

Darkness falls suddenly in the tropics, and it came upon us at Corralito, a farm where customary hospitality invited us to sleep on the living room floor and furnished supper and pasture. In the cold country, houses had ceilings which made it impossible to hang hammocks. There was nothing else to do but spread rain capes and saddle blankets on the floor and stretch out in a row. Hip bones seem unduly prominent on such occasions, since I had never become accustomed to sleeping on boards. On one occasion, I slept in De la Rosa's bed and found that he had placed boards over the top of his bed spring. The elder didn't mind smooth boards either, but that night, he slept on a part of the floor that had been patched and therefore was as restless as I.

There were four more days of travel to Salto de Agua, which lay at the northern border of our state, where we hoped to find a riverboat. The first two days were not especially difficult. We made meals at streams where there was also grass for the horses, and we found decent places to sleep. At Chilón we stopped to visit the believers and then hurried on to Yajalón, where we had an evening service. We retired after eleven o'clock that evening to be up again at four thirty in the morning for the most difficult stretch of all. Arnulfo and I had made the climb to Tumbalá a few months before, so we knew what to expect in the forenoon. But the seventy-four-year-old elder and Genaro were from the coast and had done little mountain travel. We all had to walk to save our horses' strength as we climbed higher and higher to the little town where the Ch'ol Maya were building a church on the wind-swept summit. Arnulfo and I had pried open the kitchen of a believer's home and warmed the lunch sent with us by a motherly Christian in Yajalón, before our companions reached the top.

Impatiently we waited for Chanti (J. Santiago González), our worker among the natives. I had sent a Maya runner on ahead to ask him to meet me in the village and to trade horses for a few days, since mine had been overworked during the season. But Chanti did not come, because as we learned later, he returned very late that day from a four-day missions trip. The way from Tumbalá to Salto de Agua was down the mountain we had just climbed but on a trail that was most difficult to find. Ever since my first trip in 1926, I had avoided this road.

Weary at sundown, we reached Trinidad to find the village hilarious with the fiesta of the Trinity. Again we had to sleep on a floor, this time because the owner of the house feared that the worm-eaten timbers would not hold our hammocks. By then, I could have slept on corrugated iron. Unfortunately, there was only one mosquito bar, which enabled the netting to fall in tent-like fashion over both De la Rosa and myself. We tried to make the most of the hours for rest, when I awoke suddenly to hear the horses at the door. To my question whether he was intending to give the horses their corn, Arnulfo answered that they had already finished. It was one thirty in the morning! He and the elder had not been able to sleep because of mosquitoes, raucous drunks, and firecrackers. There was nothing for us to do but to get up and start out in the pitch dark over a trail which the rest had never traveled and which I naturally did not remember at all. This time there was very little conversation. The horses, with heads drooping walked slower and slower, but all such weary journeys come to an end. By ten o'clock that morning, we sighted the river and the village of Salto de Agua. I knew then that my horse would make it and would have a few days' rest, so I did no more walking.

It was Sunday morning. We still had a week to get to Yucatán to be in time for the presbytery meeting. Would there be a boat at Salto for us, or would we have to wait day after day in the terrible heat of the lowlands?

Ezequiel Lango, who had been doing pastoral work in that northern zone, had come down the river the previous afternoon. It was good to see his hammock, but it was much better to see him and to hear him say that there were two boats, and we could leave the following day. We are slow to trust in God's providence, no matter how often he shows his hand in extraordinary ways.

After living principally on eggs and tortillas for four-and-a-half days, the turtle meat and other well-cooked food helped us forget what was behind and prepare for what lie ahead. On Monday morning, considerably rested, we bade goodbye to faithful Arnulfo, who with the three horses had to return step by step along the road we had just come. The rest of us walked the plank onto the *Nueva Esperanza*, a motor-sail boat with 235 stinky screaming hogs down below. For three days and three nights, we were to live, eat, and sleep on a little upper deck of about eight-by-ten feet.

At Lango's suggestion, we had purchased a crate of soda water which, although lukewarm, stood us in good stead. The breeze, when there was one, carried off the odor of the pigs along with the mosquitoes.

Genaro de la Rosa, Ezequiel Lango, and I endured three days
and three nights on this boat from Tabasco to Yucatan

I do not know just what watercourse we followed. The map shows
many rivers, and we must have crossed from one to another. The sun
appeared on various sides of the boat as we wound around the bends,
but on schedule, we reached Ciudad del Carmen on the Gulf of Mexico,
from which we were to travel the rougher waves to Campeche. The hogs
could not be drenched with salt water nor could they drink it, so during
these forty-eight hours of Gulf travel and forty-eight more that they
had to continue after we gladly left them, they were without water and
therefore also without food. When people traveled east from Chiapas,
Tabasco, or Campeche in these boats, they traveled with either livestock
or bananas. So had it been for generations. What could have been a
most pleasant cruise down a tropical river became almost unendurable.
Those who made this trip always complained but afterward joked about
it. Nothing, however, was ever done to improve the traveling conditions.
It is no great wonder that the daily Pan-American plane was always
full. By then I thought that someday Yucatán might be joined to the
center of the country with a railroad, but there was no reason to believe
that this would occur with Mexican capital and Mexican supervision
nor that it could be done any faster than their completion of the Pan-
American Highway.

We spent the day in Campeche resting, swimming, and eating
fish. Dozens of fishing boats spent their nights working on the gulf, so
the fish section of the market was much larger than those with other
meats.

Tabasco's rivers were their roads

By then we had another companion, and after the half-day train ride to Mérida, we were met at the station by Yucatán workers who took us to their homes. Lango and I had the privilege of being entertained at the Finleys' home (Theodore R. and Frances P. Nelson)—young Presbyterian missionaries whom I had met six years before.

We were still on our way to the presbytery meeting but had made such good time that we could spend Sunday in beautiful Mérida, with its clean, paved streets and city atmosphere, windmills on every patio, and quaint horse-drawn cabs. There were opportunities to teach Sunday school and preach in the Mérida churches. On Monday we visited the Maya ruins at Uxmal, since I had already seen the more stupendous ruins at Chichén-Itzá. That night in Ticul, I preached to an indigenous congregation using an interpreter.

Yucatán was different from all the rest of Mexico. The people called themselves Yucatecos and spoke of the rest of their countrymen as Mexicans. This was my first visit to the Maya centers, which were not native villages such as we had in Chiapas, but were well planned and could be compared to the larger towns in Chiapas in all manner but size.

Akil, where the presbytery met, had a small church, too small for this crowd, but people could stand out on the patio and listen. In fact, they were better off there because of the excessive heat. Ministers even asked those who were preaching not to be given a part in the evening service so they could sit outside or at least come without coats. The extra chairs came from the movie theatre, which showed no pictures that week because the townspeople were all at church. The postmaster opened the daily mail bag on the station platform and distributed the mail to the delegates.

Four days is not enough for Mexican presbytery meetings. One session after the evening preaching service lasted until one o'clock in the morning. On Saturday night, we rushed to close at midnight. Each worker gave a written report of his year's work. Statistical reports were presented, problems discussed, and fields assigned. Salaries could be arranged, and candidates could be examined. I took with me reading material for dull moments but did very little reading. Missionaries had no vote in the sessions, although they could express themselves freely and influence the voting. Until the last few years of the 1930s, when we were able to make Chiapas a real part of the Presbytery of the Gulf, these meetings held little interest for us, and we did not think attendance was worth the time or expense. But all that changed by the early 1940s, and meetings would have even more importance for Chiapas as our work grew and became more organized.

There were several highlights that we long remembered, such as the report of Roque May, a Maya layworker. He referred, incidentally, to his imprisonment, and upon being questioned by the president, explained that he had been sentenced to hard prison labor for eleven days for preaching the gospel in a village. Because he sang hymns while doing prison work, he was judged insane. Presbytery had no distinguished service medal, but Roque was declared honorary president of the presbytery for that year.

Another moment that touched our hearts was when the elders of the largest church in Mérida, which had separated from the presbytery several years before and which was now returning penitently, offered to share two months of their pastor's time for indigenous evangelistic work. Such a Christian spirit put quick-tempered and quick-tongued ministers to shame.

De la Rosa, with whom we had worked for fifteen years, was ordained at an evening service. Coffin, with whom De la Rosa had sustained a Timothy-Paul-like relationship all those years, pronounced the words of ordination. I led in the opening prayer, and a classmate and friend of Genaro gave a beautiful dedicatory prayer. By 1940 we had eight young people studying for the ministry, either in preparatory school, Bible schools, or the seminary. Three of these were from our own state.

Pastor Genaro de la Rosa, the first ordained minister in Chiapas,
with his son (*courtesy J. Samuel and Helen Hofman*)

I preached the Friday evening message on "Souls, lost and found."
It proved to be an inspired choice, and the consistory of the city church
in Mérida asked that I preach it there on Sunday night.

We had economized on expenses by taking the slow road to Yucatán
but had to economize on time on our return journey. So changing from
train to Gulf boats to a Pan-American plane, to an Isthmus train, and
then to an auto, I reached Tuxtla Gutiérrez on the fourth day to find my
son Roger, who had come down from San Cristóbal de Las Casas ahead
of the rest of the family, and a friend arranging our home in Tuxtla
where we were to live again until January.

Once again, we had been to a presbytery meeting. We had traveled
over mountain and plain and sea—by land, by air, by water.[1] That was
Chiapas!

---

[1]   JRK, "Over Mountain and Plain and Sea," *The Christian Intelligencer* (September 20,
1940), 10-11.

CHAPTER 62

The Priority of Evangelization

I am a missionary evangelist. As a missionary, my first responsibility is to proclaim the good news of the gospel. On the mission field, there were multiple tasks to perform, but evangelization always came first. Let there be no misunderstanding about the missiological importance of the evangelization of the people we serve. There is nothing better we can give Latin America than the gospel of Jesus Christ. Evangelization should be our first preoccupation and commitment. Goodwill missions have their place, but the good willers profit more by them than do the countries they hurriedly visit. These good willers have become such a plague, that Latin America calls them the Sixth Columnists. American capital could do much to help develop the resources of these countries, but capital has had its chance, and in Mexico at least, it was unceremoniously booted out.

In the early 1940s, a Hope College survey on foreign missions showed that less than 10 percent of the students believed evangelistic missions were important. The majority believed that medicine and education could do much more good. This, however, was not the opinion of influential mission agents at the time. Dr. Paul Harrison, serving in Arabia during those years agreed with me. This goodwill approach to missions was also not the opinion of Professor Robert A. Brown, who for forty years was director of a fine preparatory school in Mexico but ended his years of service doing evangelistic work. Nor was it the opinion of Professor Theodore A. Finley, who for years was associated with a first-rate mission school in Yucatán but gave that up to do more direct evangelistic work.

Many college students in those years evidently did not understand the meaning of the word "evangelization," confusing it with the emotional type of preaching of some so-called evangelists. Evangelistic preaching means preaching the evangel or the good news of salvation in Jesus Christ, as Christ has commanded us to do. There can be no more glorious work. One college student with sophomoric smartness said preaching was the "rah-rah" of Christianity! In other words, it was only the ballyhoo or press-agent stuff. This poor soul did not know that you cannot educate people into the Kingdom of God, nor surgically operate them in.[1] The only way to bring people into the Kingdom is to evangelize them.

Of course this was not an easy task on the mission field. The word of the Psalmist was even truer there: "Those who go out weeping, bearing the seed for sowing, shall come home with shouts of joy, carrying their sheaves" (Psalm 126:6). And the most painful reality was that the harvest was not always immediate. After we tilled the ground in Chiapas for more than thirty years, I heard people saying, "It seems too bad that after so many years of work in Chiapas, there is so little to show for it." Very few members of the Reformed Church in America have ever traveled to Chiapas to see how the mission and the church function there. Nor would we ever encourage anyone to do so. A hasty visit could give only a partial and probably a very erroneous impression of our evangelistic work.

If one thinks of a mission in terms of a plant, then the Chiapas Mission had little to show. Our mission was not interested in a large compound with numerous and imposing buildings. Visitors would find one missionary family living in one town, another in a city at a considerable distance, and others out in Maya villages in the mountains where they could be reached only by small planes and where they scarcely had room to set up a cot for a guest. When Mabel and I first arrived in Veracruz, we were shown the little wooden church and the dispensary, which to us seemed quite dilapidated. We had just come

---

[1]   JRK, "The Call of Mexican Youth," 17.

from fabulous New York. We had been brought up as Americans to think that everything had to be bigger and better. We had not yet formulated our philosophy of missions. We were quite depressed.

Surely Dr. Albert Schweitzer, with all of his worldwide contacts, could raise enough money to erect an enormous, modern, tile-floored hospital in the area of Africa where he had worked for so long. What folly that would be! What is acceptable in countries such as India and Japan may not be advisable elsewhere. If a missionary builds himself a too-large house, in some areas, he erects a barrier between himself and the people with whom he wishes to identify. One of our homes, though very economically built, was rather imposing in its setting. It did not escape criticism. No, buildings do not constitute a mission.

The Chiapas Mission was interested in seeing children, light skinned and dark skinned, scrubbed clean and in their Sunday best—more than eight thousand in 170 churches by 1960—attending Sunday school. This is what we wanted our visitors to see, too. What could warm hearts more than the sight of little children cleaned up and coming to church? We loved them all!

The Chiapas Mission was interested in young people, third generation, second generation, and the newly converted, exhorting one another in their Christian Endeavor Society meetings or at their annual convention. The young people participated in prayer meetings, outnumbering the adults, while their unbelieving fellow students or employees were diverting themselves in worldly pastimes.

The Chiapas Mission was interested in adults from every walk of life: city, village, and country people; educated and illiterate; the Spanish-speaking *ladino* and the Maya of half-a-dozen tribes. If they needed assistance in building their churches, we helped them, but we did not build churches for them. And when they designed a structure, they did not follow any type of architectural drawings; a photo of their edifice might never grace the cover of a church publication, but it would be *their* church.

The Chiapas Mission was interested in education, but due to the laws of the land, if the church was to sponsor educational work, it would have to be done through Mexican nationals. The ever-increasing number of Normal School graduates in our churches gave us hope that, in the near future, some educational endeavor might be undertaken. For two years we provided a boarding home for out-of-town students in the Tuxtla Gutiérrez city schools.

The Chiapas Mission was interested in the health of the people. It was next to impossible for a missionary to secure a license to practice medicine, but so great was the need for medical services in the indigenous areas that health authorities did permit our missionaries to dispense medicine and treat the sick and injured in outlying areas. We wanted visitors to see our clinic and to know what a tremendous influence this was in the spread of the gospel of love.

The Chiapas Mission was tremendously interested in the preparation of a national ministry, so much so that our primary focus was to train lay workers and pastors for the Spanish-speaking believers, for the Tzeltals and the Ch'ols. On one occasion, an overworked pastor pled with the presbytery to postpone organizing more churches until we had more ministers. New groups continued to form, but the number of those committing to ministry also increased. In this, we paid more attention to the men we trained than to the buildings in which we housed and taught them.

The Chiapas Mission above all was interested in the organization of a strong indigenous Mexican church, with the indigenous people integrated with the Spanish-speaking members. The highlight of each year for ministers, elders, and missionaries was the presbytery meeting to which delegates came by plane, train, car, horse, and on foot from the cities, mountains, and jungles. There they reported what had been done, and there, together, they planned what was to be done.

In simple words, evangelization was the core of our mission in Chiapas. But this evangelization was understood according to the New Testament, that is, involving "the proclamation of the gospel of the Kingdom, healing the sick and casting out demons" (Luke 9:1-6; 10:1-12). Through forty-five years of missionary work, Mabel and I have minored in brick and adobe and majored in human hearts.[2]

---

[2]   JRK, "Our Concern at Chiapas," *The Church Herald* (November 4, 1960), 4-5, 30.

CHAPTER 63

1940: A Very Special Year

By 1940 a political order stable enough to replace the Porfiriato had been found. It had taken thirty years and countless deaths, but everyone's hopes were lifted that there was at last the possibility of developing a more stable and prosperous economy. The new order consisted of a one-party state, run by a strictly temporary autocrat, pledged to an ideology of revolutionary nationalism, yet committed to a path of intensive capitalistic development. The system was to last for over fifty years. Obregón and Calles had laid the political and economic foundations. They believed in state-led development based on modern agricultural production and financed by a combination of public and foreign private investment. In this way, a period of stability and growth (1940-82) began to materialize in Mexico. Over the next four decades, the growth of the Mexican economy was prodigious. Mexico was transformed from an agricultural country into a predominantly urban and industrial society.[1]

---

[1] Williamson, *The Penguin History of Latin America*, 399-400.

This was the only way to cross the Grijalva
River before the bridge was built

Chiapas, however, was far from enjoying all these encouraging developments. In fact, during the years from 1942 to 1946, coffee plantations owned by Germans were placed under government control. Deficit and inflation were the cost of the social policies of the government of Cárdenas. Popular protests were limited, and landowners, businessmen, and entrepreneurs strengthened their resistance. The process of industrialization favored the national capital and its foreign partners (mainly the United States), but the rhythm of the agrarian reform was hampered, with serious effects on the indigenous population. The ideology of development prevailed, resulting in benefit for the cities but in economic collapse of rural regions like Chiapas. The production of coffee decreased during these years, and there were no new investments or credit.[2]

At the beginning of all these new processes affecting our state, we moved to San Cristóbal de Las Casas for a period of six months to a house on Mariano Arista N° 35. We delighted in the cool weather of the highlands and the beauty of the small city so packed with colonial history. The move, however, from Tuxtla Gutiérrez to San Cristóbal de Las Casas, was not that easy, in spite of the fact that it was only a sixty-mile trip. It took from four to six hours by car depending on the condition of the roads, but it was just a fifteen-minute trip by plane over the mountains. Such bouncing over what could be called a road

[2]   Zebadúa, *Breve historia de Chiapas*, 161-62.

The bridge over the Grijalva River was a welcome
replacement for the primitive ferry

only by the excessive use of Mexican courtesy was difficult to endure. The climb was to about six thousand feet above Tuxtla. At times, going around the spiral turns up the mountain, one almost expected to meet oneself. Part of the adventure was the crossing of the bridge over the chasm of the Grijalva River, more than one hundred feet deep, which made us hold our breath for fear that one extra pound would make the bridge sag too far down.

San Cristóbal de Las Casas was both a Spanish colonial seat of government and a Maya town. Despite the fact that the *mestizos* gave their name to the country of Mexico, Chiapas was largely inhabited by Maya who, at that time, constituted about 70 percent of the population. In the central part of the state of Chiapas, surrounding San Cristóbal de Las Casas, the indigenous Chamulas predominated. Chamulas wore a homespun woolen blanket with a hole in the middle that slipped over the head, cotton shorts, and leather sandals to which they were prone to nail a part of the tread of a rubber tire. The Chamulas constituted the farming class, carrying their garden produce all over the state. In this town of Las Casas, noted for its fanaticism for the Roman Catholic Church, at great sacrifice, the group of Christian believers endured severe hardships which impacted their bread and butter. Many Christians who engaged in business knew what it meant to be boycotted and the laborers denied work. Yet, in the face of it, they built a lovely church,

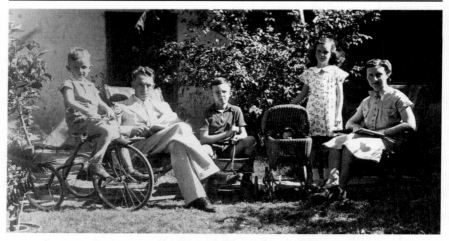

Our happy family relaxing in our Tuxtla home

graduating from holding church in a house, and by their witness to Christ, they shamed their persecutors.[3]

Finally, in June 1940, we moved back to Tuxtla because Mabel was ready to give birth to our fourth child. On July 14, our daughter Margery Ann was born at the American Hospital in Puebla. Mabel flew alone to Puebla and had to deal with all the complications of giving birth to a child by herself. We kept in permanent contact through the mail and especially the telegraph, but I wanted to be by her side on that occasion. Praise God, three weeks after her birth, Margery Ann came floating down out of the sky after a four-hour plane ride with her mother to her excited brothers, sister, and me, her father, in Tuxtla.

In addition to the arrival of Margery, the year of 1940 was very special for us as a family. Roger Dyke, our oldest son, was doing eighth-grade work in our home. He was also preparing to continue with his studies in the United States, remaining there after our next furlough in 1941. Kathleen Joy had a new interest in life being Mabel's helper, caring for our baby. David Warren loved nothing better than to race about town on my horse, although his feet didn't quite reach the stirrups. His little friend, Juanito, wore the clothes David had outgrown without any self-consciousness on the part of either.[4]

---

[3]   Frederick Zimmerman, "Domestic Missions in Mexico Begin a New Era," *The Intelligencer-Leader* (April 21, 1939), 13.

[4]   MVD, "A Home in Chiapas," *The Intelligencer-Leader* (November 22, 1940), 17.

CHAPTER 64

Isidro Estrella

The Lord blessed me with a long missionary ministry of forty-five years. Throughout these years, I faced all sorts of difficulties and challenges, none of which, however, scared me to the point of frustrating my objectives as I understood them to be set by the Lord. I have always buffered friction as much as possible so the work would not suffer any negative consequences. But that meant for me a lot of stress and preoccupation. There were, however, two coworkers who became like thorns in my side. I tried my best to work in harmony with them, but due to different visions, clashes were unavoidable. These two men were José Coffin and Isidro Estrella. I admired and respected them in many ways. I appreciated very much their talents and their many gifts. Their commitment to the work was distinguished and undisputed. But there were moments when I came to consider their attitude too negative and obstructive for the well being of the work. This was particularly true with regard to Isidro Estrella. As Paul did with Peter in Antioch, "I opposed him to his face, because he stood self condemned" (Galatians 2:11).

Isidro Estrella was a Yucatecan (from Yucatán) who came to Chiapas to mess things up. Thinking that a Maya would find the

Ch'ol language easy, I tried to get Roque May to serve in the Ch'ol region when he graduated from the seminary in Mexico City. He was a very promising young man, and I thought that he would probably have little difficulty in learning the Mayan Ch'ol language. I sent in that suggestion to a meeting of the Presbyery of the Gulf that I did not attend. Roque was a good man, so Tabasco had already laid claim to his services. Joaquín Vera got ahead of me and secured him for the Tabasco field, which already had a good number of pastors. Ezequiel Lango, although already retired from Chiapas, was at the meeting and, trying to be helpful, suggested that Isidro Estrella, another Maya, who was without a pastorate and available, might be a good substitute for Roque May to fill the vacant position in Yajalón and its neighboring area. Lango did not know at the time that Estrella had been removed from the church in Ciudad del Carmen (Campeche), but surely Lango should have looked into Estrella's past service more carefully.[1]

Estrella became the pastor in Yajalón in 1943. I believed in his commitment when he wrote me, "Both my wife and I are in the hands of God and capable to face any critical moment that may come, ready to move to Yajalón, Chiapas."[2] The only thing to be determined at that time was the amount of their salary and his preference for a rural ministry rather than an urban one. When they finally moved to Yajalón, I expressed my joy for that and our desire for him to dedicate at least half of his time to work among the Ch'ols.[3] When he arrived in Yajalón, the congregation was at the airfield to welcome him, but regretfully, they saw no one who looked like a minister get off the plane. They expected to see a tall person like Coffin or me. After a few awkward moments, they discovered that the short Maya was the man they were looking for. Estrella never forgave them for that; he often made jokes about tall ministers.

Estrella, nevertheless, started out all right, but soon his violent temper began to show itself. Although his early work was acceptable, the congregation got tired of him because of his pugnacious disposition. One time, I was in Yajalón awaiting the arrival of Mabel the next day. We had almost finished a very fine prayer meeting led by Consuelo Trujillo, when Estrella walked in and dreadfully scolded some of the people because they had moved some dirty *petates* (straw mats) into his room in an effort to clean the place up for Mabel's arrival.[4] I viewed this

---

[1]   JRK, unpublished document, n.d., in JAH.
[2]   IE to JRK, May 26, 1943, in JAH.
[3]   JRK to IE, June 22, 1943, in JAH.
[4]   *Petates* are mats made from woven reeds that many of the indigenous peoples spread on the floor to sleep on.

overreaction as an expression of jealousy. Chanti (J. Santiago González) would not work with or for Estrella because of this, and so the trouble began in the Ch'ol field. Eventually, the consistory of the Yajalón church, the governing body of the area, asked the Presbytery of the Gulf that Estrella be removed. I tried to keep myself out of the picture and uninvolved. But since the local church had also asked the presbytery not to send him back, he believed I was the main cause of the petition. He knew how much the Yajalón people relied on my counsel.

These tensions, regretfully, reached the Presbytery of the Gulf. Coffin was the only Chiapas person or representative in the presbytery and was a much-respected leader, but he did nothing to mollify the situation. At the presbytery meeting in Ciudad del Carmen (Campeche), with Coffin again as the only representative from Chiapas and with Isidro Estrella as secretary, there was an opportunity for revenge. In my absence, Estrella drummed up charges against me. Every time one of these accusations was struck down at this special meeting, Estrella remarked: "Es que sospechamos" (We are suspicious). Genaro de la Rosa was such a clever and vocal defender of my case that Roque May, the president, ruled that Genaro would no longer receive *la palabra* (the right to speak), which was highly irregular and illegal.

At the meeting of the presbytery in Comalcalco (Tabasco), March 19-23, 1947, a number of improper things happened for which I was held directly responsible. First, no Chiapas elders attended the meeting. The attendance of elders, however, was the responsibility of the ministers, not me. In fact, it was Coffin's business, not mine, to see that elder delegates were appointed. But I was blamed for their absence. Second, I was held responsible because no consistorial minutes appeared at the meeting. That also was not my responsibility. The minutes of the Second Regional Committee (Chiapas) had not reached the Presbytery of the Gulf on time because a Maya member of the church in Tuzantán had been elected secretary, and he did not know what it was all about. The inexperienced elder had neglected to send these. So, I was blamed for the late report. Third, I was accused of having sent Nehemías García to Mexico City for his second year of studies in the seminary without the previous approval of the presbytery. In reality, Nehemías had gone to the city to accompany his very sick mother. And fourth, I was accused of organizing the Chiapas Christian Endeavor Union, again without the approval of the presbytery. Alfonso Marín and I had both counseled the young people in Chiapas. Both of us helped them organize their different societies into a union for annual meetings, and at that time, it did not occur to us that we were doing anything contrary to the will of the presbytery.

Estrella, as secretary of the presbytery, wanted me to be declared a *persona non grata* and asked the board to take me out of the country. In a letter sent to the board, in the name of the Presbytery of the Gulf, and signed by Isidro Estrella as permanent secretary, Estrella mentions the resolutions adopted in the meeting at Comalcalco, Tabasco:

1 To respectfully ask the Board of Missions of the Reformed Church that they diminish the economical help which they impart in the Chiapas field of this Presbytery, thus giving us the opportunity to prepare the field for self support until we reach the total nationalization of our Presbytery, as this is the wish of all of the nationals and of the Presbytery.

2. Very attentively we ask the same Board that in the shortest possible time you retire your representative in Chiapas, Rev. John R. Kempers, because he does not suit the Presbytery and the work in Chiapas.

3. That if the Reformed Mission thinks of sending another representative to Chiapas, that this person come prepared to collaborate with the Presbytery and ready to obey the dispositions and actions of the Presbytery. This is an indispensable condition for the entrance of another missionary of the Reformed Church in Chiapas, to the field of this Presbytery.[5]

Coffin, with one word, could have put a stop to all of this, but he chose to remain silent. After all, I had been giving him a hard time because of his constant absence from the field, and he never approved of our work among young people.

When word of this action reached Chiapas, there was an immediate outcry of protest. Letters from individuals and church organizations poured into the synod office. There it was decided to call a special meeting of the Presbytery of the Gulf to reconsider the matter in Xinatitlán, equidistant from Tabasco and Chiapas delegates. The presbytery and Coffin received a tremendous surprise when elders from all but one of the Chiapas churches appeared.

The accusations were so easily refuted that the secretary was made to look ridiculous. As I said, Coffin could have prevented the whole thing had he been emphatic in the Comalcalco meeting. But he was peeved because I had reduced his salary when he spent month after month away from Chiapas, pretending that he had some *nombramiento* (appointment) to do special work, which was all a pretense. My argument

---

[5]   IE to Board of the Reformed Church in America, April 8, 1947, in JAH.

was that if people named him for work outside of Chiapas, they had to pay his salary for that period of time. Now, beyond all of this, it was clear to me that Estrella was trying to oust me from Chiapas.[6] Why?

Estrella most likely had the same reasons to put me down that Coffin had. The dominant issue in most of his letters to me in the months and years that followed his arrival in Yajalón had to do with his salary and an increase in his income. Issues of vacation (a one-month, paid vacation free of any duties) and the reimbursement of all travel expenses were issues of permanent complaint. On the other hand, he was faithful in reporting his activities in various places and particularly his slow progress in learning the Ch'ol language. Two other subjects of conversation were the construction of a church for Yajalón and a training course for Ch'ol lay workers. I admit that most of these issues caused tension and misunderstanding because I had total control of the funds sent by the Reformed Church Mission for the churches in Chiapas. People complained that I was too "thrifty," and I thought that most of them were too "abusive" and inclined to dependency.

Besides, by the end of 1943, Estrella faced two problems that discouraged him and turned him against me. On the one hand, he had asked for my recommendation on behalf of a young man named Clemente Oscar Trujillo, so that he could receive a scholarship to study at the Instituto Bíblico del Sureste (Bible Institute of the Southeast), in Xocempich, Yucatán. I thought the boy was not all there mentally and denied a recommendation. I encouraged Estrella to guide him in taking advantage of all the training opportunities open at the local congregation. I made it clear that, in my opinion, in consultation with Ezequiel Lango, who also knew him, he was not qualified for any lay or ordained ministry.[7]

On the other hand, I had received a letter from somebody by the name of Jesús Venegas with a number of complaints against brother Estrella, which I mentioned to him one by one. I pointed out the fact that Mariano Constantino was occupying a section of the parsonage with his tailor shop and that this had to be terminated.[8] Estrella responded to both issues, but somehow he was hurt by them. His letter was written in harsh terms.

> In answer to your written communication of December 7, 1943, I inform you that I have passed [this issue] to the consideration

[6]   JRK, unpublished document, n.d., in JAH.
[7]   IE to JRK, Nov. 26, 1943, in JAH.
[8]   JRK to IE, Dec.7, 1943, in JAH.

of the Executive of the H. Presbytery and the Justice Commission, due to the fact that it has been dealt with irresponsibly. Such an accusation involves a good measure of slander. Another part comes from sources that are more occupied in destruction than in construction, and they are not active members of the congregation. Besides, there is no such Jesús Venegas in the congregation. That signature is fake. The president of the Christian Endeavor Society is Don Pedro Venegas, and he is the author of the letter.

It is true that I have lodged Mariano Constantino, but there has been no discontent because of this, except from one and him only. You launched your observation on this issue without investigating how much of it is true. Are not these the same who removed the worker Ovando? Or Don Límbano Trujillo? Are these the same elements that discharged Don Febronio Lara? And now is it my turn? Besides, if Mariano Constantino lives in the house, it is because there is a reason. All of them are family. I have not lodged any stranger or pagan in the house. It is true that my brother-in-law was with me, but that was temporary and not permanent, and the brethren agreed with him living here. If you want to come to be aware, you may come with all confidence, even when I believe it will be useless, because I think that first I will come out of here as soon as possible.[9]

I perceived a wrong attitude on his part and responded to him by pointing out three things: First, he said he was writing on a "particular issue" but did it using the official stationery of the Gulf of Mexico Presbytery, subtitling his heading with N° 187 of the Permanent Secretariat and calling my personal letter "official." Second, I told him that I perceived certain emotional exaltation in his making a big issue of a rather small thing, to the point that he even suggested the possibility of leaving Yajalón "as soon as possible." I had to tell him that if a pastor intends to run out every time somebody in the congregation criticizes his work, it would be better for him to get movable furniture because he will never settle anywhere. None of us is so perfect that we do all things as they should be done, and it is natural that we will be criticized. Sometimes criticism is wrongly founded, but sometimes it has some basis, and the wise pastor, instead of defending himself, should know how to accept critique for his own good and for the well being of the work.[10]

---

9   IE to JRK, Dec. 14, 1943, in JAH.
10 JRK to IE, Dec. 24, 1943, in JAH.

Beyond the anecdotal character of these controversies and disagreements, the real problem with Estrella was that he was too close to José Coffin and his desire to control the work in Chiapas. By then I was trying my best to organize the Presbyterian churches that were emerging as a result of a dynamic process of evangelization. My vision was to establish consistories in each congregation and to try to get enough trained and ordained pastors so as to have our own presbytery in the state of Chiapas. Coffin did not share this vision and influenced leaders such as Estrella to prevent the development of local congregations to become more efficient and better organized in their work. Time after time, I had to face this type of conflict, which became even more serious because of the fact that I was the administrator of the resources placed by the Reformed Church in Chiapas. A portion of the salaries of most pastors, including Coffin's; the construction projects; the organization of the Christian Endeavor and the Women's Societies; and the printing ministry were under my responsibility and were financed by the mission.

Estrella's opposition did not end after the Comalcalco Presbytery. Later, he and Joaquín Vera still tired themselves trying to take the Tumbalá people away from the Yajalón Consistory. Also, after some years, at the riverfront in Villahermosa (Tabasco), I urged Vera one day not to install Estrella as pastor of the Villahermosa church. I told him that Estrella would cause trouble, and once installed, they would not be able to get rid of him. Vera laughed and said that, if Estrella did not behave, with one snap of the finger, he would be gone. Trouble soon developed, and after much fighting and scheming, Estrella left the Villahermosa church and took a group with him. Later he left the ministry, but his destructive work left bitter fruit.[11]

In spite of all this dissension, during those years, the Prince of Peace (Príncipe de Paz) Presbyterian Church in Yajalón was organized with its corresponding authority, the consistory. This consistory belonged to the Gulf of Mexico Presbytery because the Chiapas Presbytery was not yet organized. The pastoral work in that large Ch'ol-speaking field was coordinated from Yajalón. The pastors (presbyters) that frequently visited the new work in Tumbalá and other neighboring places like Chilón—Daniel Aguilar Ochoa and José Cruz Antonio—were sent by this dynamic congregation in Yajalón. They also received with open arms the first Reformed Church missionaries to work among the Ch'ols, Garold and Ruth Van Engen, who arrived there in 1944. Their

---

[11] JRK, unpublished document, n.d., in JAH.

arrival and work helped relieve me of the heavy burden I had borne for a good number of churches in the region.

As for the work in Chiapas, all the controversies and frustrations named above resulted in the fulfillment of my cherished dream. At a special Minatitlán meeting, all our elders declared that they wanted a Chiapas Presbytery immediately. When Coffin voiced a contrary opinion, the Las Margaritas elders, who were so subject to him, demurred. The whole affair sped up the organization of our presbytery by many years. And we were rid of Estrella, Coffin, and Joaquín Vera's opposition to the organization, development, and progress of the work of the Lord in Chiapas.[12]

---

[12]   Ibid.

CHAPTER 65

Garold and Ruth Van Engen

In the early 1940s, Mexico's political leaders relaxed their antichurch prohibitions, and the door to missionaries opened slightly. Rev. Garold and Ruth Van Engen slipped into Mexico in 1943. They became our first missionary reinforcements in Chiapas, after eighteen years of working alone. After some studies of the Spanish language in Mexico City, during the week of Easter in 1944, the Van Engens departed from friends and fellow students and began their southward journey. The four months they spent in Mexico City studying Spanish grammar helped them to understand most conversations. But when they arrived in Chiapas, they had a lot of work to do with the new language. The trip from Mexico City to Tuxtla was tiring for them, because it took two days and two nights on a train that seldom traveled more than thirty miles per hour. There was, however, a certain thrill in knowing that they were coming to a state where they hoped to have their permanent residence. The scenery on the way was charming, with different views, different vegetation, different customs in dress, and different landscapes nearly every hundred miles. Since it was the dry season, they saw many arid places, but the beauty of the mountains

I introduced Garold to the adventure and challenge
of travel on the trails of Chiapas

and numerous villages on the way removed much of the boredom and
captured their admiration and delight.[1]

When they arrived in Tuxtla Gutiérrez, they stayed with Mabel
and me for several months. They began their missionary career in
Chiapas in the spring of 1944, and they did it with great passion and
humility. In an article Ruth and Garold wrote for the *Church Herald*,
they expressed their expectations at that time: "It is impossible to say
as yet in what part of Chiapas we shall be located. . . . Our prayer is for
God's guidance. The field is so large, and there are so many places which
need Christian workers that it is difficult to know just where to go. The
final decision will be made with the aid of Mr. Kempers, who knows the
field much better than we will know it for years to come."[2] During those
months, we took basically two trips to visit the mission stations in the
northern part of the state.

We started our first trip in San Cristóbal de Las Casas and began
our wayward trek toward Chilón, which was a two-day journey by horse.
In Chilón, we had a small congregation eager to know more about the
Bible. It was here that Garold first realized the great task which was
ahead of the itinerant missionary. The people were eager to learn,

[1]   Ruth and Garold Van Engen, "The Land of Our Adoption," *The Church Herald*
(August 11, 1944), 22.
[2]   Ibid.

It took a lot of courage for Garold and Alejandro Barrios
to cross this bridge

but they did not have the opportunity. We left Chilón immediately
after Sunday school in order to help the people in Yajalón with their
afternoon meeting. From there, we went to Petalcingo and held a
service, then to Moyos, where we stayed for a couple of days having
services both evenings and also a children's hour in the morning. In
Tumbalá, a predominantly Maya town, we had a large crowd of people
ready to receive the message in their native Ch'ol language. We started
our homeward journey in Tumbalá, stopping at Yajalón where they were
laying the foundation of their new church. We finally reached Las Casas,
and these two weeks of travel were for Garold not only interesting but
also challenging. He could feel the greatness of the task and realized
that in our own strength, we would not be able to do the work that was
needed.

Our second trip took just a month. Leaving Tuxtla Gutiérrez, we
spent several days at Las Casas, getting things ready. During the month,
we held twenty-five services and called on many homes where the Bible
was read and prayers offered. Many days we had two services, and one
day we held four. Mazapa was the only place we spent more than one
evening. We used it as a central location for several short trips.[3] I tried

---

3   Garold Van Engen, "First Travels in Mexico," *The Church Herald* (November 24,
     1944), 9.

I found a dependable and faithful
partner in Garold Van Engen

to do with Garold what Coffin did with me when I had first arrived in Chiapas. Through the years, Garold thanked me for these experiences that helped him so much in affirming his missionary call and his personal commitment to serve the Lord in Chiapas.

After traveling to the various mission stations, trying to get some idea where they would be needed most, the Van Engens decided to spend their first term of service in the village of Yajalón. Their objective was to prepare themselves to serve the Ch'ol converts in that area. The first three years were difficult for them as they tried to learn the language, customs, and ways of the natives; understand the work system of the local groups; and adapt themselves to a new lifestyle and missionary strategy. Yajalón was their first home in Chiapas, and they extended their labors to neighboring Tumbalá.

Garold taught weekly classes to young people in the congregation at Tumbalá who were interested in receiving ministerial training. Through an interpreter, he shared exegetical materials for the Sunday preachers. A good number of faithful church leaders were under his tutelage. They received biblical instruction and doctrinal orientation.[4] The tropical climate, however, quickly undermined Ruth's health, and the doctor urged them to return to the United States or to at least find a cooler climate. In 1947 they moved to the city of San Cristóbal de Las Casas, located at seven thousand feet elevation. There they teamed

---

[4]   Esponda, *El presbiterianismo en Chiapas*, 60-61.

This Bible school class in San Cristóbal provided
a half-dozen ministers for Chiapas

up with a dynamic, capable Mexican minister, Rev. Daniel Aguilar
Ochoa. Together they developed a Bible school and established a press
for religious publications.[5] In San Cristóbal, Garold and Ruth assisted
in the Spanish-speaking Bible Institute of Chiapas as administrator
and teacher from 1948 to 1966. Van Engen also served as director
and treasurer of the Chiapas Mission. His work included Bible school
administration, leadership, stewardship, and evangelism workshops
and administration relating to government regulations for the
missionaries.

Garold was like a 4x4 off-road truck. Some missionaries planted
vegetable gardens and fruit trees for personal use and as demonstration
plots. For a few years, vegetable seeds were sold at a low price to encourage
the neighbors to plant their own gardens. Garold became involved by
default in this vegetable seed project. Seeds were readily available in San
Cristóbal, so he sent seeds in bulk via the Mission Aviation Fellowship
(MAF) plane to the Stegengas in Berea, to the Ch'ols, and to the Buenos
Aires Ranch among the Tzeltals to be measured and repackaged in
small envelopes for resale.[6] He was also the supplier of medicine for the
various clinics in the state. Sam Hofman, for example, ordered medicine

5   JSH, "The History of the Chiapas Mission," 7.
6   DDM, *Ministry among the Maya*, 351.

and equipment from Garold on the San Cristóbal end of this supply line. From 1965 to 1978, Garold received the paramedics' lists, boxed up the requested medicine, and took it to the MAF base for transport to the remote villages. At one time, Garold was providing medical supplies for more than eighty paramedics. He and Salomón López, a *mestizo* church leader from Las Margaritas, began a small business that provided, at a lower cost, most of the medicine used by paramedics in their dispensaries. Garold's part in the medical work made possible the growing success of the clinic program. This service was another facet of Garold's ministry in Chiapas—a task he willingly carried out.[7]

Another very important contribution he made had to do with leadership training. The answer to providing an alternative approach to leadership education lay in a specialized program—Theological Education by Extension (TEE). Since 1968, when Garold introduced the program (which pioneered in Guatemala), TEE study programs brought new life to *mestizo* and indigenous congregations. The Van Engens were closely associated with this ministry. Even their house in San Cristóbal, the spacious U-shaped house next door to the Presbyterian Church property, was donated to hold week-long leadership training courses or "Bible institutes" for the Tzotzil church leaders.

Garold was also very much involved in the ministry of the printed page. He was particularly committed to the publications of Wycliffe, more specifically, their four-page Tzeltal paper, the *True Word*, which was begun in 1956 by the Wycliffe team in Corralito. Material was sent to and from Garold in San Cristóbal by the MAF plane. Garold proofread the articles and then printed copies of the paper on the mission's linotype printing press. But when copies of the paper arrived in Corralito, they stayed there until visiting natives could carry them to distant congregations. Issued sporadically for about nine years, the *True Word* eventually died because of difficulties in delivery and payment.[8]

Garold became for me a great blessing sent by God. He had gifts that I did not, and we comprised a very effective team in the projects we carried out. His talents were many, and his gifts as an administrator were particularly outstanding. The work was growing very fast and extending to many places. I would not have been able to handle such an increasingly complex field without the assistance of this gifted man. Evangelization, leadership training, medical ministry, social assistance, church construction, and the permanent tensions related to any

[7]   Ibid., 326.
[8]   Ibid., 231.

Garold and Ruth Van Engen were ideal partners in ministry
(*courtesy J. Samuel and Helen Hofman*)

institutional and denominational development would have led me to
an early burnout. But the Lord provided our mission with Ruth and
Garold Van Engen at just the right time.

All these tasks and ministries in which I became involved through
many years of hard work needed a mind capable of administering and
organizing the resources required to carry out the work. That was
Garold Van Engen. His personal commitment to the responsibilities
assigned to him was extraordinary. For me, he was truly the choicest
ministry partner that I could have had in the years after I broke with
Coffin. I had acted as director and treasurer of the mission for thirty-
eight years and as director for two more years. Garold, who was second
in seniority, was asked to be the mission director after we moved to
Mexico City in 1966. Garold was always a good, hard-working, and
approachable administrator. The staff believed he was sensitive to their
concerns and willing to be helpful, whatever the need.[9]

The same could be said of the wonderful relationship of Ruth
and Mabel. They constituted a dynamic team, particularly working in
the promotion of women's ministries and youth organizations. Their
efforts in training young girls for ministry were honored with the
creation of the Mabel and Ruth Bible School for Women.

---

[9]   Ibid., 198.

The Van Engens were very special to Mabel and me. Garold was born in Prairie City, Iowa, on October 30, 1913, and Ruth Muyskens was born in Alton, Iowa, on October 10, 1915. Growing up on a farm near Lincoln, Nebraska, Garold received his education at Central College in Pella, Iowa. Ruth went to Northwestern Junior College (Orange City, Iowa), the same college where I had studied years before. She graduated from Central College in Pella, Iowa, in 1940 and subsequently taught school in Northwest Iowa. Garold wanted to go to China as a missionary, and Ruth wanted to join her brother, John D. Muyskens, an RCA missionary to India. But it was war time, and the RCA was not sending missionaries to either China or India.

In 1943 Garold graduated from Western Theological Seminary in Holland, Michigan. Like me, Garold also served as a summer intern in one of the RCA's Native American missions in Winnebago, Nebraska. As he was graduating, the leaders of the Board of Domestic Missions approached him and Ruth, inviting them to consider going as missionaries to Chiapas.

The Van Engens were married in 1943. They were commissioned by the RCA General Synod on June 6 of that year, and then they moved to Mexico. They were the first RCA missionaries to join us after eighteen years of our mission activities in Chiapas. Garold and Ruth had four children: Ronald John (August 20, 1944), Bernice Rose (December 9, 1945), Charles Edward (September 25, 1948), and Elizabeth Ann (January 25, 1954).[10] Retirement in 1978 took them to Orange City, Iowa, packed with wonderful memories of the mission field and with lots of spiritual fruit before the glorious throne of our Lord.

---

[10]   Adapted from a brochure published by the General Program Council of the Reformed Church, n.d., in JAH and personal conversation with Charles Van Engen, July 15, 2014.

CHAPTER 66

Persecution and Hostilities

In October 1944, Rev. Isidro Estrella wrote me reporting the difficulties he was facing in Yajalón with the local authorities. He had received a notification from the Administrador de Rentas (income administrator) to come to the Oficina de Hacienda (finance office). He went there and spent a whole morning with officials telling him that he had to submit his income taxes. He was forced to do that, which represented for him a considerable amount of money. The government wanted to tax him. They considered his very low salary "as a professional" a source of income. But my suspicion was that all this was another way of pressuring evangelical leaders and hindering their ministry. My suggestion to Estrella was for him to contact higher-level authorities, because to my knowledge, none of the nationals was paying income taxes. On the other hand, I asked him to encourage the believers in Amado Nervo who were suffering some sort of persecution. I told him that, if they were able to suffer this persecution for a while, the enemies of the gospel would get used to having evangelicals in their midst. They would leave them in peace, as was the case in Tumbalá, where believers were exempt from paying the expenses of the pagan festivities.[1]

[1]   JRK to IE, Oct. 6, 1944, in JAH.

Ch'ol prisoners were dependent on
family members for their food

These types of situations were not new in Chiapas or in the rest of the nation. We developed most of our ministry under the shadow of persecution, hostilities, and opposition. Mabel and I were still studying Spanish in Jalapa in 1926 when we received the news that laws against foreign priests and missionaries were to be enforced. That was upsetting, but little did we realize that it was the least of many blows still to come. Later our efforts at developing medical work came to naught because of Mexico's refusal to license more foreign doctors. Then the mission schools, one by one, were forced to the wall by impossible requirements. Later the number per state of Mexican ministers and priests allowed to officiate was reduced to zero or to some impossibly low number. Afterward, in several states, including Chiapas, the Catholic churches and some evangelical chapels were closed altogether, whereas a former law simply restricted religious services to church buildings. On and after November 20, 1934, images of saints were dragged from churches and publicly burned, and each government employee and teacher was forced to contribute one image to the bonfire.

That return to medievalism seems to have been the turning point. From the beginning of 1935, because of political shakeups, including the split between the former dictator Elías Calles and President Lazaro Cárdenas, and because of the return of more rational thinking, there were unmistakable signs that the storm was blowing over.

During our first ten years of service in Chiapas, however, Mabel and I continued to minister under very oppressive conditions. A lot of water had gone under the bridge of religious freedom, but instead of improving, conditions for believers and churches seemed to get worse. By 1936 we evaluated the situation in terms of what had been wrought. It is interesting to check the damage after trouble. What was left of the Protestant churches in Mexico after ten years of increasing restrictions? We tried to ascertain what the evangelical churches had lost. The answer was that practically every loss had been turned to gain. The evangelical church in Mexico, by 1936, was stronger by far, larger, and more secure than it had been ten years before.

The time to shift the responsibility for directing the work in Mexico from the missionaries to the Mexicans had to come sooner or later. Because of government rulings, the transition period came sooner than expected, but the process was less painful. Persecution weeds out the weak and strengthens all the rest, but we knew of only two or three who, for fear of losing a government position or because of another pressure, gave up their faith. Atheistic propaganda swept along a great many young people, especially among the teachers. They were mostly former Catholics, who could give no reason "for the faith that was in them," not Protestants who had thought through their beliefs before the crisis.

The one loss which we cannot as yet count as gain was the closing of our church schools and the restrictions placed on the Presbyterian Seminary in Mexico City. In those years, our prayer was for some day to know why God, in his providence, allowed that our boys and girls might attend schools where nonreligion and atheism were frankly taught. This situation naturally reduced the number of students who would be guided into the ministry by mission school teachers.

Restrictions in Mexico and the loss of support at home greatly reduced the number of missionaries in Mexico. Those of us who were able to carry on felt like veterans and were able to rejoice in victory with the Mexican believers. There were trying days and weeks and months, but with the passing of years, we sensed that we had won, although not in the sense that restrictive laws were rescinded. Catholic churches in many states were sealed for years, and those Protestant churches that were closed for one reason or another could not for decades obtain permission to reopen. But the atmosphere changed little by little in the coming years. During the 1940s and 1950s, we went about more freely preaching and distributing the Bible. All of us learned that even though there might be more serious restrictions at some time in the future, the church of Christ would prevail and progress in spite of it all.[2]

[2] JRK, "Mexico after Ten Years," p. 12.

Persecution and opposition increased when a particular group of people came to the Lord in large numbers. That was the case with the massive conversions experienced by the Ch'ol in some areas. In good measure, this was due to the work of Wycliffe translators, who put the New Testament in the Ch'ol language. This brought hundreds of new believers. The increase of evangelicals aroused the ire of the Mexican ranchers who exploited the natives for their products and labor and sold them liquor. They struck back after a Catholic church accidentally burned to the ground during a fiesta and had six Ch'ol evangelicals arrested for arson. The prisoners were soaked with gasoline and paraded before a mob. An accuser struck a match and held the flame perilously close to their clothing, while he threatened: "Confess or I'll burn you alive." Later, the Ch'ols were tricked into signing a confession in Spanish, which they could neither read nor understand.

Three of the prisoners were sentenced to long prison terms. Appeals for their release went to the highest offices in Mexico City. Scores of intellectuals signed a petition, but the last prisoner did not gain freedom until 1958.[3] Nothing, however, could hinder the advance of their Christian testimony and its undeniable transformation of the lives of people. Economic advance kept pace with the spiritual growth of the Ch'ol church. The first man in the village of Amado Nervo to wear shoes was a believer and was also the first to own a horse. That was also the case with the first man to ignore the threats of the ranchers and petition the government for land. The land rush gained such momentum that the supply of cheap Maya labor dried up, and the ranchers were forced to sell their estates to the Ch'ols.[4]

---

[3]   James C. Hefley, "The Challenge of the Ch'ols," *The Church Herald* (November 1, 1968), 7.

[4]   Ibid., 7-8.

CHAPTER 67

The Power of the Book

How magnificent is the Word of God! What God says is true and powerful. The Lord affirmed, "For as the rain and the snow come down from heaven and do not return there until they have watered the earth, making it bring forth and sprout, giving seed to the sower and bread to the eater, so shall my word be that goes out from my mouth; it shall not return to me empty, but it shall accomplish that which I purpose and succeed in the thing for which I sent it" (Isaiah 55:10-11). In Chiapas we have witnessed this again and again. The Bible has proved to be a powerful book for us.

Many have found new life in the words of truth and hope found in a Bible which had been laid providentially in their path. After committing a crime on the Mexican side of the border, Abundio Alfaro found it comparatively easy to slip across to the Guatemalan side, but such was his temper and his behavior that before long, he would have to flee again to find refuge in Mexican territory.

Even bad men occasionally make a serious effort to earn a decent living, and Abundio obtained work as a cattleman, for which he was especially fitted by early training. He worked hard, and under his care, the herd multiplied. Abundio's boss was well satisfied with his work, but another employee was envious, so when, because of his own carelessness, a young bull died, that employee shifted the blame to Abundio, who then lost his job. It was not the loss of the job that rankled Abundio so much as the mean treachery of his fellow cattlehand. So the old spirit took hold of him again, and he made plans for vengeance. Abundio was not afraid, and he knew how to kill. One morning, he explained to his wife what he was about to do, and he set out.

On the way to find his enemy, deeply engrossed in bitter thoughts, he accidentally kicked an object lying in the path. It was a small book, and Abundio, who had some knowledge of reading, examined it. The verses he read might not impress a person under ordinary circumstances. But the God of heaven was using his written Word to save a soul from hell that day, so Abundio stopped in his tracks. Soon he was home again, to the surprise of his wife. His bitterness had left him. His voice was calm. When his wife asked him for an explanation, they sat down together to read. God, through his providence and through his Word, had saved a criminal who later became an elder of the church in Tapachula.

In another case, the Bible was a book set on a post. This was the experience of Martín, a Mexican peon. The Mexican peon begins his work at early dawn and quits for the day in the early afternoon to have dinner at home. He takes the morning meal with him in a *morral* (woven twine bag) slung over his shoulder or the pommel of his saddle. Martín had been detailed to cut weeds in a pasture, so he started off to the field early with machete and *morral*. As he came to the scene of his work, he was about to hang his jacket and his *morral* on a fence post as countless peons did, but to his surprise, someone had left a little book on that particular post. He spent quite a bit of the coolest time of day reading it when he should have been hacking weeds. At lunch time, he practically forgot to eat in his eagerness to read. The stories he read produced in him conviction of sin, and he surrendered his life to Jesus Christ as Lord and Savior. Martín was born again as a result, and the others he won to Christ are now living souls.

For many people, the Bible is merely an interesting book dealing with fancy stories and religious issues. For the government of Mexico, during our years of missionary work, it was a book whose reading was not convenient for the intellectual health of a person. For most people, the Bible has been the "forgotten" book. But there was somebody who "forgot" the Bible on purpose. Land distribution has always been quite a jigsaw puzzle in Chiapas. Those who plant corn often have to travel many miles to their fields at plowing and planting time and in harvest. One believer took his large Bible with him but wrapped it in old newspapers to hide it from those hostile to the Christian faith. He found lodging in a fanatical home and hoped for some opportunity to introduce the subject of religion prudently. But to his sorrow, up to the time for taking his departure, he had failed. Though his Bible, because of its size, had cost him several pesos, he pretended to have forgotten it and went his way. The family, with a natural curiosity, unwrapped the package to see what he had left and what the nature of the book was. The Spirit of God can soften the hardest hearts. When the man returned to harvest his crop, the whole family had found Christ and had formed a little congregation in their home.

There are occasions when the Bible is a dangerous book. Doña Simona was no ordinary woman. She had a temper and a will of her own. She was a *beata* (devout Roman Catholic woman) and assisted the priest. Colporteurs came from everywhere to sell the scriptures, and one day, a brave man sold a Bible to Doña Simona's husband, a saloon keeper. His fanatical wife gave him a tongue lashing when he brought that book home. Had he not heard the priest say repeatedly that the Protestant Bible was of the devil? Strangely, the book was not destroyed, but neither was it read. Being pushed around with other stored things, it finally lost its cover; the pages, however, although unread, remained intact.

One day, the news came to Doña Simona that her saloon keeper husband had been killed. It is almost unbelievable what exaggerated grief Latins can demonstrate and apparently feel instantaneously. Doña Simona contemplated suicide but then thought better of it. She did, however, want to do something desperate, so she looked for the condemned book. Holding it at arm's length, she began to read, expecting some explosion or evil to befall her. The verse she providentially read was "sweeter than honey and drippings of the honeycomb." She sat down and read on and on. Mabel and I have long known Doña Simona as a church member, and we know some of those who are believers because of her and in turn have won others. Foolish men sit at their desks and write books and prepare lectures which reflect the doubts in their own minds about the divine origin of the scriptures, and they pound away with destructive reasoning. Meanwhile, the old Book quietly ignores them and goes right on accomplishing that to which God has destined it.[1]

Finally, there are times when the Bible becomes a defensive book. The author of Hebrews compares the Word of God with a two-edged

---

[1]   JRK, "My Word Shall Not Return unto Me Void," *The Church Herald* (November 21, 1947), 16-17, 28.

sword. The apostle Paul calls it "the sword of the Spirit" and describes it as an integral part of the armor of God that the believer has to use for both defending oneself and attacking the enemy. In Chiapas, we have seen the defensive power of the Bible being applied on more than one occasion. A friend of one of the believers was taken ill and came to the Christian's home in order to receive medical attention. As the days went by, the hostess explained the gospel to her sick friend, who gradually understood and accepted the good news and began a new life. Then a Catholic priest missionary came to see her as he passed through town. He asked her to confess her sins, but she replied, "I have already confessed my sins to Christ." The priest insisted that this was a false Protestant teaching, but the sick woman explained to him that her Christian friend had told her about Jesus and that it was not necessary to confess to men. The priest became infuriated. Just then, the hostess returned from her marketing, and hearing that the priest was there, she entered the house with fear and trembling. The priest began to upbraid her for teaching false doctrines. An elder of our church, hearing the commotion, entered the house and began to talk with the priest, who continued to rage. The nuns who accompanied him were crying, for they saw that the elder was winning in the conversation. Finally, the priest, noticing that the elder was calm and composed, changed his attitude. He asked the elder to visit him at the manse so that they might talk in private. The neighbors gathered around, for the rumor had spread that the elder was beating the priest, and the poor priest was suffering at the hands of the elder. No doubt the priest did suffer, because our dear brother in the faith used the sword of the Spirit, and the enemy could not counterattack the servant of the Lord brandishing the two-edged weapon.[2]

---

[2]   Garold Van Engen, "The Holy Spirit at Work—In Mexico," *The Church Herald* (November 13, 1953), 8.

CHAPTER 68

God Cares for His Own

What a wonderful biblical truth this was for us in Chiapas! Again and again, Mabel and I repeated together the words of the apostle Paul in Philipians 4:6: "Do not worry about anything, but in everything, by prayer and supplication with thanksgiving, let your requests be made known to God." God does care for his very own. From time to time, this has been clear and evident in our work in Mexico. Three instances come to mind that show how, in the providence of God, plots to harm his children are brought to naught.

The very first article written by us in Chiapas and distributed in the Reformed Church was illustrated with a picture of the roofless, doorless, windowless, and overgrown ruins of a huge colonial Catholic church in the Maya village of Tumbalá, in Ch'ol territory. The gospel came to the Ch'ol Maya some years later. The first services were held under an arbor, but soon a wooden church was built by the missionary and the *mestizo* layworker, some three blocks from the old Catholic church ruins. Immediately the congregation outgrew that small chapel as four or five hundred natives came to worship. Audiences in the United States have expressed audible "ah"s when shown a slide of the neglected

The huge Catholic church in Tumbalá was an abandoned shell

Catholic church building followed by a slide of the huge crowd of white-clad Ch'ols sitting on the grass near their chapel. At their own initiative and their own expense, these natives built a large, fine stone church in which to worship.

This stirred up the members of the old colonial Catholic Church. The natives, many of them unbelievers, were prodded into donating money and furnishing labor to recondition the old structure. Time, money, and energy were spent laboriously rebuilding the towers first. At that time, many predicted that in a few years, the old Roman church building would be restored to much of its former glory and splendor. This would have fostered continued drinking and superstition, which are the byproducts of the marriage of Roman Catholic ceremonies with pagan indigenous beliefs. Just when the reconstruction of the towers was completed, however, the powers of heaven sent lightning down those towers and blasted them to bits.

One of the consecrated families of the Tuxtla Gutiérrez church had a wayward daughter, Bertha. While living with her married brother, a deacon in the church, she was keeping company with a married man of very unsavory reputation. In spite of the protests of her brother and parents, she eloped with this man who had promised to secure a divorce from his wife and marry her. The divorce was obtained, and although he continued to live with Bertha, he did not marry her, and soon children were born. The man lived a bestial life, and Bertha suffered physically, mentally, and spiritually. There were more promises of marriage, but

An impressive church was built in the remote village of Tumbalá

suddenly, true to character, although he still supported and dominated the foolish Bertha, he married another woman.

At last, when conditions became unbearable, Bertha's brother, the deacon, helped her to escape with her two children to Mexico City. Somehow the man learned where she was and that her brother had aided her escape. He vowed to wreak terrible vengeance on Bertha's brother, the deacon. The man's drinking crony, knowing that this was not a vain threat, in alarm passed the word along by relatives to the deacon. The deacon's mother-in-law, a God-fearing woman, answered that no harm would befall those who trusted God. Soon after this, the threatening man complained of a severe headache. Despite sedatives, the pain increased. When the doctor arrived, the man was already dead of a cerebral hemorrhage.

These two incidents may be added to the ever-growing list of constant reminders that we are in the Lord's work and that he who controls the lightning of heaven and the sparrow's fall looks after his own and prospers his work.[1]

There is a third illustration of God's care, which is seen particularly toward those whom God has set apart for ministry. That was the case with Fancisco Gómez Nimail. In the making of a minister, many forces converge. In the separation of Francisco "unto the gospel," God used: an obedient, Spirit-led deacon; a Stanford University trained, non-

[1]   JRK, "Therefore Do Not Be Anxious," *The Church Herald* (November 14, 1952), 4.

The first two Tzeltal ministers, Francisco Gomez and Manuel López, were students in our home (*courtesy J. Samuel and Helen Hofman*)

Christian engineer; and the prayers of believers in many lands for God to raise up a man to lead Tzeltal believers.

When the call of God came to him, Francisco gave up his position as a school teacher with a good salary in a government school in his home area of Mesbilja. He had to endure the misunderstanding and gossip of neighbors and friends. His formal education leading to ordination began in 1958 with Mabel and me in Tuxtla Gutiérrez. Francisco's continued absence from home caused many problems. His wife and family were forced to assume the added burden of cutting and carrying firewood and cultivating the family's cornfield. There was sickness, too. He became discouraged and doubted the wisdom of his decision. After a few months, he felt he could not continue with his classes. He returned to his village near Corralito, long the center of church activity in the tribe. A year later, he was back in San Cristóbal de Las Casas to dedicate himself to both ministry and education.

Francisco's intelligence and ability had not gone unnoticed by government agencies. He was in demand for helping with the census and other jobs because he was bright, literate, and spoke Spanish fluently. When an engineer pressed him into service in early 1961, Francisco turned away from the call of God. He decided he should go to the town center, Oxchuc, to work. The engineer sent to survey and establish boundaries was at times as cruel as he was well educated. He insulted, mistreated, and threatened Francisco and the other native helpers. He discovered that some of the natives had surnames which were also the names of plants or animals and jeeringly called them by the Spanish equivalent.

He forced the men at gunpoint to drink beer. Francisco did drink beer once, thinking that *then* the fellow would be satisfied. But the engineer, in an effort to force Francisco to continue drinking, ordered two other men to pull Francisco's arms behind his back. He then pushed the bottle between his lips. Francisco clenched his teeth, and the second bottle of beer merely ran down over his clothes. Later, when the engineer insisted that Francisco drink wine and stronger liquor, he refused. "Go ahead and shoot," he told the furious man. Neither threats nor force could sway Francisco from his convictions. God kept him from bodily harm and from succumbing to further temptation.

The months of servitude to the demanding task master came to an end. Sorrowing and repentant, Francisco turned his thoughts back to his abandoned work. He observed, "Maybe the Lord let this happen to me to teach me what I should do." Through trying experiences, he learned that the real purpose of many trials is to "test our submission to the Lord and to deliver us from our own ways." Finally, in July 1963, in the Golgotha Presbyterian Church in Corralito, Francisco was ordained to the gospel ministry and installed as pastor of that church. He also became the officiating pastor of Bethel Presbyterian Church at Pacbilna and was charged with the care of twenty-five congregations for which these two churches were responsible.[2]

The Lord blessed this man in very special ways. Francisco became the first Tzeltal pastor ordained in the Chiapas Presbytery, after graduating from the Bible School and Seminary in San Cristóbal de Las Casas. He also became a major leader in the Tzeltal church, and later, he was one of the primary Bible translators to work with Paul Meyerink. We all felt so proud of him![3]

---

[2]   DDM, "The Making of an Indian Minister," *The Church Herald* (December 6, 1963), 4-5.

[3]   Information provided by Charles Van Engen to the author, July 15, 2014.

CHAPTER 69

Chiapas Gets a Plane!

Certain areas in Chiapas were totally unreachable by surface, particularly those lost in the middle of an impenetrable jungle. The only possibility to reach some villages and *rancherías* (small group of huts) was by air. The first plane to serve the missionaries working in Chiapas in remote territories arrived in February 1946. The Christian Airmen's Missionary Fellowship (later Mission Aviation Fellowship) was a very significant strategic ministry in this regard. In 1943 three World War II pilots began meeting for prayer, Bible study, and discussion of how to develop a ministry of missionary aviation using the skills they were learning during the war. The following year, one of those pilots was led to establish an organization as soon as possible so that missionary aviation could begin when the war ended. The ministry launched in 1945 as Christian Airmen's Missionary Fellowship.

On February 14, God gave this ministry an airplane for a Valentine. It was not a sleek, streamlined, post-war model like some magazine advertisements showed. On the contrary, the first Mission Aviation Fellowship (MAF) aircraft purchased was a comparatively slow but hard working 1933 red Waco made entirely out of wood and cloth. This four-seat cabin biplane had just recently been overhauled and was in "like new" condition. Add to that, it had a brand new 220 hp Continental engine. In an inflated market, such as existed in those days, with demand far surpassing supply, only an all-powerful God could have enabled the folks at CAMF to get so much of an airplane for so little cost.

This "beauty" was the first plane of this ministry, and it was dedicated to serve the jungle camp of Wycliffe Bible Translators, located in Chiapas. The trip from Los Angeles was an eventful one. Everything from bad weather to water in the gasoline made this trip difficult. But by God's grace, the Waco reached its field of service safely. This trip, however, started long before the Waco took off from Los Angeles in February. It began when Cameron Townsend, director of Wycliffe wrote: "I am convinced well-planned use of airplanes is absolutely essential for evangelizing inaccessible areas in this generation." The second lap of the journey was accomplished as Christians in Mexico and the United States prayed for a plane and a pilot with which to do this work.

The pilot in this first airborne missionary adventure was Betty Greene, an ex-WASP. Again, as has been the case on many occasions throughout the history of missions, a woman was the pioneer. Nine busy days were spent in giving the ship a thorough "going over" to make certain it was ready for the difficult work ahead. Then on February 23, after a crowd of CAMF members and friends had gathered around the plane for prayer, Betty Greene took control of her flying machine and turned to help her two passengers fasten their seat belts. Ethel Lambotte and Lois Schneider, two Wycliffe workers who were on their way to Mexico, "hitched" a ride on this "ferry" trip. As the little red airplane roared down the runway, took to the air, and disappeared over the horizon, heads bowed, once again asking God to bless the ministry of this plane as it assisted in "speeding the light" to Chiapas.

The Waco flew uneventfully across the southern part of Arizona, then crossed the southwest corner of New Mexico and skirted along the Texas side of the Rio Grande to Brownsville, Texas, the very bottom of the United States. Following a twenty-four-hour delay due to customs and weather, the plane took to the air once again and was soon over Mexico—the land to which it had been called. After refueling in a Mexican town, the engine began to sputter due to water in the gasoline. By switching gas tanks and using the hand primer, pilot Greene retraced her course to the point of take off. This was not only an answer to many prayers but also a testimony of God's faithfulness in keeping his own from unseen dangers.

Weather delayed the flight once more before reaching Mexico City. This tropical city, virtually surrounded by mountains, is the location of a real "weather factory." Towering cumulus clouds frequently build up around the city in the afternoon as the air over the mountains becomes extremely turbulent. Since even commercial airliners experience difficulty getting through when these conditions exist, it would be very foolish to attempt breaking through with such a small craft.

Several Wycliffe workers who were in Mexico City at the time of the plane's delayed arrival came to the airport to give it a royal welcome. But even this warm reception was eclipsed a day or two later by the celebration that took place when the plane crossed the last ridge, circled the little group of huts on the river below, and then lined up with the narrow, eighteen-hundred-foot landing strip adjacent to the jungle camp. This was down in Chiapas, near the Guatemalan border. As Betty cut the engine, people swarmed around the plane like flies. Here were some of the Wycliffe "recruits" who were just completing their training at the jungle "boot camp." There were *mestizos* and Maya who in a few days would be busily engaged in building a hangar for the little red plane. All were excited over the plane that was actually on the field after so many months of hoping and praying. Christians were extremely thankful, because they realized that this plane meant an increased ministry in winning souls for the Lord Jesus Christ. But this plane had not come all the way from Los Angeles just to be admired; there was work to do, and Betty and numerous other pilots of CAMF were fast in getting to it.[1]

This ministry, however, was not free from difficulties and accidents. Before leaving for Peru, Betty Greene tested her successor, George Wiggins, a former navy pilot who was to replace her in Mexico. Landing at the El Real ranch near the Wycliffe jungle camp, George did not see a small building and struck it with the tip of a wing, tearing off the two wings on one side of the plane and ruining the propeller and the landing gear. A Mexican bush pilot flew the damaged parts out to Tuxtla.

We welcomed Betty into our home and over time nursed her through two attacks of malaria. A young mechanic, Nate Saint, responded to her call for help in rebuilding the wings. With the help of a local carpenter and Garold Van Engen, Nate began the difficult job. It took months to build the replacement parts. When Nate became

[1]   "And Now. . . Mexico," photocopy of an article not signed (n.p., n.d.), 6-7, in JAH.

seriously ill with dysentery, the Lord provided help in the person of Phil Baer, Wycliffe missionary to the Lacandon tribe.[2]

It was a day of hope and anticipation when we loaded all the parts into a local bush plane. There was barely room in the plane for Nate with Phil's wife and their child. The take off was one of the most terrifying moments of my life and theirs. When it became obvious to us that the heavily loaded plane was not going to clear the trees at the end of the airstrip, Phil and I began running to the rescue. Miraculously, the plane lifted just enough to clear the trees and then struggled successfully to gain enough altitude to climb out of the valley. Phil went overland to the El Real ranch to help Nate assemble the wings, and Nate and George were able to fly the repaired plane out to Tuxtla. We were deeply saddened about ten years later by the news that Nate Saint had been killed by the Auca Indians of South America.

[2]   Russell T. Hitt, *Jungle Pilot: The gripping story of the life and witness of Nate Saint, martyred missionary to Ecuador* (Grand Rapids, MI: Discovery House, 1959), 101-2.

CHAPTER 70

Translators and Pilots

From May to June 1948, we went to visit our family in the United States. It was a wonderful trip packed with many memorable experiences. The saddest experience that year, however, was that my mother died. She was very special to me, even though most of my letters since I had left home in my early youth were addressed to my father. The 1940s, however, did mark another very uplifing, extraordinary, and providential development: the arrival of Wycliffe Bible Translators and Mission Aviation Fellowship (MAF).

Wycliffe Bible Translators is a multinational organization dedicated to enabling all of the world's people to discover that God speaks their language. The organization was founded in 1934 by my good friends Leonard L. Legters and William Cameron Townsend. They envisioned making God's Word available through vernacular translations. Mexico was their first challenge, particularly because of the great variety of native languages. Wycliffe received permission from the Mexican government to give the 130 indigenous languages a written form, to produce literacy materials, and then to translate the New Testament into these newly written languages.

The MAF airplanes provided transportation to the remote tribal
locations (*courtesy J. Samuel and Helen Hofman*)

Mission Aviation Fellowship (see chapter 69) came to Chiapas
to provide Wycliffe missionaries with transportation, supplies, and
communications. God raised up Wycliffe and MAF to share the gospel
with the indigenous peoples of Chiapas. Both organizations were
strongly committed to the proclamation of the gospel through the
distribution of the Bible in the various native languages.

Wycliffe translators entered the six tribes of Chiapas, living in
remote villages to learn their languages and translate the scriptures.
The work among the Ch'ol and Tzeltal prospered very quickly and
believers multiplied rapidly, but progress in the Tzotzil and Tojolabal
tribes was much slower. This was due to severe persecution. Tribal
and village authorities were determined not to permit any change
from their animistic Catholicism. After persecution in the Ch'ol and
Tzeltal tribes subsided, it began in the Tzotzil and Tojolabal tribes,
and it was persistent and violent. Wycliffe missionaries and their
converts were chased out of the villages. The Tzotzil Christian refugees
began gathering in San Cristóbal, and the Tojolabal refugees gathered
in Las Margaritas. Translations of the New Testament continued,
and eventually the Wycliffe missionaries and their Maya translation
partners produced New Testaments in Tojolabal and in five dialects of
the Tzotzil language.[1]

[1]   JSH, "The History of the Chiapas Mission," 9.

Flying with Mexican bush pilots was always risky

Mabel and I were deeply involved in the ministry of the Wycliffe missionaries. We offered them all sorts of assistance and advice. We, however, were not always in complete agreement with their strategies. All the Wycliffe translators who served among the Tojolabal and Tzotzil were from Baptist and independent churches. They were not comfortable with the idea of placing the indigenous converts under the care of the National Presbyterian Church of Mexico, preferring that the Maya converts remained independent and free to develop their own style of church government. But in the heat of persecution, it was the Mexican Presbyterian Church leaders and believers who came to the aid of the persecuted natives. In the Tzeltal, Ch'ol, and Chamula persecutions, Presbyterian pastor Rev. Daniel Aguilar Ochoa (who had studied law before becoming a pastor) was a dedicated, wise, constant, and clear voice with the state and local governing authorities, insisting on religious liberty for the new believers. As the Wycliffe missionaries completed their translations and moved on, the Tzotzil and Tojolabal believers asked the Presbyterian leaders to receive and organize them. This helped in their relationship to regional and state government officials, since the Presbyterian Church was recognized and respected.[2]

In 1945 former test pilot Betty Greene became the first MAF field pilot, serving Wycliffe missionaries in Mexico, especially in our state. They established a base in central Chiapas, at Ixtapa, with two airplanes. For thirty-eight years, they provided transportation

[2] Ibid.

and communications for the missionaries of Chiapas without suffering a serious injury or fatal accident.[3] The ministry of our Chiapas Mission would have been impossible without their assistance. Our missionaries, particularly those in more remote areas, extensively used the pilots and planes provided by MAF. The number of servants of God of these two missionary organizations that blessed our ministry in Chiapas during these years was admirable. John and Elaine Beekman arrived in Ch'ol Maya country to learn the language and translate God's Word into it. They served from 1948 to 1961. John had been born to poor but devout Reformed Church parents in Midland Park, New Jersey. A heart condition caused poor circulation and limited his physical activity. After finishing high school, he rebelled against church teaching and decided that the Bible was only a "book of myths." Providentially, he found a book on the fulfillment of Old Testament prophecies in a public library. Checking the book's claims against secular histories, he became convinced that the Bible was divine. His commitment led him to enroll in Moody Bible Institute, where he met and married Elaine Hummel, a native of Clearfield, Pennsylvania.

John and Elaine attended Wycliffe's Summer Institute of Linguistics at the University of Oklahoma, where they first heard about the Ch'ols. "Your denomination has missionaries in Chiapas," translator Ethel Wallis told them. "But they work with Mexicans and the few natives who can speak Spanish. They would welcome more help with the natives." They learned that Wycliffe was already working among the Ch'ols and Tzeltals in friendly cooperation with Reformed Church missionaries. Wycliffe translator Evelyn Woodward, who had gone to the Ch'ols in 1941, had reduced one of the Ch'ol dialects to writing and then translated the gospel of Mark. She and her husband, Wilbur Aulie, would also welcome the Beekmans. So the young couple went to Chiapas to serve the Ch'ols. A major reason for their selecting this tribe was the opportunity to work near Reformed Church missionaries.[4]

We greeted the Beekmans joyfully when they arrived in Chiapas in December 1947. Elaine stayed with Mabe, while John and I made a survey trip through the rugged Ch'ol country. On the trail, I recounted to John the history of evangelical work among the Ch'ols. We helped them settle in the mountain village of Amado Nervo. Because there was no airstip, Elaine had to be carried in on a porter's chair over a narrow trail that snaked around precipitous cliffs. They moved into a one-room hut and

---

[3]   Ibid., 7.
[4]   Hefley, "The Challenge of the Ch'ols," 5-6.

With Wycliffe missionary Marianna Slocum translating,
I taught Tzeltal lay preachers in Corralito

began learning the language. With courage and faith, they confronted all sorts of difficulties and opposition. The young couple's first big crisis came when their firstborn child died while they were home on a short study furlough. After returning to the Ch'ols, Elaine contracted malaria and had to return home for recuperation. John stayed behind in Chiapas and narrowly escaped stoning by drunken men at a fiesta.

The Beekmans' difficulties eased after the Ch'ols built them a larger house and cleared a landing strip for the MAF plane. John began making progress with translation. He first translated several Old Testament stories and then began to work on New Testament books to supplement the work of Wilbur and Evelyn Aulie, who were living in another village. The hard work and dedication of John and Elaine soon began to show results. The increase in the number of Ch'ol believers was amazing during the years of their service.

Later, when John's heart condition forced them to leave Ch'ol country, he began to teach and train translators. Paul Meyerink and an Oxchuc Tzeltal pastor, Francisco Gómez Sánchez, participated in a workshop led by Beekman before beginning revision of the Oxchuc Tzeltal New Testament. John eventually served as chief translation consultant for Wycliffe's worldwide ministry.

In the Tzeltal tribe, the Wycliffe translator was Marianna Slocum, a Presbyterian from Pennsylvania. Her partner was a nurse, Florence Gerdel. After enduring several years of hostility and suspicion, there was a gospel breakthrough in the small valley of Corralito in 1949. The missionaries moved to Corralito, and in five years, the New

Pastor Daniel Aguilar provided leadership and training for the initial
Tzeltal church leaders (*courtesy J. Samuel and Helen Hofman*)

Testament translation was complete. Florence Gerdel's medical work
also prospered. Garold Van Engen and I constructed the first clinic for
them, near the house where Marianna and Florence lived in Corralito.
Paul and Dorothy Meyerink joined Marianna and Florence in 1952
to help develop the Tzeltal leaders emerging in the growing church.
They later moved to the Bachajón area to produce a New Testament
in that dialect and continue medical work. These women left Chiapas
permanently in 1963 to begin Bible translation in the Paez language in
Colombia. Wycliffe missionaries would move on to new fields of service
when their translation of the New Testament was finished, so Reformed
Church missionaries were called to continue the work in the Ch'ol and
Tzeltal fields.

The background of these missionaries facilitated the placing of
the Ch'ol and Tzeltal work under the National Presbyterian Church
in Mexico. Rev. Daniel Aguilar Ochoa of San Cristóbal became the
officiating pastor for the Tzeltals, and Rev. Alejandro Barrios, pastor
of the church in Las Margaritas, served in the Ch'ol field. These men
prompted the selection of elders and deacons and organized the
indigenous churches, which then joined the Presbytery of Chiapas. The
welcome and respect that the natives received in the Chiapas Presbytery
was an uplifting and gratifying experience for the downtrodden Maya.[5]

5   Ibid.

Garold and I planned and participated in the construction
of the clinic and missionary residence in Corralito

CHAPTER 71

Voice without Vote

By the end of the 1940s, the pastoral ministry in Chiapas was in critical condition. For years the only ordained pastor in the National Presbyterian Church in the state was Rev. José Coffin. He had a good number of chaplains, and I was ready to do whatever ministration I was allowed to do according to Mexican laws and the request of the churches. But the work was expanding, and the needs of shepherding were increasing. I also became more and more convinced that it was necessary to organize the Presbyterian work in Chiapas and obtain an independent or autonomous status from the Presbytery of the Gulf of Mexico, which in many ways limited our opportunities for expansion and the development of our work in the state.

Ever since Plutarco Elías Calles, then president of Mexico, enforced the existing laws which restricted the religious activity of foreign priests and ministers, Protestant missionaries, at least, had acted accordingly. No one seemed to know just what the law prohibited or allowed missionaries to do, but we had interpreted the law to mean that we could do every type of work, with the exception of "officiating." I understood officiating to be the administering of the sacraments, admitting members into the church, and performing marriage ceremonies. I did take charge of countless funerals and do most other types of pastoral work, however, in addition to the many responsibilities of our ministry.

In the excitement which accompanied the original application of the law, it was thought that a foreigner should not be a member of a consistory or a presbytery. Consequently, missionaries withdrew their memberships in presbyteries, and a few Guatemalan elders were substituted for by Mexicans. By 1948, after more than twenty years of missionary service under these conditions, some missionaries were once again considering the action of joining the presbyteries, where the foreign element would not be too numerous and where the Mexican ministers earnestly desired them to do so. During all these years, however, the missionaries had been welcomed to official gatherings as corresponding members, and they had been given the privilege of the floor with *voz sin voto* (voice without vote).

This measure of voice without vote was actually a significant privilege. One's influence generally moves in inverse proportion to the ascending category of the official body. In fact, in the local church organizations and in the consistory, foreign missionaries had to employ strategy and exercise caution, lest their suggestions or opinions were accepted too hastily. In the next higher official body, the regional committee of presbytery, because of the missionaries' knowledge of the entire field and its needs and because of the respect the people of the state had for their missionaries, the influence of the missionaries on the vote was again powerful. In the presbytery and synod meetings, the ideas of foreign missionaries were considered more critically, but voting members could make the suggestions of missionaries propositions, and missionaries could debate freely. Neither was there any law against "lobbying" before and during ecclesiastical gatherings. No, aside from the fact that I could not hold office, I did not feel at all handicapped in official gatherings.

In the strategy of war, once a beachhead is taken, fighting strength is built up for the breakthrough. I had been actively working for a long time to build up strength—too long, actually, for reasons which need not be discussed in detail here. But by the end of the 1940s, I was ready to advance my ideas and promote the constitution of a Chiapas presbytery, in spite of the objections and resistance of well-respected leaders such as José Coffin. Until this time, for this entire field—a state one-half the size of Iowa—with its more than one hundred churches, congregations, and missions, the number of ordained Mexican ministers had never

Coffin, Lango, De la Rosa, and I can be found in this
photo of the Presbyterian General Assembly

been more than four. Our hope was that at the Presbytery of the Gulf meeting in February of 1949, two more men could be ordained. By then, three seminary students were on their way to graduation. After two years of practice, each of them could be ordained. This very fact encouraged me to see the constitution of a presbytery for Chiapas as something feasible.

With an increase in the number of ministers, however, I faced two new problems, and both were matters of administrative policy. First, as a foreign missionary, I could not build up anything in Mexico which the nationals would not be able to carry on, sooner or later, by themselves. The key question for me was: "Just how many ordained ministers will the Chiapas churches eventually be able to support?" Second, by increasing the number of salaried workers, volunteer workers might lose their enthusiasm, since they would naturally consider salaried men to have the responsibility to do all the work.

With the ordination of additional men in the spring of 1949, I had hoped that the Chiapaneco church would have the necessary number of ordained pastors (five) to have our own Chiapas presbytery (classis) organized. In this way, I thought, I would be able to fulfill a twenty-three-year-old dream. To attain this or to even have it come so near its fulfillment, I had to overcome opposition like the mountain of Zerubbabel's dream. The required number of ministers was not simply a matter of "calling" pastors from elsewhere for the formation of a presbytery. In Mexico, where the people of each state have distinct regional peculiarities and affinities, it is best that their ministers be people from their respective states. It took a long time for young Christians in Mexico to feel led to enter this most difficult of all professions—the preaching of the gospel of Christ. Then, too, we had to arouse and cultivate a sense of the need of a presbytery within the state. In 1948 we learned what Zerubbabel had learned so long ago, "Not by might, nor by power, but by my spirit, says the Lord of hosts" (Zech. 4:6).

In those days, I received a letter from a Maya elder of one of the consistories, in which he said: "I assure you that the Chiapas congregations will be eternally grateful to you for what you have done to obtain the organization of our own presbytery." At that moment, I thought, "I may join the Chiapas presbytery, as some of the ministers have requested, and if I do, it will not be because I desire '*voz y voto*' [voice and vote] in matters of church polity, but for their sake and for the sake of the church in Chiapas." I have been more than rewarded in all this. Most of all, because the dream I had right from the start of my ministry in Chiapas was fulfilled.[1]

---

[1]   JRK, "Voice without Vote," *The Church Herald* (November 26, 1948), 9.

CHAPTER 72

Organization of the Chiapas Presbytery

The year of 1949 was a blessed year. From May to November, we enjoyed a rather short furlough in the United States. We traveled with our veteran Chevy and visited our children and family now scattered in different places. We went to Winona, Minnesota, for board meetings. We also visited Mabel's sister, Lillian, whom we cherished. By then, Kathleen Joy was a freshman at Hope College, Holland; David Warren was a junior at Mt. Hermon, Massachussetts; Margery Ann was in Mexico with us and was part of our traveling crew; and Roger Dyke had graduated from Hope College. Later he became a graduate chemistry major at the University of Michigan.

The year of 1949 was—especially for me—the fulfillment of a long-cherished dream: the organization of the Presbytery of Chiapas. In 1925 the Presbyterian Church in the entire southeastern part of Mexico was governed by the Presbytery of the Gulf, consisting of five ordained ministers and the elders of the churches. By then José Coffin was the only minister in Chiapas and Salomón Díaz the lone Tabasco pastor. Campeche had no pastors, but there were three in Yucatán. When Rev. Asunción Blanco R., one of these three, was transferred to Mexico City,

377

In the United States, making plans for the future education
of our children (*courtesy Joy Fuder*)

there was talk of asking me to become a full member of the presbytery
to complete the necessary five. The problem was eventually solved
without this commitment on my part.

The foremost obstruction to ministry in those days was
communication. For some leaders, to attend presbytery meetings was
an absurd adventure. Congregations were scattered through a very large
and rough territory. The two means of travel between the churches at
that time were by horse and by boat. It was the same every year with the
meetings of the Presbytery of the Gulf that embraced such a vast region.
There is one trip to a presbytery meeting that I remember particularly
well. This periplus meant five days on horseback, riding from San
Cristóbal de Las Casas to Salto de Agua, and then a three-day riverboat
journey living with the stench of 235 hogs carried in the hull, followed
by a more comfortable train trip from Campeche to Mérida, in Yucatán,
where the meetings took place. And then we had to return!

When the Reformed Church exploration committee, consisting of
Mrs. Edith Allen, Mrs. Tabor Knox, Rev. Henry Sluyter, and Rev. Gerrit
Watermulder visited Chiapas in February 1925, and later accepted the
transfer of missionary responsibility in Chiapas from the Northern
Presbyterian Church, the only other people present at the Tapachula
meeting were Rev. José Coffin representing the Presbytery of the Gulf
and Rev. Harry Phillips representing the Presbyterian Mission. If any

The first meeting of the Chiapas Presbytery was a joyful occasion

minutes were taken at this transfer meeting, neither I nor the presbytery saw a copy. Since no other Mexican people were present, Coffin could and often did tell the presbytery, in defense of some action of his, that this was in agreement with the accord between mission and presbytery.

There were years when I skipped the annual meetings of the presbytery because of the time and hardship involved in travel and because Chiapas matters were seldom discussed. With no other Chiapas delegates present, Coffin managed to keep the work in this state off the agenda. When asked for the Chiapas consistory books, which had to be reviewed, he would actually go to the post office to inquire for these, knowing full well that none had been sent. As the gospel spread, the Peninsula Presbytery, the Maya Presbytery, and the Campeche Presbytery all separated from the original body, leaving only Tabasco and Chiapas as regional committees of the Presbytery of the Gulf.

At each presbytery meeting, by mail or in person, I submitted the mission plan of financial cooperation for the next year, monies which I sent directly to the people involved month by month. The plan was always approved, even when I stipulated that there would be a reduction in payments to Coffin if he persisted in being off the field for longer than the specified weeks. There were years when he spent more time in Tabasco, baptizing uninvited in other people's fields, than he did in Chiapas. Naturally there were some who screamed when I applied that reduction.

The ordination of (*l-r*) Margarito Hernández, Nehemias Garcia, and
Bartolomé Solórzano gave Chiapas the required five ministers
to form a Presbytery

Another issue that resulted from a lack of our own presbytery in Chiapas was the situation of Roque May and Isidro Estrella. Had we mattered, with a well-organized presbytery in our state, we would not have lost Roque, and Estrella might have had more limitations to his disturbing actions. At least a presbytery could have acted as mediator and judge to smooth the conflicts. The tension increased when the consistory of the Yajalón church, the governing body of the area, asked the Presbytery of the Gulf for the removal of Estrella. For many years, these controversies and tensions afflicted me and, most of all, the churches in Chiapas.

There was, however, a positive result from all this foolishness. Our Chiapas delegates were so disgusted that they insisted Chiapas should have its own presbytery. To that end, Chiapas needed five ordained ministers, and as to the two we had, Coffin was vehemently opposed. It would take time.[1]

Meanwhile, I continued to train leaders for the ministry. At the invitation of Rev. Lango, who had returned to serve in Mexico City, two young men from Chiapas, Daniel Aguilar Ochoa and Nehemías García, were sent to the Presbyterian seminary in the capital city. Two other candidates for the ministry were taught in our home. At last, in 1949, three Chiapas men were ordained at the annual meeting of

---

[1]   JRK, "Some of This and Some of That," 16-17.

Five pastors who endured in Chiapas (*l-r*): Margarito Hernández, Genaro de la Rosa, Pedro Diaz, Daniel Aguilar, and Bartolomé Solórzano

the Presbytery of the Gulf. This provided the necessary five ordained ministers to form the Presbytery of Chiapas.[2]

But we still needed the vote of the Presbytery of the Gulf for approval of the organization. Coffin was not present. Tabasco had one more voting delegate than we, and I strongly believe it was God's Spirit who moved elder Lutzow, an delegate from Tabasco, to vote for Chiapas. The name of this man must be preserved in the history of the church in Chiapas.

A letter of mine reflects the admiration and the antagonism I had toward Coffin: "Coffin the lion, a man, a great man, who was destroyed by his own jealousy. He had a way of hypnotizing the unwary to think he and he alone was right. How much did Genaro de la Rosa, Lango, and I suffer under that man! How much did the work progress in spite of him in his spiteful years!"[3] At the end, when the leaders of the Presbytery of the Gulf continued to delay the formation of the Chiapas Presbytery, the synod ordered its immediate organization. The historic day was July 14, 1949.

Later that year, Coffin and his wife Luz Otero left Tapachula and returned to Tabasco, unwilling to transfer his membership

2   JRK to JSH, Feb. 27, 1982, in JAH.
3   JRK to JSH, Sep. 4, 1971, in JAH.

Margarito Hernández served faithfully as the pastor of the Mazapa church

from the Presbytery of the Gulf to the new Chiapas Presbytery. He was received with honor in his home, and that same year was elected the first president of the General Assembly of the National Presbyterian Church of Mexico. He also was invited to speak at the General Assembly of the Presbyterian Church USA in Seattle, and received an honorary doctorate from Whitworth College.[4] In summary, the story of the organization of the Presbytery of Chiapas centers on the unrelenting opposition of José Coffin to the project. What is not generally known is that the organization of the presbytery was hastened by an unsuccessful attempt of a mean-spirited, Yucatecan indigenous preacher, whom the Yajalón church would no longer tolerate on their field, to have me declared a *persona non grata* by the presbytery. As I suggested, Coffin could have easily stopped that effort cold with one word. But he deliberately refrained, and it took a special meeting of the presbytery to right the matter, and at that meeting, all of our Chiapas consistories declared they would have no part of this scheme. It was then that the Chiapas elders, for the first time, saw how indispensable it was to have a presbytery of our own and be free from Tabasco control. One may speak of a sacrificial lamb or the blood of the martyrs, but I did pay a high price to have our presbytery.

In writing the history of the church in Chiapas, Hugo Esponda did not write about all the years of tension between José Coffin, the

---

[4]   JSH, "The History of the Chiapas Mission," 6-7.

giant of the Mexican nationals, and me, the unassuming missionary of the Reformed Church. It was not that one individual prevailed over the other. It was what each stood for that triumphed or failed. There was no joy in Coffin's leaving, only sadness that a man with so much experience and so much potential had misdirected his efforts.

This story may never have been told before, but recalling this incident might be of some value to others committed to the Presbyterian work in Chiapas.[5] To have a peek at what has gone on before may be of help to leaders to avoid the errors of the past.

[5]   JRK to Richard Vander Voet, July 10, 1985, in JAH.

CHAPTER 73

Honoris Causa Degree, a Wedding, and Christmas

Sometimes unexpected things happen. Events seemingly from another universe will appear on the horizon and shine for a moment like a shooting star crossing the high heavens. That was my experience in June 1950 when I preached at the Hope College baccalaureate service and received an honorary degree for my service in Chiapas.

In 1949 the leadership of Hope College had learned that my family and I would be traveling from Chiapas to Holland in June of that year to attend our son Roger's graduation, so they invited me to give the prayer at that ceremony in Dimnent Memorial Chapel. There I shared the stage with Everet Dirksen, senator from Illinois and member of the Reformed Church, who delivered a memorable baccalaurate address. The trustees called a meeting soon thereafter and decided to grant me an honorary degree the following year. We, however, had made plans to leave Holland shortly after our son's graduation, and when representatives of the trustees called to tell me of their decision, they learned that we had just left town to drive back to Mexico. So they drove very rapidly out of Holland, hoping to overtake us to give me the news and also to ask me to give the baccalaureate address as well the next

385

Hope College awarded me an
honorary doctorate

year. By some miracle, they did overtake us twenty miles down the road. Of course, I was stunned and honored. I told Mabel and Roger later that I had worried that whole year over the address I would have to give.[1]

On the occasion of the eighty-fifth convocation of my alma mater, the baccalaureate service was celebrated in Dimnent Chapel on Sunday, June 11, 1950. I preached the sermon "What Doth the Lord Require of Thee?" Delivering that sermon was a terrible challenge for me. Earlier that year, I had written Dr. Irwin J. Lubbers, then president of Hope College:

> You were on a mission field where, I believe, a good deal of English was used, so you cannot know how extremely difficult it is for one who has been hearing and using practically nothing but Spanish and Ch'ol to suddenly walk onto a platform and try to preach in English. On furloughs, I generally start out in some little church or one where the audience is not too critical. Then, too, there is the problem of living in this atmosphere and trying to think of something helpful to say to an audience more than three thousand miles away. If it must be done, I'll get busy and work on something, but it will be like pulling teeth. If there is anyone whom you have in mind, who could do this without working under the disadvantages I would have to labor, please assign the

[1]   Roger Dyke Kempers, email to author, July 4, 2014, in JAH.

job to him. In that case, I shall be free to go about my work here until the end of May.[2]

Obviously that did not convince the man to find a substitute, and I was scheduled to preach on that very special occasion. After the test, I received a letter from him saying, "Thanks very much for your very fine sermon last Sunday evening. We have had many compliments, but perhaps we had better not pass them on too much in detail. We don't want you to be forced to buy a new hat."[3]

When I was granted the honoris causa ad gradum divinitatis doctoris at the commencement exercises on Wednesday, June 14, 1950, I was honored by Professor Albert Timmer when he presented me to Dr. Lubbers.

> Mr. Kempers has spent almost a quarter of a century in the service of the Reformed Church in America under its Board of Domestic Missions in Mexico. Entering upon a new field in a situation that meant almost pioneer conditions, Mr. Kempers, with Mrs. Kempers, set himself to a task which in the course of the years was to demand the pastoral care of a people living under most adverse conditions. He was to develop an educative system that could train these people from young childhood through the normal education years of youth and, in many instances, to professional labors in the ministry of the church and to responsible positions as lay workers. He was to find himself confronted with administrative problems, which grew more and more complex as he developed his field.
>
> All this was to be achieved under geographic and climatic and social conditions which only the most vigorous self discipline could endure. He has met all these challenges as a worker that never needs to be ashamed, as a valiant soldier of the Cross, and as a man who has demonstrated the power of personality and persistent endeavor under resolutions for great and consecrated living.[4]

I was almost convinced that our work in Chiapas had gone unnoticed by most of our brethren in the United States and even more so in the world of academia. When the time came for Dr. Lubbers to present to me the doctor of divinity degree, he went even further.

---

2   JRK to Irwin J. Lubbers, March 20, 1950, in JAH.
3   Irwin J. Lubbers to JRK, June 15, 1950, in JAH.
4   "Commencement Week 1950," *Hope College Magazine* (1950), 9.

I always tried to work with
commitment and determination
(*courtesy Joy Fuder*)

Scion of sturdy stock, who laid firmly the foundations of true piety and purposeful living and stretched the soul to compass far horizons; son of the Reformed Church, nurtured in her schools and commissioned by her to preach in the uttermost parts of the earth; founder of a new church in an ancient land; exemplar of the gospel of love; graduate of Hope College; educator, minister, and missionary; "a workman approved of God who needeth not to be ashamed."[5]

I could not believe his words; for a moment I thought he was referring to somebody else.

What a glorious year was 1950! On June 17, shortly after I received my honorary degree from Hope College, we celebrated the wedding of our eldest son Roger. He and Marcia had asked me to perform the ceremony along with the pastor at Hope Church in Holland, Dr. Mert DeVelder. I was delighted. Although I was ordained in the Reformed Church in America, I was technically not permitted to perform wedding services alone, but I knew Mert well and worked out dual roles for the ceremony. Similarly, along with the pastors of their respective churches, I married all of our children as well as Roger's oldest daughter, Mary Christine, and one of my nieces in Iowa. Roger and Marcia's wedding was beautiful with many people in attendance since Marcia's father

[5]   Ibid., 10.

Harmon and mother Della were well known in the community. Harmon was a successful clock and furniture manufacturer, and Della's father was Rev. Henry Hospers, president of Western Theological Seminary in the 1930s. Mabel and I were also well known in the community because of our missionary ministry, and many relatives and friends of ours were invited.

How proud Mabel and I were of our son Roger! We were so thankful to the Lord that the young boy who had spent his first fourteen years with us in Chiapas was now an impressive grown man and committing himself together with Marcia to begin a new family. Following their honeymoon at the beautiful Grand Hotel on Mackinac Island in northern Michigan, Roger began medical school, and Marcia taught kindergarden. Mabel and I continued with a heavy schedule of speaking about the mission in Chiapas at numerous churches throughout the country.[6]

The year came to an end with our very special celebration of Christmas back in Chiapas. Christmas provided a perfect opportunity to share the gospel of our Lord. In a Roman Catholic setting like Chiapas, there were two Christian celebrations that offered fruitful opportunities for our testimony: Holy Week and Christmas. Mabel was an expert in making an occasion beautiful to attract people and present the message of salvation. Mabel loved poetry. She kept a file of beautiful poems, clips taken from various magazines, mostly on subjects like motherhood, Christmas, New Year's, children, love and marriage, home, and the like. She also collected sayings, phrases, and quotations taken from many sources: letters, a Mexican truck on the American side of the border, an ashtray in a restaurant, magazines, and books. She kept a brown covered notebook with hundreds of entries organized by theme. She also collected hundreds of Christmas stories and dramas.

This collection was her source material to write Christmas programs and short dramas that were published and distributed among the churches. If ever there was an occasion when we had our houses and churches packed with curious newcomers, it was Christmas. We always organized a thoughtful and well-planned use of this opportunity.

---

[6]   Roger Dyke Kempers, email to author, July 4, 2014, in JAH.

CHAPTER 74

Genealogical Tree

On the occasion of the celebration of the golden anniversary of the General Synod of the National Presbyterian Church (1951), a book was published commemorating the event. There was an interesting article accompanied by a drawing entitled "El árbol genealógico" (The genealogical tree). The author, Rev. Nicanor F. Gómez, described three stages in the development of the Presbyterian testimony in Mexico. The first stage was called the sowing, and it referred to the beginning of the proclamation of the gospel in the country by the Presbyterians. In 1872 the first northern Presbyterian missionaries arrived, and in 1873, the southern Presbyterians came. Ten years later, in 1883, the Zacatecas Presbytery was organized, with missionaries of the northern mission. The following year, in 1884, the Tamaulipas Presbytery did the same in the field of the southern mission, this time with national ministers only. In 1885 the City of Mexico Presbytery took shape with missionaries and nationals participating. And finally, by 1896, the Gulf of Mexico Presbytery came to life. With these basic structural resources, the tree of the Presbyterian work in Mexico was solidly planted.

The second stage in this process was the organization of the General Synod of Mexico. It was on July 8, 1901, that this national body was formed. The first presbyteries to form the General Synod were: Zacatecas (later disappeared), Tamaulipas (later disappeared), Mexico City (dissolved in 1953), and Gulf of Mexico. After some years of fruitful life and open cooperation with other denominations, there came the critical years of the Mexican Revolution. When order was restored, the Presbyterian Church enjoyed more and better opportunities to share the gospel of salvation. In 1919 the Cincinnati Plan was introduced and applied in the country, with the different denominations parceling out the Mexican territory as if it were a cake. Missionaries were moved from one place to another like pieces on a chess board. Southern Presbyterian missionaries went to the center of the country, and northern Presbyterian missionaries went to the southeast of the republic. Under these circumstances, the presbyteries of Zacatecas and Tamaulipas joined forces and organized the presbytery known as Nacional Fronterizo (Frontier National), which was the first to be self supporting.

In 1921 the Presbytery of the South was organized, embracing part of the field that was formerly under the Presbytery of Mexico City. This presbytery, known as "the Boys presbytery," grew in such a way that it was necessary to divide it. The result was the formation of the Presbytery of the Pacific in 1936. To overcome controversy and difficulty, a new presbytery was created out of the Nacional Fronterizo in 1941: the Presbytery of the North.

During these decades, the Progressive Movement was introduced into Mexico from the United States.[1] Together two ideological currents divided the Presbyterian Mexican family. One was in favor of fraternity and cooperation with other evangelical denominations, and the other struggled for complete isolation from them. It was a miracle that the Presbyterian harmony was not broken by this clash between factions with equal power and influence. To this ideological difference was due the request of a group in Saltillo in 1944 to organize another synod.

Thus we come to the third stage in the development of this genealogical tree. This was a time of transition. An organizing committee was appointed in order to evaluate the constitution of a second synod. This Comisión Organizadora assumed all the supreme capacities of the General Synod, acting as top authority in the church. This committee organized the new Synod of the Gulf in 1944, a vigorous

---

[1]   Progressive Movement refers to the social activism and political reform in the United States that flourished from the 1890s to the 1920s. In its foreign policy expressions, it resulted in the persistent intervention of the United States in Mexico and Central America. It also had theological implications.

branch which, with half of the Presbyterian forces, withdrew from the First Synod. This new synod authorized the formation of the Peninsula Presbytery in 1945. In a rather short period of time, other presbyteries were organized: the "twin" presbyteries of Oaxaca (1947) and Veracruz (1947) and later the Presbytery of Chiapas (1949). By 1947, however, there were enough organized presbyteries to form another synod, the third one, the Synod of the Center. This one was constituted by the Comisión Organizadora.

With the three synods already in operation—First Synod, Synod of the Gulf, and Synod of the Center—the Mexican Presbyterian national work was ripe to organize the General Assembly on November 2, 1947. By 1956 the General Assembly included the three synods: (1) the First Synod with the Presbyteries of the South, the Pacific, and the North; (2) the Gulf Synod with the Presbyteries of the Gulf, the Peninsular Presbytery, and those of Veracruz and Chiapas (in 1954, the Maya Presbytery was added); and (3) the Synod of the Center with the Presbyteries of the City of Mexico (in July 1953 it was disbanded, and the Presbytery of the Federal District was created), the Nacional Fronterizo, and that of Oaxaca.[2]

The development of the national Presbyterian work in Mexico was both complex and conflictive. Many circumstances coincided that made this process difficult to understand. The tree of the Presbyterian testimony was deeply rooted in rich soil. But it grew mostly under the terrible conditions prevailing in the country during the final years of the nineteenth century and the beginning of the twentieth century and, since 1910, within the oppressive conditions created by the Mexican Revolution. Political turmoil and economic crises deeply affected the development of the work. Besides, the fact that there were at least four different Presbyterian missions coming from the United States, each with a different agenda, made it more complicated for the nationals to organize their denominational work in their own way. On more than one occasion, the controversies prevailing in the United States were transplanted to Mexico, involving Mexicans in issues totally alien to their circumstances and understanding. Most likely, these issues were the most painful and the ones which hindered most the healthy progress of the national work.

When the Reformed Church sent us to Mexico to collaborate with the national Presbyterian work, we were very careful to leave behind the problems affecting the denomination in our country. We also tried

[2]   Nicanor F. Gómez, "El árbol genealógico," in *Libro histórico de las Bodas de Oro del Sínodo General de la Iglesia Presbiteriana en México, julio 8, 1901-1951* (Mexico: n.p., 1956), 6-8.

our best to contribute to the missionary enterprise of the National Presbyterian Church, not attempting to plant Reformed churches or conspiring to organize a parallel structure. The churches we planted, the missions we opened, the various projects we developed were not done for the Reformed Church but for the National Presbyterian Church in Mexico. This has always been a central principle of our missionary strategy in Chiapas. I myself was much involved with the Comisión de Obra Cooperativa (Cooperative Work Commission), representing the work of the RCA with the National Presbyterian Church in Mexico. This body was also integrated by representatives of the other two North American Presbyterian churches and other denominations.

Cooperation among the various denominations and ecclesiastical institutions in Chiapas was not optional. It was essential to reaching the objectives we had set for "Chiapas para Cristo" (Chiapas for Christ). Also at the core of our missionary strategy was the principle of keeping a very low profile in our work. I was 100 percent committed to keeping the church in Chiapas under the radar and out of range of both state government and public opinion. This is the reason why I tried not to promote or advertise either in Mexico or in the news media in the United States. I wanted the least possible publicity of our missionary work in Chiapas. I did the same with the national Presbyterian organization. As much as I could, I tried to keep the Mexican General Assembly of the National Presbyterian Church out of Chiapas. During the 1950s and 1960s, I was as much a protector of Chiapas as Coffin had been, just in a different time, in a different way, and with a different attitude.[3]

---

[3]   Information provided by Charles Van Engen in personal conversation, July 15, 2014.

CHAPTER 75

"¿Qué Quieres Tú de Mí?"

On November 25, 1951, I had the privilege and opportunity to preach to the graduates of the National Presbyterian Seminary in Mexico City. The title of my message was "What Do You Want from Me?" My text was Acts 9:6 in the old Reina-Valera version in Spanish, which reads "Señor, qué quieres que haga?" (Lord, what do you want me to do).

I started my message recalling a visit I had paid to a number of Ch'ol congregations in the state of Chiapas. One of the questions I had for them was about the meaning of our human existence, the purpose of our lives. It was very interesting to see their faces looking at each other in astonishment. They understood the question to be legitimate, but at the same time, it was evident that they had never considered this issue. Of course, some of them could repeat by heart, but not with a clear understanding, the traditional Presbyterian answer to the first question of the Westminster Confession: we are in this life to glorify God and to enjoy him forever.

On one particular occasion, I went with Mabel to visit a congregation in the coffee region of the Sierra Madre in Chiapas. We spent the night in the public school of a small town. With the first sunlight of the new day, we could hear the growing sound of thousands of birds in the forest. I had never heard such a marvelous and polyphonic choir of so many different vibrations. In spite of the many years that have passed, that impression remains vivid in my mind. Those birds were truly glorifying God and enjoying him. They knew very well what the purpose of their existence was.

For most human beings, however, because of our condition as sinful and lost creatures, we find it rather difficult to join with bliss that singular choir. Even religious people find it difficult to accept this challenge. Saul of Tarsus was one of them. He had rehearsed all kinds of music through the first part of his life: Greek poetry and philosophy, Hebrew religion and ways, and Roman citizenship and prestige, but all without satisfaction. And now, before the manifested Lord himself, his only question was, "Lord, what do you want me to do?"

This was the very question that I had myself when I was studying at Princeton Theological Seminary, and I began to consider the possibility of going overseas to proclaim the gospel to indigenous tribes. The first answer from the Lord that I received then was "evangelize." I understood that was the top priority in God's purpose for my life and call. In the mind of the Lord, who is love, there is no more important thing than to declare broadly and effectively the redemptive work of Christ. To that end, he needs our human assistance. I was convinced by the Holy Spirit that the most pressing responsibility of any redeemed believer is to let Christ be known as the only Savior and Lord.

In 1939 there were only some ten Ch'ols converted to Christ in Chiapas. By 1951 there were thirteen congregations, from one hundred to four hundred members each. This was not the work of missionaries and pastors, colporteurs and chaplains, but of the powerful testimony of the nationals themselves. The last letter I received in those days from that region said, "The minister does not visit us, but the brethren do not cease to go out to evangelize in the colonies."

In 1949 there was only one Tzeltal converted to the gospel. By 1951 there were about twelve hundred. Again this was not the work of ministers but of the natives themselves under the guidance of the Holy Spirit. I remember in those days receiving a visit from a Tzeltal brother who had been imprisoned because of a false accusation by a local school teacher. He was first taken to the town of Oxchuc, where he was kept for four days and succeeded in converting another inmate. Later he was taken to the see of the municipality, which was two days away. On the way, he won to Christ the policeman who was transporting him.

Traditional believers tend to be indifferent to evangelization. They seem to be lazy when it comes to the fulfillment of the mission that has been entrusted to all believers by the Lord himself. For some, it is easier to hire somebody—a pastor, an evangelist, a missionary, a colporteur—to do the job. There are also ministers who are not willing to obey the Lord's clear mandate to evangelize; they prefer to run errands and do nothing for the Kingdom, forgetting that Christ came to bring good news to all people. How many pastors are very busy preaching instead of evangelizing? There is a world of difference between these two activities. The first means that people will come to you to hear you. The second means that you will go to the people for them to hear the gospel.

For many years, Chiapas had a pastor (José Coffin) who tried to avoid the pulpit and spent his life visiting small and isolated groups of believers. His emphasis on the rural work seemed to be the cause of a fanatic. But I learned from him, from my first days in Chiapas, the importance of direct and personal evangelization. My brother Bert is a surgeon, and when he had to leave Chiapas, not being allowed to practice his profession, he told me: "I need to go somewhere to practice surgery. Otherwise, I will lose the art." With evangelization, it is the same. You can read books, take courses, participate in congresses, but if you do not practice evangelization, you will lose the art. This is the reason why the apostle Paul said: "Woe to me if I do not proclaim the gospel" (1 Corinthians 9:16). I understood evangelization to be my first responsibility as a missionary in Chiapas.

There was a second responsibility: serving my neighbors in need. I found plenty of opportunities to do this, particularly with my indigenous brothers and sisters scattered in Chiapas. I have tried to imitate as much as possible Jesus himself when he said "For the Son of Man came not to be served but to serve, and to give his life as a ransom for many" (Mark 10:45). Ch'ol women working with their weaving looms speak of woof and warp. If evangelism is the woof of ministry, service is the warp. Christ teaches us not only to serve but also *how* to serve. This was his great teaching: "Whoever serves me must follow me, and where I am, there will my servant be also. Whoever serves me, the Father will honor" (John 12:26).

The third thing we have to do is grow in Christ. This responsibility is toward ourselves, and basically it has to do with our training for ministry. Mabel and I dedicated most of our time and energy to train the *mestizo* and the indigenous leadership in Chiapas. This was a never-ending process. As a young missionary, after receiving the best education at school and seminary, I came to Mexico to teach, to train, and to share with others the depth of my knowledge. It was, however, in crossing the mountains and rivers of Chiapas and visiting the small groups of believers and sharing our Christian testimony with them that I learned the most important lessons of my life. After decades of missionary service, I continued to grow in Christ and to learn new and great things through those to whom I was sent. I have learned the meaning of Paul's admonition: "Work out your own salvation with fear and trembling" (Philippians 2:12).

In this way, the Lord's response to my initial question (Lord, what do you want me to do?) immediately after he called me into ministry was threefold: First, he gave me a responsibility to himself, which was the evangelization of those lost in the darkness of sin. Second, he gave me a responsibility to my neighbors, which meant serving them as he served us all, "giving his life as a ransom for many." And third, he gave me a responsibility to myself, which was growing in him in my knowledge, character, spiritual life, and training for ministry.[1]

---

[1]   John R. Kempers, "Nuestro púlpito: ¿Qué quieres tú de mí?" *El Faro* (January 1, 1952): 9-11.

CHAPTER 76

My One and Only Mabe

Through all the years that Mabel and I have shared, I have loved her very much. I was the only one to call her Mabe, and this was at home. I admit that I have failed to call her more endearing terms, but I have always been shy and not very romantic. She always called me Kemp, but in her letters to me, she often had more affectionate phrases. Most of our shared expressions of love through the years have traveled through the mail. Mabel's letters exceeded by far my poor penmanship and lack of romantic prose. One of her letters that quite clearly defined her was written on January 30, 1925. In it Mabel communicated her decision to accompany me in life and ministry wherever the Lord would send us. I have always admired the passion and conviction behind her decision. If I became a useful servant of the Lord in Mexico, it was entirely due to her encouragement and patience. After the Lord, she was the one who helped me most to find my way in ministry. In a letter I wrote to her on March 12, 1925, I asked:

> My Pascarita,
> Mabel, one time you wrote to me about your hoping or thinking that I would be more than just an ordinary preacher. As

Mabel Kempers, a gracious, lovely,
and warm-hearted woman
(*courtesy Joy Fuder*)

I was coming from lunch, I was thinking of that and wondering what you had meant. The only ministers that you have come in contact with, as far as I know, have been considered to be above the ordinary run. At least, they have some of the largest churches. I'll consider myself quite far up the ladder if I ever equal Martin's standing [Rev. James M. Martin, pastor of Third Reformed Church, Holland]. I don't know what your opinion of him is and I really don't have a very definite opinion myself and what I do have may be very mistaken. [Somebody] made some sort of remark about him when Garry Vander Borg was at your place, the significance of which I failed to catch. Will you or can you tell me what you had in mind then?

I don't suppose I'll ever be a big preacher in a big church, although I assure you my aspirations and ideal is beyond the Martin type. I can't imagine myself fitting in anywhere where I should need helpers. I would feel happier where I could fix my own car and repair the leak in my own roof and mend my wife's ironing board and—oh, well you know. Perhaps that's why I turn to some mission field. Could I develop into what you expect of me on a mission field, Mabel?[1]

Mabel had a beautiful soprano voice that even in her later years of retirement was quite amazing. In 1979, when she was seventy-seven, she gave a brief testimony and sang a solo which I recorded; it was quite

---

[1]   JRK to MVD, March 12, 1925, in JAH.

The Women's Society of the Tuxtla church celebrates
Mabel's birthday with flowers and gifts

remarkable.[2] I loved her voice not only when she sang but also when
she spoke. She has always had a musical, sweet tone in her voice that
communicates peace and quietness.

On June 26, 1954, Mabel received a token of appreciation for her
ministry among the women of Chiapas. It consisted of an acronym in
Spanish that had a lot of meaning. The English translation is difficult,
but the idea is more or less like this:

MABEL

Your name involves the prophecy of your life:

M *MAESTRA* (teacher), chosen by God even before your birth, he
placed in you the gift of wisdom.
A *ABNEGADA* (altruistic), able to impart your teaching, far away
from your home and here in a new land.
B *BIENHECHORA* (benevolent), you have watered your path
with the seed of love, even when sometimes your hands bleed,
wounded by the thistles of ingratitude and ignorance.
E *EVANGELISTA* (evangelist), indefatigably leading to Christ
children, young people, and adults.
L *LÍDER* (leader), of our Women's Society, you have taught us to
occupy our place in the Work of the Lord.[3]

---

[2]   Roger D. Kempers, interview with author via email, April 8, 2014, in JAH.
[3]   Acronym in JAH.

It is almost impossible to summarize her many contributions to the work of the National Presbyterian Church during the many years of our service in Chiapas. Dorothy Dickens Meyerink did this on one occasion, and I was surprised to see the results.[4]

- Guided the Women's Societies in local churches to form a State Union which holds annual conventions.
- Worked with other women to prepare bylaws and rules to govern the Union of Women's Societies.
- Member of the executive committee and secretary of the State Union for many years.
- Played the folding organ or piano for innumerable worship services, meetings, and other occasions.
- Taught Sunday school and Bible school classes.
- A role model of Christian wife and mother for Mexican and missionary women.
- A true partner and encourager in all of Kemp's activities and work.
- Arranged for and taught many short courses for young girls, often using as teachers some of the young Chiapas women, graduates of the Bible school.
- Edited *Reflejos Femeniles* (Feminine reflections), the paper published by the Union of Women's Societies and distributed the copies to its members.
- Edited *The Charm and Challenge of Chipas*, an illustrated annual booklet written by Reformed Church missionaries, from its first issue in 1955 until leaving Chiapas.
- Translated Christmas and Easter songs into Spanish and taught them to key people in the Tapachula areas who, in turn, trained others in their home churches.
- Founded the very popular *Annual Institute of Sacred Music*.

Mabel traveled occasionally with me. She was always ready to go through any discomfort or difficulties during those travels. She never complained about spending hours waiting for a delayed train or driving the dusty roads of Chiapas. Mabel never expected a five-star hotel but accepted with gratitude any hammock or bed in the most humble hut or house. In 1956 she wrote an article entitled "Riding Circuit in the Sierra Madre" that illustrates her positive attitude toward our missionary travels.

[4]   DDM, "Seventy Years of Missionary Service: Part 2," *Missionary Monthly* (October 1995), 7-8.

At noon we reached the heights of Male—cold and beautiful in towering forests (over 10,000 feet above sea level). There we worshipped with the family of an aged, bed-ridden patriarch, ate dinner in the smoke-filled kitchen, and Lolo, the bachelor son, became one of us as we headed down toward El Porvenir. Late in the afternoon, when we were weary from goading on the tired animals, El Porvenir lay before us at the end of the pass. A snug cluster of white houses and brown sheep corrals, it was a scene of Arcadian peace. Sleek slopes rose gently on three sides, close cropped by flocks that roamed shepherdless and golden brown now in the dry season. High above, their tips were lost in a frame of forest green. Alone and picturesque against a hill stood a new white church, which later we were to find crowded with believers and furnished with quaint originality and regional color.[5]

Traveling in those days was sometimes dangerous. On one occasion, I was driving southeast from Tuxtla on the old Pan-American Highway to a preaching engagement. On this route, one drove through Chiapa de Corzo and then cruised over a mile of straight highway that ran directly to a steep hillside. The road then snaked up this hillside for about two thousand feet. On a backward S-curve about half way up this hillside, my Jeep skidded as I rounded the first curve. The Jeep spun around and bumped up against a low curb at the edge of the highway. The vehicle tipped over the chasm and then fell back to put all four wheels on the highway. If it had gone over the edge, it would have rolled a thousand feet down the hillside. After I shared this experience with other missionaries, they began to call that curve "Kemp's corner." Interestingly, the sermon I had prepared to preach at the church to which I was traveling that day was about guardian angels.[6]

That was not the only occasion when my life was put at risk and Mabel nearly became a widow. Around 1960 the presbytery meeting in Los Llanos, near the ocean, went on and on into the evening, but we were determined to drive to Tuxtla after the late closing hour. One man drove our Jeep full of delegates, and I drove the Van Engen's Dodge van. Everyone was asleep except for the drivers—supposedly. At some point during the long, steep climb between Cintalapa and Ocozocoautla, there was a bang. I had fallen asleep and veered off the road to the right.

5   Mabel Van Dyke Kempers, "Riding Circuit in the Sierra Madre," quoted in "John & Mabel Kempers: They Planted Seeds of Christianity in the Mexican State of Chiapas," *The Church Herald* (February 2000), 17.

6   J. Samuel Hofman, interview with author, Holland, Michigan, April 8, 2014, in JAH.

Mabel accompanied me on one of my pastoral trips
on this sure-footed and stubborn mule

There was some fender damage and a missing light, but we were able to continue our journey. I don't think any of the passengers realized that, had I run off the road to the left, we would have fallen a thousand feet.[7]

Mabel was truly my partner on the mission field. She never lost the passion of her call to accompany me to the "ends of the world." This conviction remained with her from the first hour and was the key factor in keeping her standing in the midst of opposition and incredible difficulties. She continued onward in spite of the fact that I had warned her in the most dramatic way that our career would not be easy. Before we made the final decision to go to Mexico, I told her:

> You made me happy during my stay at your place, when you assured me with more than words that you would be happy with me in some far off country. Dr. or Sir [James C. R.] Ewing told us last week that the romance of any mission field wore off in three months, and from then on, it was the hardest kind of work. He said that, of all the missionaries he had ever talked with, and he has talked with them for forty-six years, only one had ever regretted that he had gone out. That one had a wife who was always crying for her mother. He said, "If you ever are in a situation like that,

---

[7]   JRK, "Strength through Weakness," 2.

take her back to her mother, but don't take her from her mother in the first place." Such a question or problem all must face, and my girl has assured me that if I decide or have decided for me that I am to go to South America or Central America, she will be my biggest help and will always have a cheerful and happy greeting for me "when I come home."

It's fun to think of the future that way and of all that is to come. It's all such a mystery and a question mark. But I have no doubt that it is best so. Things have turned out far better for me so far than I have deserved, and I may therefore hope that they will continue to do so. I have had to make all my decisions alone so far, but in a few years, someone will help me. Someone will help to lessen the number of mistakes I have made.[8]

Yes, Mabel was my lifesaver on more than one occasion and the one person who helped me to stay focused on my call and on reality. We truly became "one flesh," one person with one heart for missions and the Kingdom of God. Without her, it would have been impossible for me to do anything significant in the Lord's vineyard.

[8]   JRK to MVD, March 12, 1925.

CHAPTER 77

José Coffin Sánchez

José Coffin Sánchez, my mentor and boss, my friend and enemy, passed away in Monterrey, Nuevo León, under the care of his son José Coffin. In his later years, he had traveled to Monterrey looking for better conditions for his feeble health. Few were the months he could spend there, but enough to gain the appreciation of everybody in the Presbyterian church, El Divino Redentor, in Bellavista Colony. Finally, it was on the ninth day of June 1956, at five thirty in the morning that he was promoted to true glory. He had preached his last sermon to this congregation in the Easter Sunday morning service.[1]

Coffin was born in the state of Tabasco in the region of La Chontalpa, on January 21, 1881. He was wrongly considered an American; he was 100 percent Mexican. His father—Joseph Coffin Deems—was an American of Scottish descent who had come to Mexico from Kentucky with various other people after the defeat of the Confederates in the Civil War, never to return. His mother—Tomasa Sánchez—was a native of Tabasco. Both of them were first-generation Mexican Protestants in

---

[1]   "Últimos días del Dr. Coffin," *El Faro* (October 1956): 20.

The Coffin family served tirelessly in Tapachula for twenty-nine years

that Mexican state. As a child, José was raised in the evangelical faith, and early in his youth, he dedicated himself to Christian ministry. He receivd his theological training at the Presbyterian Seminary in Coyoacán, close to Mexico City. He was part of the first generation to graduate from there in 1904. As a student, he served the Presbyterian Church of Veracruz, mostly as a colporteur, and had the opportunity to visit places like Jalpan, Coatepec, Xico, Teocelo, and Huatusco selling and distributing Bibles. In Teocelo, a fanatic tried to kill him, but he managed to escape. After graduation, he became the pastor of the congregation at Veracruz, and then he, together with Newell J. Elliott and J. Miraval Lausan, established the medical work in that town.

Coffin and his wife, Professor Luz Otero, went to Paraíso, Tabasco, where they administered a school for several years. In Tabasco he also organized the work of the Red Cross during the difficult years of the Mexican Revolution, which both he and his wife supported. His revolutionary ideas were expressed in the biography of General Ignacio Gutiérrez, a Presbyterian and revolutionary *tabasqueño*.[2] Coffin's wife was a teacher in elementary schools and taught Christian doctrine in the churches that he served as pastor.[3]

---

[2]   José Coffin, *El General Gutiérrez: héroe presbiteriano de la Revolución maderista en Tabasco* (Mexico: Publicaciones El Faro, 1912).

[3]   Alberto Rosales Pérez, *Historia de la Iglesia Nacional Presbiteriana El Divino Salvador de la ciudad de México* (Mexico: published by the author, 1998).

His most celebrated endeavors of evangelism, however, were performed in Chiapas, starting in 1919. He was considered to be the one person who introduced Presbyterianism to various dispersed groups in the intricate geography of Chiapas. He called his ministry *ruralismo* (rural work), because it consisted of intense journeys throughout the state on foot and on horse. He used extensively lay leaders whom he himself had trained for ministry and whom he called chaplains.[4]

He was an outstanding Mexican pastor and an important coworker in our mission's early years. He had a great influence on me as I reviewed and pruned my concept of mission and attempted to contextualize my ministry in Chiapas to all of its inhabitants. I followed his "eight principles" and taught them to succeeding missionaries by word and by deed.[5]

Coffin moved to Chiapas in 1920, five years before we did, sponsored by the Northern Presbyterian Mission. He had ordained elders in four of the largest existing Presbyterian groups, thereby organizing these groups into churches. All groups in the area became satellite congregations, each with an appointed chaplain. The choice of a chaplain was determined by his spiritual life and not his oratorical abilities.[6] Coffin's introduction of the concept of local leadership based on one's Christian experience and pastoral skills worked well in the early years. A chaplain was appointed to be the sole head of the group and acted as under shepherd of the flock in his care. I admired Coffin's dedication to the Kingdom, the energy he invested in the work, his doctrinal zeal, his willingness to sacrifice himself for the Lord, and his moral integrity.

Throughout the years, Coffin's name was mentioned many times when the Presbyterian work in Mexico was recounted. He exceeded others in his personal convictions and his support of a conservative Calvinism. Outside the state of Chiapas, he was remembered as an outstanding Presbyterian leader. Within the state, he had some loyal support among the older people, but in fear of losing sole control, he opposed attempts at outreach and growth. His distrust of young people, with whom we had worked so intimately, was also remembered. The other Reformed Church missionaries had never had to deal with this man who had given me so many headaches. He asked me point blank one day why we had moved from Tapachula to Tuxtla Gutiérrez

---

[4]   Esponda, *El presbiterianismo en Chiapas*, 165-66.
[5]   DDM, *Ministry among the* Maya, 37. On Coffin's missionary principles see following chapter.
[6]   JRK, "Some of This and Some of That," 1.

in our second term—a wise move on our part to get away from his domineering control. Tuxtla was a central place from which we could direct work throughout the state.[7]

Coffin had a very strong personality, and it was almost impossible not to have a clash with him. On more than one occasion, he was like a nail in my shoe. The man was an enigma. He never wrote or spoke in plain language. He was a politician who trusted no one. Our problems with him were many but were especially due to the Tapachula property purchased with Northern Presbyterian money and held in Coffin's name. Without approval, he kept enlarging the property, all due to a statement made by a Presbyterian Board treasurer: "Wouldn't it be nice if we could own this whole block for school purposes?" This was merely wishful thinking, but Coffin claimed it as permission which had to hold sway even over the Reformed Church in America. His intention was, without our prior authorization, to keep adding pieces of property to enlarge Mrs. Coffin's day school, each time causing a financial mess. To keep that property from being confiscated by the government, he had to be involved in a long fight against church members and government forces.

In 1930 he lost half of the congregation, who claimed that the Presbyterian Board had given the property to the church and not to Coffin for school purposes. Since the government claimed all church property, that distinction had to be maintained. When it was finally apparent that the government would not grant permission to continue a private school, the board issued an order that all excess property not needed for a new church building and parsonage had to be sold. In the end, when the congregation was ready to construct the new church, we were proud of the place we had designed and our cooperation in building.[8]

The second problem was that Coffin, as he himself had often stated, wanted to be in charge of the whole state of Chiapas or nothing. I saw this attitude to be detrimental to the sound development and maturation of the work. This had a lot to do with the goals of self support and self government of the churches. We always had this tight rope to walk between self government and getting things done. When I look back, it is remarkable how easy it was to get consistorial approval, unless Coffin stood around with the sword of Damocles. Don Daniel Aguilar Ochoa's selfishness and stubbornness was also something to

[7]   JRK to Richard Vander Voet, July 10, 1985, in JAH.
[8]   Ibid.

When the Gulf Presbytery met in Tuxtla, Kemp and
Ezequiel Lango challenged Coffin's authority

contend with in this regard, but he was only a flea compared to Coffin the Lion.[9]

There was also the fact that Coffin had spent a quarter of his time in Tabasco. As the correspondence shows, I had one long series of problems trying to keep him on the field of Chiapas. He would neither respect the rules which limited his time off the field nor agree to a pay cut from the Reformed Church. I was criticized for not paying him when he worked in Tabasco by those who should have been paying him if they wanted him to work in their field. In fact, he received his salary from the Chiapas churches and the Reformed Church, but he spent months of unapproved time each year in Tabasco. His extended stays outside the state of Chiapas and especially in Tabasco was a constant irritant, and I was obsessed with this issue. At each yearly presbytery meeting, as director-treasurer of the mission, I would make arrangements that ministers with missionary support could have time for attending presbytery and synod meetings plus two weeks of vacation, but he would stay away for months. On one occasion, he did it with the pretense that he was gathering historical data. When this historical data did not materialize, he said that the termites had eaten his notes![10]

[9]   JRK to JSH, Sept. 4, 1971.
[10]   Ibid.

This meeting of the Synod of the Gulf was probably the last meeting
of Coffin (*back row, center*) and myself (*third from left in grey suit*).
Far right in grey suit is Genaro de la Rosa; *behind him* is Bartolomé
Solórzano; *behind him* is Margarito Hernández López; the
Executive Committee is seated in front; *third from left
seated* is Daniel Aguilar Ochoa

Our move inland to Tuxtla Gutiérrez away from Tapachula
proved wise. It paved the way for the great young people's work and
the women's ministries which Coffin had opposed. It gave us access to
the center and the north of the state, where Coffin's infrequent and
difficult visits left nothing permanent. His influence and control did
not lead beyond Comitán to the east and Pijijiapan to the west. The
board somehow helped in all of these problems due to the Depression
and their lack of understanding of the situation. It all was a washout
until Rev. Frederick Zimmerman came into the picture.

In Tabasco, Coffin was much honored for many years. He was
remembered even in the names of schools and public buildings. In
Chiapas, however, he was all but forgotten. A man who might have
done great things, but who was his own worst enemy, that was Mr.
Coffin. He lived the last fifty years of his life behind the times. I have
learned from him many good things: personal evangelism, rural work,
lay participation in the work, personal contact with the people, and
many other important issues. He fought against bringing in outside
pastors and opposed the organization of the Presbytery of Chiapas. His

love for Tabasco and the past led him to leave when our presbytery was organized.

Here was a classic case of losing one's gift if it is not used. Coffin once boasted that he had not preached for eighteen years because the people were incapable of understanding sermons. Later, when he tried to preach, he had completely lost the art, if he had ever had it. He simply told inconsequential stories. In Tuxtla, where sermons were frequently preached, he tried three successive nights and failed miserably each night. At the organization of the General Assembly of the Presbyterian Church in Mexico and as its first president, he had a crowded auditorium to preach to at the Divino Salvador church, and he failed miserably. I was on the platform and saw Eleazar Z. Pérez shake his head in disgust at the lost opportunity of preaching to that crowd. As I have always said: "Qué lastima!" What might he have been![11]

The Presbyterian Church in the United States somehow recognized Coffin's best virtues and honored him, granting him through Whitworth College, at Spokane, Washington, a doctorem in divinitate pro meritus eius, on May 31, 1948. The following day, in the afternoon, he addressed the plenary of the General Assembly of the Presbyterian Church in Seattle, on the occasion of the presentation of the banner of the Presbyterian system, ornamented with the heraldic coats of arms of Mexico and the Presbyterian Church. This was probably the utmost level of his self-glorification.[12]

Coffin's many travels throughout Chiapas were impressive. I was inspired and motivated by his account of a trip with a group of scientists to the remote region of the Lacandons that I read in *El Faro*.

> Insignificant seems to me having stayed in the beautiful border town of Las Margaritas, on the way toward my Tabasco, after transiting by foot during several weeks through the six valleys and seven *serranías* [mountainous country] of the wild Lancandonan jungle in scientific studies, and having to suffer the healing of my *colmoyotes* and the typhoid that they get there too. It also is not a great deal to converse day by day with hostile porters and *macheteros* [cutters] who curse and oppose against the wise and their humble workers bragging on their demagogy with their tobacco, their *aguardiente* [firewater, strong liquor], and the smarter with their *escapularios* [scapularies] on their necks. And to improvise jungle

[11] Typed page, n.d. or signed but found in a file of Kempers titled with the name of Coffin, in JAH.
[12] "El Dr. José Coffin," *El Faro* (July 1, 1948): 5-6.

dorms by the rivers or peaceful streams or by the grandiose falls is almost nothing, looking to the sky through the laces of branches inhabited by not that much surly pheasants, parrots, or monkeys; branches illuminated through the nights by the bonfires specially destined to drive away the beasts; tormenting branches for those who would like to see horizons even for a moment each week, and they are not able to see them.[13]

Coffin, however, made his most significant contribution in Tabasco. There he won the recognition of both the church and the state, which was no small thing. On the occasion of the inauguration of a public library named after Coffin in Puerto Ceiba, Tabasco, General Miguel Orrico de los Llanos, the governor of that state, made the following statement: "You have made a great and right decision, and there is not a better chosen person to carry the name of this library because, in all that is good, teacher Coffin is great and he symbolizes for us the best."[14]

---

[13]   José Coffin, "Un viaje a la selva lacandona," *El Faro* (July 1, 1932): 5-6.
[14]   "Un embajador es exaltado," *El Faro* (July 1, 1948): 18.

CHAPTER 78

Missionary Strategy

To evangelize and plant churches in a region as challenging as Chiapas during the first half of the twentieth century, it was necessary to develop a singular missionary strategy. The lack of communications capabilities in conjunction with a rough terrain with two major mountain ranges, created an environment plagued with difficulties. These physical and geographical factors operated together within a multiplicity of cultures and languages. Three quarters of the population in those years spoke Spanish, but the other quarter spoke five Mayan languages as their mother tongue (Tzeltal, Ch'ol, Tzotzil, Tojolabal, and Lacandon) and Zoque, an ancient pre-Columbian language coming from the neighboring Mexican state of Oaxaca. By the time of our arrival in Chiapas, four other pre-Columbian languages had already disappeared (Mam, Quiche, Chiapa, and Motozintlec).[1]

Another major challenge for the proclamation of the gospel in Chiapas was the culture of religion at that time. The region had been Christianized by the Roman Catholic Church since the days of the conquest by the Spanish Empire. But the old and traditional religions

---

[1]   Esponda, *El presbiterianismo en Chiapas*, 11-13.

of the natives remained almost intact, thus creating high levels of syncretism. On the other hand, the competition in proselytism among the evangelical denominations and missions was shameful and created new difficulties. In Chiapas the National Presbyterian Church in Mexico carried out evangelistic mission work in conflict not only with the Roman Catholic Church but also with the Adventists, Nazarenes, Baptists, and others.

A singular missionay strategy, therefore, would guarantee the best results with the most efficient use of the scarce resources available. The task of developing this strategy was first attempted by José Coffin. As mentioned, he visited Chiapas in 1919 and began missionary work a year later. In a rather short period of time, Coffin was able to develop some basic guidelines for mission in Chiapas that proved to be very contextualized and effective. His missionary strategy consisted of:

1. Personal evangelism: as opposed to public campaign evangelism, which proved to be fruitless and very difficult to organize.
2. Rural work: as opposed to church development in the cities, which was the Presbyterian pattern in much of the rest of Mexico at the time.
3. Ministry of the laity: in each small congregation of believers, Coffin would name *capellanes* (lay chaplains) who would preach, visit homes of those interested, and be organizational leaders of new believers.
4. Pastoral leaders: they were to be chosen on the basis of experience, giftedness, and leadership as recognized by their congregation. All leadership positions were to be voluntary, with no remuneration.
5. Clear ecclesiastical structures: these were taught and carefully organized along the lines of Presbyterian polity.
6. Avoid publicity: whenever possible, this should be done due to the constant harassment and persecution of believers. This persecution dated back to the beginning of the twentieth century.[2]

I learned these missionary guidelines from Coffin and by accompanying him in his missionary work. He had a deep impact on my young heart and mind. He was my early mentor, and I learned foundational mission principles for work in Chiapas from him. His teaching methodology was tough and imposing, as I soon realized

---

[2]   Ibid., 237. See Charles Van Engen, "Mission Basics 101: Lessons from Chiapas for the 21st Century," *Reformed Review* 58, no. 1 (Autumn 2004): 16.

when I went with him for almost two months on my first exploratory trip throughout the state. But I will never forget what I have learned by his side, even from his mistakes and contradictions.

To these very rich experiences, I added my own and what I had learned from my avid readings on these issues. I had read the most important thinkers of my day in this field. All this allowed me to develop my own missionary strategy, in light of more effective principles tailored to the specific needs in Chiapas. For almost thirty years, I tried to apply the missionary strategy inspired by these guidelines. These missiological principles are as follows:

1. Decentralization of church workers and missionaries, spreading them out and placing them in strategic locations.
2. The identification of the missionaries with the indigenous people (a key to success of the mission work, especially in the Maya areas).
3. Establishing only institutions that the national church could later direct and maintain without subsidies.
4. Supporting the construction of churches and pastors' homes only if the local church paid half the cost, following the principles of good stewardship.
5. Avoiding the payment of such high salaries that later the national church could not take over the complete support of its own ministers and church workers.
6. Giving preference to the training of national pastors and lay church workers, over the introduction of a growing number of expatriate missionaries.
7. Working toward having the Maya churches and the Spanish-speaking *mestizo* churches be part of one Presbytery of Chiapas for the good of the church and for the integration and empowerment of the Maya Christians.
8. Seeking the approval of local consistories and the presbytery before initiating any new mission work.[3]

In practical terms, these mission principles were expressed in at least seven specific ways.[4] First, I was convinced of the most foundational principle of classical Reformed missiology, that the biblically based goal of mission was the conversion of people to faith in Jesus Christ, the planting of churches, and the glory of God. I summarized this

---

[3] Esponda, *El presbiterianismo en Chiapas*, 238-39.
[4] What follows is a summary of Van Engen, "Mission Basics 101: Lessons from Chiapas for the 21st Century," 17-30.

principle in the motto that guided our missionary enterprise, "Chiapas para Cristo" (Chiapas for Christ). The perspective of this goal of mission permeated our vision, set our priorities, and guided our day-to-day decisions in Chiapas. This understanding of mission made it necessary to emphasize long-term identification and deep immersion on the part of the missionaries in the culture and life of the people and the churches in each place. There was no room for short-term mission endeavors, and missionaries had to be seen primarily as evangelists and as the supporters, trainers, and equippers of indigenous evangelists. To this end, it was necessary for a missionary to gain the right to be heard in becoming an integral part of the life of the new culture, enjoying close personal relationships with people in the Chiapanecan culture. In my understanding, new missionaries coming to Chiapas should spend their first four years living in a village or small town, listening to, worshiping with, and learning from the Christians there.

Second, I was convinced that when a person comes to biblical faith in Jesus Christ, there begins a process of conversion that transforms all aspects of that person's life, both personally and socially. There is no dichotomy between proclamation evangelism and social action. A split between faith and action was contrary to the Maya worldview, which understands that all of life is interconnected. It is also in contradiction to biblical truth, which teaches that conversion to Jesus Christ has an impact on every aspect of life. This holistic understanding of the gospel provided the foundation for our missionary activities in Chiapas. Our central desire was that men and women became disciples of Jesus Christ and responsible members of Christ's church. But we also worked for everybody to come to a life in abundance, to a truly human life. In our Chiapas environment, a holistic gospel and an integral approach to conversion was, in fact, powerfully subversive and transformational.

Third, I was convinced that the most effective means of evangelizing people, especially in resistant areas, was for Christians to share their newfound faith in their heart language and in culturally appropriate ways with those with whom they had a natural affinity. Personal, relational witness was the primary means by which the churches grew in Chiapas. Relational evangelism was the key to church growth in this part of the world. It was even more effective because of a pattern of constant relocation of people throughout the state. All this, together with the use of every available technological means at our disposal to share the gospel, resulted in impressive numbers of new believers.

Fourth, I was convinced that the development and growth of the church was first and foremost the spontaneous work of the Holy Spirit, and human efforts and organizations were secondary at best. In Chiapas this principle had a unique twist, because it became a principle of decentralization. As director of the Chiapas Mission, I insisted on placing the new missionaries arriving in the state in remote areas, with little contact with other expatriate missionaries. I believed that this dispersion would force the expatriate missionaries to learn from, work with, and depend upon national leadership and local people. The application of this principle resulted in the integration of the Presbyterian work and the development of a spirit of close companionship, cooperation, and interdependence. On the other side, I set almost as a rule for our missionaries the practice of not beginning anything that the national church could not continue. Chiapas Christians therefore were able to support their own pastors and pay for their buildings with their own resources as a result of this rule.

Fifth, I was convinced that congregations should be appropriate in every respect to the culture in which they were located. In Chiapas this principle was already woven into the very fabric of Reformed Church missionary life because of the patterns of decentralization and partnership. But over time, the importance of cultural indigeneity, as understood through the lens of cultural anthropology, became even more important. Our close partnership with Wycliffe Bible Translators most likely helped us in this direction. This principle was the basis for requiring that new missionary recruits spend most of their first four years getting to know the people, language, and culture of their new adopted home. Language learning was considered an integral part of their mission work, as was the case with Mabel and me at the beginning of our ministry. This also meant that missionaries had to give top priority to long-term missionary service in Chiapas.

Sixth, I was convinced that every Christian should be learning the Bible from someone and teaching the Bible to someone. I applied this principle especially in the Spanish-speaking churches. It was my practice to carry with me boxes of Bibles on every trip, distributing and selling them in the churches or leaving them on consignment with pastors, lay evangelists, elders, deacons, and church leaders. Mabel and I were very much involved in Bible teaching in the local churches and in the training of leaders. An expression of this principle was also the organization of the Union of Christian Endeavor Societies (1943) and the Union of Women's Societies (1947). We organized Bible recitation bees like spelling bees. We held competitions in on-the-spot extemporaneous

Bible expositions. There were also competitions and presentations of music and drama. And every night, there was serious Bible study. We worked hard to establish Sunday schools in every congregation. The dedication of the Chiapas Mission to the translation of the Bible into the various Mayan languages is evidence of our long-term commitment to sound biblical instruction.

Seventh, I was convinced that pastoral leaders of the church should be indigenous to their churches, the natural, culturally appropriate leaders raised up from the ranks of the faithful. They should be chosen on the basis of their experience in ministry and their giftedness, and their leadership ability should be recognized and confirmed by the congregation. Their formal theological education was important but should be viewed in a supporting role, not as the sole basis for their leadership. I had learned this principle from Coffin and consistently applied it throughout my ministry. This indigenous pattern of home-grown leadership was a wonderful fountain from which flowed a constant stream of new leaders who could respond to the explosive growth of the churches in Chiapas. In time, the creation of Bible schools and a seminary in Chiapas supplemented the experience-based, ministerial formation of these workers.

CHAPTER 79

Work with Natives

We began ministry in Chiapas with the Spanish-speaking people, but later our primary focus became the Maya tribes. In fact, I was chosen as the first missionary to this field because of my experience in the work with Native Americans, which although very limited, was judged by board leaders to be commendable. The Holy Spirit definitely guided us in Chiapas not to take the "straight road" but the "long way round" by first building up the Spanish-speaking church, which with time became the Presbytery of Chiapas. In our efforts to secure suitable national ministers for this ever-expanding work, we were severely tried. But our constant prayers were answered, and we proved to be right in expecting a considerable number of Mexican pastors to be raised up throughout the years.

As to the work with the Maya, we could do almost nothing in our first two decades of missionary work in Chiapas. We were not, however, unmindful of the Maya. At length, we were happy that by 1958, we had two couples dedicated to the work in the two largest Maya tribes. But we were fully convinced that one family could not efficiently conduct a Bible school among them. To bank on the help of Wycliffe

Bible Translators, in this phase of the work, for any length of time, was unwise because that was not the type of work they were called upon to do. Furthermore, they were not officially related to the presbytery. To expect *mestizo* ministers to do this work was almost beyond hope. So far, in all Mexico, I knew of only one *mestizo* who had learned a Mayan language so he could work among them. American missionaries had been able to adapt themselves better to this work than *mestizos*, and usually they were more acceptable to the natives because they came free of prejudice.

Throughout the years, I was very mindful that succeeding boards had the same vision and goals as the board of 1925. Already by 1958, half of the membership of the church in Chiapas was monolingual Maya, but they were not receiving the attention and help that the *mestizos* were.[1] The incorporation of new missionaries to the missionary force working among Maya tribes was necessary. This, however, was the most challenging of all ministries in the mission field.

Our goal from the first day of our labors was "Chiapas para Cristo" (Chiapas for Christ). And by Chiapas, we meant every single human being in this part of the world, no matter which language he or she spoke. We have always wanted to proclaim the good news in such a way that, by all means, we could be able to save some. By 1956 we had 150 congregations, large and small, using Spanish, Ch'ol, and Tzeltal. We kept ourselves busy visiting most of these groups at least once a year. The Chiapas missionaries, however, did not limit themselves to sermon preparation and preaching. A well-rounded program called for more than preaching.

In order that "by all means [we] might win some" much time and thought was given to other activities. One priority was the training of lay leaders both *mestizo* and Maya to serve in the scattered churches. Lay workers required instruction, and this was the reason for the various programs we developed in places like Tuxtla, San Cristóbal, and Tapachula, as well as the Bible schools for Ch'ols and Tzeltals. In addition, right from the beginning of our ministry in Chiapas, we used visual methods for education and evangelization. The old projectors used carbide and told the gospel story thousands of times in cities and villages and on plantations. Later gasoline and electric models were used. Eventually the mission purchased an Ampro soundstrip movie projector, and for some time, we featured the picture *King of Kings*, which was a success, especially among the indigenous population. Connected

---

[1]   JRK to Russell J. Redeker, August 7, 1958, in JAH.

These portable phonographs facilitated much effective evangelism

with the showing of this film were Bible sales and distribution and the offer of a simple Bible correspondence course that Garold Van Engen and his personnel in San Cristóbal administered for many years for hundreds of believers.[2]

The gospel in Mexico spread far more rapidly among the poor and less educated than among others who feared the loss of prestige resulting from a break with the Roman Catholic Church. The increase in the number of believers was explosive, particularly among the various Maya groups, and rapid growth occurred among the Ch'ols. In 1940 few Ch'ols had heard the good news of salvation. But about that time, the Lord had touched the hearts of Ch'ol men who had heard the gospel in the *ladino* (Spanish-speaking) towns of Yajalón and Tumbalá. Their hearts were opened to understanding. Directed by the Holy Spirit, they returned to their villages to tell others of the things which they had heard. *Ladino* evangelists began to travel among the Ch'ol villages, expounding upon the Word of God, teaching hymns, and preaching.

Into this Spirit-prepared setting came the newly translated hymns and scripture portions in Ch'ol from Wycliffe Bible Translators. Interested men learned to read and study the newly written scripture selections with the translators. All the while, they and others were telling

[2]   JRK, "By All Means to Save Some," *Charm and Challenge*, no. 2 (1956), 3-4.

of their newly found faith and joy. They were very much like the early Christians who said, "For we cannot keep from speaking about what we have seen and heard" (Acts 4:20). Thus, from infancy, the Ch'ol church was a missionary church. After beginning in their own villages, men began going out "two by two" to other villages to tell the good news. Soon, records were cut, with new Christians and the translators singing hymns, reading scripture, and giving testimony. It became common for men to go out each weekend with a hand-wound phonograph in a net bag. People's hearts had been prepared by the Holy Spirit, so when they heard the good news, they believed.[3]

---

[3]   Charmaine and Henry Stegenga, "Two by Two," *Charm and Challenge*, no. 12 (1966), 19.

CHAPTER 80

Chiapas Mission Meetings

The Lord gave Mabel and me the distinction of being the pioneer missionaries of the Reformed Church in Chiapas. This was a priceless privilege as well as a tremendous burden. For almost eighteen years, we felt alone in the task, without the assistance of any other missionaries sent by the board. Finally, during the 1940s and 1950s, we had the joy of welcoming several new missionary couples sent by the Reformed Church, plus those who came to serve with Wycliffe Bible Translators and the pilots of Missionary Aviation Fellowship.

Reformed Church missionaries were needed to continue the work of the translators when their translations were finished, and as pioneer missionaries, Mabel and I enjoyed the privilege and opportunity to be instrumental in getting young servants of the Lord into Mexico and placing them in their missionary fields among the Ch'ol and Tzeltal natives.

In 1952, twenty-seven years after the Reformed Church began its work in Chiapas, Albert (Al) and Nita De Voogd arrived in the Ch'ol village of Santa María with their two small children. And in 1956, in Tuxtla Gutiérrez, Mabel and I welcomed Paul and Dorothy Meyerink in preparation for their move to Corralito. In September 1959, Sam

At the 1960 meeting, the Chiapas Mission now included six couples
(*courtesy J. Samuel and Helen Hofman*)

and Helen Hofman arrived in Corralito to partner with the Meyerinks among the Oxchuc Tzeltal natives, and Henry and Charmaine Stegenga joined the De Voogds in Berea. Together they developed successful training programs for the Tzeltal and Ch'ol church leaders.

Chiapas presented a variety of responsibilities and challenges for the Meyerinks and the Hofmans who taught and trained leaders for the 150 Tzeltal congregations at the Tzeltal Bible Center. Paul and Sam worked hard to organize the Tzeltal Bible School after much consultation with Tzeltal church leaders and the Chiapas Mission. They wanted the Tzeltal Bible School to become an indigenous institution, fully supported and run by the Tzeltal church. In addition to teaching, Paul majored in Bible translation, and Sam was responsible for the supervision of the growing number of Tzeltal health clinics, each staffed by a Christian medical worker.

The presence of more missionaries and their very scattered locations in the state encouraged us to organize ourselves into the Chiapas Mission. With the arrival and partnership of the Van Engens, our labors were enriched. We developed a wonderful relationship that resulted in each one of us dedicating our energies to more specific ministries. And as more new missionary couples came, the possibilities of our work multiplied, as did the need to organize our labor and strategies. I continued to lead; I held orientations and shared my

Al De Voogd, Helen Hofman, Charles Van Engen, and myself at
the Ixtelja airstrip (*courtesy J. Samuel and Helen Hofman*)

experiences with our new partners. At the same time, I was very aware
that the continuity of our testimony in Chiapas depended upon our
capacity to delegate responsibilities to others. In this way, my singular
authority was first shared with Garold Van Engen and then with the
other arriving missionaries. This led to the development of a mission
organization that could ensure the stability of the work and its
expansion after my retirement.

Our foremost objectives were to coordinate our efforts, maintain
dynamic communication among the various stations, and assist the
missionaries as needed in their particular ministries. Our meetings
were a highlight of our time at the Chiapas Mission; we tried to hold
them on a regular schedule and with frequency. I remember every one
of these meetings with joy, but there was one in particular which I have
kept in my heart as a cherished memory. It was celebrated in 1959 at the
Ch'ol Bible School (Berea) on the banks of the Tulija River.

The Cessna had already shuttled one load—Garold and Ruth
Van Engen, with their daughter Betty, and Helen Hofman—between
San Cristóbal de Las Casas and Ixtelja. On its second flight, with Sam
Hofman, Charles Van Engen, and Mabel and me aboard, magnificent
clouds of white froth, moving persistently upward, forced our little
plane to climb to ten thousand feet, one thousand feet higher than on
the previous trip.

Our pilot, Floyd Bishop, called out, "There's Ixtelja; we're going
down." To drop in the blink of an eye from that height to a tiny, sea-
level airstrip in the choppy terrain of Chiapas was everyday business for
the skilled and dedicated men of Missionary Aviation Fellowship. And

Garold and Al guide the canoe to a safe landing on the Tulija River

we, knowing they were the Lord's annointed, flew in their care without fear and with gratitude to him and to them.

The mission meeting in Berea was a reality because of these pilots. The only alternative to the fifty-minute plane ride was an eight-day round trip of plodding horse travel. Never before had the Chiapas Mission even considered meeting outside the cities, much less in such a remote and isolated corner of the world as Berea.

We came down at Ixtelja. It was only a spot in the green jungle where a rancher had built a rough house and cleared back enough rank growth for an airstrip parallel to the river. This was Al and Nita De Voogd's point of contact with the outside world. Practically everything needed for living in that remote region was flown in here and then carried upriver to Berea in Al and Nita's small aluminum boat rigged with an outboard motor. This boat bore us up the swift Tulija, banked with tall wild cane and great tropical trees whose branches reached down to the water, forming shady bowers where white lilies grew. Bevies of raucous parrots swept overhead, their chattering breaking the wilderness silence.

Three years in building by then, Berea was, as its name suggests, a place dedicated to Bible study. Set back from the river, surrounded by a primeval forest, stood Al and Nita's stone-and-brick residence, the all-aluminum home of John and Elaine Beekman (graciously put

After the meeting, the missionaries returned to the Ixtelja airstrip
(*courtesy J. Samuel and Helen Hofman*)

at our disposal as a dormitory), the clinic, two native-type huts for the workmen, and the first homes of the students of the Ch'ol Bible School. During our two-day stay, the natives were bringing in poles for the chapel they planned to build there.

Although the Ch'ols were on the move, organizing colonies farther and farther from their original settlements, Berea was still, for the most part, centrally located for the thirty-six Ch'ol congregations existing in 1959. Henry and Charmaine Stegenga, at that time the newest recruits for the growing Chiapas Mission, were expecting to proceed to Berea for language study as soon as they secured official permission to enter Mexico. Praise God that all this happened as planned, and they could fulfill a great ministry in Berea in spite of the many challenges they had to face.

In those days, when one heard so much about "younger churches" and "fraternal workers," it may have seemed strange that we in Chiapas continued as a mission. Since its organization, however, our mission has navigated the middle road between the one extreme of disbanding altogether, practiced by some denominations, and the opposite extreme of retaining the old mission techniques of patronage and domination of nationals and protection in a compound. Although Mexico was not a country where missionaries could become integrated into the national church, the national church did not have any antipathy toward the concepts of *missionaries* and *mission*. In fact, ecclesiastical bodies frequently took official action to express gratitude for the cooperative work of the mission.

In this land where the government had so severely restricted missionary activity many decades before, relations now between missionaries and nationals in the church was more nearly ideal than that of many other countries where there had been no such pressure. Since the church in Mexico was national and independent, it was entirely natural and reasonable that she was also very protective of her sovereignty. The mission fully respected her rights and her spirit, so all new projects were presented to the national church for approval and, where possible, directed through one of her official committees or organizations. This mutual, respectful, and collegial relationship of the RCA missionaries with the national leaders and pastors was unique to the Presbyterian work in Mexico.

The General Assembly had a mixed committee, as did some of the presbyteries, where representative missionaries and nationals worked together. In the Chiapas Presbytery, however, relations were so harmonious that there was no need for such a committee. The closest contact between missionaries and nationals, outside the local churches, was on the various committees of the presbytery. Missionaries were assigned to these committees by invitation. They took a very active part in shaping the policies of the presbytery and interelating the work of the missionaries with that of the nationals. In a sense, I was "forced" to attend the Comisión de Obra Cooperativa (Cooperative Work Commission), in which, at times, the RCA area secretary created significant difficulties by making (church-to-church) agreements with the National Presbyterian Church leaders at a national level, without either me or the Chiapaneco leaders being involved.

The fall meeting of the Chiapas Mission in 1959 was largely for budget adjustment. When the last figures were approved, the minutes accepted, and the Doxology sung, there was time for a late afternoon ride up the Tulija, with Al De Voogd again as helmsman. We were reminded that the late Mason C. Alcott used to entertain church dignitaries with excursions on the Hudson River Day Line, far removed from this jungle river, which from all appearances, might have been in the Congo or a tributary of the Amazon.[1]

[1]   JRK, "Introducing Berea," *The Church Herald* (November 6, 1959), 4.

CHAPTER 81

Health Problems in the Field

One of the most serious hindrances to our work in Chiapas was our exposure to all sorts of health problems inherent in such hazardous living environments. Parasites, insects whose bites produced fever or infection, bugs that transmitted serious illnesses, and poisonous serpents multiplied in astronomic levels everywhere in the Green State. Each of us was at one time or another infected by these creatures with varying degrees of severity.

By the end of the 1920s, a most dreadful plague was spreading over the state of Chiapas. The disease was known as "onchocercosis" and was propagated by mosquitoes, ticks, and other insects. The cyst-like filaria could be removed surgically, but soon there would be another growth on a different part of the body. The most alarming effect of the disease was a weakening of the eyes, leading at times to total blindness. Many of our congregations were in the stricken areas, and in some cases, 100 percent of the people were afflicted. It was shocking to see young boys and girls trying to read a paper at a distance of two or three inches from their eyes. Whether the disease would spread over the state and beyond, we did not know. But at the moment, the government could not find a preventative.

In November 1931, there was another disease—a sort of typhoid—rapidly spreading over Suchiate (later Ciudad Hidalgo), on the Guatemala border. Four hundred of the one thousand people in the town were ill, and many died. There was no doctor in the entire town and no medicine. Those who had money went to Tapachula before they were seriously ill. On a mission tour, we encountered sick people all along the road, begging me to diagnose their disease and prescribe medicine for them, associating me with my brother Bert, a medical doctor who was there, ministering to them in 1930.

We were continually besieged by fleas at the end of the rainy season. No amount of disinfectant exterminated them entirely. Every season had its pests: ants, big and small, rifled everything in the house not placed in water, and on the patio, huge army ants destroyed all plant life. The dreaded scorpion and ugly cockroach and a great variety of other pests like the *nigua* (jigger flea) were always with us.[1]

I once made a list and described the insects that most seriously affected our health. The *zancudos* (mosquitoes) were probably the most common and the ones that transmitted the worst diseases. In Veracruz we found that there were no mosquito bars above the beds in the hotel to hold the mosquito netting, so we purchased a piece of gauze and covered our faces with that those first nights. In real mosquito country, that would have been totally ineffective. Jalapa and Mexico City, because of their altitude, were free of mosquitoes. But we were to meet them again in Tapachula. Mrs. Coffin showed us how to sew a mosquito net for a double bed. Hammock mosquito bars were made with sleeves for the rope ends. Crossing the state of Tabasco, as we worked our way to the north of Chiapas during our exploratory trip in 1926, the mosquitoes were merciless. They found their way through any small opening in a mosquito net and kept us from sleeping. In the daytime, they attacked any part of the body where clothes fit tightly. By the time I had stitched a head piece like that of a bee keeper and sewed linings in my shirt, we had exited the worst area.

Screen was available, but neither in Tapachula nor in Tuxtla Gutiérrez did people have screened homes. The long verandas and the numerous street windows took a lot of screen in the Tapachula and Tuxtla houses we occupied. As I was screening our first house in Tuxtla, I heard a soldier across the street remark to a companion how useless screens were because the flies inside would not be able to come out. One year the government, with American help, determined to spray every

---

[1]   JRK, "Missionary Trials," *The Christian Intelligencer* (February 10, 1932), 103.

house in the mosquito-infested areas. Bugs of every kind succumbed. The cats ate the dead cockroaches thus poisoning themselves. With no cockroaches, the bed bugs multiplied at an alarming rate. With no cats, the mice and rats multiplied, so people offered considerable sums for cat replacements. With a second spraying, we were mosquito free; we stored away our home mosquito nets but not those for travel.[2]

Due to the climate and the abundance of infecting insects in some areas of Chiapas, most of our missionaries suffered different sorts of maladies, and in some cases, this provoked their retirement from the mission field. Henry (Hank) and Charmaine Stegenga served in Chiapas from 1959 to 1979, working in the Ch'ol field. With the dedication and distribution of the Ch'ol New Testament in 1959, there was a growth spurt in the Ch'ol church. Hank traveled a great deal in the first years of their ministry, joining Ch'ol evangelists on weekend trips to distant congregations. The Stegengas lived in Berea during their entire missionary career. The climate was quite unhealthful because of the heat and humidity, particularly during the rainy season.

Hank had to go through serious treatment for malaria. Then in 1979, he suffered severly from typhoid and hepatitis, forcing him to seek specialized medical care in the United States, where their children Karl and Lynn were already in high school. Hank and Charmaine and their younger sons, Matt and Kurt, were forced to leave the land and people so dear to their hearts and return to Michigan to settle in Holland.

Magazine ads and tropical travel posters picture carefree individuals lying in hammocks strung under palm trees. These scenes look like paradise. What they do not show is the myriad of hostile life on the ground, ranging from insects so small as to be almost invisible to the naked eye, to slithering and venous reptiles. The grasses do not show the hungry army of ticks, ready to attach to any leg that invaded their home territory; nor can the peaceful scene reveal the flying pests from tiny gnats to stinging hornets.

An itinerant missionary avoids as many of these threats as possible and learns to live with those he cannot escape. Not all are immune to the infections these creatures can transfer from one body to another. They met us from day one of our life in Mexico and were a constant concern.[3]

---

2   JRK, "Some of This and Some of That," 19.
3   Ibid., 18.

CHAPTER 82

The First Ch'ol Minister

This is the story of Juan Trujillo and his ordination as the first Ch'ol minister. His ordination was the fulfillment of a dream and commitment I had to the Ch'ol field. When one thinks of him, one thinks of Tumbalá. To the traveler, Tumbalá was just a small town with *mestizo* homes and stores on both sides of its only street. There was a town hall, a school, and a very old Roman Catholic Church which stood roofless and windowless for many years with grass and bushes growing on its wide stone walls—symbollic of the low esteem into which the church in Mexico had fallen during the days of the Revolution. At the edge of town, where the trail dropped steeply toward Yajalón, there was another large stone church—the Protestant church—built more recently, in a spacious yard, looking out on a vast area of mountainous forested terrain.

José Coffin and I spent a cold night in Tumbalá on our initial exploratory trip across Chiapas in 1926. (Let no one describe any road as the worst ever until he has traveled from Salto de Agua to Tumbalá in the rainy season.) Tumbalá at that time was for us only a place with a house, where we could find shelter from the penetrating fog and hang

435

our hammocks. Little did we know what transformation lay ahead for the town and surrounding area and that we would be permitted to have a part in setting the change in action.

Later evangelistic tours took us near Tumbalá to the plantation of a converted woman who would relay the content of our message to Ch'ol Maya standing around. At the same time, a relative of this Doña Otilia was teaching a dozen interested Ch'ols in Tumbalá proper. When the death of this believing layman left the group leaderless, old Cristóbal was appointed to walk the three days' journey to Tuxtla Gutiérrez to ask us to name someone to teach them.

God's time for the long-neglected Maya had come. A humble *mestizo*, Ch'ol-speaking Chanti (J. Santiago González), was able and ready to become the evangelist in the area. This man, of his own initiative, had traveled all the way across Chiapas to study with us in Tapachula in our first year there.

Early meetings in Tumbalá were held in homes, or standing groups would gather in the open and, as the number increased, under branch-covered arbors. Land was secured, and a small board chapel was built. Ch'ols from the village of Allende walked eleven hours on Saturday to be at the Sunday morning services. There was no scripture in their language and no hymns. The evangelist even prayed in Spanish until we persuaded him to try Ch'ol.

There was violent opposition to the new movement. Not so much because Maya were changing their beliefs but because they were changing their lives. The sale of liquor to the natives had long been a chief source of income for the *mestizos*, and the Maya had stopped drinking. Some Ch'ols paid heavy fines rather than hopelessly fight a biased judge. Three innocent young men spent four years in the state penitentiary. The Maya had always been persecuted, and the new faith was something for which they willingly suffered persecution.

Opposition only fanned the flame. Allende, Hidalgo, Amado Nervo, and La Cueva became new centers of consecrated Christian living. The gospel tore down barriers that formerly isolated these colonies. And no longer squandering their earnings in drink, believers could live independently of the large plantation owners, who cursed us for upsetting their world.

Large families and worn-out land forced the Maya to try new settlements. Gingerly, a few made the experiment, at first only planting crops without moving their families. Before long, there were permanent colonies all over the region, which only a few years previous had been virgin forest. Each new colony meant a new chapel.

When the evangelist Chanti got himself lost in strange doctrine and discontinued his work, missionaries from Wycliffe Bible Translators came to the field. Evelyn Woodward, John and Elaine Beekman, Arabelle Anderson, and Wilbur Aulie translated the entire New Testament and some hymns. Viola Warkentin and Ruby Scott taught the Ch'ols to read. The Beekmans introduced medical care for the unnumbered sick, and they provided midweek teaching to young men who would go out to preach on Sunday. Al and Nita De Voogd of our mission took up the medical work and the training of teachers of the Word.

In the Presbyterian system, all the congregations came under the control of the nearest consistory, that of the *mestizo* church in Yajalón, smaller in membership than the newest of the indigenous congregations. The elders could not be expected to tend to the entire Ch'ol field. The presbytery, just learning to stand on its own feet, did not recognize for many years the need for Ch'ol consistories, years during which God's very special grace preserved the vast Ch'ol church. *Mestizo* ministers sporadically visited the field, officiating in Spanish to a people who understood only Ch'ol.

Juan Trujillo was not one of the early Ch'ol believers. He came much later. Juan was not even a full-blooded Ch'ol, although he was accepted as Maya. His mother had pointed out his father to him, but Juan's father never recognized him. There are many Maya of mixed blood like Juan, but Juan excelled in many ways. He was handy with tools; he could speak Spanish and Tzeltal as well as Ch'ol and frequently was our interpreter. Although he never had a day of schooling, he could read and do simple arithmetic. He was an earnest lay preacher. In the past, he had traveled to Tuxtla to ask us to teach him, but busy with other tasks, we were unable to help him. When the Tumbalá consistory was organized, Juan was elected a ruling elder and then became their candidate for the ministry.

We had always hoped for the opportunity to open a Bible school for the Ch'ols. At length, in Al and Nita De Voogd, the mission had a couple, willing, capable, and eager to fulfill that dream. But it took time to learn the Ch'ol language, to build a suitable home in the jungle, and to organize a school, and the Tumbalá consistory was insistent and in a hurry about Juan's training. Inasmuch as Juan knew some Spanish, the presbytery commissioned Mabel and me to teach Juan and two Tzeltal students who knew Spanish. After a year, this Maya group was incorporated into the regular Spanish Bible school but with separate classes and with pastor Daniel Aguilar Ochoa and Rev. Garold and Ruth Van Engen rounding out the teaching staff.

Juan Trujillo (*center in suit*) and his consistory became responsible for the entire Ch'ol field

Juan was not a brilliant student. His orthography was poor and his Spanish unpolished, but he had boundless enthusiasm, and his faith was constant. He was fearless. He was licensed and then ordained, not in his home church but in distant Las Margaritas. When preaching his trial sermon, he explained that he had not preached in Spanish for a whole year, but there was no need for him to apologize. The *mestizo* audience listened intently to every word.

Nine ministers and missionaries formed a semicircle on the platform. Seventeen elders, representatives of the nineteen organized churches, stood below and extended their right arms toward Juan, who was kneeling on a borrowed coat. The audience stood as veteran Genaro de la Rosa with unexcelled eloquence led the prayer of consecration. For Pascual, the aged elder from Tumbalá, for the other Ch'ol delegates, and for the Tzeltals present, this was something very special: one of *them*—a Maya—was being ordained to the gospel ministry.

The installation came later. We would not have missed it for anything. Elias Hatcher ("Hatch," we called him) was the Missionary Aviation Fellowship pilot who flew Mabel and me and a *mestizo* pastor to Tumbalá. Al De Voogd came up from his Berea home and Bible school in Ch'ol country. The deacons met us at the airstrip and carried the light plant, projector, and cots up the steep hill. The Maya women of the church prepared abundant delicious food. We knew that the large church could not hold all the people and that many would have to

For missionaries and Mexican pastors, the ordination of Juan Trujillo (*in suit*) was a happy occasion. *L-r, front row*: Albert De Voogd, elder from Yajalón; Juan Trujilo (just ordained), Ch'ol elder, *back row*: Rev. Pedro Diaz de la Cruz and myself

stand outside. A thousand little gift packages of sweets, prepared and distributed by the consistory, gave us a somewhat accurate count.

We recalled having had to urge the lay worker to pray in Ch'ol and how we had struggled to get an exact translation of the Lord's Prayer. We had always had the benediction pronounced in Spanish. Now it was a happy surprise to hear Juan, unprompted, terminate the installation service with the Ch'ol version of the benediction.

Juan was not the first Maya pastor in Chiapas, but he was the first to preach and officiate in his language to a monolingual tribe. He had always been plain Juan. What would they call him after ordination and installation? Surely not reverend (that was English) and not *presbítero* (that was Spanish and equally inappropriate). We heard the brethren call him *don*, Don Juan, a term of dignity, respect, and esteem—the first fellow Ch'ol they had ever called *don*.[1]

---

[1]   JRK, "Don Juan, First Ch'ol Minister," *Charm and Challenge*, no. 7 (1961), 4-7.

CHAPTER 83

Young People and Women's Ministries

Our two major contributions to the development of the Kingdom of God in Chiapas most likely had to do with our ministry to young people and the organization of women's ministries. We saw in the first group the future leadership of the Chiapaneco church and in the second, the most dynamic factor for the evangelization of the state population. Strategically speaking, with the enthusiasm and energy of the young people and the patience and courage of Christian women, the churches counted on the necessary human resources to increase in number and be strengthened.

From our first term until the final days of our residency in Mexico, there was scarcely a period of time in which boys or girls of different ages did not live in our home. Occasionally, girls were sent to us to protect them from the pursuit of suitors the parents objected to. Others were there as students in the "city" primary, secondary, or preparatory schools. Some were sent to learn how to cook for occasions when pastors or missionaries came to visit rural places.

Israel Jacob came to us as a little boy from the Maya town of Mazapa, with the hope that someday he might be the pastor of his

Margarita was one of our adopted
daughters in San Cristóbal

people. When we moved from Tapachula to Tuxtla Gutiérrez, Israel Jacob followed us and did well in school. Sadly his father died, and his elder brother became very critical of Israel "living at ease" in the city, while he was left with the responsibility of supporting their mother and numerous other brothers and sisters. Years later, Israel came back to us for a while but became disheartened when he could not get the high grades he had always been used to. He returned home to teach in rural schools. He resided in Tuxtla Gutiérrez when he retired and was instrumental in organizing an additional Presbyterian church in the city.

Heriberto López, also from Mazapa, lived with us for many years, while studying in the city schools and in Bible classes in our home. When he returned to Mazapa, we learned, after a time, that he was getting into trouble, so we asked him to return to Tuxtla, where I introduced him to a young lady, new to the church. In time they got married, with the reception held in our home. They raised a large, very special family in Mazapa. One of their sons became a prominent teacher, and two others held high positions in the National Presbyterian Church. Jorge served as the director of what became the John Kempers Seminary, serving the Spanish-speaking churches. From its founding in 1970 until 1978, Jorge worked with Garold Van Engen and then Charles Van Engen in leading that seminary. Jorge also studied at Western Theological Seminary in Holland, Michigan, for several months in 1977-78. Jorge

The Hidalgo sisters of Las Margaritas shared
our home for several years

served three times as moderator of the General Assembly of the
National Presbyterian Church in Mexico. Another son, Abner, became a
chief executive officer of the Mexican Bible Society.

Margarita Oseguera became a prominent businesswoman in San
Cristóbal de Las Casas. She was dumped on our doorstep by her irate
mother and got married while under our care. Her daughter was named
after Mabel, and all of her children considered us their grandparents.

Luz Hidalgo, who came to us from Las Margaritas fleeing a suitor,
was perhaps closer to us as a family member than any of the others. She
inherited many characteristics from her father, who was an influential
and highly respected businessman and churchman who died when Luz
was young. After finishing Bible school in Mexico City, she married a
seminary student. Our name, along with that of her mother, appeared
on the wedding invitations. Correspondence, Christmas greetings, and
Mother's Day cards continued to arrive after many years of retirement,
addressed to us as "Papá" and "Mamá" from her and many others.[1]

We sometimes wonder if we accomplished more through having
these many "children" in our home than through all the other preaching
and teaching ministries. We did not have specially appointed youth

---

[1]   There is an important collection of these in JAH.

workers during the forty-five years we spent in Chiapas. We were the youth workers in our home and in the churches.[2]

There were also a few outstanding young Christian men and women in Chiapas that inspired our admiration because of their commitment to the gospel and the devotion of their Christian life. Emilia Rincón, a very bright girl, was about to finish her work in Normal School, where she had staunchly stood alone amid the jeers and jests of her friends. Her teachers told her that she would not receive her certificate unless she renounced her religion. In spite of the threat and ridicule, she was true and brave, and in the end, of course, the diploma had to be issued. She became a fine teacher, married a splendid Christian man, and reared a family in the faith that was her joy and strength.

In Tapachula, Elodia lived with her old father, a border guard, and her younger brother and sister. There she kept the house, tended a small store in one room of her home, and conducted classes for small children of the neighborhood. Her father strongly opposed her interest in the Protestant church and the Bible. Elodia, in order to attend the young girls meetings at the missionary's home or even the regular church services, was compelled to cover her movements with falsehoods. She never ceased, however, to talk to her father of Christ and the gospel, although he ridiculed and scolded her. Upon his death bed, he called for José Coffin, the pastor, and confessing the Christ his daughter had introduced to him, he admonished Elodia to never depart from Christ's path nor allow her brother and sister to reject him. Sometime later, a friend of her father, who had attended the little home funeral, called upon Coffin asking for "one of those books that teach one how to die."

Alfonso Marín was a young man who was called *guerito* (blond one) because his skin was remarkably light, his cheeks pink, and his hair auburn—all features not at all common but quite desirable among that dark-skinned people. He held an elevated school position under government employ, and at the same time, was a central figure in the Tuxtla Gutiérrez congregation. Since early childhood, he had been stamped in a Roman Catholic community as "that little blond Protestant." On one occasion, someone created a general panic in a Catholic church, while a large crowd was gathered, by exclaiming falsely, "That little Protestant is within our walls!" Through the years of childhood and adolescence, he had stood firm with opposition and temptation on all sides, and he had become our most dependable and capable church worker in the capital of the state.

[2]   JRK, "Some of This and Some of That," 2.

This group of Christian Endeavor leaders includes myself (*third from left*), Alfonso Marin (*third man to the right of Kemp*), Pastor Genaro de la Rosa (*to the right of Marin*), future pastor Pedro Diaz de la Cruz (*second from right, standing*), and Pastor Daniel Aguilar Ochoa (*front row, right with books*)

Consuelo Marín was the most active girl in this same church. Tall, dark, with flashing eyes, she was very attractive. She attended Normal School, hoping to be a Christian teacher and leader in some needy *pueblo*. Her faith was very real to her, and she proved it. When examinations were in progress, she asked her mother, upon leaving the house in the morning, to pray for her either during her science examination or at her ten o'clock history test. Such faith in prayer in the life of a young Mexican girl was an inspiration to her American Christian peers.

Gilberto Marín, Consuelo's brother, graduated from the same school. When starting his course with non-Protestant companions, he asked his mother, Doña Guadalupe, to help him. "What? How can I, who can barely read and write, help you in school!" His answer was beautiful, "Help me with your prayers, Mother!" He graduated with honors, and his companions followed a year or two later. Gilberto was a successful teacher in government schools.

Of another race they were—another color, another language, other customs, different ages and levels of experience—but all of them were followers of our Lord, who recognizes no such distinctions.[3]

As to our commitment to develop the potential of our sisters in the church, Mabel should receive top recognition and credit. Mabel

---

[3]   JRK, "Mexican Young People I Know," 477.

Mabel and her companions are ready for a train
trip to a Women's Society meeting

and Genaro de la Rosa led in the organization of various women's societies in the state of Chiapas into a union. These societies had met for conventions with the young people, sharing programs and entertainment, but with separate business sessions. The first convention of the Unión de Sociedades Femeniles de Chiapas (Chiapas Women's Societies Union) took place in Tuxtla Gutiérrez, from January 29 to February 2, 1947. Rev. de la Rosa and I served as advisors. On this occasion, they set seven goals: (1) to organize new societies; (2) to create a fund for the union; (3) to subscribe each society to the periodical of the union, *Reflejos Femeniles*; (4) to cultivate family Bible study in each home of our churches; (5) to establish a prayer circle in each society; (6) to promote a literacy campaign in each society; and (7) to put into practice the calendar of activities of the Progressive Movement by 1947.[4]

When attendance became so numerous that no church could feed all the delegates, to the surprise of some doubters, the women successfully held their own conventions, which they continued to do throughout the years. Mabel, as a leader in the union for years, edited a bulletin called *El Noticiero* for the women. It began in April 1962. Later it became *Reflejos Femeniles*. In 1963 the Chiapas Presbyterian women held the First Women's Convention as a separate entity from the

---

[4]   Minutes of the First Convention of the Union of Women's Societies in Chiapas, in JAH. The Progressive Movement emphasized the social implications of the gospel.

Mabel and Ruth contributed greatly to the development of the Women's Societies in the Chiapas churches

National Presbyterian Church. The following year, the union assumed responsibility for the publication of *El Noticiero* with the same name. In 1964 the Institute for Ministers' Wives was organized in Tuxtla Gutiérrez.

In ensuing years, Ruth Van Engen took an active part in the union as did Jean Van Engen when she joined the mission. Garold Van Engen and I, officially appointed by the presbytery, served as counselors for the Women's Union and for the Youth Union at different times.[5]

The work with women in the churches was always one of the most successful ministries we could develop in Chiapas. Most societies had a day in the week when they celebrated their meetings. Each society had its own name. For example, in San Cristóbal de Las Casas, they chose the name "The Star of Bethlehem." After a devotional period of hymns, prayer, and scripture reading, the president gave a short meditation. Then she requested that as each member responded to roll call, she would read, recite, or sing a stanza of her favorite hymn. It was stimulating and very interesting to hear their responses. As they gathered to chat briefly after the meeting, they expressed joy and satisfaction at having taken part in the service.

These little bands of women represented only a small part of the larger group who comprised the National Presbyterian Union of

[5]   JRK, "Some of This and Some of That," 6.

At the annual gathering of the Women's societies,
the delegates displayed their banners

Women's Societies in Mexico. The National Union was composed of all the societies within the various presbyteries and was responsible for connecting women's ministries in these presbyteries. They published a yearly study book in which themes were planned and developed for each weekly meeting. The National Union also published a small monthly periodical, which was designed to keep the individual societies informed of various activities carried out by women in other parts of the country. In addition to the literature program, the national organization maintained the Girls Bible School in Mexico City, sponsored a traveling secretary who visited and assisted the various presbyterial unions, and encouraged giving to a foreign mission program.

Each year the National Union held leadership training classes of one week in each presbytery. Each society within the presbytery was permitted one delegate whose expenses for food, lodging, and travel were paid by the National Union. Classes were presented on the life of Christ, Old Testament history, stewardship, instruction of the child in the home, and first aid. At the close of the week, the delegates were given an examination on the material studied, and they were encouraged to present this material to their fellow members upon return to their societies.

The presbyterial unions, like ours in Chiapas, as well as the local societies, were organized under the same plan as that of the National Union, having an executive committee and four chairpersons who supervised the departments of work: spiritual life, missionary, home, and social work. The Presbyterial Women's Union of Chiapas, organized in 1947, included eighteen societies with approximately two hundred active members by 1961. Every year in January, an annual convention was held to encourage the women in their spiritual lives, as well as in the activities of their individual societies.

Thus the women's ministries of the church in Chiapas were carried out. In the Spanish-speaking churches in Chiapas, the women were always the primary evangelists. They were the front-line presenters of the gospel, even in the face of severe persecution. Mabel was an integral part of that movement. The same is true with regard to the brave Maya women who served the Kingdom of God with courage and dedication in spite of their many limitations. To the humble women who had little training or education, all the details of organization and procedure seemed difficult to understand. Nevertheless, they loved the Lord and desired to serve him. They were constantly stimulated and encouraged in their Christian lives and service by the national motto: "Ardientes en espíritu, sirviendo al Señor" (Ardent in spirit, serving the Lord).[6]

---

6   Ruth Van Engen, "Thus We Serve," *Charm and Challenge*, no. 7 (1961), 12-13.

CHAPTER 84

Board and Mission

In 1925 our mission board—the combined Women's and Men's Boards of Domestic Missions—promised to send someone down to Chiapas as soon as we were settled in order to help plan a program of operation. But because of the Mexican government's new antimissionary and antichurch stand, and due to the financial depression in the United States, nobody came to investigate or counsel for fourteen years. We were very unhappy with the lack of understanding and the lack of cooperation from the early board secretaries who succeeded the talented and energetic Mrs. Edith Allen, one of the four in the delegation that consummated the transfer of mission responsibility in the state of Chiapas from the Northern Presbyterian Church to the Reformed Church in America.

In 1928 Dr. and Mrs. James Martin, pastor of Mabel's home church (Third Reformed Church, Holland) were our guests during the meeting of the National Synod, functioning as a General Assembly at the time. Dr. David Watermulder came in 1932 to visit San Cristóbal de Las Casas and Tuxtla Gutiérrez as possible future places of operation for us. Although their visits were welcomed, their help, of course, was minimal.

451

In 1939 Dr. Frederick Zimmerman made the first of his two visits to Chiapas and experienced the inconveniences of travel at that time. I recall that on his first visit, I awoke one morning in the chapel of the congregation in Ciudad Hidalgo, then known as Suchiate, and saw that the ropes of his hammock had stretched so much that he was actually sitting on the dirt floor in a V posture. During his second visit for a special meeting of the Presbytery of the Gulf in Tuxtla Gutiérrez, his winning personality and tactful speech influenced the presbytery to insist that José Coffin share some of the vast field of Chiapas with Ezequiel Lango, whom Coffin selfishly and bitterly opposed. Lango had worked zealously and always harmoniously with us in the northern half of the state for seven years. Our children loved Zimmerman's visits, and he was a great friend and help to us. He often stated, "You make the decision. You know more about it than I do. I'll back you up, and I am sure my Board will give me backing."

Another former secretary, frequently in correspondence, once wrote, "When you come to New York, we must sit down together and have a long chat." When I arrived, she informed me that she was busy with a "committee meeting," so I wasted my time seeing movies in the theatres around Times Square. She treated me as if I were coming from around the corner and not from a mission field located three thousand miles away!

In 1932, when our second child was due, we made hospital arrangements in Guatemala City. Rev. Lenn P. Sullenberger, pastor of the large Presbyterian Church in that city, was preparing to leave for furlough with his family. When he learned of our coming, he invited me to pastor the congregation on the central square during his absence. We agreed to stay six months, a time that resulted in a most valuable experience, which only God in his providence could have planned. The Presbyterians paid our salary, and we lived in the manse. The two boards, however, never came to any understanding of the arrangement until we were returning to Chiapas.

Recently, in reading the board correspondence I kept in my files, I noted on what a high plane and how friendly our correspondence was with Dr. Beth Marcus during all these years. Very special relations also existed between us and Dr. Richard Vanden Berg during his time as secretary. Perhaps his ethnic background made the relationship more comfortable, frank, and candid. He visited Chiapas in 1950 when he participated in the ceremony at which the presbytery honored Mabel and me and presented us with a silver plaque on completing twenty-five years with the Chiapas church. Missionary contributions to Social

Dr. Richard Vanden Berg endured a trip to Mazapa with me in 1950

Security began in his years, and there was improvement in mission organization and procedures. When Vanden Berg finished, I wrote him a letter thanking him and stating that he had done everything that could be expected of a secretary.[1]

When both Dr. Zimmerman and Dr. Vanden Berg introduced me to audiences in the United States, they would tell a story considerably embellished. For example, Vanden Berg said that he was assigned such a small mule to ride from the airport to the village of Mazapa that his feet scraped the ground. Such tales would captivate the audience, in contrast to my twenty-minute talk on the problems and progress of church work in Chiapas.

Then followed Dr. Russell Redeker, whose inexperience was evident. When he carried out my suggestions for the Mexican work, he did all right, but when he ventured out on his own, he fell flat on his face every time. Even so, our correspondence was friendly and gentlemanly.[2] As secretary, he came to attend a mission meeting and read off all of Mabel's assignments and mine in Chiapas, giving them to other people. We did not know what was going on or what the problem was: board secretaries did not assign work. These were all presbyterial appointments. Somehow, after an uncomfortable silence, he exclaimed, "Then you are only sixty-four years of age and not sixty-five!" Even if I

[1]   JRK to JSH, Sept. 4, 1971.
[2]   Ibid.

had been sixty-five, retirement was voluntary at sixty-five and mandatory only at sixty-eight.

Then came Rev. Howard Schade who, while he was serving as secretary, attended the synod meeting with us in the city of Oaxaca. Schade had messed things up from the very beginning by announcing what days he would be in Chiapas. I answered that it was surprising that he should announce a visit without first consulting what date would be convenient, since we were scattered all over in many places, some in the United States, some on the way down, and some with planned schedules.[3] During the synod, at the time when I was presenting an important study on which I had worked long and hard, he was visiting the city Rotary Club. He pressed us hard to accept the invitation to join the teaching staff of the National Presbyterian Seminary in Mexico City. Now we see that transfer as the providence of God's planning. At that time, we resisted until the last moment. Our heart was in Chiapas, and our people were saying, "You can't leave us. You belong to us." When we reached sixty-eight and had finished our original appointment, we were invited to continue teaching, which we did, living on retirement pay, with Sioux Center First Reformed Church paying our rent.

Some years ago, Richard Bass, a former Methodist seminary professor, and a good one, wrote to me prior to a lecture he was to give. He said it was obvious that we had been more successful than they in our mission project and wanted me to explain what our policies were. That was easy. In writing and in innumerable speeches, I have given the reasons, as I saw them, for the unbelievable growth of the church in Chiapas.[4] In summarized fashion, these principles were three. I started out in Chiapas with (1) identification (living *with* the people, which was easy for us since there was no other choice); (2) nationalization (we always played second fiddle to the Mexican leadership); and (3) decentralization (our missionaries were scattered throughout the state).[5]

Another important aspect to the success of our commitment to bring Chiapas to Christ was our resistance to any foreign interference. In this particular, there was a big difference between our work and the Presbyterian work. We were free from interference from the New York board all those years. Both Presbyterian churches (north and south) had secretaries who insisted missions should be done their way. Howard Schade, our secretary of the board, was a man who tried to take

3   Ibid.
4   JRK to JSH, Jan. 8, 1990.
5   JRK to JSH, June 18, 1994.

I joined the staff at the seminary in Mexico City;
Howard Schade is at my left

over my responsibilities as director, and I fought him tooth and nail. Shorty Brown and Richard Vander Voet took over the work of director, which became necessary when each station had different interests and expectations. Shorty did a good job, and so did Vander Voet.[6]

We have always said that the hand of the Lord was evident in our work, just as we saw clear evidence in our young lives of his calling us to Chiapas with the timing of various incidents. We have always known that it was his initiative to have us ready to go to Mexico at the exact time when the board decided to undertake work there. We were convinced of his providence in bringing us to Mexico just before the door to missionary entrance was closed by federal orders and by the confirmation of choice when the people accepted us. We recognized God's work in our lack of any homesickness ever and the absence of health problems like malaria and typhoid fever, to which missionaries were prone. We were sure the Lord would show us as clearly when to leave Mexico. The invitation to continue teaching on the national level was there. Finances were no problem, even though we were retired. Our health was as good as ever, but again, there were the many providential events that confirmed our decision.

When the Reformed Church General Synod celebrated fifty years of ministry in Chiapas in 1975, we were honored and presented with a

6   JRK to JSH, Jan. 8, 1990.

plaque by Dr. Redeker as board secretary. He recalled that, at a board meeting some years earlier, I had said, "Board secretaries come and go, but the Kempers go on forever."[7] And Mabel and I are convinced this "forever" is real, because even when we pass away, we will be remembered with love and gratitude by our Chiapanecan brothers and sisters.

Every Mexican pastor and American missionary in Chiapas has made his or her contribution to the development of that remarkable church. Hesitatingly and humbly, Mabel and I have jotted down a bit of the legacy we leave, and now we turn our pens over to others to add their chapters. We join with joy the Psalmist in his song: "You have made my days a few handbreadths, and my lifetime is as nothing in your sight. Surely everyone goes about like a shadow. Surely for nothing they are in turmoil; they heap up, and do not know who will gather. . . . For I am your passing guest, an alien, like all my forebears" (Psalm 39:5-6, 12).

[7]   JRK, "Some of This and Some of That," 13-15.

CHAPTER 85

At Sixty-Five Years of Age

What is there about reaching sixty-five years of age? Nothing special, save that in most parts of the world, that is retirement age, which is important to most people. For me, it presented the opportunity not only to go back to my homeland and rest but also to put an end to the task to which I had committed myself for most of my life. As such, my sixty-fifth birthday in 1965 was an appropriate occasion to evaluate my ministry in Chiapas. Sitting in my rocking chair on the veranda of our home in Tuxtla Gutiérrez, as the sun was disappearing on the horizon, my mind rolled back and brought wonderful memories. Flashes of hundreds of events began to explode like fireworks and show their multiple colors.

A Tzeltal Maya, presbyter Francisco Gómez, was elected to the presidency of the Chiapas Presbytery. When it was voted to license two Tzeltal candidates for the ministry, it was his responsibility to officiate. To see a Maya president licensing two fellow Tzeltals in a large Ch'ol church in the presence of Ch'ols, Tzeltals, and Spanish-speaking *mestizos* was a dream fulfilled. For me, as a North American missionary, it was a thrilling sight because, through the years, I had insisted on the parity

457

of the ministers and on equal treatment of all elements in the church. There could be no more convincing proof for the natives that they were part of the presbytery than this historical Christian event. The licensure of these two men meant that, very probably, within the next year or two, they would be added to the four indigenous pastors already ordained. They were very much needed to share some of the tremendous load the four men were carrying by then.

The statistics of 1965 showed that the Chiapas Presbytery had a membership of 8,414 *mestizos*, 8,171 Ch'ols, and 10,191 Tzeltals. The Zoque and Tzotzil converts were fewer in number. The total membership was approximately twenty-seven thousand. During 1964 the thirteen pastors in our presbytery baptized 1,100 children and received 989 adults into the church by confession of faith. The primary focus of the work of the church continued to be evangelism, Christian education, and stewardship. Growth in the indigenous fields had been astronomical. Without any formal training or guidance, the believing nationals won others by personal testimony. The medical program, too, had been an instrument for showing Christian love and compassion and for breaking down walls of opposition and suspicion. The *mestizo* churches gave instruction in personal work and made constant efforts to keep alive or rekindle the passion for lost souls.

The missionaries of our Chiapas Mission gave much of their time to the training of church workers, teaching in the Tzeltal Bible Center, the Berea Bible Institute, and Las Casas Bible School for Spanish-speaking students, and since 1964, teaching the Girls Bible Course. In addition to *El Despertador*, the presbytery paper, by then in its thirty-fourth year, and *El Esforzador* of the Christian Endeavor Union, the Women's Union published a monthly paper, *Reflejos Femeniles*, which won instant popularity.

The goal set by the Mexican church for complete self support of all its ministers, by the centennial year (1972), seemed almost unattainable in Chiapas (the Reformed Church mission responsibility) due to the increase in the cost of living. But we were trying to teach the grace of giving by emphasizing stewardship in the churches and in regional institutes.

By 1965 persecution was strong, often violent, when the gospel took hold in a new village or a new tribe. This could be seen when the few Tzotzil believers fearlessly witnessed to their people. While one man was playing gospel records in an effort to persuade others, he was shot through the eye. There were threats to kill all the Chamula Tzotzil believers. God, in his providence, had placed in official positions men who, although not evangelical, offered what protection they could to those who wished to follow the Christian road.

Each year the Chiapas Mission, through the presbytery, assisted with the building of five or six new churches. By 1965, 170 of the 240 worshipping groups had their own church buildings and chapels. All of these became government property by federal law, but since 1935, no group has been denied the use of its building for worship purposes.

As Mabel and I came to the end of our missionary commitment in Chiapas, the presbytery was asking for two more couples and two pairs of nurses so badly needed in this indigenous country. I remember my prayer at the end of 1965: "Lord, may your Holy Spirit, whom we recognize as the Builder of this great church, touch the hearts of American youth to offer themselves as instruments in your hands to serve in this precious land."[1]

[1]   JRK, "The Chiapas Mission," brochure published by the North American Missions of the Reformed Church in America, 1965, in JAH.

CHAPTER 86

Retirement from the Chiapas Mission

During the last five or six years of our ministry in Chiapas, there was some conflict between Rev. Alejandro Barrios de León and myself. Alejandro had Bible school training and some advanced education before his ordination. But he insisted on having a complete seminary education in Mexico City. The presbytery and I reluctantly gave him permission. So from 1960 to 1963, Barrios completed his studies at Presbyterian Seminary in Mexico City, serving in Chiapas during the summer months and other interims.

Later Barrios served in the Las Margaritas church and had the opportunity to teach a class in English at the local school. I opposed this, insisting that he should give all his time to the churches under his care. As a result of this conflict, I had to pay a price. At the beginning of each presbytery meeting, the new executive committee would make the committee assignments for the delegates and missionaries. In those years, the missionaries served not as voting members but by invitation (*por invitación*). It was already a long tradition that I would be assigned to the finance committee, which had the task of deciding on the location and financial support of the pastors and workers for the coming year. I

Pastor Alejandro Barrios was a fervent preacher and a fearless leader

admit that my influence in that committee was very strong, since I knew the men and the churches intimately and could match them effectively (at least, I believed so).

I think it was at the presbytery meeting in Tuzantán in 1964 that I was not named to the finance committee. The executive committee named Garold Van Engen to the finance committee in my place, and Garold continued to serve on that committee in the following years. I was named to a much less significant committee. I remember myself sitting in a chair in the evening when the finance committee was meeting and commenting on how strange it felt not to be involved. I felt so discouraged and frustrated that I left the presbytery meeting a day before the closing service. Alejandro Barrios felt offended, saying that this was a breach in our fellowship. In my return to Tuxtla that night, I fell asleep at the wheel momentarily and had a minor accident. Thanks to the Lord, I was not alone. The frightening situation woke me up and helped me to realize that I was wrong. I had been obsessed with the responsibilities that I had been assigned and thought that nobody else could manage them. On the other hand, this over sensitivity was most likely due to my approaching retirement.

In fact, as I was nearing retirement age (February 1965), I appealed to the Reformed Church Mission Board for an extension of our service in Chiapas, assuring them that I had the necessary health and strength to continue with the task and that we still had a lot of

These four men were the officers of the Chiapas Presbytery in 1964
(*left to right*): Daniel Aguilar Ochoa, Oliveros Garcia López,
Genaro Mendez M., Alejandro Barrios de Leon

work to do in Chiapas. I don't think Mabel shared my desire to go on with our ministry in Chiapas. She was losing her hearing and stamina and longed for a change. Later I came to know that the executive committee of the Chiapas Presbytery met secretly with the Reformed Church Area Secretary, Rev. Howard Schade. They urged him not to extend my time of service. I assume that Barrios was the spokesman for the executive committee. Schade was able to confirm my retirement and made the necessary arrangements for me to teach at the Presbyterian Seminary in Mexico City for three additional years. This was considered an alternative to immediate retirement and our return to the United States. I reluctantly accepted the offer, conscious that there were no other possibilities. In the end, this provided us a gracious and much less painful departure from Chiapas. I, however, resented Schade's insistence on our leaving Chiapas, and at that time, I did not understand why he was so insistent.[1]

It took me a good while to understand my feelings as I approached retirement. When you have invested your life as deeply as I had in Chiapas, you feel torn to the bones by retirement. This painful process stretches you in two different directions: your past and your future. As to the past, you feel that you lose the activity where you have invested the best part of your life and where, in spite of many conflicts, you have received lots of recognition and reward. This is particularly true

---

[1]   JSH interview with the author, April 8, 2014.

in Christian work. Through the many years we spent in Mexico, we received numerous expressions of gratitude and acknowledgment:

The First Regional Convention of Christian Endeavor Societies, San Cristóbal de Las Casas, March 18, 1943.

The National Presbyterian Church in Chiapas, Tuxtla Gutiérrez, December 1945.

The National Presbyterian Church in Tapachula, on the occasion of our silver anniversary as missionaries in Chiapas, Tapachula, January 27, 1951.

The Presbyterian Evangelical Church "Getsemaní," Tuxtla Gutiérrez, December 5, 1955.

The Honorable Presbytery of Chiapas, Tuxtla Gutiérrez, September 1968.

The R. Synod of the Gulf of Mexico, September 25, 1968.[2]

As to the future, this process of retirement brings closer the shadow of fear and anxiety. In my case, it was not so much a preoccupation with regard to our income; I have never worried about God's financial provision. What I feared was the ambiguity of the role of a retired person. To be sure, society does have some definite cultural expectations about the behaviors and attitudes of retirees. Retired people are supposed to live independent lives, to pay their own way, to show a reasonable degree of self-respect, and to exhibit social responsibility. These few role prescriptions, however, still leave the retired individual in a rather ill-defined position. This is even more serious when you have been serving as a missionary, a preacher of the Word of God. Unlike the roles of homemaker, worker, and parent, the role of the retired missionary, at least in my case, is essentially unstructured with regard to daily activities and obligations. And adjustments proved to be somewhat difficult.

Clearly a major loss occurred when I stopped serving as a missionary in Chiapas and did not replace this responsibility or activity with a new one. Teaching at the Presbyterian Seminary in Mexico City was not the same as visiting the scattered congregations in Chiapas. It was this withdrawal without replacement that made my transition to retirement different from any earlier occupational change in my life. Thanks to the Lord, my leaving the mission field was not due to illness

---

[2]   These parchments are in JAH.

or disability. Independence and social responsibility are critical aspects of the role of a retiree, and I had a great deal of these two. Nevertheless, although the role of a retiree begins when one quits work, the process typically starts before that. In fact, we had been working long enough to be able to form some judgments about how we might feel when we came to the end of our working lives. In a sense, one's attitude toward retirement can be predicted by one's attitude toward work. I did not want to retire from my missionary commitment in Chiapas because I felt it was the greatest source of joy and satisfaction that I had ever had, in spite of everything.

Attitudes shape decisions about when to retire. And the forces that influence attitudes—income, educational and occupational status, and age—prove to be the most important predictors of what your stand will be at the time of retirement. When I reached retirement age (65), I wanted to stay in the work force. I felt that I was in better shape than ever before in my life. I considered the many years of collected missionary experiences to be an asset that worked positively for me to gather the fruit of my labor. But in 1965, mandatory retirement policies forced me to leave the land of my dreams and the place where I was happy. And, believe me, as an event, retirement is not a particularly comforting rite of passage. I saw this event as involving significant loss, and major losses are often viewed as crises. The teaching position at the seminary in Mexico City could not fill the vacuum left in my heart with our departure from Chiapas.

CHAPTER 87

Seminario Presbiteriano Nacional

I praise the Lord that after my retirement from the Chiapas Mission, I did not remain jobless. There is nothing worse than spending sixty-five years of your life in active work and then, all of a sudden, becoming an inactive fellow when you still have a lot of energy to work and gifts and talents to invest in profitable tasks. The prospect that Mabel and I could stay in Mexico for a few more years was a great blessing in our lives. It helped us in the transition to our final return to the United States in 1969.

The opportunity to serve at the Seminario Presbiteriano Nacional in Mexico City and to join its faculty was the coronation of almost forty years of missionary service in Chiapas. This gave us the chance to continue with our passion, which was our ministry of training young people for Christian service. We had the knowledge, experience, and enthusiasm to inspire and guide the next generation of Mexican servants of the Lord, who were now enjoying more freedom and opportunities to share the gospel than we had during our own missionary adventure.

Mabel and I were convinced that the training of a national ministry was indispensable for the survival and growth of any missionary work.

On this particular point, we were in full agreement with the vision of the Presbyterian missionary pioneers that had planted this church in Mexico. As early as 1872, the first Presbyterian missionaries in Mexico started Bible schools which, in 1885, merged into a seminary located in San Luis, Potosí, from where it later transferred to Tlalpan, a suburb of Mexico City. In 1897 it moved to the picturesque village of Coyoacán, also in the Federal District.

In 1917 Presbyterians, Congregationalists, Methodists, and Disciples of Christ joined teachers and students to form the Union Seminary, from which several of the most outstanding ministers of the Mexican evangelical churches graduated. By order of the General Synod of the Mexican Presbyterian Church, its own seminary was reorganized in 1931. José Coffin, the Mexican pastor whom we joined in Chiapas in 1926, was a graduate of this institution, as were other Chiapas pastors.

Because of the very urgent need for ordained men in the vast and growing Presbyterian field in Mexico, augmented by the fact that, for many years, foreign ministers could not legally officiate in Mexican churches, students with limited academic training were accepted and graduated by the seminary. Later when representatives of the Mexican church attended a conference in Brazil and saw the high standards of the seminaries in that country, they resolved to upgrade their school in Mexico. In the coming years, the seminary accepted only college graduates and made constant efforts to improve the quality of the teaching staff.

When we began our service at the seminary, Mexican laws required that all religious courses had to be taught in church buildings. Therefore, single students, housed in a very fine dormitory, and married men, housed in cottages on the campus, would walk five blocks to classes in the Getsemani Presbyterian Church. In addition to the theological department, the seminary had a very excellent school of music with a growing enrollment and staff of teachers.

The number of North American missionaries on the faculties of both departments was out of proportion compared to the Mexican teachers. This was partly because of the need for pastors in the churches, partly because missionaries sometimes had more academic and specialized training, and also, perhaps, because the seminary did not have to pay the salaries of missionary teachers. As the National Presbyterian Church in Mexico looked forward to celebrating her centennial in 1972, the seminary had an important role in the attainment of goals set for that occasion.

After forty years of evangelistic work in Chiapas, at the urgent request of the seminary board and faculty, and by official transfer by the Board of North American Missions of the Reformed Church, my wife and I were incorporated into the teaching staff of the two departments of the seminary. There we helped to prepare ministers and leaders in music for the church in Chiapas and also for the other presbyteries.

We were honored with many privileges, and we feel deeply grateful for the task commended to us. We participated in the development of the church in Chiapas from small beginnings to three hundred congregations, with a membership of thirty thousand by the time of our retirement. We were involved in the preparation of workers in Bible schools. We published a good amount of literature. We preached the Word of God Sunday after Sunday in all parts of the state of Chiapas. We took the initiative in developing children's, young people's, and women's ministries and the Constitution of the presbytery and its various organizations. All the accumulated experiences of those forty years of service in Chiapas could then be shared at a national level in the training of ministers for the evangelical churches in Mexico.

In 1965 we left the lonely mountain trails of Chiapas for life in a modern city of six million inhabitants. Fortunately, Coyoacán was relatively quiet. It had been the center of an ancient Maya civilization, then the site from which Hernán Cortés directed the Spaniards' destructive attack on the Aztec Empire, and later it became the seat of colonial government. Its tree-lined streets, its shaded parks filled with flowers, its air, then called the purest in Mexico City, and its historical and picturesque charm were an invitation to restful living. For us, it was a kind of preparation and transition to the next and final stage of our lives.[1]

---

[1]   JRK, "Ministers for the Mexican Church," *The Church Herald* (November 4, 1966), 14-15.

CHAPTER 88

Last Evaluation

Nobody can stop the course of time. It flows inexorably and sweeps you and your dreams away to the unknown dimension of the future. When the year 1969 came, Mabel and I knew for sure that the time for us to leave Mexico was at the gate. We were about to initiate a new stage in our lives, totally different from anything that we had experienced in the past. On an occasion like this, there is only one thing to do: evaluate your work and the context in which you have invested your life and energy.

On June 29, 1969, I enjoyed the privilege of preaching the graduation sermon at the Presbyterian Theological Seminary, where Mabel and I had taught for four years. My text was Daniel 2:44-45: "It shall crush all these kingdoms and bring them to an end, and it shall stand forever. . . . The dream is certain, and its interpretation trustworthy." Starting with an explanation of the historical context of these words, I referred to the present situation of the Christian testimony in the world. I affirmed that the Christian church was going through a time of crisis. Statistics on church attendance, offerings, and most of all, missionary work and the number of candidates for ministry, were diminishing. Some observers were talking of a post-Christian era and asking if Protestantism could survive at all.

The condition of the Roman Catholic Church was not much better. I remember a priest raising the same question in view of the exodus of hundreds of priests from the ministry. On a television program, a well-known priest in Mexico City said: "God has shaken the tree, and the rotten apples have fallen. The faithful remain in their posts, and the Church continues onward." Regretfully, in the Protestant churches, the doctrinally rotten apples did not fall. They remained and came to occupy leading positions, claiming to speak for the whole church. I considered the situation to be chaotic. The cause was not the ceaseless ecumenism that in those days was making a lot of noise. Neither was it the exaggerated emphasis on the social gospel or the unrest and dissatisfaction expressed in protests by the new generation. All these factors were the result of a bankrupt theology and the consequence of holding the Word of God in a very low esteem and as a human product.

What in my perception was the condition of the National Presbyterian Church? I praised God because it was a conservative church which held the Bible as the only authority for faith and practice. The National Presbyterian Church felt neither compelled to change its doctrinal confessions nor to renounce its social commitments to those in need. It was essentially a community that understood its primary mission was to share the good news of personal salvation to those still without Christ. This church assumed its responsibility to shepherd the sheep and was not involved in leading the politics of the country. It was a church that examined those who were teaching and supervised the curriculum of its seminary and Bible schools. Proof of this was the fact that it did not accept the invitation to be a part of the Theological Community (United Seminary) which, because of its theological liberalism, would have meant the liquidation of the National Presbyterian Church in Mexico.

Eternal vigilance, however, is the price of success. Although many of our strongest defenders of true Presbyterianism and orthodoxy had passed away to be with the Head of the Church, others remained. Our church's doctrine was not a major preoccupation, in spite of the continuous controversies between those of a more conservative stance and the more liberal. Problems of a more serious nature affected us, and it was necessary to recognize them and work to solve them. I learned missionary work by the side of a great Presbyterian, Dr. José Coffin, a zealous man in doctrine and Presbyterianism. And as I was leaving

Mexico, I trembled to look at a church with an eclectic liturgy, an improvised government, Pentecostal customs, and without discipline.

The next generation did not have the conviction that to be a disciple of Christ, one must leave the world; it is impossible to have one foot in the world and the other in the church. This generation made fun of the Puritanism of their parents who knew how to raise a church in the midst of adverse circumstances. In my understanding, this was the reason why our churches did not believe, in spite of so many evangelistic campaigns. This was also true with inactivity. We were approaching the centennial of the Presbyterian work in Mexico in 1972, and there were presbyteries closing some institutions and diminishing the number of its workers. Old projects were forgotten, left in oblivion; goals were not achieved, and new challenges did not appear. My prayer then was that, by the centennial, we would be able to celebrate not only the heroic past and the promising future but also an explosive present full of activity.

My conviction is that the evil one has no aspiration other than to destroy the church founded by Christ himself for the extension of his Kingdom. The crisis that I perceived in 1969 resulted only in the enemy's glee and satisfaction in the context of a confused doctrine, worldliness in the church, and the inaction of its members. In the light of the text of Daniel 2:44-45, however, my conviction was that, on every occasion that the church was in the midst of a crisis, seemingly defeated, God would show up in unexpected ways and redeem the situation.

From the human side of the equation, however, there were some things that we had to do to survive the crisis. To my audience of faculty and students I asked: (1) to be dynamic missionaries and ministers, (2) to be studious, (3) to be upright, and, (4) to love their people. I told them that I had received lots of certificates, plaques, medals, and tokens of affection and gratitude from innumerable ecclesiastical bodies, organizations, unions, societies, and churches. I remarked, however, that nobody had seen the growing collection of personal letters written with tears, which I kept in a folder in my personal archive. What caught my attention in these letters—and this is why I mentioned them—was the repetition by the various authors of the characteristics outlined above that they had seen in my own missionary ministry. And I continued to tell them that when they came to be my age, they did not need to go to books in search of illustrations for their sermons or to seek advice from others. They could go to the immense field of their own experience. The above-mentioned characteristics are the only thing remaining of all our labors when we are forced to retire from the field of ministry.

I closed my message stating that I would like to leave Mexico with the church at its best. Regretfully, in my understanding, that was not the case. There were too many deficiencies. The church at that time was just simply idling instead of moving ahead with enthusiasm and effort. My comfort and joy was that the situation in Chiapas was totally different. When Mabel and I arrived in the state, there were few believers, and the testimony among the natives was almost nonexistent. But by the time we were ready to leave the country, various portions of scripture had been translated into a number of indigenous languages, ten thousand Ch'ols and fifteen thousand Tzeltals were members of Presbyterian churches, and hundreds of *mestizos* and natives were receiving leadership training. The local churches were well organized with their consistories, and the Chiapas Presbytery was running at full swing. The Chiapanecan church was ready to be launched into astronomical growth in the years to come, to become the fastest growing church on the continent.[1]

Praise be the Lord, Mabel and I could leave Mexico with the voice of our Master whispering in our ears those sweet and encouraging words: "Well done, good and trustworthy slave; you have been trustworthy in a few things, I will put you in charge of many things; enter into the joy of your master" (Matthew 25:21).

---

[1]   JRK, graduation sermon, Presbyterian Theological Seminary, Coyoacán, Mexico (June 29, 1969), in JAH.

CHAPTER 89

Let Me Go Back!

As new missionaries were arriving in Chiapas, Mabel and I were thinking about our definitive retirement from Mexico. It was a very difficult decision to make. By 1968 we had spent forty-three years in the field. We were more used to the Mexican ways than to our American ways. Just to think of going back to live in the United States created in us a lot of anxiety. In February of that year, I had reached the age of sixty-eight, which was the age of mandatory retirement in the Reformed Church. The Board of Domestic Missions was permitting us to finish the school year at the seminary in Coyoacán, outside of Mexico City, with salary and allowance for rent through June. Missionaries were generally given a terminal furlough which meant that their salary was paid during their final furlough. Accordingly, our board would pay our salary until December 31, and we were permitted to spend those "vacation" months wherever we wished.

The faculty and the board of the seminary in which we were teaching had asked us to continue teaching for another year. We were in perfect health, and although we were not as youthful as we once were or as the new Chiapas missionaries were, physically and mentally there was no reason why we should not favor their request. In fact, we wanted to do so since there was no replacement for us there in either the Bible Department, of which I was the head, or the English Department, of which Mabel was the head.

Finally, in March, we planned to take a trip to the United States in late July, immediately after the close of the seminary academic year, and then return for the opening of the school year in October. Our plan was to live on our retirement income beginning in January. We did not want the board to make an exception in our case and continue to pay our salary for the next year. Rules should be followed whenever possible. In this way, our supporting churches would be free to contribute to the support of some other missionary family beginning in 1969.[1]

Nevertheless, how difficult it was for Mabel and me to leave Mexico! I kept a poem that I had read in 1928, and forty years later, in 1968, it helped us to express our deep feelings as we left our missionary field of almost forty-five years. It was truly for us "The Prayer of a Veteran Missionary."

> Let me go back! I am homesick
> For the land of my love and my toil,
> Though I thrill at the sight of my native hills,
> The touch of my native soil.
> Thank God for the dear home country,
> Unconquered and free and grand!
> But the far-off land of Chiapas, for me
> Is the territory of the Promised Land.
>
> No longer young—I know it—
> And battered and worn and gray,
> I bear in my body the marks that tell
> Of many a toil-filled day.
> But 'tis long to the end of a lifetime,
> And the hour for the sun to set.
> My heart is eager for years to come;
> Let me work for the Master yet.
>
> My brain is dazed and wearied
> With the New World's stress and strife,
> With the race for money and place and power,

---

[1]   JRK to First Reformed Church in Sioux Center, Iowa (March 29, 1968), in JAH.

And the whirl of the nation's life.
Let me go back! Such pleasure
And gains are not for me;
But, oh, for a share in the Harvest Home
Of the fields beyond the sea.

For there are my chosen people,
And that is my place to fill,
To spend the last of my life and strength
In doing my Master's will.
Let me go back! 'Tis nothing
To suffer and do and dare;
For the Lord has faithfully kept his Word,
He is "with me always" there.[2]

Our return to the United States was inevitable. We had to go back to a country that, by now, was almost unknown to us. After forty-four years of living in the tropics, we had no interest in living in the cold snow-and-ice country. Residents at the Presbyterian missionary compound in Santa Fe, New Mexico, urged us to join them. We also considered Tucson, Arizona, with its warm climate and beautiful surroundings. There were two Leisure Worlds in California, but circumstances pointed to the one in Seal Beach. A fully furnished apartment was for sale at a modest price by a Salvation Army couple who had been asked to return to duty in San Francisco. We grasped the offer eagerly.

Once word spread in Coyoacán that we would be leaving, there were buyers for everything we did not plan to take with us. Matilde Hidalgo, who as a Mexican daughter was living with us while she did her medical studies at the National University, was able to find another home. We gave the moving truck that took what we retained an extra day before we left by passenger bus to El Paso. There we stored our bags in Greyhound lockers and took a taxi back across the border to Ciudad Juárez, where the moving truck was parked on the city square waiting for us, already empty but for our goods. We transferred our possessions to a small pickup and were on our way to the border crossing where a "tip" (*mordida*) allowed us to pass without going through Mexican customs. When I was ready to open the trunks for American customs, I realized I had my keys in our bags at the Greyhound station. I offered

---

[2]   Woman's Missionary Friend, "Let Me Go Back! The Prayer of a Veteran Missionary," *Missionary Monthly* (May 1928): 215.

to break the locks, but the officer with a curt— "Get the stuff out of here!"—dismissed us.

U-Haul agents assured us there were no U-Haul vans in El Paso, so I was prepared to drive a truck all the way to California. But surprisingly, two new U-Haul vans had just come in from the east. When there are that many seeming coincidences, you know that Divine Providence is working things out. By now we knew that the God who had sent us to Mexico in due time was now telling us to say goodbye to that beloved land. It took us some five years to become Americanized again. Even now after so many years, almost all of my dreams at night are of Mexico and our life there.[3]

---

[3]   JRK, "Some of This and Some of That," 15.

CHAPTER 90

Centennial of the National Presbyterian Church

The National Presbyterian Church in Mexico celebrated its centennial in November 1972, which was also the occasion to rejoice in the twenty-fifth anniversary of the General Assembly. This year of celebration marked a time for change in every sphere of the national work. Church buildings were remodeled and improved, and educational buildings were furnished and equipped, mostly in urban areas. These changes were a reflection of the fact that in most of Mexico there was a major migration from rural areas to cities. Emphasis was placed on urban evangelization and massive evangelistic crusades. Churches were planted, and church buildings were built in major cities. The seminary was doing well, and the publishing house was very active. The Central Biblical School for women with a call to missions was running successfully, and there were twenty-eight presbyteries (three times more than when the General Assembly was organized) and five synods throughout the country. The number of churches was acceptable after forty years as an organized national work, with a good number of pastors and missionaries. Numerous lay leaders, both men and women, were involved in the work of the church.[1]

In Chiapas, however, things were a little different. The rural field increasingly became more important that the urban one. Churches and chapels were built, but this was not the major thrust of the believers. Massive evangelistic crusades were not the most effective way of reaching people with the gospel: personal contacts were. The most striking contrast, however, was in the statistics. Whereas the growth of churches in most of Mexico by 1972 was not entirely satisfactory, in Chiapas, the numbers increased from 10 to 12 percent per year, especially among the Maya population.

It was under these particular circumstances that, to our disappointment, the General Assembly of the National Presbyterian Church in Mexico at Veracruz in April 1971, voted to put an end to missionary cooperation. The church expressed the desire that "some missionary work," as it had been traditionally conducted in the country, should come to an end at the beginning of 1973. The national church believed it was strong and mature, and assistance from foreign missionary agencies was unnecessary.

There was more than one reason for the General Assembly's decision. First, there was the ever-present nationalist feeling prevalent in all of the smaller countries, augmented in Mexico because of the approaching centennial celebration. Since the very beginning of our missionary partnership, extreme nationalists had resented us. The very presence of missionaries had bothered them. There were those who believed that, even though the missionaries had no vote in official bodies, the missionary financial cooperation in some way controlled the work. Such protests were usually sporadic and more a public display of oratory skill than personal conviction. But as the centennial approached, the belief that the national church should be not only self-governing but also self-financing and self-propagating gained ground.

Second, the Presbyterian Church in Mexico was a very conservative, fundamentalist church, and because of the liberal teaching in many Presbyterian seminaries in the United States, it was suspicious of all North American missionaries, until they proved themselves to be conservative.

Third, the Mexican Presbyterian Church had been strongly antiecumenical ever since a well-meant attempt at ecumenicity among

---

[1]   Saúl Tijerina González, *Peregrinaje de un pueblo* (San Cristóbal de Las Casas: Centro de Comunicaciones Audiovisuales del Sureste, 1993), 205-8.

Protestant churches in Mexico was forced on them by mission boards through the "infamous" (to them) Cincinnati Plan of 1917 (chapter 16). This theoretically "splendid" plan for the evangelization of Mexico was carefully worked out in church offices in the United States, but it did not take into consideration human nature, much less, the particular cultural and ecclesiastical framework of Mexico. The Cincinnati Plan backfired and was the cause of disharmony between the signing boards and the National Presbyterian Church throughout the years.

Modern ecumenicity with the Roman Catholic Church was inconceivable for the church in Chiapas, even after the changes produced in this church with the Second Vatican Council. Most members of our churches came out of the Catholic Church and were entirely familiar with, and utterly opposed to, the doctrines peculiar to that church. The memory of persecution in all of its forms—including martyrdom—was still fresh in their minds. In Chiapas, to be evangelical meant to be anti-Roman Catholic.

The fact that one American Presbyterian missionary had been asked to leave the work in Mexico because of his modernistic views and another because of his ecumenical emphasis, made all missionaries in the Mexican church suspect. These dismissals also irked the sending boards who, ironically, were eager to withdraw their missionaries because of the antiecumenical position of the Mexican church and because of their own financial bind. Some of these missionaries were doing excellent work and were thoroughly sympathetic to the people of the Mexican church, who lamented their leaving. Some presbyteries wanted their missionaries to continue working among the churches but did not know how to retain them. It should be noted that Pioneer Mission Agency, which had cooperated with the Presbyterian Church in Yucatán for many years, had no plan or intention to withdraw its missionaries.

The Presbytery of Chiapas, however, strongly and unanimously opposed this action by the General Assembly, who then in turn made an exception in the case of Chiapas. The missionaries in Chiapas were conservative in theology and biblical interpretation, and the kind of ecumenicity they believed in was inoffensive to the church there. The nationals in Chiapas knew that the Reformed Church missionaries were completely at one with their church. They knew that the heart of their missionaries was to build a strong national church. What was said of one missionary, namely, that "he loves the church more than his own life," could be said of all of the missionary families; they worked in full agreement with the nationals. From the time the Presbytery of

In 1973 I was the guest of honor at the 24th annual meeting
of the Chiapas Presbytery at the Mazapa church
(*courtesy J. Samuel and Helen Hofman*)

Chiapas was formed (1949), the mission upheld the rule to never have any missionaries start a new work or project without the approval of the presbytery or one of its official committees.

The work in Chiapas was unique in that two-thirds of the church membership was made up of monolingual Maya. Six of the seven missionary families that were serving there when the centennial was celebrated lived and worked among the dialect-speaking Maya. Fifteen of the twenty-one pastors at that time were Maya. The unusual fact that the Maya and Spanish-speaking churches were in one presbytery—the largest in the nation—was not a matter of course or accident but rather a missionary triumph which was little understood. In fact, it has always been my deep desire that there be one church, all in one presbytery, bridging cultures and joining people of several languages. The nature and character of the work in Chiapas was unique, fantastic, amazing, and a very special reality—especially amazing given the racism and classism of the cultures of Chiapas. I was determined and intentional on this matter, and I tried my best to promote the unity of the work.

The monolingual Maya was at best a second-class citizen and was discriminated against by the Spanish-speaking *mestizo*. This class system was so inbred that it was most difficult for a *mestizo* to treat a Maya as an equal, even when, as a Christian, he tried. A native could immediately spot pretense in the *mestizo*. Therefore, when it was suggested at the General Assembly that the missionaries be given seven or eight years to train the *mestizo* pastors to do indigenous work, the reaction of the missionaries was, "Why not just train the Maya themselves?" The truth is that, among the hundreds of members of Wycliffe Bible Translators living in indigenous villages throughout Mexico, there was only one Mexican *mestizo* (a lovely Mexico City lady) on a translating team at that time. The missionary who lived with the Maya and spoke their language had won their confidence and their hearts.

Mexico still needed missionary help in many areas during the 1970s. The Presbyterian Church in Mexico had been the leading Protestant church in that country but was in danger of retrenching for a time, closing institutions and departments of the church. In areas where the church was weak, other denominations or sects could potentially take over. At the time of the centennial, there was a dearth of capable leaders in the church, so the assembly's decision seemed to come at an inopportune time. Some believed that, within a few years, the church would again ask for missionaries, but that by then, these experienced missionaries would be working elsewhere and would have lost their residency papers.

Even though the rapidly growing church in Chiapas needed ministers, two of the most capable Spanish-speaking pastors had left the state in 1972 for family reasons. Missionaries were needed to train more lay workers to guide youth work and women's ministries. The Mexican pastor generally limited his vision to his own parish and soon got into a rut. It was the well-read missionary with a broad base of contacts who had a better overall understanding of the needs and possibilities and could therefore suggest new ideas.

With one hundred years on her shoulders, the National Presbyterian Church in Mexico continued to need missionary help, especially in indigenous work. The Chiapas Maya leaders needed to be trained in the monolingual Bible schools. Literature had to be provided and translations made. The moral support alone of the missionaries was a tremendous influence and a powerful factor in the advance and growth of the work. New ministries were needed, and there were plenty of opportunities to develop them. Charles and Jean Van Engen were invited to come to Chiapas by the Chiapas Presbytery in violation of the "moratorium" because of these needs. They arrived in the fall of 1973 to serve the Spanish-speaking churches, form a new generation of pastors and evangelists in the Extension Bible School and Seminary, and build a conference center for youth and university evangelism.

The Chiapas Christians respected and loved the Reformed Church missionaries. The Mexican church had no quarrel with the Reformed Church. We had plenty of opportunities and challenges to continue to cooperate in the Maya work and in the Spanish-speaking areas. The need demanded it, and the opportunity was there. The church in Chiapas prayed that we would continue together. The plaintive protest which I heard before retiring from the Chiapas Mission in 1965 was once again heard by the faithful Chiapas missionaries, "You can't leave us; you belong to us."[2]

---

[2]   JRK, "Chiapas Needs and Wants Our Missionaries," *The Church Herald* (May 26, 1972), 5-6, 21.

CHAPTER 91

Leisure World

We finally arrived at our new home in Leisure World, in Seal Beach, California. The place was not paradise, but we were happy. As soon as we got settled, we became involved in missionary conferences and other similar events. I believe that these programs were carried out with sincere conviction, but there was often not a speck of missionary literature on hand, and there was a dire scarcity of speakers. Six Reformed churches planned their own separate missionary conferences, and on one occasion, Mabel spoke in one church, while I preached in three others. We repeated this schedule on several occasions.[1] I preached often and with great joy in my "retirement," and since I still considered teaching an important obligation, I taught the Keenagers Sunday school class in our local congregation. Singing was Mabel's primary ministry. She did this well, and although she was the congregation's preferred soloist, she accepted the invitation only when the others were unavailable.[2]

---

[1]   JRK to JSH, Nov. 3, 1969.
[2]   Ibid., Oct. 21. 1972.

Mabel and I also enjoyed traveling during our golden years. We completed a European tour with thirty-four others, visiting England, Holland, France, Switzerland, Italy, Spain, and Austria. We traveled four thousand miles by bus, took two train rides, sailed the Amsterdam canals and the river Rhine, and we were delighted to swim in the Mediterranean. We could do this not because we were rich, but because we had saved pennies and pesos from our puny salaries throughout the years, so the money was there when the opportunity came to travel to Europe. I recommend this practice to everyone. Regretfully, after a few weeks, we were back to the humdrum of life in Leisure World.[3] The retired routine, however, did not last long, since in September, we joined some forty people on a bus tour to the Pomona Los Angeles County Fair for one day. "A good time was had by all."[4]

We were seasoned travelers during our ministry in Chiapas, and we became so also in our retirement. In January 1972, we got our camper ready for our first trip to Mexico with the Keunings. I was scheduled to teach a course at the Presbyterian Seminary in Mexico City from February 21 to March 3, and we wanted to continue on to Chiapas.[5] In August of that year, we and the Keunings went to Alaska in our campers. We returned with thirty-seven pounds of colorful stones and hundreds of pressed flowers. We enjoyed the fresh fish we caught and the blueberries we picked. I lost twenty pounds on the Mexican and Alaskan trips and had to look for my older belts to keep my pants up.[6] Nevertheless, by September, we were again loading up the camper for another trip. This time we headed for the Midwest. We stopped in Iowa, Minnesota, Michigan, and Tenessee, especially to visit our kids and grandkids.[7] In 1974 Mabel and I went on a Holy Land tour with a group from Lake Hills Community Church, our local church. All our expenses were paid by a wealthy member of our class. This tour was very educational but not as emotional and inspirational as some people portray. Little was added to my knowledge of the life of Jesus, but I learned a great deal about Paul, his days, and his world.[8] A more memorable trip was the one Mabel and I made to Mexico to participate as guests at the General Assembly in 1975. On that occasion, the fiftieth anniversary celebration of the beginning of our mission to Chiapas

---

[3]   Ibid., Aug. 1, 1971.
[4]   Ibid., Sept. 23, 1971.
[5]   JRK to JSH, Jan. 23, 1972.
[6]   Ibid., Aug. 13, 1972.
[7]   Ibid., Sept. 11, 1972; Oct. 21, 1972.
[8]   Ibid., March 7, 1974; June 10, 1974.

took place, and we were honored in many very special ways.[9] We went back to Mexico with our camper in 1976, traveling to Chiapas with the Vander Ploegs of Sioux Center, Iowa.[10]

Retirement gave us more freedom and opportunity to visit our children and their families who were scattered throughout the United States. We spent restful time at the home of our son, Dr. Roger Kempers, on the shores of Lake Michigan. We had fun picking blueberries at farms north of Holland, and Mabel made her first blueberry pie ever. Mabel appreciated having time to sew (for our daughter Margie's girls), and we enjoyed bicycling, reading a lot, and making new friends at Leisure World.[11] We had the enormous satisfaction of rejoicing with frequent family gatherings in our place and the many visits of sons, daughters, spouses, and grandchildren.

Everywhere we went, we tried to promote the missionary work in Chiapas. I was invited to show my slides with taped lecture and marimba music to the men of Lake Hills Community Church at their weekly breakfast. I worked hard in preparation of this presentation, and we hoped it either generated or fanned interest in missions in Chiapas. On some occasions, men were in tears, and many women kissed us both. We did not try to be emotional, and we did not know what brought this on.[12] Maybe it was the Holy Spirit.

Another wonderful activity in which I invested time and energy was sports. Basketball was of special interest, not so much to play, but to watch. I have always been a fan of Los Angeles Lakers basketball and Los Angeles Dodgers baseball. And in 1971, I won an award as the most improved bowler of the year in the local league! With the passing of time, our life settled into an even pace. To the two afternoons of bowling, we added a morning of shuffleboard, which Mabel enjoyed and took quite seriously. We were not expected to win our first tournament, but we did, and with this triumph, Mabel had her first athletic trophy![13] Otherwise, our lives continued to be very quiet and home centered. We spent most of our Sundays right there on the campus of Leisure World, and we walked to church whenever possible. The new assistant pastor at that time was a former classmate of mine from Princeton.[14]

Church membership was quite an issue for both of us. The associate pastor of Dr. Robert Schuller's Garden Grove church, Rev.

---

[9]   JRK to JSH, June 1975.
[10] JRK to JSH, Feb. 1976.
[11] MVD to JSH, Sept. 12, 1973.
[12] JRK to JSH, Dec. 14, 1975.
[13] Ibid., Jan. 16, 1982; April 29, 1982.
[14] Ibid., Sept. 27, 1982.

Leetsma, began a new church in Lake Hills. This new congregation started out with a bang. There were nine hundred present in the two services of their first meeting. They already had a regular choir and were getting the Sunday school organized. Some wanted me to take the adult class, but that would have meant getting tied down and a weekly drive out there of forty-five minutes. We planned to join the Lake Hills Community Church with a dual membership if possible, in my case at least. I wanted to continue to be a member of the First Reformed Church in Sioux Center, Iowa, which had always supported us and where the bulletin listed me as their missionary emeritus. We even purchased a burial plot in the cemetery there.[15] Mabel also thought of keeping her membership with Third Reformed Church in Holland, but finally she asked for a letter of transfer of membership. She wrote a heartfelt letter to the consistory:

> There is deep gratitude in my heart to the Lord for his allowing me to be part of Third Church for a lifetime. . . . From the time of our becoming missionaries in Mexico, Third Church was our generous and loyal supporter, in prayer and financially. You held my membership in trust all those years, and I am so very grateful. Third Church will always be my "home church." But now, retired and living in Southern California, my husband and I feel the need of becoming active members in a church in this area. And so, not without emotion, I am asking you to transfer my membership to the new Lake Hills Community Church.[16]

In Lake Hills church, Mabel soon became active with the Women's Fellowship and also continued to be active in a group at the Leisure World Community Church. I managed a good number of speaking engagements in different places, including the Garden Grove Keenagers monthly potlucks. My most successful presentations were those in which I showed slides of Chiapas and our work there. My adult Sunday school class was a source of continued satisfaction, and to all these tasks I added the teaching of a college group on Tuesday nights for a while. The senior Keenagers made me their president for the year of 1977, which meant that Mabel and I had to attend the monthly potlucks and meetings of the executive board of that group.[17]

---

[15]   Ibid., April 2, 1973; Oct. 11, 1973.
[16]   MVK to the Consistory of Third Reformed Church, Holland, Michigan, Oct. 18, 1973, in JAH.
[17]   JRK to JSH, Sept. 20, 1977.

Another turn of events had to do with our health. Both Mabel and I had always been very strong, physically speaking. When, however, you become an octogenarian, a number of pains, difficulties, and physical limitations begin to interfere with your abilities. In July 1980, we were just about to set out for Michigan with our camper, when I had a strong dizzy spell—much worse than my earlier ones. We flew to Michigan instead, and upon returning to Leisure World, I sold the camper and gave up teaching my class at Lake Hills Church. We also decided to walk to the Leisure World Community Church for worship. Later in August 1981, I began to suffer severe back pain with sciatica pain down both legs. At this point, we cut back on our travel and increased our participation in activities at Leisure World.[18]

As you get old, everything around you also ages. By 1986 I felt the weight of my years as my circulation problems were advancing. At times, not enough blood got to my brain causing momentary dizziness. Mabel suffered a lot with her eyes (macular degeneration of both retinas). With a magnifying glass, she could read slowly, but she still went through several laser treatments. By 1990 she had given up piano, sewing, crossword puzzles, reading, and tricycle riding, and extra care was required to cross streets. Church singing was no problem since she sang all the stanzas of familiar hymns from memory.[19]

Also the institutions of which we were active members began to change and no longer held our interest. We had to disband our Iowa Club. Members were getting old and did not want to take executive responsibilities. Many had died, so what earlier was a club with over three hundred members was reduced to fewer than one hundred. I gave up bowling in 1985; I tried a game later but decided not to rejoin the league. Mabel gave up shuffleboard, but I continued as long as I could.[20] I had a cataract removed from my left eye; the right one had been removed about two years before. Nevertheless, when I was eighty-eight, I renewed my driver's license with a perfect score on the written exam, so I was authorized to drive until age ninety-two. And this without glasses! I also took a two-day, ten-hour class for drivers age fifty-five and older, which gained me a 10 percent discount on our car insurance.[21]

Mabel became more and more involved in women's ministries in the church at Leisure World, and she led studies on the women of the Bible in her local circle for some time; the women were very

[18]   Ibid., July 12, 1980; August 29, 1981.
[19]   Ibid., Christmas, 1990.
[20]   JRK to JSH, Oct. 1, 1986.
[21]   Ibid., March 1988.

impressed. They passed the word along, so she was asked to speak at the monthly meetings of the entire fellowship, up to seven hundred members. She gave a study entitled "Hagar, Tragedy and Promise," relating Hagar to the Arabs of today. She worked hard on this study and gave practically the whole thing without referring to her notes. I sneaked in to get it on tape. She really impressed the women. She also impressed the director of our local choir. He, who had never heard her sing, asked her to give a two-minute, older-Christian testimony and sing "The Longer I Serve Him, the Sweeter He Grows," from *Alleluia* by Bill and Gloria Gaither. She accepted with fear and trembling. Mabel practiced long and hard; she prayed and then performed beautifully. The audience burst into prolonged applause as did the choir members themselves. Many have told us that she "stole the show." Not that her voice compared with the top women singers in the choir, but for her to do it all flawlessly and with a radiant face seemed to thrill them. One boy said afterward: "I hope I can sing that way when I am seventy-seven."[22]

These long years of retirement have been wonderful in terms of the time available to do some things that have been postponed for years. In particular to organize the astronomical amount of documents collected throughout our years in Chiapas. I went through all of my mission correspondence and many other documents. I threw some away but still have at least a two-foot stack remaining. These papers mean more to me than to any other reader, because I remember the circumstances in which the letters were written and the people who wrote them. Throughout those letters runs a thread of the problems I had with Coffin. What a pain in the neck he was, and how we had to fight for the progress that he opposed at every turn. He was highly overrated by people outside of Chiapas, and this fact always made them suspicious of us. Joaquin Vera in Tabasco especially did us a great deal of harm by always backing Coffin and holding back our work. Once they had Coffin in Tabasco, after he left Chiapas, they did not know what to do with him, since by then, he was all talk and no action. Tabasco honors Coffin; Chiapas has forgotten him.[23] My hope is that someday somebody will go through all these pages and do justice to our enormous effort to build up the Kingdom of God in Chiapas, in spite of the many difficulties we had to face. I have been preparing these documents for that person who will accept the challenge to write about Mabel and me and recover from the past our commitment to proclaim the gospel until Chiapas belongs to Christ, "Chiapas para Cristo."

[22]   Ibid., April 6, 1979.
[23]   Ibid., Sept. 27, 1982.

CHAPTER 92

Golden Wedding Anniversary

I remember quite well that afternoon in 1975 when Mabel and I drove into the Tapachula Conference Center in our road-weary camper, unannounced and totally unexpected. I got out of the vehicle to survey the little two-bedroom house that Charles Van Engen had just finished building and where he and his wife Jean would make their home for the next six years. Carlitos was very pleased when I said, "It looks good," and immediately his face changed when I remarked, "But it needs to be painted!" Color came back to his face when I asked, "Where's the paint?" During the following days, in hot and humid Tapachula, the four of us painted that little "missionary home." Yes, I have always been convinced that these expressions of love and concern for missionaries on the field are a significant way of doing missions.[1]

Looking at the Van Engens—so young, so much in love with each other and so passionate for doing missions—I remembered with joy and gratitude to the Lord the fifty years of matrimony that he had given to Mabel and me. On August 15, 1975, we had a great celebration with our

---

[1] Van Engen, "John Kempers: A Modern Day Apostle."

children, grandchildren, friends, and brethren in Christ. A deep sense of thankfulness overwhelmed Mabel and me for all these years dedicated to his service in the Kingdom.

The celebration was performed at Third Reformed Church in Holland, Michigan, a place packed with precious memories for Mabel and me. The sanctuary—the second oldest church building in Holland and the third oldest among the architecturally significant and historic public buildings in this city—was radiant after the restoration work finished in 1968. Mabel and I had the opportunity to confirm our covenant of love under the marvelous Gothic pillars and arches, while the audience was sitting on the cushioned original pews. The two spiral staircases were beautiful, blending in with the style of the church. The blessed ceremony was lit by old lanterns and colored by the rich, stained-glass windows and the rose window on the north end of the sanctuary, all embellished by the chancel furniture, particularly the pulpit, from the St. Nicholas Collegiate Church in New York.[2]

Listening to ministers retell of the amount of time spent in marriage counseling and to the reports of professional counselors, one would conclude that one-per-lifetime marriages are collectors' items. Not so! When the time of our fiftieth anniversary came, Mabel and I were living in a retirement community where golden anniversaries were an almost daily event. Judging by announcements I have read in the *Holland Sentinel*, fifty years is hardly worth a celebration.

On the day of our wedding, we had a cherished group of people who signed our wedding certificate guest book and played important roles in that event: Lillian, Mabel's sister and maid of honor; Ed and Edmonia, parents of our little flower girl; the bride's niece, Dorothy Ann Van Dyke Michola; Margaret Trompen Beuker, dear friend of my wife's since their Hope College days, who played the traditional marches and *Country Gardens* and *Etude Mignonne*.[3] What a glorious and exciting day and night that was!

At the time of our marriage, we arranged a memory book with pictures and mementoes of our courting days and ending with our wedding picture. On the introductory page, we wrote these words: "I am one of those who by the luck of life and God's goodness have found their mates."

[2]   Elton J. Bruins, *The Americanization of a Congregation*, 2nd ed. (Grand Rapids: Eerdmans, 1995), 98-102.
[3]   MVD, "Thoughts on Our Golden Wedding Anniversary," unpublished document, n.d., 2, in JAH.

It may not be Christian to speak of the "luck of life," but the lines do speak of the providence of God. It should surprise no one that marriages which God's providence has arranged should last until life's end. In my talks on Chiapas, I have often related how the Lord would hold back in difficult situations and then at the last moment, when we were at the breaking point and had been tested, he came with a clear answer.

I dated frequently in high school and all through college, but prayers for the right life's partner were not being answered. I was becoming quite concerned in my senior year and prayed all the harder and then, at long last, in the pattern that was to become so familiar in later life, the clear answer appeared. Onto the campus and into my life there walked a freshman whom God was preparing for our life and work together.

When the offer to begin a new missionary work in Chiapas came—which was another of those held-back-to-the-last-minute answers to prayer that came toward the end of my senior year—and by mail or by wire, I asked for her okay, Mabe's answer was immediate, decisive, and Ruth like. Later as our sailing date was drawing near, one night in bed in New York, both of us suddenly had some qualms about the unknown, the untried, and the unaccompanied life ahead. Then one of us, and to this day we do not know who, spoke the words which voiced the thought of both of us: "But we have each other." For more than fifty years, those words have given us the needed lift in troubled times, and in the work and world we lived in, there have been troubled times.

Mabel's glorious ministry was not only as a partner in missions but also as the one who kept our family together through times of testing. After the ceremony in celebration of our fiftieth wedding anniversary, our children made merry in our honor. The four girls and four boys planned a very happy party, and the boys presided and took the floor to present the program. We hoped that some day all of our children may experience the exhilaration, pride, and satisfaction that we did in our family. We were also grateful to God who had seen us through a half century—and more—together and who has held us in our golden years in the loving security of his hands.[4]

What a companion Mabel has been! What a trooper! Never any *zaniken*: never a complaint about housing but always ready to make any house into a home; never a complaint about climate, either in the heat of Tapachula or in the cold of San Cristóbal de Las Casas, in the

---

[4] MVD to JSH, Sept. 11, 1975.

aridity of Tuxtla Gutiérrez or in the soaking wet of other places; never a complaint about the pace of my travels or work; never a complaint about the too frequent and lengthy periods of separation during field trips.

More often than deserved, I have been honored for what I supposedly have done. The admiration, the acclaim, the love she so richly merits is for what she has done and for who she is. I think I'll keep her forever![5]

[5]   JRK, "Golden Wedding Anniversary," unpublished document, n.d., in JAH.

Epilogue

I have often wondered about my departure from this world. As I grow older and more limited in my thoughts and actions, I long to go to the Lord rather than to remain here on earth where there is not much that I can do for him. The departure of former comrades and friends has accelerated this longing. One of my few remaining Princeton classmates died in September 1994; he had served as an associate pastor in California and was much admired, and the church was full for his memorial service in 1995. My high school (academy) classmates are all gone. There might be two or three women left of the college class and four Princetonians at the most. All of them (myself included) are like the "last rose of summer."[1]

And now, I am ninety-five years old. A person is granted but one ninety-fifth birthday celebration. Mine was a very special one. There were many cards and phone calls. Now we have learned to live a day, a week, a month, a year at a time.[2] We have also learned to depend more and more on the decisions of others, particularly our children. They

---

[1] JRK to JSH, Sept. 24, 1994.
[2] Ibid., Feb. 20, 1995.

Mabel and I were partners in ministry for seventy years
(*courtesy J. Samuel and Helen Hofman*)

made up their minds that it was time for us to move to where they could look after us, especially Mabe, if I were to die first. So we left Leisure World and moved to Holland, Michigan. Our move to Holland was another example of God's providence. We settled comfortably near our daughter Joy. Both of us kept keenness of mind and clear memories. But Chiapas always occupied the choicest place in our thoughts.

Packing, shipping, unloading, and rearranging, everything was hectic, but the children helped, and now all seems to be in order. I sold the car, so I was left with the trike, which is sort of a novelty in this town. I use the trike to go to a large grocery store in one direction and to a bank in the other direction, a mile and a half—no bus system here. The noon meal is served in our place, so Mabel is free from the heavy cooking. We get especially good meals when our children invite us to their homes. I miss all the comfort and convenience of Leisure World and the nearby shopping areas, but I had a minority vote, so we will adjust to the living conditions here. Fortunately, we have some months to get used to our surroundings before the cold of winter sets in.[3]

As winter approaches and we celebrate Thanksgiving, I am thinking about what seventy years of Thanksgivings have meant to us. Seventy years ago, we were in New York City, getting ready to leave for

---

[3]   JRK to Pearl Calix and her husband Cal, July 27, 1995.

Mexico. When we were commissioned in Flatbush, New York, in my speech, I put on a brave front contemplating dangers involved, quoting: "Man is immortal until his task is done." We continue to be eager for news from Chiapas, the place in the world that has always been in our hearts and prayers. Now we look forward to Christmas. May there be joy in the churches in Chiapas![4]

As we approach the end of this year of 1995, I am very much like the apostle Paul, when he said, "As for me, I am already being poured out as a libation, and the time of my departure has come. I have fought the good fight; I have finished the race; I have kept the faith. From now on there is reserved for me the crown of righteousness, which the Lord, the righteous judge, will give me on that day, and not only to me but also to all who have longed for his appearing" (2 Timothy 4:6-8).

*John R. Kempers went to be with his Lord and Savior Jesus Christ
on November 27, 1995,
and on December 13, 2003,
his wife Mabel joined him to worship eternally
in the presence of their Heavenly Father.*

[4]   JRK to JSH, Nov. 22, 1995. Kemp died five days after writing this letter.

Works Cited

Arciniegas, Germán. *Latin America: A Cultural History*. New York: Alfred A. Knopf, 1966.

Báez-Camargo, Gonzalo, and Kenneth G. Grubb. *Religion in the Republic of Mexico* London: World Dominion Press, 1935.

Barbieri, Sante Uberto. *El país de Eldorado*. Buenos Aires: La Aurora, 1962.

Brown, Arthur Judson. *One Hundred Years: A History of the Foreign Missionary Work of the Presbyterian Church in the U.S.A., with Some Account of Countries,*

Peoples and the Policies and Problems of Modern Missions. Book One. New

York: Fleming H. Revell, 1936.

Browning, Webster E. *New Days in Latin America*. New York: Missionary Education Movement of the United States and Canada, 1925.

Browning, Webster E. *Roman Christianity in Latin America*. New York: Fleming H. Revell, 1924.

Clark, Francis E. and Harriet A. Clark. *The Gospel in Latin Lands: Outline Studies of Protestant Work in the Latin Countries of Europe and America.* New York: The Macmillan Company, 1909.

Comisión de Historia. *Bodas de Oro: 1902-1952.* Tuxtla Gutiérrez, Chiapas: Iglesia Evangélica Presbiteriana Nacional "Getsemaní," 1952.

Crow, John A. *The Epic of Latin America.* 4th ed. Berkeley: University of California Press, 1992.

Esponda, Hugo. *El presbiterianismo en Chiapas: orígenes y desarrollo.* Mexico: Publicaciones El Faro, 1986.

Grubb, Kenneth G. *An Advancing Church in Latin America.* London: World Dominion Press, 1936.

Keen, Benjamin. *A History of Latin America.* 4th ed. Boston: Houghton Mifflin, 1992.

Lacy, Creighton. *The Word Carrying Giant: The Growth of the American Bible Society.* Pasadena, CA: William Carey Library, 1977.

Mackay, Juan A. *El otro Cristo español: un estudio de la historia espiritual de España e Hispanoamérica.* Mexico: Casa Unida de Publicaciones, 1952.

Martínez López, Joel. *Orígenes del presbiterianismo en México.* Matamoros, Tamaulipas: n.p., 1972.

Meyerink, Dorothy Dickens. *Ministry among the Maya: A Missionary Memoir.* Grand Rapids: Eerdmans, 2011.

Moreau, A. Scott, ed. *Evangelical Dictionary of World Missions.* Grand Rapids: Baker Books, 2000.

Nida, Eugene A. *Understanding Latin Americans: With Special Reference to Religious Values and Movements.* Pasadena, CA: William Carey Library, 1974.

Orr, J. Edwin. *Evangelical Awakenings in Latin America.* Minneapolis, MN: Bethany Fellowship, 1978.

Ortega Aguilar, Penélope. "El *Abogado Cristiano Ilustrado* y *El Faro*: la prensa protestante de la época ante el Porfiriato." Lic. in History diss., Universidad Nacional Autónoma de México, 2011.

Pendle, George. *A History of Latin America.* London: Penguin Books, 1990.

Read, William R., Victor M. Monterroso, and Harmon A. Johnson. *Latin American Church Growth.* Grand Rapids: Eerdmans, 1969.

Williamson, Edwin. *The Penguin History of Latin America*. London: Allen Lane-The Penguin Press, 1992.

Zebadúa, Emilio. *Breve historia de Chiapas*. Mexico: El Colegio de México and Fondo de Cultura Económica, 2003.

Index

The subjects, places, and names index are combined into one list. All places are in Mexico unless otherwise indicated. United States locations use standard postal abbreviations for the state. Pictures are indicated by italic page numbers. A list is also included under "Images."

212, 214, 447, 254, 337, 339–
46, 437; arrival in Tuxtla, 340;
settle in San Cristobal, 342;
first trips with Kempers, 340–
42; introduces Theological
Education by Extension, 344
Van Engen, Ronald John, 346
Vasconcelos, José, 122
Venegas, Don Pedro, 336
Venegas, Jesús, 335–36
Veracruz, 33, 35, 57, 80, 94, 127,
153, 157, 162-63, 175, 220,
308-9, 324, 408, 432, 480;
American landing in, 60, 176
Veracruz Presbytery. *See* Presbytery of Veracruz
Vera, Joaquín, 332, 337, 490
Verdusco, David, 252
Vidal, Silvino, 50
Villa, Francisco, 80
Villahermosa, Tabasco, 179, 188,
198, 202, 226, 337
Villa, Pancho, 155, 175
Virgin of Guadalupe, 161, 268

W

Wallace, William, 60
Wallis, Ethel, 368
Warkentin, Viola, 437
War of Independence of 1810, 96
War of the Cristeros, 130
Watermulder, David, 451
Watermulder, Gerrit, 127, 135, 378
Watermulder, Gustavus A., 49, 54,
244
Weathers, Ken, 309
Western Theological Seminary,
346, 442
Whitworth College, 413
Wichert, 254
Wiggins, George, 363

Wilson, Woodrow, 175–76
Winnebago, NE, 346
Winona, MN, 377
Wolfe, Vera E., 164
Women's Board of Domestic Missions, 84-85, 105, 126, 133-34,
145, 146, 153, 451; Kempers'
connection with, 84–85
Women's Convention, first, 446
women's society group, *447, 448*
Women's Spanish Club, 67
Women's Union of Chiapas, 447,
448
women's work in Chiapas, 445–49
Woodward, Evelyn, 368, 437
World Missionary Congress, 87
World War I, 75–77, 296; missions after, 173–74
Wycliffe Bible Translators, 178,
224, 257, 350, 362, 419, 421,
423, 425, 437, 483; arrival in
Chiapas, 365–70
Wyngaarden, Rev., 152

X

Xico, 408
Xinatitlán, 334
Xocempich, 335

Y

Yajalón, 23, 195, 197-99, 230,
238, 268, 311, 314, 316, 332-
33, 335-36, 341, 347, 380, 382,
423, 435, 437; construction of
church in, 278; organization
of church in, 337; settlement
of Van Engens in, 342
Yaxhuatán, 303
Youth Union, 447
youth work, 227–31, 441–44, 447
Yucatán, 33, 57, 80, 94, 103, 161,